D1526398

Stopping Pickett

The History of the Philadelphia Brigade

by

Bradley M. Gottfried

WHITE MANE BOOKS

Maps drawn by Bradley M. Gottfried.

This White Mane Books publication
was printed by
Beidel Printing House, Inc.
63 West Burd Street
Shippensburg, PA 17257-0152 USA

In respect for the scholarship contained herein, the acid-free paper used in this book meets the guidelines for permanence and durability of the Committee on Production Guidelines for Book Longevity of the Council on Library Resources.

For a complete list of available publications
please write
White Mane Books
Division of White Mane Publishing Company, Inc.
P.O. Box 152
Shippensburg, PA 17257-0152 USA

Library of Congress Cataloging-in-Publication Data

Gottfried, Bradley M.
    Stopping Pickett : the history of the Philadelphia Brigade / by
Bradley M. Gottfried.
        p.   cm.
    Includes bibliographical references (p.   ) and index.
    ISBN 1-57249-164-7 (alk. paper)
    1. United States. Army. Philadelphia Brigade (1861-1865)
2. United States--History--Civil War, 1861-1865--Regimental
histories.   3. Pennsylvania--History--Civil War, 1861-1865-
-Regimental histories.   4. United States--History--Civil War,
1861-1865--Campaigns.   I. Title.
E527.5.P48G68   1999
973.7'448--dc21   99-11301
                                                                CIP

To my parents:

Edward and Bernice Gottfried

Samuel and Selma Hoffman

CONTENTS

ILLUSTRATIONS

MAPS

ix

FOREWORD

Like many units formed at the outbreak of the Civil War, the ranks of the Philadelphia Brigade were filled with soldiers with limited military experience. The brigade differed from others because most of the men hailed from one small geographic area. Despite this fact, the unit had the distinction of being initially mustered into service under the banner of a distant state.

From its baptism of fire, the brigade participated in every campaign involving the Army of the Potomac, until it was mustered out during the siege of Petersburg. This book is more than merely a history of the actions of this brigade—it is the story of how civilians were forged into an effective fighting unit that gained lasting fame on the Gettysburg battlefield. I have attempted to take a balanced approach, giving both credit and criticism when warranted.

Like most things in life, this book was born of a compromise between my desire to write a long and comprehensive history, and my editor's (Harold Collier) interest in publishing a book that would not be prohibitively expensive. He has my thanks for his patience in seeing this project through to completion.

Many other people helped to make this project a reality. Steve Wright of the Civil War Library and Museum (CWLM) in Philadelphia, Pa., patiently answered my endless questions with humor and charm, and pointed out many valuable sources of information. The 69th Pennsylvania re-enactors graciously allowed me access to their primary source material, and I spent a stimulating afternoon with George Levens, while going through the archives. Patrick Purcell, of the CWLM also lent valuable assistance. Greg Acken provided a preliminary peek at his transcript of the Frank Donaldson papers. I am also grateful for the help extended by the United States Army Military History Institute (USAMHI). Dr. Richard Sommers and his staff made the wealth of manuscripts available to me, and Randy Hackenburg patiently pulled out photographs for my use. JoAnna McDonald of the Pennsylvania Preservation Committee allowed me to view and photograph the regimental flags. Daryl Smoker of the Gettysburg National Military Park retrieved files for me from their library's vertical files. Philip Lapanski provided access to the Philadelphia Library Company's collection of recruiting posters. Permission to use quotes and photographs were also granted by the CWLM, Robert Vanderslice, Robert Mundy of the Union League of Philadelphia, Donald Enders, and Jeff Kowalis.

Finally, and most importantly, my most heartfelt thanks go to my family, Adele, Mara, and Emily, for their patience and support as I slogged through a long journey that often took me far from home.

Commanders of the Philadelphia Brigade, from Ward's *History of the One Hundred and Sixth Pennsylvania Reserves*

CHAPTER 1

ORGANIZING THE FIRST CALIFORNIA

The fall of Fort Sumter caused President Abraham Lincoln to issue a call for 75,000 men to quell the rebellion. Each state received a quota, and Pennsylvania Governor Andrew Curtin decided to use his militia first. The years of neglect soon became evident; the units were poorly equipped, trained, and led. Nevertheless, the militia was reorganized into three-month regiments and shipped out.[1]

Two of these regiments, the 22nd and the 24th Pennsylvania Volunteers, were the forerunners of the Philadelphia Brigade. Beginning as the Second Regiment, Second Brigade, First Division of the Pennsylvania Militia, the 24th Pennsylvania Volunteers were mustered into service on May 7, 1861. The regiment, which would later form the nucleus of the 69th Pennsylvania, moved to Chambersburg in early June, and then to Hagerstown on June 21. Here it joined General Robert Patterson's army, and moved to Virginia's Shenandoah Valley. The unit made many marches, but never engaged the enemy. Because the government had not yet gained proficiency in supplying its troops with necessities, the men suffered from not enough food, and inadequate supplies and clothing. Utterly frustrated, the regiment's colonel wrote to the commander of the Pennsylvania militia, "You know well, sir, how shamefully the men have been treated...how injuriously the reputation of the Commonwealth has been affected by the ragged conduct of our Regiments...The men must have what they are entitled to, or I'll know the reason why." At the conclusion of its three-months' service, Patterson made an "earnest appeal" for the regiment to remain in service until other troops could replace it. The regiment agreed, and spent two additional weeks under Patterson. When the regiment reached Philadelphia on August 9, its men were reluctant to march through the streets, as most did not have shoes, and underwear formed the outer attire for more than a few. So embarrassed were the men that they insisted on wearing their heavy overcoats despite the sweltering heat.[2]

The 22nd Pennsylvania Volunteers formed as the Philadelphia Life Guards during the summer of 1857, but were officially known as the First Regiment, Third Brigade, First Division of Pennsylvania Militia. The unit was ordered to Baltimore about the middle of May 1861. Soon after, they were dispatched to find and confiscate contraband arms hidden around the city. The mission was successfully completed, and upon their return, they were "greeted by their companions with cheers." The regiment remained in Baltimore for the remainder of their service, and was mustered out on August 7, 1861.[3]

On May 8, President Abraham Lincoln granted his close friend, well-known Senator Edward D. Baker of Oregon, permission to raise the First California Volunteers, one of the first three-year regiments. Born in England around 1800, Baker came to America as a child and settled in Philadelphia. When his father died, Baker was forced to fend for himself and his younger brother. He worked in the city's mills until the age of twenty-one, when he moved West to seek his fortune. Settling in Illinois, he studied law. After establishing a practice, he met another young lawyer in Springfield— Abraham Lincoln, and the two became close friends. This was apparent during Lincoln's first inauguration, when Baker rode with the new president in his carriage and introduced him on the podium.

Baker was a veteran of the Black Hawk War of 1832, and was elected to the U.S. Congress in 1846. When the war broke out with Mexico, he raised the 4th Illinois Volunteer regiment, and joined General Winfield Scott on his march to Mexico City. Baker commanded a brigade after the battle of Cerro Gordo. At the conclusion of the war, Baker resumed his career in the House of Representatives. He left Washington in 1851 for San Francisco, and became a prominent lawyer. At the behest of many Oregonians, Baker moved again in 1860, and was elected to represent the state in the U.S. Senate.[4]

In 1861, Baker was a well-known and distinguished figure. About fifty years old, with a high forehead and a cleanly shaven face, Baker was an outstanding orator who had a fondness for reciting poetry. His two fatal flaws were his impulsiveness and reluctance to change his decisions. Despite commanding a regiment, Baker frequently returned to the Senate chambers in full dress uniform. Upon arriving, he slowly and ceremonially unbuckled his sword and laid it across his desk. There was no room for compromise with secessionists. During the spring of 1861, he told his colleagues, "I want sudden, bold, forward, determined war." Although Lincoln offered him a brigadier general's star, and subsequently a major general's commission, he declined both as it would have forced him to resign his seat from his beloved Senate.[5]

Soon after the Sumter bombardment, Baker became impatient with the trickle of troops arriving at the capital, and decided to stir things up a bit. One of twenty distinguished individuals who spoke at a meeting at Union Square on April 19, he entranced the crowd purported to number 100,000. Mincing no

Colonel Edward Baker, commander of the California Brigade

words, he said the "hour for conciliation was past; the gathering for battle is at hand, and the country requires that every man shall do his duty."

The following day, a group of Californians met with Baker at the Metropolitan Hotel to discuss the possibility of organizing a regiment to serve under the California flag. Hoarse from his speech the day before, Baker quietly listened to their ideas, but quickly agreed. He would show the country that even a U.S. Senator could join the army to quell the rebellion.[6]

Baker returned to Washington, and probably discussed the matter with President Lincoln, for on May 8 Secretary of War Simon Cameron provided the authority necessary to raise the California regiment with Baker as its commander. "You are authorized to raise for the service of the United States, a regiment of troops (infantry) with yourself as Colonel, to be taken as a portion of any troops that may be called from the State of California by the United States, and to be known as the California Regiment." This would be the first three-year regiment recruited. Realizing the problems he would encounter trying to recruit a thousand Californians, Baker decided to raise the regiment back East.[7]

Baker was torn between his love of the Senate and the potential glory he would receive as a soldier, leading his men into Richmond. With luck, it could propel him into the presidency. Pondering how to do both, Baker recalled his former law partner from his San Francisco days. Isaac Wistar was a Philadelphian, who had gained a wealth of military experiences, from his command of Indian Rangers in California, and as a volunteer aide-de-camp to General George Cadwalader. Summoning Wistar to New York City, Baker laid out his plan—help him raise and command the regiment, and he would see to it that Wistar received a general's star. Wistar was asked, "Can you raise this regiment?" to which he replied, "Not in New York, I have no acquaintances there." Baker then asked "Can you raise it in Philadelphia?" Wistar replied, "I think I can, but I am not sure." With a broad smile, Baker knew he had Wistar hooked, and said, "Very well; your private business is sure to be broken up and not worth following for a while at least. Abandon it. Go to work and raise this regiment in Philadelphia, bringing the men over here to be mustered."[8]

Wistar enthusiastically recruited men, enlisting 630 by April 25. Hiring men to play the drums and fifes, he tirelessly roamed the city in search of recruits. Some men volunteered out of patriotic duty, others out of boredom, and many because they needed work. One soldier wrote to his mother in August 1861, "...you asked why I enlisted. When I left I had not the least idea of it. I thought I would get employment. Not finding it, I thought I would enlist. I get $11 per month."

Wistar realized that he would have most success at saloons. He later wrote, "It is impossible to remember how many of these last I had to visit, or how many drinks of bad whiskey I was obliged to consume and bestow in the service of my country..."

Colonel Isaac Wistar, 71st Pennsylvania

Wistar repeated this routine several times a week. Upon arrival in New York City, the men were marched to a large building at 4th and Broadway, where they were locked up. Wistar then rushed back to Philadelphia to recruit more men. He was quick to learn that a verbal commitment meant little to some of the men, so he administered an "*ex tempore* devised oath" while the recruit placed his right hand on a bible or on an old volume of state reports that "bore sufficient external resemblance to that venerable volume." Both parties usually knew it was not legally binding, and Wistar realized that 150 men must be recruited for every 100 that actually arrived in New York. Getting the men onto the midnight train was not cause for relief, as many hopped overboard when the chance permitted. He wrote, "...even after the trains were in motion, many jumped off, with courage worthy of a better cause, and were left scattered promiscuously in a wide swath across the State of New Jersey."[9]

Some of the recruits were already formed into companies, which drilled on a daily basis, all hoping to be mustered into the army. These groups attracted Wistar's attention, and he decided to accept the three best-drilled companies. In this way, Companies A, B, and C were selected and mustered into service.

After ten companies were formed, the regiment was mustered into service in a ritualistic service. The unit was ordered to stand at attention, and after a Regular Army officer inspected the men and their equipment, the induction ceremony began. After reciting the oath of allegiance, as mandated by the tenth article of war, they were read all of the articles of war. The unit was now officially part of the Union army. Most of the companies were mustered in while they occupied their quarters at 4th and Broadway.

The regiment was recruited in less than 20 days. So great was the desire to enlist under the distinguished senator that an additional five companies were authorized (L, M, N, O, and P) bringing the number to fifteen, totalling 1,650 men.[10]

The regiment was transported fifteen miles upriver to Fort Schuyler, where the men were clothed, armed, and drilled. While the *New York Times* referred to the fort as "fit for millionaires—cool, breezy, and delightful" some of the men thought it was little better than a sty. One new soldier reported that the first night the men slept on mattresses without blankets in tents outside the fort. When he entered the fort, he found "a more filthy, disagreeable, and detestable place I can scarcely ever set foot upon." Baker, who during this time lived at the Hotel Aster in New York City, partially made up for the surroundings by being "very particular in regard to the comfort of his men."

Some of the men's enthusiasm for the soldier's life caused them to overlook the fort's shortcomings. George Beidelman wrote home, "Our quarters are as good as could be desired. We are domiciled in fine rooms, between which are thick stone walls (not damp), and have good straw mattresses to lie

Private George Beidelman, 71st Pennsylvania, wearing his gray uniform

on, with our blankets to cover us." The men also liked it because they could fish from the walls of the fort. The officers liked the fort because it did not permit anyone to slip away, and provided ample room for drilling. Because rifles were in short supply, the men used 500 old muskets stored there.[11]

The regiment's first uniform was gray in color. One soldier described the uniforms as being composed of "suits and caps of stout gray cloth, blue overcoats with large caps, and an array of shiny buttons and each man has two shirts, two pairs of stockings, two pairs of drawers, shoes, and all the necessary accouterments of war." A red stripe ran down each leg. The overcoats were light blue and the shirts were made of flannel. So intent on uniformity, Baker insisted on providing the men's undergarments as well. The gray uniforms were easily confused with those of the enemy, and were replaced several months later.[12]

The men were finally exposed to drilling and discipline while at the fort, spending six to eight hours a day in these activities. Wistar wrote, "...for the first time it was possible to introduce some order, discipline and obedience, to inure officers and men to regimental duty and life in the field, and to communicate such military instruction by day as could be extracted from text books at night." A private proudly wrote home, "It is an awfully grand sight to witness a thousand men in one line, charging bayonets at the double quick." After three weeks of hard work, Wistar was satisfied that the regiment was ready to take the field.[13]

During the regiment's stay at Fort Schuyler, the medical staff decided to inoculate the regiment against smallpox. Within a week, almost fifty men were stricken with the disease. While most cases were light, a wagon load of men with the most virulent cases were sent to a special smallpox hospital established at Blackwell's Island."[14]

As the regiment trained at Fort Schuyler, Lincoln asked Colonel Baker to report on the condition of General Benjamin Butler's troops at Fortress Monroe. Upon his return, Baker filed his report, dated June 11, 1861, which praised General Butler's overall efforts, but concluded that the troops' morale was low, and the officers were unreliable. Baker suggested an immediate shipment of equipment, and that he be elevated to second in command, the latter at the request of General Butler.

During his return trip, Baker was interviewed by a correspondent from the *Cincinnati Commercial*. In calm and even tones, Baker told the correspondent that he would never see the shores of the Pacific again because his inexperienced troops would require the officers to expose themselves to enemy fire. Baker was convinced that he would be singled out by enemy sharpshooters, and killed at the head of his regiment. "This was said without any bitterness or self-pity, but he made the prediction with calmness as though it would have been a most insignificant observation. After saying it he took leave...went to the cabin and seated himself at the piano and played a song."[15]

If the newly recruited men of the First California had any second thoughts about fighting under the banner of a distant state, they were never mentioned. Instead, the men were excited about the prospect of being led by a distinguished senator, who had at least some ties to Philadelphia. "The fact that he is an intimate friend of the President and of all the high officials is an assurance that the California Regiment will not go into the field unprepared," wrote George Beidelman. Above all, they were anxious to go to war.[16]

Pennsylvania's governor, Andrew Curtin, was upset with the arrangement, and complained to the secretary of war, Simon Cameron, on September 18, 1861. "Under authority given by the War Department to citizens of other States than Pennsylvania to raise troops, sundry persons are recruiting men in Pennsylvania to the great detriment of the service here... It is urgently desired that such proceedings may be stopped without delay..."

Realizing the potential fallout from this situation, Cameron hastily replied on September 23, 1861, that his department had not given permission for these actions. Cameron seemed reluctant to stop these violations, writing, "The remedy for the difficulty referred to rests with the Executives of the different States."

Perhaps after giving the matter further consideration, or because of mounting political pressure, Cameron decided to take a more direct role. On September 25 he wrote to Curtin that all men mustered from his state would be placed under the command of the governor of Pennsylvania, "who shall organize or reorganize them as he may deem most advantageous to the interests of the General Government." Cameron also wrote that his department would continue to provide "camp equipage, clothing, &c" to these troops. Closing the communication, he wrote that in the future, "all volunteers for the service of the United States shall be raised in Pennsylvania only under requisitions made on the Governor." The recruitment of Pennsylvanians to serve under the flags of other states thus came to an end.[17]

The stay at Fort Schuyler ended on June 28, when after five weeks of training, the regiment was ordered to Fortress Monroe. Boarding steamers, the men were transported down the East River to New York City, arriving there at 3:30 p.m. As the men marched down Broadway on their way to the Jersey City Ferry, crowds lined the streets to see the regiment pass. The scene was captured by a *New York Times* correspondent.

> The balconies and windows of the hotels and residences were filled with ladies and citizens, who cheered and waved to them as they passed. Col. Baker rode upon a black horse, and the adjutant and surgeon were also handsomely mounted and rode in front of the regiment....The men gave evidence of the superior discipline and drill to which they had been subjected while in camp. They halted for a brief space in front of the Astor House, where the guests treated them with prolonged cheers— the ladies waving their complements from the windows.[18]

The men boarded the waiting ferry at 5:30 p.m., and an hour later, they arrived in Jersey City. After another hour, the regiment boarded a special train bound for Philadelphia.

The quiet of the hot and sunny Saturday, June 29, 1861, was broken by the sounds of drums that became louder with each passing moment. Soon a regiment of men clothed in strange gray uniforms under a California banner, swung into view. It did not take long for the citizens to recognize Colonel Baker in the lead, and their friends and acquaintances in the ranks. Although the regiment was mustered into service in New York, it was permitted to return to Philadelphia before being shipped to the front. Furloughs were freely distributed to the men, who were expected to return by the following Wednesday, when the unit would leave for Baltimore. While here, an additional company was added to the regiment, raising its number to sixteen and permitting it to be subdivided into two battalions.[19]

Prior to leaving Philadelphia, a silk U.S. flag was presented to the regiment by Lt. William Todd of Company C. The flag was made by Mrs. A. E. Yerger, whose husband was a member of the company. This flag would not see the onset of winter.[20]

The regiment was to sail by steamer for Baltimore, but after everyone was on board, Baker felt that the quarters were not comfortable enough, so he ordered them to disembark and march to the railroad station. Here they boarded cars for Baltimore. The regiment did not remain here long, for Brigadier General Benjamin Butler, commander of the Virginia District, desperately needed men to counter the build-up of Southern troops on the "Peninsula." Butler feared an attack against Fortress Monroe by the eight thousand rebels at Yorktown, and ten thousand in the vicinity of Norfolk. According to Butler, the number of men in the area was "too few for safety, unless under the guns of the fort, and too many for comfort or health even within the fort!" The First California, along with the Third, Fourth, and Fifth New York Regiments, totalling about 4,000 men, were crammed into steamers for the trip to Fortress Monroe on the tip of the peninsula. Butler called these newly arriving regiments "among the very best I have, and, with the exception of their equipments, will compare favorably with any other volunteers in the service."[21]

The *Philadelphia Inquirer* reported that soon after the regiment arrived, a group of forty men "seized the entire stock" of a grocery store owned by a poor man and had to be dispersed "at the point of the bayonet by the Provost Marshal." The correspondent indicated that this was but one of several misdeeds committed by the regiment. A week later, the newspaper carried the angry response by a member of the unit, who assured the readers that the bill had been paid in full. "It is reasonable to suppose that in a regiment of 1300 men there will be some unruly, but, as a general thing, our regiment is made up of high-toned men, whose integrity can be relied upon." This would not be the last time that the actions of the brigade would be the subject of controversy in the media.[22]

The regiment camped in an oatfield adjacent to the town of Hampton, approximately 100 yards from the home of President John Tyler. One soldier wrote, "This house is furnished magnificently, but I greatly fear it will suff somewhat from the contaminating presence of the abolitionist soldiers." The earliest arriving troops were quartered in some of the houses; troops arriving later set up camps around the town. Christening theirs, "Camp Oregon" in honor of their commander, the men of the First California spent these early and middle weeks of July in picket and scouting duty. Some of the men helped erect a sand battery. Across the river, the rebels were visible drilling on the beach at Sewall's Point. So concerned were the officers for their men's safety, that they told them to remain in camp when not on duty, and to remain alert. For the first time since its formation, Colonel Baker took command of the regiment. Prior to this time he was engrossed in his Senate chores.[23]

During the regiment's stay on the Peninsula, some of the men's old smoothbore muskets were replaced with rifled muskets. Private Beidelman wrote home, "We are as proud of them as a small boy with a new whip." For most Philadelphians, who did not generally own or use guns, rifles were an oddity. Upon receiving his musket, Frank Donaldson wrote that it "strike[s] me as being heavy, but it may be because I do not know much about such impediments."

The Union debacle at the battle of Bull Run put an end to the regiment's stay on the Peninsula. Sergeant Frank Donaldson wrote, "I can scarcely bring myself to write about the news of our defeat at Manassas. It was most disgraceful, most disastrous, and weighs us all down with sorrow and mortification." Leaving the fort during the last few days of July, the regiment headed for Washington, by way of Baltimore. Upon their arrival, they camped about one mile from the Capitol, at the foot of Meridian Hill. Here they formed one of the units assembled to beat back the anticipated attack on the city. Being so close to Washington, Baker returned to the Senate every day, except for one. After the panic subsided, the regiment was ordered across the Potomac at the Chain Bridge and continued for about a mile. Here they assisted in constructing Fort Ethan Allen, one of the many forts that sprung up that summer to protect Washington. The men also built a series of roads that served to connect the forts. As with their stay at Fortress Monroe, the rebel troops were close by, and the men could often see their flag fluttering in the breeze.[24]

While camped here, the First California received a number of visitors. President Lincoln, and Secretaries Seward and Welles reviewed the troops one Sunday during the latter part of August. "The boys never did better and complements were bestowed and were of the most flattering character," wrote one of the men. Another visitor came in the form of the paymaster, who was also well received. The privates of the regiment received $27.50 for the period between the time the men were mustered into service until July 1.

A correspondent from the *Philadelphia Bulletin* visited Camp Advance and wrote "it is certainly one of the tidiest camps I have yet seen on the banks

he tents are large and regularly laid out, and around the
ul growth of cedar and small pine trees." He also com-
iettlesome problems: "Although the honor of the name is
iia, it is by a sort of pious fraud, for a great majority of the
ιαι.. / from Pennsylvania. Colonel Baker himself is almost a Philadelphian, having spent the early years of his manhood in your city at the
most exacting and sedentary labor. The uniform is gray, like that of the southern regiments, which is a misfortune, and should be for many reasons be
changed."

The health of the men up to this point was excellent. Only two deaths
were recorded—the death of a drummer due to illness, and a corporal from
an accidental shooting.[25]

CHAPTER 2

ORGANIZING THE REMAINDER OF THE CALIFORNIA BRIGADE AND ITS FIRST CAMPAIGN

As the First California toiled at Fortress Monroe and Washington, three regiments that were later to join it to form the "California Brigade" were being organized back in Philadelphia. The Second California (later the 72nd Pennsylvania Volunteers), took merely a week, from August 3 to August 10, to reach regulation strength. Called the Fire Zouaves, the regiment contained fifteen companies and 1,487 men, drawn from almost every fire company in Philadelphia. The regiment was organized by Colonel DeWitt Clinton Baxter, a man known for his knowledge of drill and tactics through his experience as colonel of the 19th Pennsylvania, a three-month regiment. Watching the Zouave's bayonet exercises and "fancy drill" was a popular pastime for many Philadelphians. Prior to leaving for the front, Baxter actually rented the Philadelphia Academy of Music to put on shows.

The Third California (later the 69th Pennsylvania Volunteers) took a little longer to recruit, but unlike the First and Second California, the nucleus was built around an experienced militia unit, the 24th Pennsylvania. Known for his "generous and genial spirit," the 24th's colonel, Welsh-born Joshua T. Owen, or "Paddy," established a rendezvous camp for the Third California near his residence in Chestnut Hill, a fashionable section of the city. Nicknamed, the "rigulars," the regiment did not reach its full complement until the autumn, when it was joined by two formerly independent commands, called the "Baker Guards."[1]

Artillery and cavalry were to form the Fourth California, but these units were never organized.

The nucleus of the Fifth California (later the 106th Pennsylvania Volunteers) was a three-month militia regiment, the 22nd Pennsylvania. After mustering out the 22nd, its colonel, Turner G. Morehead, immediately began recruiting the Fifth. It took over a month to assemble the minimum number of men needed for the regiment, nicknamed, the "blazers." But it was not until the following February 28, that its organization was completed, with the addition of Company K. This assignment was not without controversy. Organized as an independent company of sappers and miners, it refused to become part of the regiment. The brigade commander at the time, General William Burns, did not tolerate this behavior, and ordered the rebellious men discharged. Combining the men from this company who chose to remain in camp with about twenty men from the Third California, Company K was formally mustered into 106th Pennsylvania. Another unique characteristic of this regiment was that it was not wholly composed of Philadelphians—three companies hailed from the state's coal mining counties.[2]

The brigade was fairly heterogeneous despite the fact that most were from Philadelphia. Professionals, such as lawyers and accountants, shared messes with laborers. All faiths were represented. An exception was the Third California, which contained a large contingent of men of Irish descent, and later carried a green flag emblazoned with the Arms of Ireland.

Each regiment had its muster point at a different site around the city— Camp Lyon for the Second California, Chestnut Hill for the Third, and Bull's Head for the Fifth.[3]

The uniforms of Baxter's Second California or Fire Zouaves were among the most colorful in the army. A red stripe ran down each leg of the wide cut, light blue pants. The cutaway jacket contained rows of bell buttons, but only the one at the neck was functional. This kept the throat warm in the summer and exposed the chest and abdomen to the winter elements. The shirt was the same color as the jacket, with the letter of the company embroidered on the breast pocket. No other pockets were present, much to the disdain of the men. Completing the uniform was a cap, and white leggings. The latter was conspicuousness to friend and foe, particularly on the picket line. Early on, the men tried to keep their leggings clean by avoiding muddy areas. As the months dragged on, many men discarded these "costumes" for the regulation Union uniform. For many years, the leggings could be found adorning the shapely legs of the camp followers. Some soldiers retained at least part of the uniform. Private James Wilson recalled that at Gettysburg "some of the Seventy-Second regiment had on that day the pants of the old zouaves, some pants and jackets, and some of the regulation blouse and sky blue pants. The blouses preponderated, but they nearly all wore the white leggins." The Third and Fifth California Volunteers wore the regulation blue uniforms from the start. The Fifth California hated their high black felt hats, adorned with a bugle ornament on the front, and a long black feather plume on one side fastened by a gilt eagle. The Fifth California's Baker Guards uniforms were similar to those of the Fire Zouaves, except for green trimmings, instead of red.[4]

The officer's uniform was a different shade of blue than the enlisted men's, and included shoulder boards, sword and pistol. Many would have preferred to be as inconspicuously dressed as possible, especially when in battle or on the picket line. The sword proved to be the most troublesome part of the attire. One officer wrote that it "...is of no more practical value

Unidentified Fire Zouave (72nd Pennsylvania)

than a stout club, except to a notice to an enemy sharpshooter that the wearer has rank." The scabbard interfered with the officer's movement through brush and dense woods, and at night, its rattling helped enemy sharpshooters locate its wearer.

Each unit's early days were devoted to drilling and generally learning the art of being a soldier. Because of the poor conditions of the muskets and lack of ammunition, few Union troops received target practice during the early days of the war. As a result, they usually fared poorly when they first faced the enemy. The officers also learned their craft during this time, with more seasoned officers acting as mentors.[5]

Unlike the First California (71st Pennsylvania) which received its national flag before leaving for the front, the other regiments did not receive theirs until the autumn of 1861, when the brigade was stationed in Maryland. The flags, made by Horstmann Brothers and Company, were sent to the state agency in Washington, and hand delivered by the agency's director, J. H. Puleston. The Second and Third California received their flags in November; the Fifth California received its flag in December. While there were several close calls, none of these flags were ever lost to the enemy.

In addition to the national colors, each regiment carried its own regimental flag. Several companies of the Second California contributed their own funds to purchase a stand of colors that included a regimental flag. The flag had the state arms on one side and the national arms on the other, and was inscribed "The Philadelphia Zouaves, by the Fire Department of the City of Philadelphia, September 16, 1861." Affixed to the staff was a silver plate that contained the names of the companies that had contributed to the fund.[6]

True to its Irish heritage, the Third California carried a green flag with the Irish coat of arms on one side, and a wolfhound, round tower, and sunburst on the other. Purchased by the citizens of Philadelphia, it was presented to the regiment in the vicinity of Winchester, Virginia on March 20, 1862. Little is known about the Fifth California's regimental flag, except that it was blue in color.

Orders to move to the front from the mustering points were usually received with surprise, and expected to be obeyed immediately. The Second California received orders on Sunday, September 15. As the men prepared to depart, fire bells around the city rang out to alert the men on leave to return to the encampment. The Fifth California was given a bit more time, about twenty-four hours, to prepare for their departure. This allowed details to be sent out to find those men on leave.[7]

The regiments tended to leave the city at night. The Fifth California left at 9:00 p.m.; the Second California left at midnight. In most cases, throngs of family, friends, and curious onlookers lined the streets to watch the regiments march by. The Fire Zouaves' trek was marked by the ringing of every fire bell in the city. Bonfires were lit, and cheers and wishes for a safe return erupted from the crowd. The Fifth California's historian recalled the march to the railroad station at Broad and Prime Streets:

> A perfect ovation greeted us along the whole route, the people on the sidewalks cheering and applauding as we passed, the excitement increasing as we reached the depot, the crowd already there greatly augmented by the throng that accompanied us on the pavements.

Such was not the case for the Irish-dominated Third California. "Hisses, derisive cries and shouts of contempt were freely bestowed on us, and on more than one occasion something harder, in the shape of bricks and stones, fell thick and fast in the ranks of the organization, as it marched through the streets of that city—the city of brotherly love," recalled one soldier.[8]

After the seven-hour train ride, the Fifth California reached Baltimore at 8 a.m., left the cars, and marched through the streets. After completing breakfast, they marched back to the railroad at 11:00 a.m., to complete their journey to Washington. Gone now were the comfortable cars, and in their places were dirty cattle cars with rough pine boards slid through the slates to serve as seats. So many men were crammed into each car that at least a third were forced to stand. The tired men reached Washington at 5:00 p.m. and marched through the city, all the while complaining about their "hardships."

After a short march, the men of the Fifth California reached the "Soldier's Retreat," where they found long greasy pine tables with buckets spaced ten feet apart. The buckets had held soup from a prior meal, but had not been cleaned before being used for coffee. The result was a disgusting concoction containing globs of grease and other objects floating on the top. At each place along the table, hunks of boiled salt beef sat atop chunks of bread, with the fat and juices of the former leaking into the latter. A tin cup completed the place setting. No napkins, utensils, or chairs were present, so the men stood in line, and gobbled down the food with their fingers.[9]

The First California was joined outside of Washington on September 18 by the Second California. They were soon followed by the Third California. Here, the three regiments were organized into the California Brigade, commanded by Colonel Baker. Both days and nights were devoted to laboring and picketing. Except for an occasional company drill, entire regiments did not practice because there were no fields in the vicinity large enough to accommodate the large units. The area had been heavily forested before the war, but all that now remained were stumps.[10]

Realizing that they had much to learn, the men of the Second and Third California spent considerable time talking with the "veterans" of the First California. Advice was freely given and received during this period of high apprehension. Picket duty was taken seriously because the enemy lines were nearby. Some men probably questioned whether they had made the right decision when they volunteered.

The growing army put a strain on the War Department's ability to provide food and supplies. William Manley of the Second California wrote home, "We don't get enough to eat. I get so hungry sometimes that I could eat a brick batt." In desperation, some men took to "exploring" the contents of nearby houses. On one such expedition, Manley found corn, cabbage, and beans. The officers frowned on these actions, and the pickets were ordered to arrest any man found plundering a private residence. Manley wrote, "The pickets arrested us, but we gave them the slip near the woods. They fired and the balls went over our heads." Stealing sometimes led to the perpetrator being mustered out.[11]

Fresh water was also a problem, as the men were forced to take turns carrying buckets of it from a distant spring. Frank Donaldson of the First wrote, "...as it is my turn to bring the water today my legs feel tired already from the very thought of it." The nearby Potomac River permitted the men to freely bath and wash their clothes. Cleanliness was important to the men during this period of the war. After one of his clothes-washing excursions, Donaldson wrote, "My poor hands are sore and bleeding with rubbing and squeezing. This is about the most disagreeable thing I have experienced in the life of a soldier, but I cannot go dirty and I presume I will have to get used to it."

The lack of adequate arms was also troublesome. Unlike the First California, which seemed to get the best of everything because of Baker's friendship with President Lincoln, the men of the other three regiments were equipped with old smoothbore muskets. Some even carried modified, but still ancient flintlock muskets, which proved hazardous to the shooter as they occasionally blew out the nipple when fired. The truly unlucky soldiers arrived at the front without any type of firearms. On one reconnaissance, the Second California's Company H was supplied with axes, and designated as a "pioneer" corps.

Each tent held five men. Upon turning in for the night, the men first spread out their India rubber blankets, which kept them dry. Using knapsacks as pillows, the men wrapped themselves in their blankets, and if especially cold, their greatcoats were thrown over the blankets. The men always slept with their pants on, and many kept their shoes on as well.

The routine became monotonous:

> We are awakened by the shrill fife and rolling drums at half past four in the morning...breakfast at 5; company drill, 6 to 7; guardmounting [guard duty] takes place at 8...At 9 o'clock is the surgeon's call;...At $9^{1}/_{2}$ o'clock is battalion drill, which lasts till 11...; at 12 dinner; at $4^{1}/_{2}$ company or battalion drill again which lasts an hour or so,—when we get supper immediately, and prepare for dress parade, which takes place at $6^{1}/_{2}$ o'clock, and is perhaps the most important exercise of the day...After dress parade, we have the evening to ourselves until 9 o'clock, when "tattoo" is beat, which is the last rollcall in the evening, and which

everyone must be present. 10 minutes later is "taps," ...then all lights must be put out and everyone is expected to be in bed, and quiet.[12]

Rumors flew everywhere. At first the men believed everything they heard. One day the brigade was moving to Missouri, and the next, that they were about to be attacked. The latter rumor was prevalent in the early days, as the men had a strong fear that a rebel lurked behind every tree. With time, the men became more proficient in detecting the nuances of rumors, placing them into two categories. "Cookhouse news" was usually disseminated by the cooks serving out the food. As these stories were retold, they became less accurate and more outrageous. The more plausible rumors were called "chin-chin." After awhile, soldiers usually asked whether it was "cookhouse" or "chin" when told a rumor.

Some of the rumors reached the newspapers. One reported that the men of the First California were on the verge of mutiny in mid-August. This was actually true. Seeing several three-month regiments leaving for home, and feeling homesick, many questioned the legality of their three-year enlistments. To make matters worse, Senator John Breckinridge, who had already resigned his seat to take up arms for the Confederacy, told the men that Congress had authorized three-year regiments *after* they had been mustered in, so they were not bound to the agreement. Others questioned whether they had officially been mustered in, as their service was conducted by Colonel Baker, not by a regular army officer. Dubbed the "fencibles," these men were placed under guard. When Baker arrived, he formed the regiment into three sides of a hollow square with the mutineers in the center, and spoke to the men of his love for the Union, the danger it was in, and the need for their loyal services. Then hardening his stand, he told the men that anyone who left without a discharge would be treated as a deserter. Baker listened to the men's grievances, and was able to convince all but the most steadfast to join their comrades. The rest were exposed to the elements while under guard, and periodically run through the countryside, until they too capitulated.

Another problem surfaced in the Second California. One soldier wrote home, "The regiment is in a flutter just at present about the State not recognizing us and we were out this morning in good earnest bound to find out or go home. But the colonel came and told us that it was not so, so we were satisfied about that and are now quiet."[13]

With these problems resolved, most of the men were anxious to fight the rebels. Many were dismayed when they heard a rumor that they were to return to Camp Oregon around Washington. Frank Donaldson wrote home, "I do not want to be a home soldier. I do not want to be in the defenses of Washington, I want to be in the field; to march to the front; to meet the enemy; to fight him...[and] personally aid in crushing out the defiant and boastful foe." The rumor proved to be false. Another wrote home, "I think that we will have a battle soon fore [*sic*] General Johnson [*sic*] is going to attempt to cross the river from all accounts and if he does he will have a hot reception."

The brigade's first war-related death occurred on September 21, 1861. Company B of the First California was on picket duty when thirty to thirty-five rebels appeared, causing the unit to flee for safety. Regaining their courage, they ventured back again. Soon Captain Lingenfelter exclaimed, "Here come the *damned rebels*" and shot one with his pistol. He then fell to his knees to take aim again, but before he could fire, he was hit in the temple and fell over, dead. The stunned Union soldiers recovered the captain's body and returned to camp.

The monotony of labor and picket duty was broken on September 24, when the California Brigade was ordered to participate in a reconnaissance-in-force toward Lewinsville. Led by General William F. Smith, the men were ordered to carry two-days' rations, overcoats and blankets. The rest of their supplies were left in camp. "Baldy" Smith had ventured forth toward Lewinsville before, on September 11, when he ran into a detachment of the 13th Virginia Infantry and J.E.B. Stuart's cavalry. After getting the worst of it, Smith withdrew his men to safety.[14]

Now Smith was intent on returning to the area with a larger force—approximately 5,100 men, 16 pieces of artillery, and 150 cavalry. The California Brigade left camp at 9:00 a.m. on September 25, 1861, and upon arriving near Lewinsville, Smith separated the First California's two battalions, sending each to a different part of the field. After painstakingly arranging his units in strong defensive positions, Smith realized that the enemy was not going to accept his challenge, and reluctantly ordered his ninety forage-laden wagons back to camp. Just then, a rebel column was seen in the distance, and small bodies of cavalry appeared in the cornfields on the Union right flank. At about 4:30 p.m. the rebels unlimbered two guns and began shelling the Union line. One of the first shots flew by Colonel Baker, who had a good laugh at his staff who involuntarily ducked their heads as the cannon ball flew by. A long-range artillery duel now began, with the infantry on both sides acting as spectators. Lieutenant Colonel Wistar of the First California recalled later, "During this artillery action the battery became so crowded with infantry colonels and field officers anxious to get under fire for the first time, that they had to be requested to move away. It is fair to our intelligence to add that most of us soon became able to restrain such curiosity with great success." After the Union guns had fired approximately thirty rounds, the enemy battery apparently had enough, and limbered to the rear. Realizing that the Southern troops were not going to attack, Smith again ordered his troops back to camp at 5:30 p.m. Only one man from the Third California was wounded—with shell fragments. While the men had not been directly engaged with the enemy, they had come under hostile artillery fire. During the march home, many bragged about how they had survived their first "baptism of fire."[15]

The men did not have long to wait for another chance to face the enemy. The Confederates had launched several attacks from their forward outpost on Munson's Hill, which was the headquarters of General J.E.B.

Stuart's cavalry. Lieutenant Colonel Wistar wrote later, "...their skirmishes [*sic*] and patrols began to exhibit an annoying amount of enterprise, closely searching our picket line every night, in one of which affairs Capt. Lingenfelter of the 71st [First California] was killed."

General Smith was again ordered to assemble his force and capture Munson's Hill. Colonel Baker was in Philadelphia arranging for the transport of the Fifth California, so the California Brigade was commanded by Wistar. Baker's absence apparently caused some confusion over orders. The officers believed that they were to begin their march to the assembly point at Poolesville at 8:00 a.m. on Sunday, September 29. General Smith galloped into their camp on Saturday evening at 11:15 p.m. and demanded to know why the men were sleeping in their tents and not following orders. Pleading ignorance, Wistar quickly assembled his troops, ammunition was issued, and the men marched out of camp in the direction of Falls Church before midnight. So began a mission fraught with miscues and tragedy.[16]

Smith provided Wistar with the outline of his plan, then quickly dashed off. While on the march, the men could not control their excitement, forcing the officers to frequently order them to maintain strict silence. At first the night was very dark, but later the moon rose in the sky. As the troops approached their destination, Wistar was ordered to move the First California to the head of the column, together with a battery of four guns. This accomplished, Wistar ordered his men to load their muskets and threw out three companies as skirmishers, 150 yards in advance of the rest of the regiment. As the column moved forward again, the men were surprised to find the picket guard of a New York regiment in their front. The First California was supposed to be leading the column, but here were Union troops where there shouldn't have been any. Another quarter of a mile down the narrow road, Wistar's skirmishers collided with pickets from the Fourth Michigan. The combination of the dark night and the deep woods on the left, and thick bushes skirting open fields on the right, caused growing apprehension. One soldier recalled, "The moon was now shining bright and our regiment, with its gray uniforms, looked, for all the world, like the rebels."

Suddenly, a volley erupted from the woods on the left. At first, Wistar thought that the unknown force was rebels, but then fearing that they could be Union troops, he rode between his men and the woods, imploring the hidden troops to cease firing. The woods were engulfed in deep shadows and only the musket flashes from the phantom troops could be seen. To the green Union troops in the woods itching for a fight with the rebs, the First California's gray uniforms were an inviting target. Wistar's horse was shot, as pandemonium erupted. Some men dropped their guns in panic and fled, others raised their muskets and returned the fire, "acting as if their first duty was to discharge their rifles at some imaginary object," wrote one soldier after the engagement. After about two minutes, the unidentified troops disappeared, and Colonel Wistar, now on foot, "swearing most outrageously and ordered the companies out on the road again," recalled John Baltz.

Before Wistar could again order his troops forward, the unknown troops returned to the woods, and fired another volley into the First California at a distance of under forty feet. This fire was quickly returned by his first battalion. The horses transporting a battery directly in front of the battalion panicked, and dashed off to the rear, in some cases running full speed over the men of Wistar's second battalion. To avoid injury, some of the men shot the onrushing horses. A bit later, Major Parrish and Adjutant Newlin rode along the road, "calling loudly for the California regiment to fall in and 'cease firing.'"

Wistar now dispatched several companies to secure the woods on the left, and fearing a repeat of this fiasco on the right flank, ordered several companies from the second battalion to enter and secure these woods as well. The column was now ordered forward again. Up ahead they spied the campfires of the enemy. However, they soon realized that the troops were not rebels, but the 9th Massachusetts, a regiment that had been marching on a parallel road before it was ordered to bivouac for the remainder of the night. No Confederate troops were ever seen during this march.

The First California's losses were fairly heavy—four men were killed and fourteen wounded. The Third California fared somewhat better. As it moved along the road, third in column behind the First and Second California, it heard volleys being fired into the head of the line. Just then, three cavalrymen rode up, exclaiming, "Take care, boys; here they come." Seeing some figures emerging along their flank, the men fired. Unfortunately, these men were their own pickets. Lt. Col. Dennis O'Kane stopped the firing, but not before one of his men was killed and three more wounded. The losses could have been much higher. General Smith apparently ordered a battery to open fire and sweep the road with canister, but its commander, Captain Barr, wisely waited until he could ascertain the identity of the troops in his front, which was the Third California. The officers also reduced the number of losses by ordering their men to lie down.[17]

The troops remained here until 4:00 p.m. the following day, when they were ordered back to camp. So ended the brigade's second mission, which some called the "Midnight Horror at Munson's Hill." This march back to camp was not nearly as exuberant as after the first. It was one thing to die in battle against the hated rebels, but it was quite another to be maimed by your own men. The stupidity of their officers was also discussed—no one with an ounce of sense would send green troops along parallel roads through unfamiliar and heavily wooded terrain at midnight. Frank Donaldson concluded, "Was there ever such a mixed up affair, was there ever in the annals of war, such a disgraceful disorder... Who is responsible for sending upon such an expedition *men dressed in the garb of the enemy*?" Lieutenant Colonel Wistar also questioned the intelligence of the officer who ordered the attack on his men. "It is hard to imagine the muddled condition of the officer's mind who thus ambushed his command against the head of a heavy column coming from the direction of his own rear." Morale also suffered when the men later heard that Munson's Hill had been evacuated by the enemy even before the expedition began.[18]

The following day, the brigade struck their tents, crossed the Potomac, and marched nine miles to Great Falls, Maryland. At noon on October 1, the brigade set off for Rockville, Maryland, arriving there by nightfall. On October 2 the brigade marched to Seneca Mills through a heavy rainfall. The following day, the men reached a point four miles beyond Poolesville where they were ordered to pitch their tents. Each company was permitted to use ten fence rails to fuel their fires.

The town of Poolesville was a pleasant little community composed of one small street and about 200 inhabitants. One soldier from the First California wrote: "Negroes were thick as flies, and seemed to form the chief part of the inhabitants."[19]

The brigade's camp, which was named "Camp Observation," was on a high elevation overlooking the Potomac River. The abundance of open fields and the distance from the enemy, allowed the brigade to finally drill on a regular basis. Colonel Baker took it upon himself to teach many of his officers how to drill their men. It soon became clear that Baker had a thorough knowledge of the manual of arms. During one instance, Baker showed his officers the importance of following orders. With the officers of his brigade assembled before him, Baker ordered an "arms at order" followed by "support arms." The officers realized that he had left out a step—"arms at shoulder." Some followed his command, while others rested their arms on the ground and smiled at him. With "grim determination," Baker growled, "I want the officers to understand that when an order is given, it must be obeyed."

Attached to General Charles Stone's Division, the California Brigade was designated the Third Brigade. On October 5, 1861, the Fifth California Volunteers arrived from Philadelphia, and the brigade was now complete. Upon its arrival, it was reunited with Company A, under Captain John Sperry, which had temporarily been attached to the First California with the designation of Company S. Other companies also joined the regiments here. For example, the Second California received additional companies raising its number to fifteen with a total strength of 1,487.

Besides drills at the company, regiment, and brigade levels, picket duty was also performed. The brigade was assigned the ten mile area along the Potomac River between Edward's Ferry and Point of Rocks. Two companies were sent out by each regiment that remained on duty for two weeks. There were no losses here, except for a soldier who died of disease in the camp hospital. As the historian of the brigade put it: "He had all of the attention the surgeon could give him, but in his case, as in many others, there was a dearth of women's care."

Sites of most Philadelphia Brigade activities, 1861–64

Harper's *Pictorial History of the Civil War*

After the Munson Hill fiasco, the First California received new regulation uniforms to replace their original gray ones. As Baker visited each company, he was asked if the men should wear their new overalls. One man recalled his answer, "'Yes,' said he, 'put on all the uniform you have as it will be none too good to die in.' This remark rather surprised us at the time..." The men would soon enter a battle that would leave an indelible mark on them for the rest of their lives.[20]

CHAPTER 3

BALL'S BLUFF

General George McClellan, fresh from his victory in West Virginia, now commanded the army. His thirteen divisions stretched from Williamsport, Maryland, to Liverpool Point, Virginia, guarding the forts around Washington, and the fords and ferries across the Potomac River. McClellan was under growing political pressure, particularly from the Radical Republicans, to mount an offensive against General Joseph Johnston's Confederate army, which was entrenched in front of him. This was no easy task. Heavy river batteries defended the lower Potomac, and the enemy's center at Centreville was heavily fortified. Johnston's left flank, near the city of Leesburg, Virginia, looked more promising. McClellan realized that a Union force in the Leesburg area would threaten Johnston's left flank, possibly causing the entire rebel army to abandon its position.

General George McCall's division was ordered to leave its camp at Langley, Maryland, and strike north toward Leesburg. Upon reaching Dranesville, about ten miles from Leesburg on October 19, 1861, McCall halted his troops, and sent out strong reconnaissance parties toward Leesburg. Realizing that a move from the east against Leesburg might hasten the withdrawal of the Confederates from the area, McClellan ordered General Stone to make a demonstration with his division at the nearby river crossings. At the same time, McClellan ordered General Baldy Smith to move his division against Southern troops on Freedom Hill, Vienna, Flint Hill, and Peacock Hill.[1]

On October 20, General Stone received the following telegram from McClellan, "...General McCall occupied Dranesville yesterday and is still there...The general desires that you keep a good lookout upon Leesburg, to see if this movement has the effect to drive them away. Perhaps a slight demonstration on your part would have the effect to move them."

McClellan later wrote, "I wished General Stone...to make some display of an intention to cross, and also to watch the enemy more closely than usual. I did not direct him to cross, nor did I intend that he should cross the river in force for the purpose of fighting."[2]

But Stone interpreted this order differently from its original intent, and issued orders to cross the river and engage the enemy. Stone did not know that McCall's division had been ordered back to camp, which was accomplished on October 21. During the evening of October 20, 1861, Stone sent the following message back to McClellan, "Made a feint of crossing at this place this afternoon, and at the same time started a reconnoitering party towards Leesburg from Harrison's Island. Enemy's pickets retired to entrenchments. Report of reconnoitering party not yet received. I have means of crossing 125 men once in ten minutes at each of two points." Pleased that Stone had complied with his wishes, McClellan retired for the evening. He would not have slept well had he known what Stone had in mind for the next day.

Stone ordered Gorman's Brigade to march to Edward's Ferry and demonstrate in full view of the enemy on the Virginia side of the Potomac. At the same time, five companies of the 15th Massachusetts, a battalion of the 20th Massachusetts, and a section of Vaughan's Rhode Island Battery were sent to Harrison's Island, a small island in the Potomac opposite Leesburg. The 42nd New York or Tammany Regiment, a section of Bunting's New York State Militia battery, and Rickett's battery were stationed at Conrad's Ferry, just north of Harrison's Island. Baker's California Brigade was also ordered to march to Harrison's Island from its camp near Poolesville. Stone ordered three flatboats to be moved from the nearby canal into the river, and at the same time, ordered his artillery to commence firing in the direction of Leesburg. Between the artillery fire and the movement of the boats, Stone conveyed a strong message that an advance against Leesburg was in the making.[3]

Because the river was too deep to ford, boats were the only mode of transportation to the Virginia shore. Further complicating matters was the presence of Harrison's Island, which forced two boat trips—from the Maryland shore to the island, a march across the island, and then another boat ride to the Virginia shore. Two large scowls, each with a capacity of fifty to sixty men, transported the troops from the Maryland shore to Harrison's Island. Between Harrison's Island and the Virginia shore were four boats. One large boat, propelled with poles, could transport sixty to seventy men. Two smaller wooden boats could carry a total of thirty men each trip, and a metal lifeboat was found that could carry fewer than half a dozen. The round trip journey between the island and the Virginia shore took about ten minutes. The math was against the Union forces—just over 100 men could be transported during each trip, and if a round trip took twenty minutes, then at best, only 325 men could be transported each hour.[4]

During October 20, Stone had sent two scouting parties across the Potomac to determine the location of the enemy. A small detachment from the 15th Massachusetts crossed the river at Harrison's Island, while elements of the Gorman's Brigade crossed at Edward's Ferry. Both groups returned after dark. The following day, Stone ordered five companies, numbering 300 men, from Colonel Charles Devens' 15th Massachusetts to cross the river, and attack an enemy camp the scouts had seen that night.[5]

The 15th Massachusetts began crossing at midnight, but all 300 men were not across until 4 a.m. As the men arrived on the Virginia shore, they craned their necks to look up at the steep and foreboding 100-foot bluff overlooking the river. Some said it was called "Ball's Bluff." The steepness of the bluff, coupled with the many rocks and fallen trees, made climbing it difficult. Troops arriving later found a meandering cow path that made their trip to the top much easier. At the top of the bluff, the men rested in an eight to ten-acre trapezoidal-shaped open field whose shortest parallel side lie adjacent and parallel to the edge of the bluff. On three sides of the clearing were dense woods. Looking at the woods around them and the steep bluff behind them, more than one soldier realized that this was a precarious place to be with rebels lurking nearby. Little did they know that the clearing would be stained with the blood of hundreds before the sun set.

A small detachment from the First Minnesota crossed downriver at Edward's Ford to draw attention away from the 15th Massachusetts. Stumbling upon the 13th Mississippi, they retreated until they were joined by additional units from Gorman's and Lander's Brigades which dug rifle pits on the Virginia side of the river and hunkered down in them.[6]

When Colonel Devens' battalion finally reached the area with the enemy camp, he learned that the green troops had mistaken bales of hay for tents. Undeterred, Devens continued on toward Leesburg.

As Devens transported his men to the Virginia side of the river during the early morning hours of October 21, 1861, Colonel Baker received a message from Stone sometime between midnight and 1:00 a.m. ordering him to rush the right battalion of the First California to Harrison's Island before daybreak. His remaining troops were to follow later. Baker aroused all four of his regiments at 3:00 a.m. The First California were served breakfast; the other regiments were told to be ready to move later. One soldier recalled that Baker, alternated between being pale, "as if from some indefinable apprehension" and flushed with extraordinary excitement. The First California's right battalion was ordered into line at 4:00 a.m., and marched toward Harrison's Island. The remaining regiments had a quiet breakfast at 6:00 a.m. while their arms were stacked in the nearby parade grounds. The First California's left battalion broke camp after breakfast for detached duty north of Poolesville. The remaining three regiments would remain here all day, waiting in intense anticipation for the order to move out. At 3:00 p.m., the order finally arrived, and the remainder of the brigade marched rapidly toward the river. The Second California led the march, followed by the Third and the Fifth California.[7]

At daybreak, Baker rode down to Edward's Ferry to meet with General Stone. A fateful decision was made by Stone when he placed Baker in command of the expedition at Harrison's Island. Why a seasoned professional soldier entrusted green troops undertaking a complex mission to a politician with limited wartime experience will never be known.

Explaining the position of the division, and the location of McCall's division at Dranesville, Stone told Baker that it was extremely important to determine the exact position and strength of the enemy in their front. After viewing the ground across the river, Baker was given the discretion to withdraw the troops back across the Potomac, or to send for reinforcements and engage the enemy. The former action was to be taken if the enemy was in heavy force. Baker left Stone sometime between 9:00 and 9:30 a.m., and returned to Harrison's Island.

Without first inspecting the ground on the Virginia side of the river, or attempting to determine the size of the enemy force between Leesburg and the Potomac River, Baker decided to send all of the available men across the river. To expedite matters, Baker supervised the movement of another flatboat from the canal to the river, which wasted another valuable hour.[8]

Baker made a second crucial mistake when he neglected to station an officer at each crossing point to coordinate the transport of the men. The result was mass confusion. Colonel Milton Cogswell of the 42nd New York later wrote, "Arrived at the landing opposite Harrison's Island, I found the greatest confusion existing. No one seemed to be in charge..." Stone later added that had an "efficient officer with one company remained at each landing guarding the boats, their full capacity would have been made serviceable, and sufficient men would have passed on to secure the success of his operation." Such an officer did appear later in the form of Colonel Edward Hinks of the 19th Massachusetts, who arrived with his regiment at 1:30 p.m., and immediately put some semblance of order to the crossing. After Hinks arrived, he sent over the last part of the First California, the 42nd New York, and finally, his own 19th Massachusetts. The infantry also was forced to wait while the artillery was loaded onto the boats. As the troops impatiently waited to cross, rebel infantry began massing in the woods in front of Ball's Bluff.

While Baker was making arrangements to cross his command, the 15th Massachusetts' five companies moved cautiously toward Leesburg. A skirmish broke out with a detachment of the 17th Mississippi, and while the Union forces drove away the Confederates, Devens decided to stop, hold his ground, and await the remainder of his regiment, which arrived soon after.[9]

About 12:30 p.m., Devens was attacked by units of two Confederate regiments and a small force of cavalry. One of the Confederates later wrote, "Here was the fatal mistake of the day on the Federal side... [the Confederate line was] so thin...that nearly every man could have the shelter of a tree or stump; whereas their own shots could hardly miss the dense line of blue coats. The Virginians and Mississippians being accustomed to the rifle, most of them old hunters, rarely missed their man. Climbing into the tops of trees, creeping through the tall grass, or concealed in the gullies, they applied their weapons with murderous havoc, especially among the Federal officers. It was very poor management to allow this to go on. Had Baker ordered a couple of regiments to sweep the woods he would have cleared his path of these death-stinging hornets and marched into Leesburg."

Although the 15th Massachusetts was able to beat back this attack, Devens grew increasingly concerned about his exposed position. Since reinforcements had not arrived, Devens pulled his regiment back sixty feet to a better defensive position, and prepared to receive another attack. At about 1:30 p.m., Devens pulled the regiment back again, this time to the main Union line.[10]

Baker arrived on the bluff at about 2:15 p.m. Marching up to Colonel Lee of the 20th Massachusetts and shaking his hand, he exclaimed: "I congratulate you sir, on the prospect of a battle." Then turning to Lee's troops, he shouted, "Boys, you want to fight, don't you?" This was met with cheers and yells in the affirmative. Baker clearly was very confident of his troops' ability to push the rebels aside and take Leesburg.

By 2 p.m., one company of the First California had reached the Virginia side of the river, and six more were on Harrison's Island. As the men marched across Harrison's Island to the boat landing opposite the Virginia shore, they saw large heaps of haversacks, overcoats, blankets, and tents that had been left by the troops who had already crossed. The First California soldiers were likewise ordered to "throw our overcoats and blankets into a heap and keep nothing but our cartridge boxes and muskets." As the men were ferried across, their thoughts ranged from excitement to extreme anguish. Few had faced the enemy before, and they did not like the look of the almost perpendicular bluff that rose up before them. One of the soldiers wrote soon after the battle that the hill was "too steep for horses to climb, and we had to go up holding to bushes, etc."[11]

As the First California arrived on the bluff they were ordered to stack arms and sit down. Soon the men were visited by Colonel Baker who provided reassuring words. Private William Burns recalled that when he came to Company G, he said that "...he had great confidence...as we were the color company."

Baker ordered the Union line to resemble a letter "L" lying on its side. Devens' 15th Massachusetts held the right flank, and to his left, and at a right angle were 300 men from the 20th Massachusetts under Colonel Lee. On Lee's left were the 600 men of the First California's right battalion under Lieutenant Colonel Wistar. Three cannon were deployed in front of the line, supported by two companies of the 15th Massachusetts. This deployment scheme was flawed. By positioning the 15th Massachusetts at right angles to the rest of the line, it faced enemy troops in both its front and flanks. Baker should have also moved his line farther away from the edge of the bluff, as there was too little space for the Union troops to fall back and regroup if the need arose.

Baker soon spied the arrival of another contingent of men—the 42nd New York under Colonel Milton Cogswell. As he greeted Cogswell, Baker is purported to have quoted Sir Walter Scott, "One blast upon your bugle horn is worth a thousand men." Cogswell was not in good humor. The crossing had been a fiasco, as Baker had not established any semblance of order at the ferry sites, and he definitely did not like the looks of the situation on the field. Now, he was greeted by the field commander reciting Sir Walter Scott. Baker's confidence must have been shaken when he asked Colonel Cogswell his opinion of the troop dispositions, and the West Pointer frankly told him that "I deemed them very defective, as the wooded hills beyond the ravine commanded the whole so perfectly, that should they be occupied by the enemy he would be destroyed, and I advised an immediate advance of the whole force to occupy the hills, which were not then occupied by the enemy. I told him that the whole action must be on our left, and that we must occupy those hills." At this point, the high ground on the left

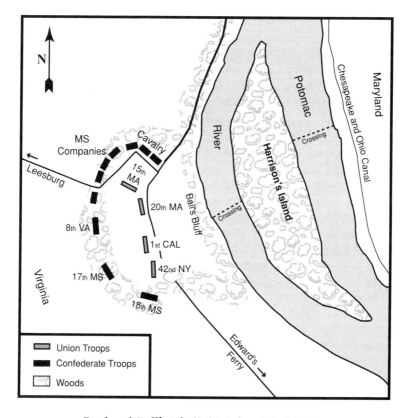

Battle of Ball's Bluff (October 21, 1861)

flank that Cogswell referred to was not occupied by the enemy, and it could have been taken by a small force. The suggestion was apparently ignored by Baker, who continued to inspect his lines and encourage his men.[12]

Colonel Baker's small command of about 1,700 men was up against a similarly sized Southern force led by Colonel Nathan Evans. Three Mississippi regiments (13th, 17th, 18th) and the 8th Virginia made up Evans' Seventh Brigade. These were veteran troops—well armed and ready for a fight. Expecting action, Evans had given the troops a rousing speech the day before, saying that he was prepared to die with the troops.

Skirmishing now erupted along the center and left of Baker's line. Wistar wrote, "...the enemy's first fire was scattering, some of it from tree-tops around the field, where they had placed some marksmen—our men lying down for shelter by my command." The men of the 20th Massachusetts were protected from injury during this exchange because they had taken off their coats with their brilliant scarlet linings, and hung them on branches so they would not get soiled. Thinking the coats contained bodies, the Confederates let loose a volley that sent balls flying through them.[13]

The 8th Virginia arrived in position at about the same time as the First California. Straddling the dirt road along which a Mississippi regiment would soon arrive, the Virginians were ordered to move all but one company to the right of the path. Ever vigilant, Wistar noticed that an isolated company of enemy soldiers occupied the woods in front of him, and at about 3:00 p.m., he requested permission to attack it. Wistar did not realize that immediately to this company's right was the remainder of the 8th Virginia. According to Wistar:

> ...I requested permission to make a change in the deposition of our skirmishers on the left, and make any dispositions I saw fit. In pursuance of this order I returned, and after a brief consultation with Col. Cogswell and myself, he directed me to throw out two companies as skirmishers to feel the woods in front for the precise location of the enemy's right...In the execution of this order Captain John Markoe (A), immediately moved out, Co. D followed him in support under Lt. Wade...The two companies moved rapidly up under cover of the woods on the left, until reaching the triangular open space before mentioned, when they were met by a galling fire from the riflemen on their front. Company A led by Markoe and closely followed by D, rushed quickly over the open ground and entered the woods when a whole regiment of the enemy [8th VA] rose up from the ground at 30 paces distant and charged with bayonet. A severe contest ensued, but our skirmishers somewhat checked the enemy's charge by taking trees and throwing effective fire into the crowded ranks at close distance. The right of our skirmishers was soon destroyed, but the left continued to hold ground for some time until Markoe was wounded and taken prisoner, when the survivors slowly fell back, bringing with them several prisoners.

Markoe's losses were heavy—about two-thirds of his men. But the survivors carried back twenty rebel prisoners, including an officer from the 8th Virginia. The battlefield now became quiet, but off in the distance the men could hear the sound of a regiment double-quicking down the dirt path leading to the open field. The men of both armies held their collective breaths in anticipation—the Union side hoping it was help from Edward's Ferry; the Confederates wishing it was the Mississippi regiment that was in the vicinity. Soon the 18th Mississippi Regiment swung into view, marching in column of fours. As they arrived, they quickly formed into a line of battle and let loose with a "wild, terror-striking yell" that was quickly followed by the simultaneous crash of 1,100 muskets. With no time to reconnoiter, the regiment's colonel led his men forward into the open field. The charge

Colonel John Markoe,
71st Pennsylvania

Massachusetts Commandery Military
Order of the Loyal Legion and USAMHI

was gallant, but doomed. Moving toward the angle between the 15th and 20th Massachusetts, his men were hit in their flank and front by small arms and cannon fire that blew his line apart. The regiment's commander, Colonel E. Burt, fell from his horse, mortally wounded, and his regiment retreated to the safety of the woods.

The three cannon boomed away at the enemy troops in their front, but one by one, the gun crews were picked off by Southern sharpshooters. At times, Colonels Lee, Baker, and Cogswell, and members of their staffs, assisted in manning the guns. Before long, the guns grew silent.[14]

During lulls in the battle, the Federal troops could hear bands incongruously playing on Harrison's Island. They could not have enjoyed the music given the mayhem around them, and the fact that their muskets frequently fouled. All through the afternoon, boat loads of men arrived on the Virginia shore. Wounded were ferried back to Harrison's Island on the return trip. As these fresh troops arrived on the bluff, they added to the blue mass. So thick were the troops that few Confederate bullets missed their mark, and some likened the situation to a "turkey shoot."

After their repulse, the 18th Mississippi moved south, past the 8th Virginia, and formed on the right flank of the Southern line, occupying the high ground that Cogswell felt so strongly that must be taken and held by the Union troops. The Mississippians continued extending their line south toward the river. Seeing this movement, and the threat it posed to the Union line, two companies from the 42nd New York and Company A from the First California were ordered to attack the head of the column and stop the movement. Cheering as they charged, these three companies smashed into the Mississippians, halting their advance.[15]

Colonel Baker was everywhere along the Union line, encouraging his men to hold their positions. Apparently realizing that he would soon need to order a general withdrawal, Baker gave the men "instructions how to fire and retire and load again." Arriving at the left of his line at about 4:00 p.m., Baker was present when the Confederates launched another desperate attack. Lieutenant Colonel Wistar was wounded a third time during this charge. The first was from a spent ball that hit his jaw, causing excessive bleeding, the second was a flesh wound, and finally, a ball hit his left elbow, shattering the ends of the three bones. Baker was the first to arrive at his side, saying, "What, Wistar, hit again?" To which Wistar replied, "Yes, I am afraid badly this time." After helping him sheath his sword, Baker called for a soldier to assist Wistar, saying, "Here, my man, catch hold of Colonel Wistar and get him to the boat somehow, if you have to carry him."

The rebel attack was driven back, and Baker now ordered a counterattack. As the line moved forward, he watched as a Southern officer was shot while riding into the field from the woods. As he fell, Colonel Baker turned to an aide and said, "See, he falls." These were the last words that

Death of Colonel Baker at Ball's Bluff

Massachusetts Commandery Military
Order of the Loyal Legion and USAMHI

Baker ever uttered. Riddled with four bullets, including one to his brain, Baker was probably dead before he hit the ground. Baker's body was momentarily lost to the onsurging rebels. Rushing to the scene, Captain Louis Bierel screamed, "Do you wish to leave the body of our beloved colonel in the hands of the enemy?" The men launched into the group of rebels, but not before Baker had been robbed of his overcoat and hat.

The loss of Baker and Wistar in such a short time unnerved the men. They had fought well all day, but were increasingly concerned about their precarious position along the edge of the bluff. The Austrian flintlock rifles carried by some of the men also proved to be highly inaccurate. The Southern troops all appeared to have rifled muskets, and their bullets usually found their mark. The men realized that reinforcements were needed. With each passing moment, the number of yells and the volume of firing from the enemy side increased, suggesting the arrival of additional enemy troops. The 17th Mississippi Regiment had arrived on the field, and now took its position between the 8th Virginia and 18th Mississippi. A strongly posted Confederate line now enveloped the Union forces as night began to fall. William Burns simply wrote, "The firing was very hot. The place was too hot for us as the rebels had completely flanked us." The Union line began to fall back.[16]

Colonel Cogswell, now senior officer on the field, hastily assembled a council of war with Colonels Devens and Lee. All realized that further resistance was foolhardy and a retreat was warranted. But here they disagreed. The two Massachusetts' colonels favored a retreat down the bluff and across the river. But as senior officer, Cogswell overruled them, and ordered an attempt to punch a hole through the 18th Mississippi, and a hookup with Gorman's and Lander's Brigades at Edward's Ferry to the south. The 15th Massachusetts on the right side of the line was to move diagonally across the field, form next to 42nd New York, and the two regiments were to attack. The First California and 20th Massachusetts were to support the attack.

For some reason, only two regiments, his own 42nd New York and the First California, actually attacked the enemy. Unsupported, they were repulsed with heavy losses. Cogswell was furious that the 15th and 20th Massachusetts did not join in the attack. All hope was lost, and Cogswell reluctantly ordered a general retreat toward the river.

With a cry of "charge and drive the enemy into the river or drive them to eternity," the Southern line charged. Colonel Winfield Featherston of the 17th Mississippi later wrote: "The two regiments [17th and 18th Mississippi] moved forward slowly and steadily under a heavy fire, but without returning it, until we had crossed the field and penetrated the woods in which the enemy were posted, and to within 40 or 50 yards of their line, when we poured in a close and deadly fire, which drove them back, and continued to advance, loading and firing until the enemy were driven to seek shelter beneath a high bluff immediately upon the brink of the river, and some of them in the river itself."[17]

The Union line melted away. One Union soldier wrote: "Now for the first time in four hours of hard fighting, I say the men Flinched." A Southern soldier recalled, "Then ensued an awful spectacle! A kind of shiver ran through the huddled mass upon the brow of the cliff; it gave way; rushed a few steps; then, in wild, panic-stricken herd, rolled, leaped, tumbled over the precipice! The descent is nearly perpendicular, with ragged, jutting crags, and the water-laced base. Screams of pain and terror filled the air. Men suddenly seemed bereft of reason; they jumped over the bluff with muskets still in their clutch,...Others sprang down upon the heads and bayonets of those below—a gray haired private of the First California was found with his head mashed between two rocks by the heavy boots of a ponderous Tammany man who had broken his own neck by the fall. The side of the bluff was worn smooth by the number of men sliding down."

Others realizing the hopelessness of retreat, tied white handkerchiefs to their bayonets and surrendered. Among them was Colonel Lee, who calmly sat behind a tree, awaiting his capture. He told his officers that there was nothing to be done but "surrender and save the men from being murdered."[18]

On both flanks, bands of Union soldiers counterattacked to buy time for their comrades to reach safety. On the left flank, the 15th Massachusetts attempted to stem the tide, but was overwhelmed. They were replaced by two companies of the 42nd New York that had recently arrived, but they fared no better. On the right, a company of the 20th Massachusetts moved against the enemy. Its captain recalled, "I called...for one last rally. Every man that was left sprang forward...We came upon two fresh companies of the enemy which had just come out of the woods...Both sides were so surprised to see each other...that each side forgot to fire...for some 20 seconds, and then they let fly their volley at the same time we did. If bullets had rained before, they came in sheets now. It is surprising that anyone could avoid being hit—we were driven back again. I had to order sharply one or two of my brave fellows before they would go back. Everything was lost now."

Not content with their victory, the Confederate troops rushed to the edge of the bluff and poured a heavy fire into the retreating yanks. Upon reaching the riverbank, the men were ordered to throw their muskets into the river rather than permit their capture by the enemy. Some men, like Colonel Devens, ran along the riverbank and hid in the brush. Captain William Bartlett of the 20th Massachusetts personally led about eighty men along the shore until they came to a large mill where they found a small skiff which they used to cross the river. Private William Burns of the First California was among these men, and recorded in his diary: "I and a few others walked a half mile up the shore at dark where we overtook another party on the same errand. Came to a mill and went inside where we found a flatboat belonging to a nigger. Capt. Bartlett and two officers of the 20th MA gave the nigger $5 for the use of the boat. There were about 90 or 100 of us to cross. We all got over to the island and to the Maryland shore in safety."[19]

Most men sought safety in the boats. Just as the large flatboat had pushed off with a fresh load of wounded, a mass of uninjured men climbed on board, pulling the little craft down. With the boat sitting dangerously low in the water, several of the polers were shot as the small craft approached the middle of the river. Falling on the gunwales, the boat quickly capsized. Only one man was known to have survived. One by one, the other boats were lost as well.

Watching the boats sink, one Confederate observer wrote, "The surface of the river seemed full of heads. Man clutched at man and the strong, who might have escaped, were dragged down by the weaker. Voices that strove to shout for help were stifled by the turbid, sullen waters of the swollen river and died away in gurgles. It is strange how persons about to die turn to their fellows for strength; they may be in mid-ocean, with no chance for any, yet will they grasp one another and sink in pairs."

With the boats gone, most of the men remaining on the riverbank knew it was time to surrender. A Confederate soldier recalled, "A feeble return fire came from some 5 or 600 men at the landing place. Then a voice was heard calling: 'Cease firing! My God, men, cease firing! We surrender!' An old officer hobbled forward, waving a white handkerchief. He proved to be Colonel Cogswell, of the Tammany Regiment."[20]

Rejecting the idea of surrender, some tried to swim the 150-yard channel. Some stopped to strip off their belongings, except their shirts and pants, before jumping into the water. Others, mad with fear, plunged in with all of their equipment, only to be pulled down to a watery grave by the excess weight. Men were drowning by the scores, some quietly, others shouting for help or crying for their wives or mothers. When the color sergeant of the First California, Sgt. Charles Vanzant, reached the shore, he quickly ripped the flag from its staff, wound it around his body, and plunged into the river. After a time, he became so exhausted that he was forced to throw the flag away as it was weighing him down. The sergeant lived to fight another day; the flag was never seen again. A number of men got across by pulling down dead tree limbs or throwing boards into the river and grasping onto them.

The remaining three regiments of the California Brigade watched the events with anticipation as the sounds of battle intensified. Soon they could see men rushing down the steep slope, heading toward the river. Rebels appeared along the edge of the bluff, sending forth a storm of death into the retreating men. The Fifth California on Harrison's Island did not attempt to aid the fleeing men, as they were forced to withdraw from the edge of the island "...very quietly so as not to attract their fire, as they could have done us great damage, especially with their artillery."[21]

The inexperienced Pennsylvanians were just as happy not to cross the river. Lieutenant John Lynch of the Fifth California wrote home, "...we were not able to cross the river—if we had my darling I should not have been here to write these few lines. Perhaps I would be in eternity—God only knows."

One of the mysteries of Ball's Bluff is Stone's use of Gorman's Brigade. Ordered to move his 2,250-man brigade across the Potomac at Edward's Ferry, one regiment had reached the Virginia shore as the battle was just beginning. Within the next several hours, Gorman crossed a second and part of a third regiment. Yet, he was never ordered to move north to assist Baker's embattled troops. Instead, he was ordered to entrench on the Virginia side of the river.[22]

The Union losses were horrendous. The Union regiments lost about 910 men, or almost half of their effectives. Many of the units' officers were counted among the losses, including Colonels Baker, Wistar, Lee and Cogswell. The citizens of Washington were reminded of the bloodbath for several days after the battle, as bodies continued to wash up along the city's piers. Of the 520 men of the First California that crossed over the river, 281 were lost. Four officers were killed (Colonel Baker, Captains Harvey and Otter, and Lieutenant Williams) and ten men were killed, three officers and 37 men wounded, and six officers and 222 men were captured. The death of Baker, and the wounding of Wistar and Markoe, were especially painful.

Colonel Baker was rewarded for his blunders by being made a national hero. He was not the first, and certainly would not be the last man, whose incompetence was misconstrued and subsequently rewarded with lasting fame. General Stone's promising career was ruined. He deserved some censure for giving so much responsibility to Baker, and for not effectively using Gorman's Brigade. Called before a congressional subcommittee to investigate the fiasco, Stone became the scapegoat. Stone's biggest mistake was not at Ball's Bluff—it was when he antagonized powerful political figures a few months earlier. Later arrested and confined to solitary confinement, he spent 189 days at Fort Lafayette in New York harbor. No charges were ever filed against him, but he was a broken man when he was finally released. Although he served as a staff officer for several months, he retired from the military before the end of the war.[23]

Cogwell's official report was especially complementary to the First California. "Lieutenant-Colonel Wistar, First California Regiment, after displaying great gallantry, was severely wounded and carried from the field, and his regiment did gallant service before and after his loss. In that regiment I would particularly mention...the color bearer...boldly held fast to his colors, waved them in front of the line, cheering the men to the defense of their flag."

The California Brigade returned to camp late that night. William Burns of the First California wrote, "Marched to camp. Got there about 2 o'clock in the morning. Very tired, but thankful for being spared." During the march through a torrential downpour, many a man probably reflected on the bad luck the brigade had experienced during the last month. First, the losses at the hands of their own men at Munson's Hill, and now the heavy losses from the veteran Southern troops. Morale suffered as the men questioned the abilities of their officers and the ineffectiveness of their own muskets. Yet, until the final moments of the battle, the men of the First California had performed well and had little cause for embarrassment.[24]

While most of the California Brigade were marching back to camp, the prisoners were moving in the opposite direction. The journey to Richmond began at 11:00 p.m. The men marched all night, and through the next day in a drenching rain, until they finally were permitted to rest on the Bull Run battlefield. During the morning of October 23, they continued their march to Manassas, arriving there in the afternoon. Corporal James Hufty of the First California, wrote home, "Soon after arrival our names were taken, and we were put in the guard house, where we remained until about 8:00 o'clock, when we took the cars for Richmond. We arrived here the next morning, soon after sunrise, and took up our quarters on the river, at the lower end of the town, in a tobacco warehouse. We have moved twice since our arrival, but keep in the same neighborhood."[25]

One regiment of the brigade had now "seen the elephant." It would be about six months before the remainder of the brigade shared the experience.

CHAPTER 4

WINTER OF 1861–62

The losses at Ball's Bluff were mourned for several weeks. In Colonel Baker the men had found a kind and wise guardian. "We miss him as we would a father, for he was a father for us here. He died as a soldier, cheering and leading us on, encouraging and showing us by example how to meet the enemy," wrote one of the men. Many referred to him as "Father Baker," and wore pictures of him on their uniforms as a sort of badge to indicate their mourning and loss. Despite this reverence, most of the men understood the shortcomings of their beloved leader. John Lynch wrote home, "...but there was one great fault which cost him his life and that was too headstrong."

The men captured at Ball's Bluff were sent to Libby Prison in Richmond. Most described themselves as being in good spirits, and hoped for the chance to be released so they could return to the ranks and repay the Southerners for their "hospitality." Corporal James Hufty of the First California wrote, "...took up our quarters on the river...in a tobacco warehouse...We get two meals a day; in the morning about 8:00 o'clock we get half a loaf of baker's bread, and as much meat as one can eat; about 3 o'clock in the afternoon we get our supper, consisting of another half loaf and tin cup full of soup." Hufty reported that officers and men occupied different floors of the same building, but complained, "They are all getting fat, as they get rather better food than we do."[1]

The ordeal left a deep-seated fear in many of the men. Private William Manley of the Second California wrote home, "There were more officers killed and wounded than I want to hear of again in my life or the war, if I live, which I know that I won't if they take us over there again. Our regiment could not get over to them or we would all be dead or taken prisoners as our beloved Colonel [Baxter] wanted to get over there as bad as anybody else did...We have just now received marching orders and perhaps will be cut to pieces so I will bid you goodby as I may never live to get out of this battle."

Colonel Baker's replacement arrived on October 31. Only 36 years old, General William W. Burns was already a seasoned officer. Graduating from West Point in 1847, he had fought the Indians in the West. A captain in the Commissary of Subsistence at the outbreak of the war, he served as General McClellan's chief commissary during the West Virginia campaign. McClellan rewarded him with a general's star, and the California Brigade.[2]

The contrasts between Burns and Baker were obvious. The younger Burns had a full beard and was much more reserved than Baker. Gone were the days when the brigade commander wandered through the camps ensuring that the men were in good spirits and comfortable. In its place, Burns instituted strict military discipline. He was constantly on the lookout for infractions, and when detected, administered swift and harsh discipline. "I don't know what his military merits are, but he is not very popular with the men," wrote one of his new soldiers. Comparing Burns with Baker, another soldier wrote, "He [Burns] is not near so sociable and kindly dispositioned." This viewpoint was not universal, however. One soldier from the Third California wrote that Burns was "eagle-eyed." "This by no means is an ill-title. It has been given to him on account of his quickness of sight to see a fault. The well-disciplined troops admire him for it; those who are not condemn him, and say he is too severe." A soldier from the First California summed up the change when he wrote home, "I do not know what military experience he has had, but I do know that our regiment drills a great deal more than it did."

One incident could not be forgotten by the soldiers of the Fifth California. "As he [Burns] was crossing the guard line into our camp, Private Collum, of Company E, was walking from him with his gun on his shoulder; the general slipped up behind him, snatched the gun from his shoulder, read the man a lecture on his duty while on guard, told him to call the corporal, then sent for the officer of the guard and had Collum put in the guard house and kept him there three days." In time, most of the men realized that Burns was merely preparing them to survive a harsh war. Private Manley of the Second California wrote home, "He is very strict indeed, but we don't care. We are getting used to it for he drills us enough. He says, 'Victory or Death.' That is the kind of man

General William W. Burns, second commander of the Philadelphia Brigade

Massachusetts Commandery Military Order of the Loyal Legion and USAMHI

I like—bully for him." The men became better soldiers under Burns, and his spirit was emulated by the officers of the brigade. Within six weeks, Burns gained popularity with most of the men. A soldier from the Second California wrote to a newspaper that Burns "...grows in favor with the men. He will become a popular general and one calculated to make his mark, should an opportunity present itself."[3]

After the war, Burns explained his behavior upon assuming command of the brigade:

> I came to you when in the deepest mourning for your dead father [Colonel Baker]—stricken on the field of battle before your eyes— when your hearts refused to be comforted... You had been reared under patriarchal rule; I brought the iron autocratical rule of stern discipline. How you hated the despot! who, if not a usurper, used all the forms of tyranny. I had to be cruel, only to be kind, to arouse your lethargy to a sense of duty...You forgave me when you knew.

Soon after Baker's death, the brigade dropped its affiliation with the state of California, and became known as the Philadelphia Brigade. The First California became the 71st Pennsylvania, the Second California became the 72nd Pennsylvania, and the Fifth California became the 106th Pennsylvania. The Third California was to became the 68th Pennsylvania, but Owen formally requested it be designated the 69th Pennsylvania as a way of linking "the two Irish regiments of the Empire and Key-Stone states."[4]

Prior to the Burns' arrival, Colonel Owen commanded the brigade, and spent some time determining the status of the units. In a letter to Governor Curtin, Owen wrote, "You may well imagine my surprise when I found that not one of the Regiments had been full organized, and that we were entirely at the mercy of the War Department as to our pay for the period of service already rendered by the officers and men." A hastily arranged trip to Washington remedied the situation, and the paymaster arrived a few days later.

Other changes occurred in the First California (71st Pennsylvania). Since Colonel Wistar was wounded, command of the regiment fell to Majors Robert Parrish and R. Penn Smith. One of the men wrote home that Parrish, "is a stern strict disciplinarian who requires the closest attention to his orders."

On November 4, 1861, the brigade shifted its camp from its exposed position in an open field at the top of a hill, to a spot beyond a large woods that provided some protection from the winter winds and storms. It also took them out of range of the enemy guns on the other side of the Potomac. What was to be a short stay, became winter quarters as the men were issued large Sibley tents around mid-December to replace their small "A" tents. Although provided with plenty of straw to sleep on and extra blankets, the men groused about the tents. "We all considered them a nuisance, although I am aware that they are thought to be the best tent in use" wrote a soldier in the 106th Pennsylvania. Part of the problem was that "only four tents were issued to a company of 80 men." Twenty in a tent proved to be a bit tight for even the most sociable. One soldier from the 71st wrote home, "We sleep 18 in one tent. Perhaps you can imagine what kind of a conversation is carried on about bedtime. Each one thinks his neighbor has got the most room."

Each tent was also to be equipped with a small sheet iron stove shaped like a funnel. Like so many other promises made by the government, the stoves did not arrive. Instead, the men of the 71st received only promises that "they are coming." About a third of the men became so impatient that they chipped in to buy their own stoves. What incensed the men of the 71st was that the 72nd and 106th regiments received their stoves with their tents.[5]

The men could not complain about the rations, though. Ovens were built in the camps, and the men were supplied with a constant flow of fresh bread. Many ate their full-day's bread rations in the morning while it was still hot and soft. Gone were the cast iron "camp crackers" that the men had endured. Other rations were also in adequate supply, as was additional clothing. As the men became accustomed to army life, they were less likely to complain about small matters. One soldier wrote home in December, "We have had rather short allowances the last few days, but it is all in a lifetime." The men had ample access to newspapers and other reading material, and mail from home arrived on a regular basis. One soldier wrote to the *Philadelphia Inquirer*, "Your instructive and entertaining paper forms a part of our daily literature. It reaches us at 2:30 p.m. the same day as published."

With time on their hands, and easy access to the news, rumors flew like the wind. One day they were going to North Carolina to join General Burnside's expedition; the next they were headed for Harpers Ferry or Washington for provost duty. Each rumor was tagged as being from a "reliable source" and caused a certain amount of anxiety among the men. But virtually all proved false, and as the winter wore on, the men became much more cynical.[6]

Each delivery of mail brought boxes from the folks back home. Lovingly packed inside were warm underclothes, stockings, gloves, and boots. Food was also a common item, and often included poultry, bread, cakes, pickles, and preserves. After carefully examining the contents of the box, the men usually shared the largess with their tent mates. Food and clothes were not the only contents that the men craved—they also wanted whiskey. At first there were no restrictions, but when drunkenness became a problem, all boxes were subject to inspection. If the offending liquid was found, the entire contents of the box was confiscated, whose contents were no doubt enjoyed by the officers. One soldier from the 71st felt the need to make this policy known to the folks back home by way of information provided to the local newspaper. "The friends of the soldiers in this regiment sending boxes here need never put anything in them in the shape of whisky, unless the person for whom the box is intended is fortunate enough to be an officer, as all boxes coming into camp now are searched, and all 'red eye' directed to privates is confiscated."

After heated protests, the officers relented and confiscated only the whisky. Families became proficient at disguising it in cans of tomatoes and peaches. Bottles were carefully slid into turkeys, and baked bread also at times had a "special ingredient." When the baking was almost complete, the bread was removed from the oven, one end carefully opened, its contents scooped out, and a bottle put in. The bread was then returned to the oven for final baking. Cakes were also manipulated in this manner.

Drunkenness was a problem. One soldier in the 106th wrote, "The men were so happy that they had to get drunk and as a natural consequence ended the day in the 'Guard House' which is the same to a soldier as the 'Station House' to unruly citizens." The officers dealt with these infractions harshly, but it seemed to make little impact on the men. Unfortunately, drunkenness was not restricted to the men, and was especially prevalent among the officers of the 71st, which was without Colonel Wistar. One private wrote home, "The officers get drunk every day....There was not a sober one in the regiment except the Major. Our captain was drunk, the lieutenant was drunk and fell into the fire and burned his uniform. The doctor was drunk and broke the bottles."[7]

The winter of 1861–62 was fairly mild. Little snow fell, and temperatures remained well above normal. This permitted the men to undertake activities not normally common during the winter months. Drilling became part of the routine. Every officer had a copy of *Hardee's Tactics*, which was used as the bible for drilling. The regiments were furnished with bands that played during the evening parades. This was not true of the 69th, which instead had a drum and fife corps. The bands played at other times as well. Private Alfred Wheeler of the 71st wrote home, "When it is moonlight, the bands go out on the parade ground and play dancing toons and the dancers go at it til 6 o'clock." Weather permitting, brigade review followed by inspection occurred on Sundays. This left little time for the men to read their bibles. One soldier groused, "McClellan's order to observe the Sabbath with respect is little regarded."[8]

The men remained in their tents during storms. George Beidelman of the 71st wrote home during one stormy period, "All we had to do was get up and eat breakfast, lay down and wait anxiously for dinner, and that over, to wait again for supper, and so on till breakfast. In fact, one is half inclined to say, 'If this is war, may there never be peace.'"

Roll call was also a daily event. One soldier from the 71st described the early routine:

> We were awoke at 5:00 in the morning, and come out in break neck style to answer the 'roll call' and stand shaking and shivering, teeth chattering, knees knocking, until that common but detestable duty is performed; and break for our camp fire or crowd the cook from his stove, and thereby receive his curses upon our devoted heads.

Before we can get washed and have shaken ourselves warm, the bugle sounds for morning parade...[9]

The men were also put to work digging trenches, building hospitals and constructing batteries near Conrad's Ferry. Many resented this hard manual labor, and felt that they should receive additional compensation for it. The corporals had little sympathy, for any man not wishing to participate would "have the privilege of sleeping in the guard house instead of your own tent."[10]

Picket and guard duty were commonplace. Each company guarded the regimental camp every three to seven days. The brigade's picket responsibility was the stretch along the Potomac from Conrad's Ferry north to the Point of Rocks, where they connected with Colonel John Geary's 28th Pennsylvania. Four companies patrolled this portion at any given time, spending one to two weeks on duty. Each company performed this duty every four to six weeks. Hourly reports from the picket senior officer were sent hourly to General Stone's headquarters. Private Beidelman described another form of picket duty—"vidette" duty, which was "something like picket, only not so hard or so dangerous; it is merely a lookout from a secret place....it was sort of vacation to us; in fact, we would have liked to have stayed all winter."

While on picket duty an unofficial armistice existed between the two sides. Lieutenant Lynch wrote home, "Secessionists are as thick as flies on the other side [of the Potomac], but as you know, pickets are not allowed to fire on one another except for self-defence or invasion of one another's grounds." The presence of an officer was also another reason to break the truce.

Because they were out in the elements, and vulnerable to enemy gunfire, many men tried to avoid picket duty. It was not uncommon for many a healthy man to turn out for sick call, often without success. Night picket duty was especially stressful to the men. Not all of the soldiers disliked picket duty. James Welch of the 71st wrote, "I like to be out here for, we dispense with the strict routine of camp duty and get away from the sound of that confounded bugler, who, just as sure as a fellow sat down to read the news or write a letter, would sound the assembly; then everything must be laid aside, while we go out and drill or do police work."[11]

Despite the fiasco at Ball's Bluff, there was frequent fraternization with the rebels across the river. Private Welch found that the rebel pickets from a Mississippi regiment, "...are very sociable...They came down to the shore yesterday morning and wished us a merry Christmas. Tis very interesting, though singular to hear them and us talk, make speeches, argue, laugh, and so on. More like *friends* than deadly *foes*! When we quit conversing each bids the other a friendly goodbye." In describing the Southerners across the river, another soldier in the 71st wrote, "They were quite merry, and exulted in having plenty of whiskey, offering to share it with us if we thought it proper to go over to obtain it." The conversation often turned to the duration of the war. "We asked them how long they were going to fight—they said until hell was frozen over and then to fight us on the ice. They seemed very sanguine about gaining their independence, as they call it," Private Burns recorded in his diary.

Not all of the troops across the river were friendly. The famous Louisiana Tigers "cursed us and called us all the names they could think of. Their favorite expression was 'low life,' 'scum of the earth,' 'abolition hounds,' and other endearing epithets which we took very coolly, and expressed our opinion of them in cool, contemptuous words that set them to swearing and striking the air and vowing vengeance on us," wrote one of the men. The days following the battle of Ball's Bluff were tense. Private Alfred Wheeler wrote home, "Their pickets, which had been very peaceable, commenced firing at ours yesterday, and say 'go bury your dead you Yankee sons of bitchs.' The day before they asked us to give them some salt."[12]

Sickness during the first winter was remarkably low. Less than three percent of the brigade were confined to the hospital during the latter part of the winter. With only 15 men in the hospital, the 106th Pennsylvania had one of the lowest sickness rates in the Army (1.5%). At the other extreme was the 72nd with 50 ill (3.5%). The 71st's and 69th's numbers were 26 (2.3%) and 29 (3.4%) respectively. One soldier from the 69th wrote to the *Philadelphia Inquirer*, "The health of the regiment is remarkable. We have in the hospital not more than eight, at an average since we left Philadelphia, and but two deaths—one that of an *old man* and the other one who contracted disease before joining the regiment. Our hospital accommodations are meager, nothing in our possession capable of comforting the sick." Writing to the same newspaper, a soldier in the 71st wrote, "We have but few sick, and they are all convalescents; our sick are well provided for, and as comfortable as can well be made in canvas tents." There was a scare in the early part of January, however, when a case of smallpox was diagnosed in the camp. This led to immediate vaccinations of all the men. There were also outbreaks of measles and typhoid fever during the winter.[13]

The medical report also showed that the brigade numbered over 4,532 men. Variations in strengths between the regiments were great. The 72nd with 1,415 men was by far the largest; the 69th was the smallest with 952. Despite the losses at Ball's Bluff, the 71st with its fifteen companies was still the second largest regiment in the brigade with 1,129. The 106th rounded out the brigade with a strength of 1,036.

As October turned into November, and December approached, the men grumbled louder and more frequently about not being paid. This posed great anxiety for many of the men, as most were expected to send money home to their hard-pressed families. Letters from home became increasingly urgent about the need for money. The delay was apparently related to a misunderstanding between the state of Pennsylvania and the War

Department about whether they belonged to California or Pennsylvania. This issue was finally resolved, and the paymaster arrived on December 6. The men of the 106th were still not satisfied, as they were only paid for part of August, September, and October. They were not paid again until February 5.

The sutlers and area farmers now took renewed interest in the men. Realizing the money to be made, some enterprising farmers loaded up their wagons and sold their wares to the soldiers at the boundary of the guard line. Active negotiations were common at this invisible line that neither soldier nor visitor could cross. Sometimes the dealings were less than honorable. In one instance, a soldier purchased a pie, only to later find that it was devoid of fruit filling. Other times some of soldiers tried to get more food than they paid for. In some cases, the officers paid off the farmer, in others, the food was returned. If the thievery was severe, or the soldier was a repeat offender, he was forced to wear a placard around his neck that read "thief" while marched back and forth under guard. One soldier in the 106th named "Yankee" Sullivan pushed his deceit too far. After negotiating a deal for a roasted turkey, he took the bird to his tent, telling the farmer that he would soon return with the money. When Sullivan did not return, the farmer alerted the guard, and with the farmer in tow, soon fingered the thief. After being forced to pay the farmer, the turkey was tied to Sullivan's back, and for the next several days he was forced to march through the camp. After this experience, his nickname changed from "Yankee" to "Turkey Sullivan."[14]

In addition to spending time in the guard house or wearing placards, the men were disciplined in other ways. When "riding the horse," the soldier was forced to straddle a horizontal log perched six feet off the ground. "Carrying a knapsack" all day filled with thirty to forty pounds of rocks also sent a strong message to the soldier. Other men were forced to carry a log on their shoulders.

The first Christmas away from home was difficult for most of the men. "Our Christmas wasn't very 'merry' in comparison with the same occasion of former years; and our minds naturally turned back to those scenes and we wondered whether by the next anniversary...we would be able to occupy our former places in the home circle," wrote George Beidelman. Dinner that night consisted of roast pig, turkey and mince pie.

As time went on, the letters from home took on a more desperate tone, and many men requested furloughs. To the men's delight, they were freely granted during the month of November. However, when several men failed to return at the required time, General Burns became agitated, and denied all requests. It was common for a soldier to receive the following statement on his request, "Refused. On account of the frequent absence without leave, no more furloughs will be granted until the troops learn that duty is a sentiment of honor." The men now became creative when making their requests. Many affixed telegrams from sick friends or documents from lawyers requesting the presence of clients. Burns continued to stand firm, granting furloughs only under the most extreme circumstances.

Several events helped to break up the monotony of camp life. During the early days of January, the men transferred boats from the canal to the Potomac to prepare for a crossing. Given the fiasco in October, the men warily obeyed these orders. Finally, to everyone's great relief, they were ordered to return the boats and "stand down." On the last day of 1861, General Burns ordered a grand parade, brigade drill, review, inspection, and muster. General Ambrose Burnside's great success in North Carolina caused Colonel Morehead of the 106th to assemble his regiment on February 12, 1862, to read the official report of the campaign. After giving three cheers for the "Union," the men gave three more for the army, navy, the flag, General Burns, and Colonel Morehead. The band played "Yankee Doodle" and the "Star Spangled Banner," and many men went to bed hoarse from all the cheering. Ten days later, the men were drawn up in a hollow square to celebrate Washington's Birthday. After firing thirty-four rounds, one of the officers read Washington's farewell address to the men. The ceremonies ended with cheers from the men and music from the bands.

The soldiers' morale varied among the four regiments. The 106th's morale was among the highest, and can be partially attributed to Colonel Morehead, who was idolized by his troops. One of his men wrote home, "...[I] think we have one of the best colonels in the army. On Thanksgiving day he would allow us to do no drilling or duty of any kind. He gave us a day for rational enjoyment." Another wrote, "...he is a soldier in every sense of the word, and sees that his men are properly cared for. He is well liked by all..." On January 10, 1862, he was presented with a sword and belt as a "token of esteem for him as an officer and a gentleman." Morehead responded with a short speech, assuring the men of his determination to wear it with honor to them and himself. Little did he know that the sword would almost cost him his life at Antietam. Several captains also received swords from the men of their companies later that winter.[15]

At the opposite extreme was the 71st, which had been decimated at Ball's Bluff. Over 300 of its men were gone, as were its most effective and popular officers, Baker, Wistar, and Markoe. A soldier wrote on January 16, "We are in no condition to fight, yet we are willing to follow whoever shall choose to lead us to the conflict. The truth as regards the regiment is, we are completely demoralized, and each day that passes over us makes us lower. The glory of the California Regiment is past, the moving spirit is gone, and we must rest satisfied as being ranked as a second-rate regiment of the old Keystone State."

Many men of the old First California hoped that morale would increase with the return of Colonel Wistar. One wrote to the *Philadelphia Inquirer*, "We daily look for his return among us, and when he does arrive we hope to see a vast change in the regiment to the benefit of both officers and men—a re-establishment of the discipline and good feeling which at one time existed in the old California Regiment under our late lamented

Colonel...Baker." Another referred to Wistar as "one who will stand no non-sense from anyone. We all like him for it, and he can lead the regiment anywhere—they will follow him to the death." Wistar finally returned on February 15, but the results were not immediate. One soldier wrote, "Colonel Wistar returned last Wednesday. He was not received with that elan that a commanding officer would like." The same soldier wrote a month later, "We are all in high spirits, and we have congratulated ourselves on the improved condition of our regiment. For this we are indebted to the fearless Wistar..."

The men were also buoyed by the return of their comrades released from Libby Prison. Prior to their return, the regiment received many new recruits from Philadelphia. While this added to their strength, the veterans of the 71st were ambivalent about the situation. One wrote about their captured comrades, "We hope they may return before our regiment is filled up, for we would of course sooner enter the field with those we knew to be of the right material than with strangers, throwing aside the many warm tides of friendship which we would again like to see united."

The men were relieved to hear that General Stone was arrested for his "transgressions" at Ball's Bluff. One soldier from the 71st wrote, "The arrest of General Stone has given us renewed confidence in war policy. Almost daily for a month previous to his arrest, rumors of some new treachery would reach our ears. When the order for his arrest was published, a murmur of satisfaction was heard along our lines."[16]

As a result of the strict military discipline imposed by General Burns, the unit was being forged into a cohesive fighting force. The men now accepted the fact that they were soldiers and to disobey orders meant swift and harsh punishment. Attachments between the men and the officers grew here, resulting in the formation of trust that would be critical during the heat of battle. The brigade's historian wrote that the name of the camp could have just as easily been called "Camp Preparation."

As the winter wore on, and periods of inactivity increased, the men became more restless. "Camp life has become quite monotonous" wrote William Lynch of the 106th. "Nothing to do and eager to move. How willingly would every mouth in this brigade welcome the orders to march into 'Sacred Soil.' It is indeed tantalizing to be so near and not do anything."[17]

To make matters worse, the mild weather caused rain to fall, rather than snow. One soldier wrote home, "The wet weather has caused the camp ground to become covered with soft yellow mud, six inches deep." This made any movement difficult, particularly drilling.

On a cold and blustery February 23, 1862, the men of the brigade got their wish—they were ordered to break camp and prepare to move the next day. This was no easy task. Being in camp for about five months, the men accumulated a wealth of material. Since there were only two wagons for each company, the men were forced to make tough choices about what was critical to retain, and what was not. The material in the latter category was either boxed and sent home, or discarded. The remaining belongings were packed and repacked in the hope that additional "vital" items could be retained. The men's perception of what was vital quickly changed when they had to carry them around on their backs during marches. "A few months later the brigade passed over the same camp, the men carrying no knapsacks and only a woolen blanket with one change of underclothing wrapped within it, and the officers had thrown away their extra baggage; the roads were no longer blocked with overloaded wagons, and the march, though more rapid, was not near so fatiguing" wrote the brigade historian.[18]

The men were issued forty rounds of ammunition, and told to be ready to move out the next day. Awakened on the 24th by distant cannon fire, no orders were received, but the men continued to pack and hastily write letters home.

On February 25, orders were finally received to move out at 10:00 a.m. As the men marched out of Camp Observation, the bands played "Yankee Doodle Dandy" and "The Girl I Left Behind." The brigade now moved north. Although few men knew it, their brigade, and the rest of the division, now under General John Sedgwick, were ordered to Harpers Ferry. Here they would join General Nathanial Banks' 8,500 infantry and eighteen guns, which was facing about 4,000 men under General Stonewall Jackson. Banks' orders were to hold the area around Harpers Ferry, preventing the Confederates from cutting the Baltimore and Ohio Railroad, and block Jackson's route into Pennsylvania. With these reinforcements, Banks was ordered to push Jackson up the Shenandoah Valley.[19]

After marching thirteen miles the first day, the men camped at Adamstown. The men had grown soft during their stay in winter quarters, and many had trouble keeping up with the column. "A very hard and severe march to me" wrote William Burns in his diary. Most of the men now realized that their knapsacks were too heavy, and relieved themselves of all but their most essential belongings. The road behind the column was subsequently littered with all kinds of articles.

That night the men slept in the open, without their tents. Each had been issued a six feet by three feet rubber or gum blanket that separated them from the frozen ground, and a single blanket to keep them warm. Few slept that night.

The next day at 2:00 p.m., the column reformed and marched to Point of Rocks, where the men waited for railroad cars that would take them to Sandy Hook, Maryland, situated directly across the Potomac from Harpers Ferry. While waiting, a storm moved in, soaking the men to the skin. The thoroughly drenched and shivering men cheered as the first railroad cars swung into view. Although these were the same type of dirty and cramped cars that had transported the 106th from Baltimore five months earlier, the men climbed in as though they had entered luxury accommodations.[20]

Arriving at Sandy Hook at 1:30 a.m., the men were grateful to learn that they could stay in the cars until daylight, catching up on the sleep they had lost the night before. Lieutenant Lynch wrote home about being "...boxed up all night in the cars, raining hard and the roof of the cars leaking so badly that we were soaking wet before morning." The men tumbled out of the cars at 8 a.m. on February 27, stiff, wet, cramped, and cold. The discomfort was soon forgotten as the men formed into a line, and with flags unsheathed and bands playing, marched across the river on a pontoon bridge.

As the 106th crossed the river, a hat flew off the head of one of the men and landed in the river. Soon another, and another followed it. One observer wrote, "Their number increased as each succeeding company stepped on the bridge, until it presented the appearance of a large flock of ducks or other waterfowls quietly floating downstream, or as if an army had been swept overboard and lost, with nothing left to tell the tale but their hats." The men hated these tall black hats, but they could not be blamed if the wind knocked them off their heads and into the river. The authorities got the message, and the men subsequently received more traditional head gear.[21]

The troops now entered Harpers Ferry, which had been recaptured by Banks' men a few days before. All of the soldiers were familiar with the town's history, but few had been there before. Lieutenant Frank Donaldson of the 71st wrote home, "This is a wretched town and I cannot see where the beauty is I have heard some much of." Quartered in the town's houses, the men were permitted to sightsee. Some sent home small bits of the Engine House where John Brown was captured, along with Confederate stamps, script, and buttons. The latter were cut off the jackets of captured soldiers. The town, particularly the government buildings, were in bad shape. Most were burned to the ground with only an occasional blackened wall to show the building's original location. One soldier from the 106th wrote home, "...[the] town is alive with soldiers and every house is occupied by them...The noble buildings that must have cost millions are now a mass of blackened ruins. Thousands of musket barrels lie in piles, broken, bent, and melted together, and utterly worthless. There are here and in the vicinity between 20,000 and 30,000 men."

While the brigade occupied the town, Colonel Morehead of the 106th was appointed provost marshal and his men, the provost guard. The brigade remained in the town until March 2, when it was ordered to climb Bolivar Heights during a severe snowstorm. The men were not happy about the prospect of leaving their warm houses in Harpers Ferry to sleep in exposed areas. Within an hour of arriving on the Heights, their Sibley tents arrived, and were set up with much difficulty.[22]

The 106th was again called for special duty on March 3, when five companies and two pieces of artillery were ordered to relieve a detachment from Colonel John Geary's 28th Pennsylvania on Loudoun Heights on the opposite side of the Shenandoah River. Since no pontoon bridges spanned this river, the men were transported, thirty at a time, in a large, flat-bottomed boat that was attached to a rope with a pulley stretched across the river. By nightfall, the men climbed the steep slope in a nasty sleet storm. Upon reaching the summit, they found to their disgust that Geary's men had not had proper shelter. Instead, they had piled logs and brush together to make "rude" shelters that did little to keep out the elements. The men later regretted using these shelters, for in a few days, "...to our horror and disgust, we found that our predecessors had not taken away all that belonged to them, but left some of the huts well inhabited; and it was here that many of us for the first time made the acquaintance of the 'grayback,' that subsequently stuck so close to us during our tramp through Virginia; neither intense heat nor bitter cold had any effect to shorten their existence or drive them away from us." The regiment remained here until March 10.

Hunger was as prevalent as the cold. Throughout the campaign, men could be seen roaming the countryside in search of food. The historian of the 106th wrote, "Chickens, ducks and geese fell an easy prey to the 'advancing hosts.' Soon not one could be found; then the remaining "porkers" were similarly disposed of, and finally the beehives were carried to the camp...It seemed to me that ... men became as children, and thought it no harm to help one's self, or in other words to steal anything to eat...if they were at home, they would never think of doing." The officers were under orders to stop this thievery, but they were more likely to look away, because the men were not adequately supplied with food.[23]

The remainder of the brigade camped on Bolivar Heights until March 7, when Sedgwick was ordered to advance on the Winchester Pike toward Charlestown, a distance of twelve miles. The brigade arrived at Charlestown at 4:00 p.m. with the 72nd in the lead. "We went in at fixed bayonet with the band playing 'Pop Goes The Weasel' on the double quick...the people all were in the houses and locked the doors...," wrote Private Manley of the 72nd. William Burns of the 71st wrote, "The inhabitants are red-hot secessionists and gave us some very black looks, especially the ladies (the dear creatures)." As the brigade prepared to camp for the night, pickets were thrown out and a reconnaissance was made to the left of the column. Because the enemy was nearby, no fires were permitted that cold night. The brigade remained here until March 10, when they struck their tents and prepared to march for Berryville at 8:00 a.m. The order never came, so they pitched their tents again that evening in the same place. The eleven-mile march to Berryville finally commenced the next morning. Passing through the town, which William Burns called a "very dirty and dilapidated place," they camped about a mile and a half on the other side.

About nine miles in front of them was Winchester, and Stonewall Jackson's Confederate division. The men were aware of his feats, and were anxious to do battle. After a day's rest, the long roll sounded at 9:00 p.m., and the brigade marched in the moonlight toward Winchester. They hadn't gone far, when the column was halted, about faced, and returned to the campground they had vacated not a few moments before. The following day, March 13, the booming of cannon suggested that they would be in action before long. After a march of about six miles, they could just see parts of the town in the distance. Suddenly, the column was halted, and the brigade was ordered to "about face" and bivouacked at Berryville.[24]

Many expressed disappointment about not entering Winchester, but there was no reason to do so. With General Johnston's withdrawal from Centreville, Stonewall Jackson was ordered to fall back up the Shenandoah Valley, while continuing to guard the army's left flank and the eastern passes of the Blue Ridge Mountains. When Banks'

Colonel Turner Morehead,
106th Pennsylvania

Roger D. Hunt Collection, USAMHI

troops entered Winchester, the enemy was gone. There was now no need for Sedgwick's division, so it was ordered back to Harpers Ferry.

The brigade reached Charlestown on March 14, and after spending the night there, returned to its old camp at Bolivar Heights. It rained most of the time. "Felt horrible and very wet, wet," William Burns recorded in his diary. St. Patrick's Day helped relieve some of the men's low morale. Burns recorded, "There was some fun. All the Paddys got drunk that could. One of Company K's men shot another of the same company while drunk. Wounded him badly."

After spending a tedious week here, the men received orders on March 23 to strike their tents and prepare to move. The column recrossed the Potomac to Sandy Hook, boarded trains, and were transported south toward Washington, where they camped on the side of a small hill, about two miles from the city, on March 24. During the trip, the men were treated to an unusual sight—a fight between two high-ranking officers. "In the cars, Colonel Miles (of Harpers Ferry fame) and Colonel Owen [69th Pennsylvania] had a fight. Owen got a black eye and run" recorded William Burns in his diary.[25]

The campaign was now over, and although the brigade had lost not a man, and gained some proficiency in marching, morale suffered. Many men felt that the campaign was a waste of time and energy. They were probably right, for Jackson would have abandoned Winchester whether there had been a buildup of Union troops or not.

General Burns could barely hide his disgust when he later described the campaign:

> This brigade had barely two months of drill and discipline after the demoralizing effects of Ball's Bluff...precluding exercise of muscle or morals, both thereby becoming relaxed, when in midwinter, February, the ill-judged campaign across the Potomac... was ordered, in snow, rain, and mud, without shelter or supplies...Burns' Brigade lost in confidence and morale most of the good of the two months' discipline, blighting the self-reliance and ambition which go to make the true soldier...[26]

CHAPTER 5

YORKTOWN

While the men of the Philadelphia Brigade were snug in Camp Observation at the end of the autumn, tension was rising in Washington for another "On To Richmond" campaign. McClellan's response was that the army was not ready, and besides, he was outnumbered by Joseph Johnston's Confederate army. Both were patently false, but McClellan believed them, and no amount of information and arguments to the contrary could change his mind. While no one could deny that General Joseph Johnston's Confederate army had taken up strong defensive positions around Manassas and Centreville, the rebel army numbered just over 40,000 men—about half of McClellan's numbers.

Under increasing pressure, McClellan finally planned an innovative and complicated strategy. Boarding his troops, artillery, cavalry, and supplies onto transports, he would sail south, around the enemy's right flank, disembarking at Fortress Monroe, well behind Johnston. A seventy-five-mile march would put the army in Richmond, well before it could be rescued by Johnston. Such an undertaking would require months of planning, but McClellan was in no hurry.

As McClellan planned his grand movement, Johnston was making his own plans to pull his troops back from the vicinity of Washington. He was increasingly worried about being overwhelmed by the growing Federal army, and his ability to defend Richmond. The withdrawal began on March 8, 1862.[1]

During the period of discord with McClellan, Lincoln assumed the initiative by reorganizing the Army of the Potomac into four corps, and took the extraordinary step of selecting their commanders without consulting McClellan. The move was intended to send a strong message, and it got McClellan's attention. Sedgwick's division was assigned to Major General Edwin Sumner's II Corps, along with the divisions of Israel Richardson and Louis Blenker. The Philadelphia Brigade now became the Second Brigade of the Second Division, of the II Corps.

Born in the eighteenth century, "Bull" Sumner had spent almost forty years in the army, and was one of its oldest officers. Despite being sixty-five years old, he was solidly built, with gray hair and beard, and he still rode ram rod straight in the saddle. Men knew when he was near because his booming voice usually preceded him. Given his advanced age, and failing mental capacities, he was probably not the best choice to command a corps. Although he had difficulty adjusting to the ways of the "new" army, his men came to respect him. One soldier in the 106th wrote home, "His skill and daring courage should ensure success, well does he deserve promotion. During the...battle of [Glendale]...the shells flying in every direction. One fell within ten feet of the General, but fortunately did not explode. His staff hurried out of that but Sumner never seemed to notice, but went on calm and cool." Later, the men learned to judge an officer on leadership and motivating abilities, rather than on the basis of coolness under fire.[2]

The Philadelphia Brigade's journey from Harpers Ferry to Washington seemed endless. Crammed into railroad cars, the men were unable to sit down. "[I] was quite used up when we arrived, being scarcely able to move one foot before the other," wrote Frank Donaldson of the 71st. Reaching Washington on March 24, the men were granted permission to visit the city, and some chose to see the Senate and Congress. After a few days of rest, the brigade left Washington on March 27, and marched to Alexandria, Virginia.

Normally, the number of circulating rumors is proportional to the number of men in an area. Yet, despite the large number of troops around Alexandria, the men were unaware of their destination. Lieutenant William Lynch of the 106th wrote home on March 28, "Part of our brigade was stowed away..., but our destination is not known. We will be off, I think today for Dixie." The harbor was loaded with hundreds of ships—the largest assemblage in United States history. Schooners, barges, side-wheelers, ferryboats, excursion boats, and transatlantic packets, almost 400 in number, carried men and their equipment to the front. In less than three weeks, the armada carried 121,500 men, 14,592 animals, 1,224 wagons and ambulances, 44 artillery batteries, and all of the equipment needed to service an army. The cost for using the ships was staggering—over $30,000 a day.[3]

Because of the cost of using the ships, the activity around the piers was frantic. The brigade was aboard the transports and under way by 8:00 a.m. on March 28. The 69th sailed on the ferry, *Champion*, while the 106th was transported in the steamers, *Naushon* and *Long Branch*. Realizing that the entire 69th, numbering about 900 men, were aboard a boat registered for a limit of 500, the captain of the *Champion* balked at shoving off. Turning a deaf ear to his protests, he was forced to shove off. The large oceanic steamers towed large barges behind them carrying men, horses, and artillery. The men of the 71st on the steamer, *Louisiana*, could look back on a menagerie behind them, and be thankful for some shelter from the elements. It did not take long for the men of the 71st to realize that the engineer was drunk. William Burns merely recorded in his diary, "Capt. P. J. Neil takes charge of the engine."

The three days aboard these boats were anything but pleasant. With men crammed into every nook and cranny of the *Champion*, the ship began taking on water. Pumps were manned day and night, and men calculated their chances of survival if the small craft went down. Because overcrowding made steering difficult, the boats dropped anchor each night, and continued on their way after daybreak.

On the second day of the trip, the weather turned so nasty that all fires had to be extinguished. Details were sent ashore to cook the food and return it to the men. Some men waded into the Chesapeake Bay in search of oysters. Even on good days, cooking posed a problem. Large cauldrons were provided to boil coffee, but there were no other facilities for cooking. The innovative Yankees soon came up with novel ways of preparing their food. The men cut their raw bacon into strips, stuck pieces on their bayonets, and used the ship's steam stacks as a broiler. The brigade historian wrote, "It was an amusing sight to see the men stand in turns around this greasy pipe and press their pork against its sides until it was done to a crisp; but the food was relished just as well as if it had been prepared in the regular way, and the operation, along with other funny doings, helped to while away the tedious hours spent on the passage down the Potomac."

The ships carrying the Philadelphia Brigade disembarked their men between March 29 and March 31. After several days on the boats, the men were overjoyed to again touch firm ground. Upon arriving here on March 29, William Lynch of the 106th wrote home, "We have just arrived here [Fortress Monroe]...we are now awaiting orders...no one knows our destination...this is indeed a large fortification—much larger than I had anticipated finding. There is an immense quantity of shipping here." William Burns recorded in his diary that "the fort looks as if it could stand a long bombardment before it would surrender."[4]

The men were treated to a sight of the U.S.S. *Monitor*, which had already attained legendary status. "Arrived at the fort and anchored near the little *Monitor*. It was a curious looking boat. It looked like a raft sharpened at both ends with a cheese box on it. There were two indentures on its side, received in its encounter with the rebel ram *Merrimack*," recorded William Burns in his diary.

As the men emerged from the boats they were formed into columns and marched to Hampton, where they camped. The scene was quite different from when the men of the 71st had been here the year before. Frank Donaldson wrote that the town, "whose neat white houses,...magnificent shade trees which so impressed me when here before, is now one vast charcoal heap, having been destroyed by General Magruder, shortly after we withdrew from it last summer." But ten families now lived in the former resort town that had boasted a population of 3,000. Another change was the number of troops and equipment that stretched as far as the eye could see. Gone was the sleepy encampment the men had enjoyed during the summer of 1861. By the time that the Philadelphia Brigade reached the "Sacred Soil" of Virginia, over 50,000 men had already landed.

During this time, General Burns reported the brigade's strength to be 3,624 men. The breakdown was: 69th=726; 71st=904; 72nd=1,215; 106th=779. An additional 357 men or 9% of the brigade were listed as absent. These men were presumably sick, wounded, prisoners, had deserted or were home on leave. The size of the brigade had shrunk considerably from its strength of 4,532 during the early winter. Since the brigade had not engaged the enemy during winter, and deaths due to illness were uncommon, virtually all of these 551 (12%) men must have been discharged, transferred to other units, or deserted.

The brigade remained here during the first few days of April, and spent considerable time drilling. In addition to the regular army fare, the men's diet was supplemented with oysters and other ocean delicacies they caught. While in this camp, the men had the chance to try out their new "shelter tents" that replaced the large and unwieldy Sibley tents. These were merely six feet square pieces of canvas with regularly spaced buttons and button holes along the sides. The men were also provided with a forked upright and a ridge pole. The "tents" were worthless individually, but when combined with a second "tent," made an inverted V-shaped tent that was open on two sides. The two uprights were thrust into the ground with the forks facing upward, and the ridge pole was laid between them. The two pieces were then buttoned together and draped over the ridge pole to form an open tent. A third soldier's contribution would make a tent closed on three sides, and a completely closed tent would require four men. The tents proved to be too small for four men, but as losses mounted in the campaign, the men had access to additional tent pieces.[5]

McClellan's grand strategy was working perfectly. With General Joe Johnston's army still miles away, along the Rappahannock River, all that stood between Richmond and McClellan's growing army, was 10,000 men under General John Magruder. On paper, McClellan's 50,000 plus troops already on the Peninsula, could shove Magruder out of the way, and easily take Richmond. Many residents of the Southern capital understood their dilemma and made plans for a hasty departure. They did not know that speed was not part of McClellan's repertoire of skills, however. Orders for the advance on Yorktown were issued at first light on April 4, 1862, abruptly ending the brigade's comfortable stay at Hampton. General Eramus Keyes' IV Corps moved northward on Lee's Mill Road while General Samuel Heintzelman's III Corps, followed by Sumner's II Corps, moved north on the parallel Yorktown Road. The brigade marched six miles, then halted for several hours. While resting along the road, the men had their first opportunity to see McClellan, as he galloped by with his staff. As he approached, the men jumped to their feet and cheer after cheer followed him as he dashed by. Private William Manley wrote home that the men cheered McClellan so much that he "...stopped and asked what regiment it was. We told him—he tipped his hat and told us we could have a chance at them this time. We told him that was what we wanted." So began a long admiration with their commanding officer. One old soldier remembered, "No matter how tired—covered with dust or trampling through mud, would respond the same way—each man would straighten up, take his position in line, and cheer as he passed. It helped them to forget their fatigue and would give them a fresh start."[6]

Most were surprised by the light Southern opposition along the route. The men camped that night at heavily fortified Big Bethel, the site of the rebel's winter quarters. A soldier from the 106th wrote home, "The works were of the strongest kind, and mounted some heavy guns, but were left without a shot being fired. Near our camp there were also some earthworks, and the barracks were winter quarters. The barracks were good log houses with fireplaces in them, well close by, stables, etc. In fact they were a good deal better quarters than we had 200 miles farther north." Private Manley also spent the night in these log houses and commented on their sturdy construction. "We slept very soundly that night for the boys were very tired from their march through the mud." The march continued at 5:00 a.m. the next morning. After covering only five miles in four hours, the column halted, and the men rested. At 2:00 p.m., the column reformed and marched to within four miles of Yorktown.[7]

Taking Richmond would not be as easy as it looked from afar. Few roads were present to carry McClellan's immense army toward Richmond, resulting in frequent bottlenecks and delays. The roads themselves were in fairly good shape as long as it didn't rain. But rain it did during the campaign, short squalls and long-drenching rains that turned the roads into mush. Men often marched along roads with mud up to their knees, and it was virtually impossible to move wagons and artillery. Then there were the Confederate fortifications which Magruder's men had busily constructed for months. The first line of defense was the Yorktown line, which stretched the entire width of the Peninsula from Mulberry Island on the James River to the west, to Yorktown on the York River to the east. This formidable line contained eighty-five heavy artillery pieces and fifty-five field guns. Because the line was behind the marshy Warwick River, any Union attack would get bogged down when it moved through this wet area. Many Union soldiers became discouraged when they first saw these formidable works. To attack them would mean a certain repulse with hundreds or thousands of casualties. The Confederates were also constructing a second line at Williamsburg, six miles north. Magruder planned to slow the Union advance by forcing McClellan to overcome both lines of fortifications, allowing time for Johnston's army to arrive.

Magruder's major problem was not enough men—he commanded only half the number needed to defend the Yorktown line. What he lacked in manpower, he made up in creativity. Several times he marched the same regiments back and forth within view of the Union troops to suggest a larger force than the one he actually had. The bluff worked, for McClellan decided that the only way to reduce the line was through siege warfare. The Union commander was an expert on this type of operation, having witnessed it during the war with Mexico and during the Crimean War. McClellan did not know it, but he had already lost the campaign, as he frittered away his golden opportunity to take Richmond. While he planned the siege, Joe Johnston's Confederate troops began to arrive to reinforce Magruder on April 6.[8]

The Philadelphia Brigade arrived at Yorktown on April 5, and camped for the night. At dawn the next day, the men of the 72nd and 106th were roused from their sleep and ordered to prepare to make a reconnaissance of the enemy line from Yorktown to Lee's Mill, a distance of about six miles. This was the first reconnaissance of the enemy's position, and the men took their selection as an honor. Formed into a column, each man was loaded down with his rations, shelter tents, and knapsacks, and marched to the extreme right flank of the army where Heintzelman's III Corps faced the strongly entrenched Confederate position at Yorktown. Their mission was to reveal the location of masked batteries, and the best way to do it was by exposing themselves as decoys to draw the artillery fire. General Burns was excited to be given this honor, and personally led the two regiments.

Upon arriving in position, Burns threw out a strong skirmish line in his front, and along both flanks, and moved forward toward the strongly held Confederate line. They drove in the rebel skirmishers, and approached the fortifications. Soon the concealed batteries opened fire. "We were not more than 100 yards from the battery and could hear the secesh hurrahing as the shell burst" wrote William Manley of the 72nd. As officers noted the position of the batteries, the troops were pulled back, moved to the left and then advanced toward the rebel works again. As soon as the hidden rebel artillery opened fire, they fell back and repeated the maneuver. In this way, the men gradually moved along the entire line of the rebel fortifications. Surprisingly, the two regiments sustained no losses during this cat and mouse game, probably because no sooner had the masked batteries opened than the two regiments withdrew, and moved to the left. One Massachusetts soldier was, however, killed by an artillery shell during this time.[9]

As the regiments slowly moved through a dense woods in the afternoon they stumbled upon rifle pits occupied by the enemy. Receiving a misdirected volley, they fired two in return, and scattered the enemy force in front of them. The men waited, expecting an attack, but when none materialized, they continued their movement to the left.

The two regiments returned to their camps after nightfall, having marched sixteen miles that day. The exhausted men fell by the campfires, sore and tired from their excursion with full packs, but proud of their accomplishments. Although these men would participate in many such exploits during the war, they never forgot the excitement of this, their first reconnaissance.[10]

The next three days were cold, rainy, and generally miserable. While trying to stay warm and dry in their "shelter" tents, the men could hear the

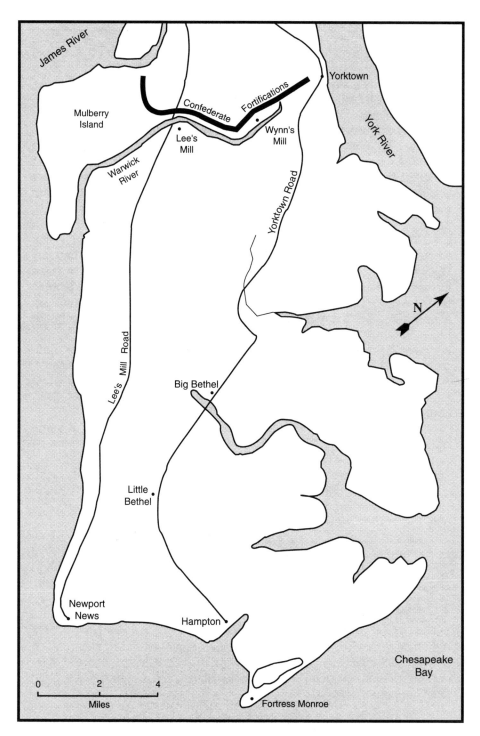

James River

Mulberry
Island

Confederate   Fortifications

Yorktown

Lee's
Mill

Wynn's
Mill

Warwick
River

York River

Yorktown Road

N

Lee's Mill Road

Big Bethel

Little
Bethel

Newport
News

Hampton

Chesapeake
Bay

Fortress Monroe

0   2   4
        Miles

Yorktown Campaign

Southerners continuing to fortify their works. Because of the Philadelphia Brigade's reconnaissance, and his own observations, McClellan ordered preparation for a siege, and soon orders were issued to begin erecting earthworks. McClellan also planned to bring up heavy siege guns. As the storms continued, however, the roads become more impassable by the hour, and what had been small marshy areas or small streams, were now becoming bottomless pits. The men were ordered out to construct bridges over these areas, and "corduroy" roads leading to and from them. To construct these roads, the men chopped down trees twelve to eighteen inches in diameter, and laid them across the roads where they were secured in place with stakes. A total of fourteen redoubts for artillery were constructed, connected with lines of earthworks and rifle pits for the infantry.

The men established camp behind the front lines at Shipping Point, where they continued the task of building corduroy roads and small bridges. Drills and campwork were a thing of the past now, as the men often toiled in knee-deep mud and driving rain. During this period of strenuous labor in rainy weather, the men seldom felt dry clothes on their backs. Mud was everywhere, and many a miserable soldier's thoughts returned to better times. Still, most believed that they were on the verge of ending the war, so they took it in good spirits. One soldier from the 106th wrote home, "...our clothes and blankets were continually wet. It was anything but comfortable. A pause in life's pleasures." Private William Townsend sarcastically wrote to his uncle, "[We have] good beds on the ground. Bark for a sheet, overcoat for a bolster, knapsack for a pillow, blankets for a quilt."[11]

The men had cause to question the abilities of their leaders, as some orders made no sense. For example, the 106th was sent out at noon on April 9 to build roads. Accompanied by the 71st and the 15th Massachusetts to protect them, the 106th started off at noon and tramped through woods, mud, and underbrush in a heavy rainstorm. With the onset of darkness they were marched back to camp without having done any work that day. The next day, the brigade built roads close to their camp.

Observation balloons under the able guidance of Professor Thaddeus Lowe were an ever-present part of the siege. Perhaps to relieve some of the monotony, General Fitz John Porter never tired of going up alone to observe the Confederate lines. On April 11, the men of the Philadelphia Brigade anxiously watched as the ropes holding Porter's balloon broke, sending him toward Fortress Monroe. Suddenly, the winds shifted, and the balloon sailed over their heads, and toward the Confederate lines. As the men held their breaths, the winds changed again, and the balloon again headed back over Union lines. The balloon now began a rapid descent. Writing soon after the incident, William Manley of the 72nd graphically described what happened next:

> We seen him coming down and expected every minute the basket would upset but he was spared for a better purpose. He came down with the balloon at a smashing rate and struck one of the tents with

the basket and smashed it in half. As soon as the basket struck there was a hundred men there and kept the balloon from turning over on the basket and smothering him [Porter]. He was taken out of the basket and stood on his feet almost insensible. The first thing he said was 'where am I?' We told him and he then asked, 'where are your officers' to which the Colonel [Baxter] replied, 'I am here.' They both walked up to old Billy Burns' headquarters where he got something to drink and felt all right again. The next minute or more there were horsemen coming in all directions to find the General and also Professor Lowe asking 'is the General hurt much.' We told him 'no' and he then went to see him. The balloon was hauled up to Yorktown in a half an hour afterwards and is now up over the rebel fortifications looking and watching what the rebels are about.[12]

Perhaps detecting a growing demoralization among the men as a result of being forced to work under these difficult circumstances, Burns had his General Order #13 read to the men on April 12:

The General commanding, after an intimate service with the brigade for nearly half a year—in camp—on march—through vicissitudes of winter hardships—in the face of danger, has had the proud satisfaction of seeing day by day the constant improvement in all of the essential elements of soldierly endurance, patience, energy, skill, and discipline; and now he is about to lead you into action, has full confidence in you, and feels and knows that you will march on the foe, while knowing that hundreds are killed in retreat, but while few fall while advancing. *Fortune favors the brave.*

Soldiers; our war cry is 'onward' our reward victory, our future of proud satisfaction that we won our laurels in the Army of the Potomac. The eyes of your General, your relations, and your country are upon you.[13]

The order probably only had a minor effect on morale.

On April 16, the Philadelphia Brigade was moved to the front line at Wynn's Mills, where it established Camp Winfield Scott. The men remained here for the remainder of the siege, helping to construct Battery #8, and the roads leading to it. Although a belt of dense woods lie between the rebels and their new position, a "shell now and then finds its way into our camp, very greatly to the annoyance of the soldiers and to the utter demoralization of the camp followers and servants," wrote Frank Donaldson.

This was a very stressful period for the men, because in addition to the rain and mud, they were constantly vulnerable to enemy fire. When the fatigued work crews returned from work on the battery, they were often "saluted" by an enemy artillery barrage, punctuated by rebel sharpshooters. Sometimes, the rebel artillery pounded the brigade's position. After one such occasion, Frank Donaldson wrote, "They [his men] were completely demoralized and driven off by the fire and took shelter further in the woods."

Artillery duels were fought daily, and the enemy often sallied forward to test the strength of the Union forces in front of them. William Townsend of the 106th wrote, "There is plenty of men here—to look at them when there is an alarm—you ought to see the men turn out and form. I thought the ball would open last Sunday. The rebels fired on our pickets and drove them in. Then you ought to have seen the glistening guns in the sunlight form in line of battle to meet the rebels. But they didn't come out. They [rebels] come out nights and try to take our batteries but they catch it at the time and have to retreat."

As time went on, these attacks were frequently made at night as well. This took its toll on the men's nerves as they worked all day, but could not get a full night's rest. Instead, they were called out two or three times a night to protect against an attack. As enemy sharpshooters became more active during the day, more work on the fortifications was done at night. For example, the 106th spent the entire night of April 25 throwing up earthworks, and after a few nights' "rest," did it again on April 28.

To reduce the amount of artillery fire against them, the men of the Philadelphia Brigade perfected a new strategy. Details of men were sent out at night to dig rifle pits. Upon completion, the men climbed into them and camouflaged themselves. Remaining in them for the rest of the night, they quietly took aim at the rebel gunners as they prepared their pieces for action the next day, driving them away from their pieces. The enemy soon copied this strategy, and artillery duels became less frequent during the latter stages of the siege.[14]

William Manley observed that the Union lines were less than half a mile from the Confederate fortifications, so the soldiers of the opposing armies could see each other. "They [the rebels] would shell him if they could but the sharpshooters keep the guns clear. They would pick the gunners off as soon as they showed their heads above the fort... They could not work them at all and therefore had to keep mum and say nothing for if they would show themselves they would surely drop. The sharpshooters say they draw them as close to them that they can shake hands with them. They all have the spy glass on the barrel of their rifles."

William Myers of the 106th agreed with Manley's assessment of the sharpshooter prowess, and added, "...and our artillery are dismounting their guns almost as fast as they put them up. They have quite a lively time, sometimes, but our men are the best shots. They can put a shell just where they want them and it is a good thing as they will have to do all the fighting at least the worst of it."

The periods of earthwork construction around Battery #8 were broken up by picket duty. Rather than the usual two companies performing this duty, an entire regiment spent a day on the picket line every three days. Units were also dispatched to protect the men working on the fortifications. These men were the first to see the gigantic siege guns that McClellan was bringing up and installing in the fortifications.[15]

Strict discipline was maintained during this period. "No permits being granted to leave camp, no beating of drums, no sounding bugles, no cheering—no demonstration of any kind allowed whereby the enemy can gain a knowledge of our numbers and what we are doing," wrote Frank Donaldson of the 71st. Colonel Morehead of the 106th ordered his men not to fire their guns prior to cleaning them. When some of the men persisted, resulting in casualties among some of the unfortunate men in the path of the discharges, Morehead's punishment was fast and strict. Most were ordered to stand on barrels under guard for a day or two.

Getting provisions to the men were a problem for the quartermasters. When the brigade left Hampton, each man was issued ten days' rations for their haversacks, and three days "on the hoof," which meant in the wagons. Because of the condition of the roads, wagons had difficulty getting to the front, so supplies were limited. It was not unusual for the men to miss a meal. One soldier renamed the camp, "Camp Starvation." "Sunday morning with nothing to eat since Saturday morning and marched up to the General Porter's Division," wrote William Manley. For the first time in the war, the supply of whiskey for the enlisted men became scarce. This posed severe concerns to the men who had developed an affinity for this form of distraction. The officers were the only ones who possessed whiskey, and this drove some of the enlisted men to extreme measures. "Officers' servants were bribed, sickness feigned to get it from the surgeons, and stolen when it could be got [sic] no other way" wrote the historian of the 106th. Several instances were reported of soldiers crawling up behind officers and taking a nip out of their canteens.[16]

During this portion of the siege, the men were constantly dirty, hungry, and apprehensive of being killed and wounded. Frank Donaldson wrote home that, "[I] have not washed my face, or had my clothes off since Wednesday, and for the last two weeks have lived on crackers and coffee, eaten out of vessels which it was impossible to find time to clean other than by a wipe now and then with dead leaves, and fed myself with hands black with dirt and smoke."

The weather was exceptionally warm during this period, and water was often scarce. The surface water was less than savory, and even attempts to dig down three to five feet in search of fresh water proved fruitless. Most of the men suffered from diarrhea as a result of drinking the polluted water. Some later estimated that the sick list during this time was almost the entire army. To counteract this growing problem, the troops were later issued whiskey two times a day, sometimes containing quinine.

Colonel Wistar later wrote about this period, "The result of hard work, constant exposure by night as well as by day, with inadequate food caused wholesale sickness; which kept the actual strength and mobility of the army reduced to a low figure." Not only was the water tainted and the food scant, the wet conditions facilitated the spread of diseases like malaria and typhoid fever. Making matters worse was the fact that many of the men did not hold the medical personnel in highest regard. Private Alfred Wheeler of the 71st wrote home, "I am pretty well but rather billious [*sic*]. Tell mother that she should send me some pills that she knows are good. We have doctors here, but they are nothing but common murderers, and I will not go to them."[17]

As the end of April approached, most of the Union heavy siege guns were in position, and McClellan set May 5 as the date for the big guns to open fire. He was able to accumulate a tremendous amount of firepower into 15 batteries—70 heavy rifled pieces, including two that weighed eight tons and fired 200-pound cannonballs, and 41 heavy mortars, some weighing ten tons. No one, Northerner or Southerner, doubted that the Confederate works would be reduced within a short time. "There is an awful lot of artillery going out all the time" wrote William Manley. "I think it will be an artillery fight... The first five [shells] they will think heaven and hell have come together if they don't soon surrender." William Myers agreed, "I think, and not only me, but others, that they will leave inside of three hours when the boys get to work at them." As the fortifications were built, care was taken to hide the guns. John Lynch of the 106th wrote home, "We have some enormous guns here and when the order comes to clear away the trees and brushwork in front of our forts it will take secesh by surprise."

As time passed, the dread of having to storm the enemy's fortifications mingled with their personal discomfort of constantly being wet, tired, and hungry. Still, most believed what they were doing was right. "I wish this fight was over and my skin whole. But if I fall, I fall in a good cause," wrote William Townsend at the end of April.[18]

Realizing that the Union attack on Yorktown was imminent, General Joseph Johnston, whose men had now arrived, gave orders to withdraw to the next line of fortifications, around Williamsburg. If the Union troops even suspected a withdrawal, they would immediately attack, and with their vastly superior numbers, crush the Southerners when they were most vulnerable. To cover the withdrawal, Johnston ordered the Southern guns to open a tremendous bombardment during the night of May 3, which had the effect of driving the Union troops to cover.

When daylight arrived on May 4, the front was curiously quiet, and it was not too long before the Union forces realized that the Southerners had fled before the blow had been delivered. While Johnston had extracted his army without losing a man, he was forced to leave behind valuable equipment that he could ill afford to lose, including all 72 pieces of his heavy artillery. To decoy the enemy, most of the tents were also left intact. As the Union troops cautiously entered the fortifications, they found that the Southerners had used charcoal to write messages on the white tents. One said, "1:00 a.m.- May 4, 1862—Goodbye, Yanks, You call us Rebels, we call you Vandals."[19]

As word of the Confederate retreat reached the troops, and they realized that they would not be ordered to storm the works, cheers erupted. Bands that had been quiet during the entire campaign played in every camp.

Suddenly in a moment, the men forgot their fatigue and extreme discomfort. William Myers wrote home, "...our Colonel [Morehead] proposed three cheers for our noble commander, and then three cheers for our glorious union. The boys were wild with excitement."

Thousands of men now surged forward to see the formidable enemy works and collect souvenirs. Before long, an explosion shattered the quiet, and Private John Green of the 69th flew through the air. He lost both legs in the explosion, and died while receiving medical attention. The officers and men were initially puzzled—the enemy were nowhere to be seen and none of their own artillery were firing. It did not take the men long to realize that the fleeing Southerners had used percussion shells with pressure sensitive fuses to "booby trap" articles of interest, as well as certain entrances into the fortifications, and the roads leading to Williamsburg. This dampened the men's scavenger impulses, causing them to return to their lines, but a dozen men ultimately succumbed to these "infernal contrivances." So angry were the officers that they made captured rebel prisoners disarm them. Other mines were marked with stakes and pieces of cloth, and soldiers were stationed nearby to warn the men to keep their distance.[20]

The hidden shells caused many rumors to be generated. One was that the rebels had poisoned the water and the food left behind. This rumor reached members of the 106th who had procured some rare flour from the rebel fortifications, and were now about to sit down and enjoy some "slap-jacks." All of the men looked at each other, and at the steaming hot delicacies, and wondered what to do. Finally, one man could not take it any longer, grabbed a pancake and informed the group that he would "test" it. The men watched as he devoured the first slap-jack, quickly followed by a second. Realizing that he was about the devour the entire stack, the men dove in to get their share.[21]

The brigade's losses during the Yorktown campaign were light. However, exposure to the elements took a much greater toll. Most of the regiments were depleted because so many men were in the dispensary suffering from sickness and disease.

The pursuit began about twelve hours after the last rebel had left the fortifications. General Joseph Johnston's goal was simply to get his army as close to Richmond as he could. Leaving a small rear guard at the strongly fortified town of Williamsburg, about six miles north of Yorktown, he moved the remainder of his army northward. The bloody battle of Williamsburg was fought on May 5, which resulted in a Southern victory, as it halted the Union pursuit. Although none of his troops were on hand, General Sumner was given command of the field by virtue of his seniority. The battle would have turned out differently had Sumner adopted a more aggressive stance. Instead, he prevented his commanders from taking advantage of weak points in the Southern line. The result was a lost opportunity to crush Johnston's rear guard.[22]

CHAPTER 6

FAIR OAKS

As the battle of Williamsburg raged, Sedgwick's division was held in readiness to provide assistance, if needed. The division began its northward march toward the battlefield on the Yorktown Road at 8:30 a.m. Although the men were anxious to get to the battlefield, heavy rains had made the road all but impassable. The Philadelphia Brigade marched only seven miles in four hours, some of them in mud and water up to the men's knees. The men were grateful when the order was given at noon to fall out and rest. They soon learned, however, that they could not sit down by the side of the road, so the men were forced to stand in the road from noon until after dark. The night was cold, rainy, and dark, and the miserable men huddled together to keep warm and hold each other up. Just as the men were about to break, Baxter's Zouaves spontaneously began singing the coronation anthem, which was taken up by the other troops as well, which helped the men forget their "dismal plight." At midnight, the men were ordered back to camp after standing in the muddy road for ten hours. Many never forgot this ordeal and the stupidity of their officers.

The following day dawned bright and sunny. An added bonus was that the troops were permitted to remain in camp to rest. The men changed into dry clothes, and washed and dried their filthy, wet ones. Farther to the north at Williamsburg, the Union skirmishers advancing early in the morning found the rebel works abandoned as the Confederate rear guard again made good its escape.[1]

During the battle of Williamsburg, McClellan planned another bold move. Five divisions would continue marching northward along the two parallel roads, while the remaining four divisions, including Sedgwick's, embarked upon ships to be transported up the York River to Eltham Landing, about twenty-five miles from Yorktown. The move was designed to bottle up all or part of the Confederate army between two Union pincers, causing its ultimate destruction. However, by the time the first troops under General William Franklin disembarked at Eltham Landing on May 6, most of the Confederate troops were already beyond this point. To distract Franklin while his troops reached safety, Johnston dispatched General John Hood and his brigade of Texans to hold back the enemy's advance, which he successfully accomplished after a sharp skirmish.

While Hood was battling Franklin's troops at Eltham Landing, the Philadelphia Brigade marched to the Yorktown wharfs at 6:00 a.m. on May 7. After waiting several hours for the steamboats to arrive, they embarked on the *Daniel Webster*, *John Brooke*, and *State of Maine* which towed the schooner *Smithsonian* and the propeller *Salvador*.

A gunboat proceeded the transports, occasionally throwing shells into the thickets, "to the consternation of the few people who still remained in this part of the country," recalled Frank Donaldson. Several houses were passed along the route, "and hanging from the windows of which, white flags hung out in token of submission."

The boats arrived at Eltham Landing at 4:00 p.m., too late to participate in a fight with Hood's brigade. The men were marched off the boats and camps were established by the banks of the river. The following day, the men moved to a new camp nearby. The brigade marched three miles inland to Eltham on the Pamunkey River on May 9, where it remained several days.[2]

During this period, the Union high command was more concerned about getting the men to Eltham Landing than feeding them, resulting in a scarcity of food. When food finally arrived at the docks, it accumulated there because the roads had become all but impassable to wagons. This forced officers, like Colonel Wistar, to take matters into their own hands. "It was frequently necessary to march a regiment several miles back to the landing to carry back a few days' rations on their own backs," he later wrote.

After awhile, supplies again became plentiful for the enlisted men. It was a different story for the officers. Instead of drawing rations from the government, officers were expected to provide their own. Many went hungry during this period, especially those who were too proud to accept the offers of the enlisted men to share their rations. The brigade historian wrote, "...captains of companies were unwilling to reduce the allowance of the men by accepting their proffered rations, were known to eke out their scanty supplies by gathering on the march, food that had been thrown away." It was hard for the men to see their respected officers being forced to behave this way. The situation improved with the appearance of the sutlers once again. Many officers also "employed" contraband slaves who acted as their servants, and who, in return, received protection and shelter. These individuals knew the land and became proficient foragers.[3]

On May 15, the brigade marched twelve miles to New Kent Court House amid a heavy rainfall. Many veterans later recalled this difficult march. The mud was sticky and slippery, and when a man took a step, his foot slid back part of the way. This reduced the men's stride and fatigued them as it felt like marching in peanut butter. The heavy mud occasionally pulled off the men's shoes, forcing the soldiers to break ranks to retrieve them. To make matters worse, the woolen uniforms soaked up the water, making them very heavy. The road, which was also heavily cut up by the prior movement of artillery and wagons, was dotted with vehicles and caisson's stuck in the mud, in some cases above their axles.

The unhealthy conditions that bred disease continued to take its toll on the men. Many officers made matters worse when they indiscriminately chose places for the troops to camp—many being within marshy areas. To attempt to stop the spread of disease, whiskey was freely issued to the men. While many undoubtedly liked this allocation, others were not so sure. Joseph Watt of the 71st wrote home,

> On account of the very swampy ground by which all the camps are surrounded, and the unhealthy air which pervades the atmosphere, Gen. McClellan has ordered each man a half-gill of whiskey with quinine in it after breakfast and after dinner, as a preventative for the chill and fever. I have not taken any as yet... I am afraid it will do more harm than good in the long run for it will give young men a taste for liquor and when they get home they will look for it an 'eye-opener' before breakfast.

Straggling was severe, as the long fatiguing marches in the intense heat took its toll. Upon nearing New Kent Court House, the brigade was given almost three days' rest. Starting off again on May 18, the column passed through New Kent Court House and camped four miles beyond it. After resting for several more days, the brigade made a fifteen-mile march on May 21 to finally reach the Chickahominy River and a reunion with the wing of the army that had been moving north on foot after the battle at Williamsburg. Because of the long marches in the intense heat, some men fell out to get water. Among them was William Burns who wrote, "Very warm day and very severe march. Fell out to get a drink of water. Had to stand one hour on guard for doing it." That night the brigade camped near Bottom's Bridge on the Chickahominy on the plantation of former ex-President John Tyler. The brigade was moved a short distance on May 23.[4]

The Chickahominy River, which was destined to play a major role in this campaign, became etched into many men's minds until they died. The historian of the 106th Pennsylvania later wrote: "What's in a name? Yet the mention of that name causes a shudder to run through the survivors of the Army of the Potomac, and brings many sad memories to thousands of households throughout the land. Many contracted diseases there that took their lives or lingered throughout their lives."

McClellan placed his army in a precarious position when he ordered Keyes' and Heintzelman's corps to occupy the western or Richmond side of the river, while the other three corps were on the opposite shore. Each wing was therefore vulnerable to attack without aid from the other side. To compensate, McClellan ordered the construction of two new bridges (Grapevine and Sumner's Lower) and the repair of two others.

During this period, Sumner's two divisions linked with Porter's corps on their right, and Franklin's corps on their left. All three corps faced the river. The Philadelphia Brigade was stationed about three miles above Bottom's Bridge, and around fifteen miles from Richmond. The men were confident that they would soon be in Richmond as Joe Johnston did not show a propensity to hold his ground, much less attack. Private Jacob Pyewell of the 106th wrote home, "...and when we get there [Richmond] I think it will about wind up this rebellion. I think in a week or two Richmond will be ours. I tell you when we do get at them at Richmond we will give them fits. 'The Yankees with horns' as they call us will show them what they are made out of." About a week later, Pyewell's optimism continued to rise unabated, "...and I think we will be there [Richmond] before another week. Suppose it will be as hard to take as Yorktown was. I am beginning to think there will not be much more fighting. I don't think the cowards will stand and show fight." Pyewell could not have known that Confederate General Joe Johnston was planning a small reception for the Yankees.[5]

The routine was broken by a variety of activities, including picket duty and reconnaissances. For example, on May 23, the 106th Pennsylvania together with the 20th Massachusetts made a fourteen-mile reconnaissance along the Richmond and York Railroad, but encountered no enemy soldiers. On May 27, the men were drawn up to witness the punishment of an officer. "Capt. Oswald of the 34th New York was publicly disgraced this afternoon in the presence of the whole division. Having his buttons cut from his coat, his kassants torn from his shoulders, and his sword broken before his face for mutiny," wrote Joseph Elliott of the 71st Pennsylvania in his diary that day.

The following morning, the entire division was ordered under arms, and within ten minutes of the sounding of assembly we were on the march without breakfast or coffee. The men could hear the sounds of battle coming from Hanover Court House. After marching a few hours, the division was halted in a large field, where it spent the night, as well as the morning of May 29. The division returned to its camp that afternoon.[6]

With his back to Richmond, the Union army divided by the Chickahominy River, and reinforcements poised to join McClellan, General Joe Johnston realized that it was time to take the offensive. The blow would be made against Keyes' corps on McClellan's right flank at Seven Pines on the Richmond side of the river. After destroying Keyes, Johnston would turn his attention to Heintzelman's corps. All the while, the troops on the opposite side of the river would be unable to assist their comrades. The topography favored the Confederates. Three roads converged on Seven Pines, and Johnston deployed his divisions on all of them. General W. H. Whiting's division was expected to hit the right flank of the Union line, while General D. H. Hill took on the center, and General Benjamin Huger's division attacked the left. Hit on three sides, Keyes' corps would be crushed in a coordinated attack.

The attack was set to begin at 8:00 a.m. on May 31. A strong storm hit the area the day before, much to the delight of Johnston, who knew it would swell the Chickahominy, making it all but impossible for McClellan to send help to Keyes' and Heintzelmen's beleaguered troops. Frank Donaldson could never recall such a severe storm. "Dazzling flashes and great blinding sheets of rain fell and rushed through our camp turning the country around us into a perfect river. We speedily soaked to the skin, but made every exertion to keep dry our muskets and ammunition."

Johnston's plan was a good one, and if implemented properly, 40 percent of McClellan's army would be destroyed. However, the operation went awry from the start. A combination of misconstrued verbal orders and recalcitrant generals caused a delay in the Confederate attack, and when it finally came, it was piecemeal and uncoordinated. General D. H. Hill's division, making up the center of the Confederate line, smashed through the General Silas Casey's division composed of raw troops at Seven Pines. Keyes' other division, under General Darius Couch, acquitted itself more gallantly, reforming its ranks again and again, in an attempt to stem the enemy tide. In the late afternoon, a flank attack by Confederate General Micah Jenkins' brigade broke the resistance and the men fled for safety. Cut off from the rest of Couch's division were several regiments of Brigadier General John Abercrombie's brigade, and a battery. Abercrombie wisely ordered his men to march for the bridges over the Chickahominy, where they might find safety.

Because of blunders on the part of the Confederate general officers, only D. H. Hill's troops had participated in the attack up to this point—the thrusts against both flanks were delayed. Finally, during the afternoon, General W. H. Whiting's division moved along the Nine Mile Road, and stumbled upon General Abercrombie's small force at Fair Oaks Station, which was only interested in fleeing to safety. Realizing his dilemma, Abercrombie quickly deployed his men. Expecting to easily push these troops aside, Whiting ordered the first brigade, Colonel Evander Law's, to charge. After a bloody repulse, Whiting called up the next brigade, which launched another, unsupported attack.[7]

From their position across the Chickahominy River, the men of the Philadelphia Brigade heard firing coming from the direction of Seven Pines at 10 a.m. A clearly agitated "Bull" Sumner galloped back and forth among the camps, impatient that his men were inactive while the hated rebels were close by. When orders to advance did not come by 1 p.m., he ordered his two divisions to assemble at the Chickahominy River bridges to await further developments. Sumner's division marched to the Grapevine Bridge and Richardson's division assembled behind Sumner's Lower Bridge. Because of the heavy rains, the Chickahominy River rushed past in a mad torrent. Sumner's Lower Bridge had all but washed away, and the Grapevine Bridge was not in much better shape. Most of the logs leading to the

Grapevine Bridge were afloat, and were only kept in place by the stumps to which they were fastened. The bridge itself was twisting and turning, and about ready to break lose and fall into the water. The historian of the II Corps later wrote, "The condition of that part of the bridge which crossed the channel of the river was impossible to ascertain except by actual trial; but its timbers could be seen rising and falling, swaying to and fro, under the impulses of the swollen floods."[8]

Sumner finally got his orders to cross sometime between 2:30 and 3:00 p.m., but before he could issue the necessary orders, he was accosted by an engineer who insisted that the bridges were in no condition to be safely used. Still smarting from the criticisms of how he handled the troops at the battle of Williamsburg, Sumner was not about to let an engineer get in the way of his redemption. Shouting to the engineer, "Can't cross this bridge? I can, sir; I will sir!" When the engineer persisted, saying the crossing was impossible, Sumner roared, "Sir, I tell you I *can* cross. I am ordered!" That was that, and the order was given to cross. The men were incredulous that they were to be sacrificed this way. There was just no way that the bridge could hold. The brigade historian later wrote, "The bridge itself was suspended from the trunks of the trees by ropes and on their strength depended the safety of the structure...as the first part of our division marched on the bridge, it seemed impossible that it could stand; but the very weight of the troops while crossing made it temporarily secure by settling it against the solid stumps." While the bridge seemed secure, the water rose to the waists of the men. Sumner's Lower Bridge did not fare as well, washing out soon after. This forced Richardson's division to assemble behind Sedgwick's at the Grapevine Bridge.

When it was time for the Philadelphia Brigade to cross, General Burns halted the men, and ordered them to first help Lt. Edmund Kirby's Battery I, First United States Artillery get across the bridge. Long ropes helped to pull the pieces up the bank. Sumner was not happy about this delay, and sent three separate messages to Burns to get his brigade across. But Burns knew the importance of artillery, so he ordered his men to continue helping get the guns across the river. Just as the last gun was crossing the bridge, Sumner rode up and personally ordered the brigade to double-quick to the battlefield. Later, Sumner rode up to the men of the 71st Pennsylvania and suggested that "[we] throw away our [gray] overcoats for our own men would shoot us."[9]

General Gorman's brigade, with the First Minnesota in the lead, spearheaded the II Corps' column as it rushed to Abercrombie's aid. Emerging through a belt of timber at about 5:30 p.m., the Minnesotans could see Abercrombie's regiments hotly engaged with the enemy, and about to be overcome by superior numbers. As they formed on Abercombie's right, Kirby's battery galloped up and unlimbered at the Adams House. No sooner were these units in place that the Southerners launched another attack on the weakly held Union line. As Gorman's other regiments arrived, they were thrown on Abercrombie's left.

The Philadelphia Brigade was second in line behind Gorman's brigade with Baxter's 72nd in the lead. As they approached the vicinity of the Adams House, they could discern the Union line of battle just beyond a thin strip of woods in front of them. "Here we met numbers of wounded men coming from the fight," wrote the brigade historian. "Stray balls were flying about us, and before we realized it, and while some were discussing whether the bullets that were whizzing past us were spent or not, we were in our first battle as an entire brigade."

This was the first time that most of the men were under fire. Burns later described the moment:

> The mass was petrified. A shiver ran through the ranks. I turned and saw a sea of upturned faces, pale as the dead. I was shocked. My outburst of 'Steady men' was like a thunder-clap in a clear sky...The reaction was instantaneous. A shout arose in answering confidence...

The brigade initially formed behind Gorman's, but enfilading fire on Gorman's

Private George Beidelman, 71st Pennsylvania. Photograph probably taken during the winter of 1862–63.

Catherine Vanderslice Collection, USMHI

right flank caused Sedgwick to worry about an attack from that direction. Riding up to the brigade, he ordered Burns to take the 69th and 72nd and form a line of battle at a right angle to the First Minnesota. Burns complied, leading the two regiments forward in line of battle through a swampy woodlands for about 300 yards in search of the First Minnesota.[10]

Leaving Colonel Baxter in charge of completing this movement, Burns rode back to his two remaining regiments. He was met by Sedgwick's assistant adjutant, who impatiently informed him that the two regiments had not yet completed their mission. Learning that the First Minnesota had changed front, and was now in an open field nearly parallel to his two regiments, Burns galloped back to redirect his men's movement. The 69th's left flank finally connected with the First Minnesota, and the 72nd extended the line to the right.

The battle now raged along the First Minnesota's front. As enemy volleys reached the flank of the 72nd, Colonel Baxter yelled out, "That's the music, boys, now for three cheers!" General Burns swung his hat in the air and yelled, "Let them be hearty!" The two regiments responded with a deafening cheer that was soon emulated by Gorman's brigade. With the roar of Kirby's guns as punctuation, the Union troops desperately holding the line felt more confident now that help was at hand. "Our men were just giving way when they heard our loud hurrahs and rallied and fought manfully until we were able to get to their support," wrote John Lynch of the 106th.[11]

Soon after Burns left the road with the 69th and 72nd, General Sedgwick personally led the 71st and 106th to the Adams House where they were ordered to support Kirby's battery and the remainder of Gorman's troops. The Philadelphia Brigade was destined to fight its first battle in different parts of the field.

Colonel DeWitt Baxter,
72nd Pennsylvania

Massachusetts Commandery Military Order of the Loyal Legion and the USAMHI

As the 71st followed Sedgwick to its position, a cannonball came hurling in the direction of Company H, causing half the company to stampede to the rear. Their newly appointed lieutenant, Frank Donaldson, ran after them with his pistol drawn. Seizing one of the soldiers by the throat and flourishing his pistol, he was able to bring the men back into the column. To prevent this from happening again, Donaldson threatened instant death to any man "who made the slightest movement toward the rear." The 71st eventually took position just to the right of Kirby's battery, about fifty yards from the woods that harbored the Confederates. The men were ordered to lie down as the rebels fired a storm of lead over them. Those officers standing, including Lieutenant Donaldson and Lieutenant Colonel Markoe were hit and quickly carried to the rear.

The Confederates had many obstacles to overcome if they were to take the Union position. Confederate general G. W. Smith wrote, "The generals of brigades, colonels, and other commanding officers were laboring under great disadvantages, the thickness of the woods and undergrowth and the smoke preventing them from seeing more than a very limited

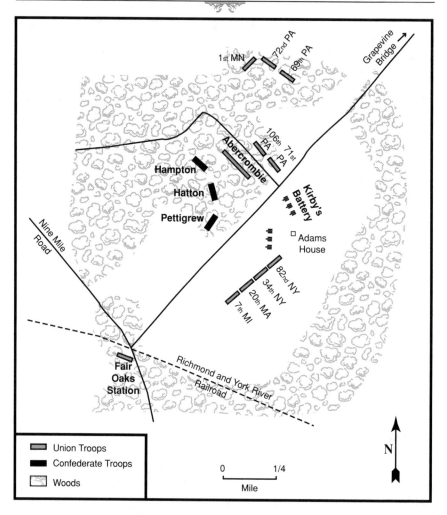

Battle of Fair Oaks (May 31, 1862)

number of their men at any one time, while the roar of musketry was almost deafening."[12]

Enamored with the idea of capturing enemy artillery, the Confederates made three bloody charges against Kirby's battery. The gunners responded by firing 343 rounds from their five pieces. During one charge, the Southerners came within a few feet of the guns, and one officer actually rested his hand on one of the pieces, yelling, "This is my gun." "Not yet," screamed Captain Kirby, as the Southern officer was knocked senseless by one of the cannoneers. To complicate matters, the guns were mired in mud up to their axles, and had to be pushed out of the muck every time they fired. Between the double canister, and the volleys from parts of the

71st and the 106th, the charges were beaten back. After the battle, one man counted thirty "graybacks" within a space of eighteen square feet that had been taken down by Kirby's canister.

As night descended upon the battlefield, the Confederates prepared to make one last charge. Before they could launch their attack, Sumner ordered three regiments from Gorman's brigade and two from Dana's brigade to immediately form into line of battle and charge the enemy. The troops fired as they advanced, and when they were within fifty yards of the rebel troops, they fixed bayonets and charged. Receiving a deadly artillery fire from Kirby's guns, galling volleys along both flanks, and now a bayonet charge, the Southerners called it quits for the day.[13]

The first day's battle can actually be considered to be two separate battles. To the south at Seven Pines, the Confederates had smashed Keyes' two divisions. But just north at Fair Oaks, the sudden appearance of Sedgwick's division spelled doom to General Whiting's advance against Keyes' right flank. Not only were Whiting's troops outnumbered, 8,700 to 10,700, they were poorly led, being thrown into the fray in a piecemeal manner as they arrived on the field. Whiting's commander, General G. W. Smith, later wrote after the battle, "Various attempts were made to charge the enemy, but without that concert of action almost absolutely necessary to success, and the gallant spirits who attempted it were very many of them shot down, when the rest would fall back into the line and resume the firing. Our troops held their position close to the enemy's line until it was too dark to distinguish friend from foe." Whiting also blundered by not bringing up his artillery. Yet, he assumed the role of the attacker, and time after time his attacks were beaten back with heavy losses.

That night, several companies from the 71st and 106th were thrown out as skirmishers. Moving slowly across the field towards the woods that harbored the rebels, they passed over large numbers of dead and dying men who fell during the afternoon fighting. Equipment was strewn everywhere, and groans and cries of the wounded filled the air. The men of the Philadelphia Brigade had never been on a battlefield at its conclusion, and were greatly affected by what they saw and heard. They were extremely careful not to step on the wounded and dead as they slowly moved through the field.[14]

In the darkness, Burns thought he heard rebel pickets to the right of the 72nd. Worrying that this might presage a rebel attempt to get into Sumner's rear, Burns moved the 69th to the right and rear of the line, where it remained during the night and next morning without incident. Sometime between 11:30 p.m. and midnight, Burns was ordered to take the 72nd, 19th Massachusetts, 42nd New York, and 63rd New York back to the Grapevine Bridge to help get additional artillery across the Chickahominy, and to keep the lines of communication open.

While the battle was renewed at dawn the next day at Seven Pines, the opposing troops at Fair Oaks Station warily watched each other, but made no effort to continue the fight. Later that morning, the Philadelphia Brigade was ordered to move to Seven Pines to support Hooker's and Richardson's divisions that were hotly engaged. The brigade arrived there toward the close of the battle, and at one point, received orders to fix bayonets and prepare to charge the enemy. The order to execute this action never came, and later in the day, Burns was ordered to turn the brigade around, and again move back to protect the army's communications. The brigade remained here for another two days, when it received orders to double-quick to the left flank where Hooker was expecting a momentary attack. The attack never materialized, and the men spent a miserable night, thoroughly drenched in a heavy rainstorm.[15]

Early the next morning, the men were marched across the marshy ground where some of the heaviest fighting had occurred. The dead lay everywhere in large numbers. Some of the bodies were partially buried. Most were not. "...in places where the swamps were deep, dead Confederates were standing erect, shot as they were retreating, and the mire had prevented their fall," wrote the brigade historian. Worse was the odor of the rotting flesh that "penetrated our wet clothes, and even tainted the food in the haversacks. Strong men grew sick and turned aside with horror."

During the battle of Fair Oaks, the Philadelphia Brigade acted principally as support to other troops, so its losses were light—five killed and thirty wounded. Sedgwick had high praise for the brigade in his official report, "It was not the fortune of any of the regiments in this brigade to meet the enemy at close quarters, but all gave unmistakable evidence of being ready if ordered forward to rush to the support of their comrades with alacrity and unshrinking firmness. The One Hundred and Sixth Pennsylvania...and the Seventy-second Pennsylvania..., held in reserve, were several times moved from their positions to different portions of the field at double-quick, evincing their eagerness to become engaged." Burns indicated his pleasure in his report, writing, "I am entirely satisfied with the conduct of my brigade. It has been christened under fire, and will do what is required of it."[16]

Private Alfred Wheeler of the 71st Pennsylvania wrote after the battle,

> We were under fire for three hours, had several killed and wounded among them was a lieutenant and a sergeant... After we crossed the Chickahominy, went double-quick to the battlefield. As we passed through the woods into the open field the whole regiment yelling like so many crazy men. The excitement was so great that there was no such thing as fear. I have often felt more frightened at the sound of musketry in the still night air when on picket than when I did while the roar of the cannons and thousands of muskets were thundering around me. The scene of the battlefield for three or four days was horrible. The roads were strewn with all kinds of implements of war. All the dead and wounded were lying in every direction. Some with hands off, and some with their eyes out. Some with

head smashed and lying in all sorts of positions. Some sitting, some standing, others kneeling or in the act of loading their piece...

The brigade remained in the vicinity of the battlefield and its "unwholesome atmosphere" for several days. On June 3, the brigade was ordered to "feel" the enemy at Old Tavern, and cover the movement of troops arriving on the field. Post-battle stress replaced the euphoria of the battle, and this coupled with the growing incidence of disease, weighed on the men. Many contracted malaria, and when they went to the hospital, found to their dismay that they were treated with disdain. Because of the large number of wounded from the battle, the surgeons could not spare time to care for the sick. "It was almost as though a soldier has no business to become sick in the surgeons' head," wrote the brigade historian. The sick and wounded alike suffered during this time as the army had great difficulty getting needed medical supplies up to the front.[17]

General Baldy Smith's division relieved Sumner's men on June 6, and Sedgwick's division was reunited with Richardson's division. Richardson's division was positioned on Sedgwick's left and the Chickahominy River anchored their right. About a mile opposite the Philadelphia Brigade were the rebel lines in the heavily wooded Garnett Farm. Upon arriving here, General Sumner ordered the brigade forward to clear the woods of rebel soldiers. Encountering the enemy in rifle pits, a charge was ordered, and the rebels fled to safety. Leaving skirmishers to occupy the pits, the brigade returned to its lines. The next day, they were joined by the skirmishers, who had been thrown out of the pits by Confederate artillery fire. That evening, the brigade sallied forward again to recapture the rifle pits, only to have their skirmishers lose them again the following day. So it went for the three weeks that the brigade occupied this area.

As the picket line composed of one company from the 69th, two from the 71st, and two from the 106th moved forward, two days later, it was attacked by the enemy, who poured an enfilading fire into the ranks. The line could not withstand this fire, and fell back, leaving several dead and wounded on the field. The narrowest part of the woods in front of the Confederate position lay directly in front of the Garnett House. This put some of the pickets, which were advanced about half a mile from the Union line, in heavy woods, while others were at the edge of the open field in front of the house. Because of the proximity of the enemy, extraordinary care needed to be exercised. Unfortunately, this did not always occur. Around dawn of June 9, Lieutenant Colonel Curry of the 106th went to inspect his pickets, but instead found Confederates, and was captured. Unbeknownst to Curry, his pickets had fallen back, and he fell into Confederate hands while searching for his men. He remained a prisoner for about three months before returning to the regiment. Until the officers and men understood the ground and the close proximity of the enemy, other losses occurred. On June 8 and 9 alone, two officers were killed and one wounded.[18]

Lieutenant Colonel William Curry,
106th Pennsylvania, killed during
the Spotsylvania campaign, 1864

Massachusetts Commandery Military Order
of the Loyal Legion and USAMHI

During most of June, the brigade was in almost continual contact with the enemy. Entries from the diaries of William Burns and Joseph Elliott, of the 71st, suggest that between June 6 and June 27, the regiment was attacked or engaged in a firefight with the enemy eight times (June 6, 7, 8, 9, 12, 21, 25, 27). Elliott thought that June 21 was especially eventful, "In the afternoon a body of the enemy was discovered approaching the works, in the adjoining camp, on their hands and knees. The pickets fired and fell back, when the batteries opened and the rebels retired. Quite an excitement took place and all thought a general engagement was about to take place. Alarms were frequent during the night." On June 27, Elliott disgustingly wrote, "Our pickets were thrice attacked through the day and night and no place stood their ground."[19]

Because of the enemy's close proximity, General Burns' men dug rifle pits that they topped off with logs and brush. The woods directly in front of these pits were cleared so the men had a clear view of the ground in front of them. The men usually slept on their arms, as an attack could be expected at any moment. Seldom did a night pass when the skirmish line was not attacked, or some other form of threat materialized. Sometimes the pickets dashed back with news that an attack was imminent, or began firing in the direction of the enemy lines. During these times, the men were ordered to take their positions to thwart attacks that usually never came. The men soon came to realize that some of the pickets were more prone to give false alarms than others. As the men turned in for the night, the question, "who's on picket duty tonight," would be asked to ascertain how well the men would sleep that night.

Some dangers were not imagined—enemy sharpshooters, concealed in trees, took their toll on the men's bodies and nerves. When their positions were identified, the snipers were killed, wounded, or driven out of the trees. The use of sharpshooters was not restricted to the Southern side, however. Burns occasionally used his own men in this capacity to harry the enemy troops. When the Union snipers were particularly effective on one Sunday morning, the relative quiet was broken when the rebels let lose an artillery barrage on the brigade, killing and wounding a number of men from the 72nd.

Only one report on the actions involving the Philadelphia Brigade can be found in the *Official Records*—Colonel J. D. Kennedy, of the 2nd South Carolina, reported on a skirmish that took place on June 18:

> The officers...report[ed] what they supposed to be a masked breast-work in the woods facing toward the road on which my regiment was formed, running from the Nine-mile road. They drove the enemy's line of pickets and picket reserve in and advanced to within 200 yards of what appear[ed] to some of the officers to be a line of fortifications. They heard officers giving orders very distinctly and cursing their men. There seemed to be a great deal of confusion among the enemy...Two or three Enfield rifles were captured, several off-cloths, marked 69 Pennsylvania, 72 Pennsylvania, Baxter's Fire Zouaves, Burns' or Barns' brigade, and Baker's California regiment, and other trophies. The conduct of the enemy is reported by officers in charge of the skirmishers as most cowardly.

Curiously, none of the Union diaries or letters from this period mention this action.[20]

The practice of providing whiskey to the men continued here. The men took to calling it their "commissary." Less happy about the practice were the officers, who were often confronted by unruly men. The officers began lobbying against this practice, saying that hot coffee would be a better substitute, especially for those men about to go out on the picket line at night.

The almost continual fighting played on the nerves of the men. This feeling of fear often extended to the officers as well. On June 8, William Burns of the 71st recorded in his diary, "Lieutenant Peter Hagen left the company pretending that he was sick. I guess the rifle pit took all the spunk out of him. The dirty *cur.*" On June 13, Burns casually reported, "Lt. Peter Hagen deserted."[21]

CHAPTER 7

THE SEVEN DAYS

The men of the Philadelphia Brigade could hear the sounds of battle coming from the direction of Gaines Mill to their right for most of June 27. This was the second engagement of the Seven Days' Campaign—a series of battles that the Confederate army's new commander, General Robert E. Lee, planned to send McClellan's troops reeling back toward the James River. The men were expected to be ordered to the right at any time, but the order never came. All was quiet along their own front, until General McClellan rode along the line, and was greeted by the cheers of his men. The brigade historian described what happened next: "This unusual excitement appeared to the enemy as if a movement of some character was intended by our division, and led to a severe artillery duel, followed by a heavy attack of infantry upon our pickets." Additional troops were rushed forward, and the enemy was repulsed.

The following day, June 28, the quartermasters informed the men that all extra clothes and supplies kept in the brigade wagons would be sent back to the White House depot. In their place, the wagons would be filled with ammunition and rations. The men were to destroy all other supplies and equipment to prevent their falling into the enemy's hands. New clothing was distributed to the men and the old were torn into tatters. Axes were used to cut up iron kettles, canteens, cups, tents, tent poles, and muskets. Barrels of meat and crackers were broken open, and the contents destroyed. After dark, the tents were struck, knapsacks filled with provisions, and the guns stacked.[1]

The men knew that the stalemate was now over—the question was whether they would move on to Richmond, or retreat. The question was answered at 4:00 a.m. on June 29, when General Burns was ordered to retire to Savage Station. Before the first streaks of light were visible, the men were ordered to erect their tents again, to make their retreat less noticeable. General Burns rode through the camps to encourage his bitterly disappointed men. After coming all this way and defeating the rebels in several battles, the men only wanted a crack at Richmond. But McClellan had lost his nerve, and settled on a retreat to the James River, and the safety of the gunboats. It would be a very difficult retreat as the long column of troops, artillery, and supplies would be forced to travel over the single road through the White Oak Swamp. Five divisions, including Sedgwick's, were assigned to cover the retreat.

A small detail of men under Captain Edward Roussel of the 72nd remained behind to slow the Confederate advance. Aided by fog and good luck, Roussel was able to finally extract his small force and join the brigade without sustaining casualties. Upon realizing that the Union works were unoccupied, the Confederate soldiers surged forward in search of "trophies." Although most of the supplies had been destroyed, they were able to gather up clothing, food, and personal items. These were discarded later, during what would be a very long and hot day. Prior to leaving the works, the rebels chopped down a large Union flag that had been left flying at the camp to deceive the rebels.[2]

Lee now ordered General Magruder and his two divisions forward along the Williamsburg Road to crush the retreating Union army's rear guard. At the same time, Stonewall Jackson's force, newly arrived from the Shenandoah Valley, was to cross the Chickahominy via the Grapevine Bridge and fall on the enemy's right flank. It was a good plan that would destroy the Federal rear guard, but once again Lee's lieutenants let their commander down.

When about two miles from Savage Station, the Philadelphia Brigade halted at Allen's Farm near Orchard Station, and formed a line of battle on both sides of the Richmond and York River Railroad. The brigade, now the rear guard of the army, was ordered to hold back the Confederate advance until the rest of the army had crossed the White Oak Swamp. Soon after their arrival here, the 71st was sent back to the brigade's old position by General Sumner to establish a picket line. Lieutenant Colonel W. Jones of the Regular Army was now in command of the regiment. Because of the importance Jones placed on discipline, "He was not liked at first and he was very strict. Made the officers and men stand around and mind their p's and q's," wrote William Burns.[3]

Cautiously advancing, the men of the 71st picked up two prisoners near their former position. Farther on, they found Louisiana Tigers in their old rifle pits. Jones advanced and drove them out of the pits, capturing several in the process. Rebels now advanced against their front, while another column moved down the railroad to threaten his left flank. Realizing that to remain here invited disaster, Jones ordered his men back to the brigade. As he approached the Allen Farm at about 9:00 a.m., he halted his men and deployed them in the woods to await the enemy's advance. Before long, elements of General George Anderson's brigade appeared in his front, and launched an attack. This was beaten back, but additional Southern troops reached the field, forcing Jones to continue his retreat.

General Burns arrived at about this time, and took command of the field. Pettit's and Hazzard's batteries galloped up and unlimbered. Dashing back to find additional help, Burns encountered Colonel Brooke's 53rd Pennsylvania of Richardson's division behind a house, about 100 yards away from the action. Burns ordered it to advance against the enemy, but Brooke declined, saying that his commanding officer had placed him here, and here he would stay. His voice rising in anger, Burns informed him that *he* commanded the sector and his orders must be obeyed. Brooke reluctantly advanced his men, and the 71st coming up behind him, formed on his left.[4]

One soldier later wrote, "At times the musketry would almost cease, as the rebels defeated at one point, would try another and the battle would be renewed with more violence than ever." The two batteries, with the help of the two Pennsylvania regiments, beat back the Southern attacks. During this engagement, Pettit's battery fired 200 rounds and was able to silence the rebel batteries. Soon additional support was brought forward in the form of the 63rd New York, 20th Massachusetts, and the 5th New Hampshire. By this time, the battle of the Peach Orchard, or Allen's Farm, was all but over, having lasted about two hours.

The casualties were relatively light on both sides (the Georgians lost 28; the Pennsylvanians, 119), although a Confederate brigade commander, General Richard Griffith, was killed by a rifled shell while his brigade occupied a position in the rear. Ninety-six of the 119 killed and wounded on the Union side were from the 71st. One soldier wrote home, "We fought at a disadvantage, they being in a wood behind trees, and we in a clear field where their bullets were certain." The remainder of the Philadelphia Brigade only played a supporting role in this battle. Burns had high praise for Lieutenant Colonel Jones, "The Seventy-first Pennsylvania Volunteers, under its gallant young lieutenant-colonel, won high encomiums from the corps commander, who knows what hard fighting means."[5]

Sumner's position around Allen's Farm was a precarious one. The right of his corps was to connect with the left of Smith's division, but a large gap existed between them. Although Sumner stubbornly wanted to maintain his position as a point of honor, General Franklin convinced him to pull back the two miles to Savage Station, where he would unite with Smith's flank. Sumner ordered this move at about noon. Part of the march was made at the "double-quick." Since the day was hot, some of the men could not keep up, and fell by the wayside, only to be captured by the advancing rebels. The growing number of rebels in their rear weighed heavily on the men. "Our only thought being to get there [Savage Station] as soon as possible, and as none were anxious to be left behind, everything that in any way hindered our march was hastily dispensed with, and the road was strewn with knapsacks, blankets, tents, overcoats, etc., no time being taken to even destroy them," wrote a soldier from the 106th. Another soldier from the 71st added, "On this march I had to throw away my knapsack. I took my blanket and Indian rubber out and left the rest of my things to the rebels for I was so exhausted that I nearly dropt [*sic*] with the heat and excitement."

The brigade arrived at Savage Station at 3:00 p.m., stacked arms, and rested along the edge of a woods. McClellan had established this area as a supply and distribution center, and while resting, the men watched as massive amounts of supplies were burned.[6]

When the II Corps reached Savage Station, General Heintzelman ordered his men to continue their retreat toward the White Oak Swamp. General Sumner later bluntly described this movement in his official report of the campaign: "When the enemy appeared on the Williamsburg road I could not imagine why General Heintzelman did not attack him, and not till some time afterward did I learn, to my utter amazement, that General Heintzelman had left the field and retreated with his whole corps (about 15,000 men) before the action commenced. This defection might have been attended with the most disastrous consequences, and although we beat the enemy signally and drove him from the field, we should certainly have given him a more crushing blow if General Heintzelman had been there with his corps."

The effect of this movement was a three-quarter of a mile gap between Sumner's and Franklin's corps. The Confederates were not slow in perceiving this weakness, and moved forward at about 4:30 p.m. to exploit it. One soldier from the 106th wrote, "Fresh from their Capital, under the belief that we were retreating and demoralized, stimulated by bad whiskey and gunpowder, they expected, by a sudden dash, to overpower our troops, whom they knew to be wearied and almost exhausted from picket and outpost duty."[7]

Sumner ordered the 72nd and 106th to move about half a mile toward the enemy and hold the woods between the Williamsburg Road and the railroad. General Burns supervised this move, which was made as if the regiments were on parade. Prior to entering the woods, the troops had to cross a clearing between the railroad and the Williamsburg Road about half a mile long and the same distance wide. As the two regiments approached the woods, each threw out two companies of skirmishers, which entered the tangled masses. One Southern soldier described the woods as, "...the thickest undergrowth of bushes you ever saw...you could not see a man ten paces ahead of you and it was utterly impossible to keep anything like a line of battle." The Union officers told the men on the skirmish line to fire when they saw enemy soldiers or if the brush moved in front of them. When the Confederate line had advanced to within twenty-five paces of the picket line, the Pennsylvanians could finally see their approach, and fired a volley into them.

The remainder of the two regiments waited anxiously in the open field. The volume of small arms fire increased in the woods, and soon several of their pickets returned, dragging wounded men. Burns was just

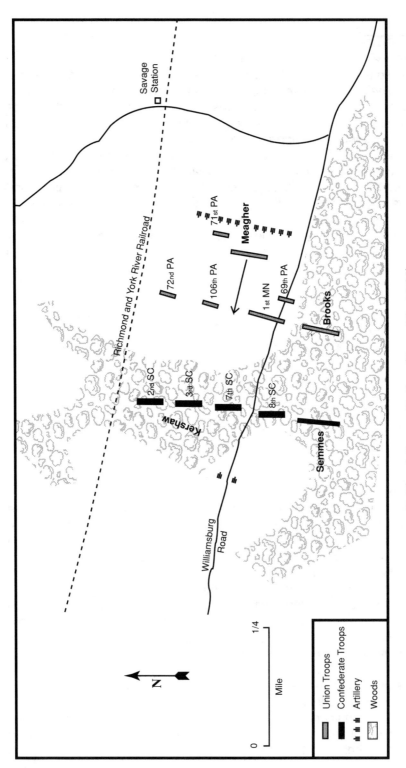

Battle of Savage Station (June 29, 1862)

Savage Station

Richmond and York River Railroad

71st PA

Meagher

72nd PA

106th PA

1st MN

69th PA

Brooks

2nd SC

3rd SC

7th SC

Kershaw

8th SC

Semmes

Williamsburg Road

N

Mile

1/4

0

Union Troops

Confederate Troops

Artillery

Woods

about to order the two regiments forward, when he realized that the rebels were moving toward his left flank. Requesting immediate assistance from Sumner, Burns was sent the First Minnesota, which deployed on the left of the 106th across the Williamsburg Road. The 72nd was on the right of the 106th, with its right-most companies refused to protect the right flank.

Because Burns was forced to cover such a long line, a gap existed between the 72nd and the 106th. Pettit's, Hazzard's, Osborne's, and Bramhall's batteries were also present.[8]

As the line of battle formed, rebel batteries near the railroad pounded the line, causing considerable losses. The newly deployed Union batteries quickly silenced these guns. Before long, the grey infantry broke through the woods, and attacked. The rebels drove toward the gap between the 72nd and 106th, and against the First Minnesota. "The rebels had advanced within 30 yards of our line, and the lines were discernable by two sheets of flame, three-fourths of a mile long. When one rebel regiment was cut up or exhausted, it was soon replaced by a new one. A desperate charge by fresh troops was made on the left of Baxter's, and on the right of the 106th," wrote a member of the 106th. As the 2nd and 3rd South Carolina rushed forward, they reached a fence directly in front of the Philadelphia Brigade. Waving their flags over it, almost in the faces of the Philadelphians, they scaled this last obstacle and lunged forward. Burns went down with a deep flesh wound to his cheek, received while trying to steady the 72nd. Refusing to leave the field, he quickly had his face bandaged with a handkerchief. At about the same time, the commander of the left-most company of the 72nd was killed.

"The enemy fought with great energy and vigor, while the Confederates pressed them hard," wrote Augustus Dickert of Kershaw's Brigade. The pressure on the weakly held center of the Union line was just too great, however. The left flank of the 72nd faltered, the men breaking for the rear. The movement further exposed the right flank of the 106th, forcing it to retire as well. "That portion of the line charged upon fell back eight or ten feet, but by order of their commander, they rallied, and, at the point of the bayonet, regained the rod of ground they had lost before," recalled a veteran of the 106th. After stubborn fighting, the South Carolinians were slowly pushed back to the woods, and the Union line was subsequently re-established. The 82nd New York arrived, and Burns sent it to reinforce the weakened area between the 72nd and 106th.[9]

The battle also raged along the Williamsburg Road, where a dangerous gap opened between the left of the 106th and the right of the First Minnesota. Kershaw attempted to take advantage of this situation by throwing two other regiments against the front and flank of the First Minnesota. The two Federal regiments poured volleys into the 7th South Carolina in their front. At the same time, the seven companies of the First Minnesota on the left flank were bent back almost to a right angle to the rest of the line to cope with the threat on its flank. A Minnesota soldier wrote: "The shells sounded wickedly as they passed over our heads, and plowed up the earth around us. Now and then, a man would reel from the ranks and be borne to the rear...besides the musket balls that filled the air..., the Rebs sent grape and canister about our ears in 'delightful profusion,' and the dead and wounded soon strewed the ground." Just as the line was about to break, General Thomas Meagher's Irish Brigade arrived on the scene, cheering while marching at the double-quick, to fill the gap. As they approached, they were greeted by Burns, who took up the distinctive green flag of the lead regiment. The 69th New York "poured in an oblique fire upon them with a rapid precision and an incessant vigor which had the effect of almost instantly staggering and silencing for some moments a fire which seemed to be almost overwhelming," wrote Meagher in his report. The 88th New York formed on the 69th New York's right, and together they charged the enemy, forcing them backward. In referring to the 88th New York, Burns wrote, "I threw them into the gap on the road, when the enemy opened artillery and infantry upon them, but they never faltered...and drove secesh before them. William Burns of the 71st also observed the charge and wrote, "It was a splendid sight to see them with the American, Irish, and state flag at the head with Meagher's brigade with Meagher leading them on."

Soon other regiments arrived from Gorman's and Dana's brigades to further reinforce the line. The 15th Massachusetts relieved the 106th Pennsylvania and the 20th Massachusetts took the place of the 72nd. When the 71st and the 7th Michigan arrived, they were placed in reserve, and the 69th was led to the left of the First Minnesota. The Northerners now had a 2 to 1 superiority in numbers north of the Williamsburg Road. Still, Kershaw's 2nd and 3rd South Carolina held their ground.[10]

The First Minnesota's left flank was reinforced by Brooks' Vermont brigade on the left of the Williamsburg Road. Engaging the 8th South Carolina of Kershaw's brigade and the newly arriving regiments from General Paul Semmes' Brigade, the Vermonters held firm despite receiving a withering fire. After repelling the attack, the Vermonters attacked, throwing back the rebels. Although the attack was successful, it was costly, as some units lost half of their men.

The men fired so rapidly that many regiments had all but depleted their ammunition. This was one of the reasons why the 72nd and 106th were pulled out of line when reinforcements arrived. The rapid fire, combined with the extreme heat of the day, had also rendered the arms "well-nigh unserviceable" and some commanders asked permission for their regiments to be "relieved until such time as his fire-arms would be so sufficiently cooled as to render them efficient."[11]

While the 71st only played a supporting role, first on the left of the line, and then in the center, it had some exciting experiences. According to William Burns' diary, "We soon after deployed into line and marched to where the rebels were in a closed woods. The bullets were flying very thick, but all over our heads. The firing soon after stopped when we left the woods and marched in the open field. The firing commenced again. When we advanced to the edge of the woods again and laid down. The firing was terrible just before dark. We remained on post about four hours. This was the first time I heard the cries and groans of the wounded begging for water and praying for help. Poor fellows. They had to be left to the tender care of the rebels."

The battle of Savage Station ended at about 7:00 p.m., after about three hours of heavy fighting. Summing up the outcome, General Burns wrote, "Our men showed their superiority, and the victory can fairly be claimed by us. He was the attacking party, and was not only checked, but repulsed and driven from the ground." The exhausted 72nd and 106th remained in line of battle in the rear for another two hours, when they were ordered to continue the retreat. The 106th lost 9 killed, 24 wounded, and 12 missing. The 72nd lost "about" 15 killed and as many wounded. The 69th and the 71st were not engaged, so their losses were light. The 71st supported the center of the line, and the 69th supported the left flank. Toward the end of the engagement, the 69th was ordered to double-quick to the opposite flank to support Pettit's battery, which anticipated an attack from the direction of the railroad.[12]

During the course of the battle, the Confederates moved up a massive gun on a specially made iron-plated railroad platform. Called the "Land Merrimac," it sent "monstrous missles" into the Union lines. One Southern soldier later recalled, "Nor was the railroad battery idle, for I could see the great black, grim monster puffing out heaps of gray smoke, then the red flash, then the report, sending the engine and car back along the track with a fearful recoil."

When it seemed that the rebels would successfully pierce the Union lines, ammunition-filled railroad cars at Savage Station were set on fire. As the battle raged, the men heard tremendous explosions behind them, and looking back, were relieved to see that the cause of the noise was not rebels in their rear. Dense columns of smoke rose high into the sky.

As night descended upon the battlefield, the fighting continued, and the opposing lines could be delineated by the rifle flashes. Sumner's fighting blood was still up, and he was determined to continue making a stand at Savage Station. McClellan's cooler, more rational head prevailed, however, and he ordered the retreat to continue at 9:00 p.m. that night. His goal was to reach the safety of the gunboats on the James River, not to fight the rebels. As the men left Savage Station, they were dismayed to learn that over 2,500 sick and wounded men in the hospital were being abandoned as there was no way to remove them to safety. To tend to their needs, a medical staff of 500 was left behind. The men recalled this to be one of the saddest moments of the retreat. "When it became known that the troops must leave these helpless fellows, some of whom had fallen only a few hours before, there were many hearts filled with sorrow, and as the brigade passed the hospital tents, comrades rushed in to take a fare-well leave of some familiar face, and to receive a message for loved ones at home," wrote the brigade's historian.[13]

The night march was dark and dreary. They hadn't gone far when a rainstorm hit the area. Fortunately, it was short-lived, ending at midnight, and the men could again see the moon and stars which guided their "lag-ging and weary footsteps." The march was uneventful, except for the burn-ing wagons and caissons that lit up the night. Many men thought about the battles they had just fought, the men they left behind, and the battles that lie ahead. One soldier remembered this march in his later years "...save for the tramp, tramp of the men and the rumble of artillery wheels, there was an unusual absence of noise incidental to a march. Occasionally some would murmur, 'my knapsack cuts my shoulder,' and received a reply, 'you will forget all about it when you have your grandchildren on your knee'..." William Burns recorded in his diary, "Marched about four hours [that night]. We came to a bridge. As soon as we crossed, I threw myself on the ground and went to sleep."

The men were surprised to see General Richardson supervising the crossing of the troops over White Oak Swamp when they arrived some-time before 5:00 a.m. Standing by the road with his coat unbuttoned and sleeves rolled up, the men appreciated his words of encouragement. After crossing, the bridge was cut away, so that it couldn't be used by the rebels. Before long, rebels could be seen on the opposite bank of the river.[14]

While Richardson's and Smith's divisions remained by the river to contest the crossing of the enemy, Sedgwick's division marched two miles farther along Long Bridge Road to the small crossroads community of Glen-dale. Moving south on the Quaker Road, the column reached Nelson's Farm, where the men of the Philadelphia Brigade were permitted to rest, being completely exhausted from the battles fought the day before and the all-night march. The division took up a position behind General George McCall's Pennsylvania Reserves in a large field between the New Market and the Charles City Roads. Because of the road system, all of the retreat-ing troops had to move through Glendale. Its defense thus became a criti-cal factor if the Union army was to make good its escape.

Realizing this fact, Lee decided to throw six divisions, numbering about 45,000 men, against the strategic crossroads. If successful, the Federal army would be split in two and each could be destroyed separately. His plan was again a good one, as no less than four roads approached Glen-dale from the north and west. Lee put troops on all of them, including Stone-wall Jackson's men moving in from the north. Guarding the crossroads were just over 36,000 Union troops from the II, III, IV, and V Corps, and thirteen batteries of artillery. As these troops nervously scanned their front for signs of rebels, an unbroken line of wagons moved along the Quaker Road in their rear to safety. One soldier watching this movement wrote, "If anything broke about wagon or harness, the mules were detached from the wagon and it was pulled out of the line and burned, together with its contents." A quartermaster from the 71st wrote, "The grandest skedaddling ever I saw. Each team trying to pass the other."[15]

After waiting for most of June 30 for Stonewall Jackson to arrive on his left flank, Lee realized that he had but four hours of daylight remaining to attack the Union troops. Deciding that he could delay his attack no longer, he ordered the battle to commence at 5:00 p.m. His initial target was General McCall's 7,500-man Pennsylvania Reserve Division. The choice of McCall's division to face the initial onslaught of the enemy was a curious one. The division had already fought two battles in the last four days, and was decimated. Yet other divisions which marched past the crossroads to safety had barely been engaged at all. On McCall's right was Kearny's division. Hooker's division formed on McCall's left, and Sedgwick's division was in reserve. "Bull" Sumner once again was in overall command.

Some skirmishing developed on the Union right around midday involving Kearney's division. Believing this signalled an attack, Sumner ordered Gorman's and Dana's brigades of Sedgwick's division to the area, leaving the Philadelphia Brigade to support McCall, who was not yet engaged. The battle of Glendale began when two Confederate brigades drove toward General Truman Seymour's brigade, forming McCall's left flank. General James Kemper's brigade captured an exposed Union battery and then engaged Seymour's infantry. Within a few minutes, Seymour's left regiments broke and ran through Burns' and Hooker's troops, causing considerable confusion. McCall's reserve brigade under Colonel Seneca Simmons now rushed forward to stabilize the remainder of Seymour's line. Fighting was vicious and at times, hand to hand. Colonel Simmons went down, and slowly, General Micah Jenkins' brigade, along with part of General Cadmus Wilcox's brigade, pushed back McCall's two brigades.

The remainder of Wilcox's brigade slammed into General George Meade's brigade, which was holding McCall's right flank. The fighting was desperate, and included hand-to-hand combat. Each side charged and counterattacked. In the end, McCall's division was wrecked. All three of his brigade commanders were killed or wounded, and all twenty-six cannon were captured or withdrawn. To make matters worse, fresh troops from Longstreet's and A. P. Hill's divisions were arriving to exploit the breach in the Federal line.[16]

Hooker's and Kearny's divisions on both flanks became engaged as well. Although slightly wounded, General Sumner rode back to the only brigade of Sedgwick's division that could provide immediate assistance to McCall. The Philadelphia Brigade was ready. The 72nd occupied the right of the line of battle, the 69th the center, and the 106th the left. In the rear

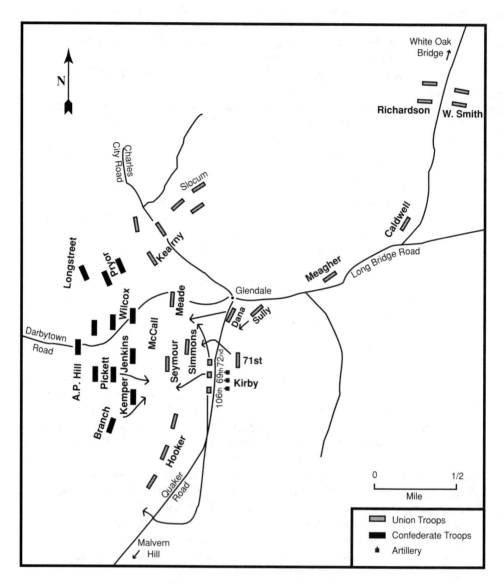

Battle of Glendale (June 30, 1862)

was the 71st, supporting Kirby's battery. Before engaging the enemy, the brigade was broken up—destined to fight yet another battle in parts, rather than as a whole. In response to a desperate plea from Hooker for a brigade, the 69th was rushed forward to his right to help plug the hole created by Seymour's flight. Riding up to Hooker, Sumner said, "General, I cannot spare you a brigade, but I have brought you the 69th, one of the best regiments in my corps; place them where you wish, for this is your fight, Hooker." The men responded with three cheers for their gallant old commander. As he left, Sumner yelled out to them, "Wait til you can see the whites of the enemy's eyes, and aim low."[17]

As the 69th moved slowly forward through the smoke and deafening explosions, they expected to see the rebels appear in front of them at any moment. Colonel Owen ordered the regiment to form into line of battle in a ravine at the foot of a hill upon which were posted two Union batteries. Owen now ordered the men to lie down and wait for the enemy to emerge from the woods. They did not have long to wait before another attack broke McCall's line, and its men began streaming through the ranks of the 69th on their way to the rear. In front of them, the Irishmen could see the rebels turning the captured cannon to fire into the fleeing Union troops. Owen ordered the 69th to kneel and open fire, which drove the rebels from the guns. Rebel infantry could be seen advancing on their position, and when within fifty yards, the Philadelphians fired a volley that staggered the approaching Confederate line. The situation was becoming desperate for the 69th as Confederate units from Pickett's and Branch's brigades were pressing forward on both flanks. Owen ordered his men to fix bayonets, and the 69th's historian described what happened next:

> The regiment instinctively jumped to their feet and advanced in wedge-shape, charged up the hill with a cheer, and met the enemy at close quarters, drove them from the captured guns and hurled them back on their supporting lines, changing what had but a short time before seemed to be a disastrous defeat into a glorious victory.

Hooker's report was almost as exuberant. He wrote that the 69th "heroically led by Owen, advanced in the open field on their flank with almost reckless daring." He also suggested that this was the first successful bayonet charge of the war, which was probably a slight overgeneralization. Burns summed it up when he wrote: "Gallant Sixty-ninth!"

The 106th had initially followed the 69th, and in response to Hooker's plea, Sumner also released this regiment to his care. Hooker immediately sent it to the extreme left of his line, manned by General Daniel Sickles' Excelsior Brigade, which was hotly engaged with the enemy. Sickles feared an attempt on his left, which never materialized.[18]

Burns personally led the 72nd toward the area held by Simmons' and Meade's brigades. Additional regiments from Dana's brigade also arrived and were thrown forward as well. The battle line forming behind McCall's

Charge of the 69th Pennsylvania at Glendale

McDermott's and Reilly's *History of the 69th Pennsylvania*

troops was, from left to right: 7th Michigan, 20th Massachusetts, 72nd Pennsylvania, and 42nd New York. As the 71st Pennsylvania and 19th Massachusetts arrived, they formed a reserve behind this line. Just as Burns established this line, Simmons' brigade broke. Burns wrote in his report, "Another heavy attack broke McCall's center and sent the fugitives shamefully through our ranks." The 7th Michigan and 20th Massachusetts rushed forward to plug this gap, but the pressure was just too great, and these two regiments also broke, creating a gap that the enemy rapidly exploited. Only the two reserve regiments now stood between the vital Quaker Road and the Confederates. Throwing the 71st Pennsylvania and the 19th Massachusetts into the breach, Burns later wrote in his report, "...and nobly did they redeem the faults of their comrades. These two noble regiments met the enemy face to face, and for nearly one hour poured into them such tremendous volleys that no further attack was had at that vital point."

While in reserve, the 71st had been ordered to support Kirby's battery. William Burns wrote, "They worked so fast at their guns that we could not see the sun for the smoke. We made a charge here. Had quite a smart fight." During this time, the 72nd Pennsylvania and 42nd New York continued to support Meade's men. General Sedgwick praised his men in his report, saying, "Not only did these troops meet and repulse the assaults of the enemy, but were forced to withstand the demoralizing influence of the panic among those of the first line, who in many instances broke through our ranks in their haste to move out of reach of the enemy's fire."[19]

Nightfall ended the battle of Glendale. As with the battle of Savage Station the day before, the Union line had just barely held back the Confederate advance. Barely or not, it was a Northern victory, but one that was not savored by anyone. McCall's division was all but destroyed. The losses to the Philadelphia Brigade were fairly modest, given the severity of the contest. The 69th sustained the highest losses: 13 killed, 36 wounded, and 5 missing. General Burns continued to win the admiration of his men. The brigade historian wrote, "Wherever the fight seemed to be the hottest, there was Burns with his face stained with blood, cheering and rallying the men."

The march toward the James River continued around midnight. With the enemy so close to their lines, each regiment used utmost care when leaving its position. Pickets were left behind for about an hour to cover the retreat. One of the men left behind later wrote, "While waiting for an order to join the column, listened with sad hearts to the groans of the wounded, mingled with the soft hum of insects and the cries of the whip-poor-will."[20]

The night march was especially difficult because the men were utterly exhausted from fighting by day and retreating by night during the past week. The desire to fall out of the column was strong, but the men knew it meant certain capture by the enemy, and an uncertain fate. A soldier from the 106th described this march in a letter to home, "We marched nearly all night, part of the time in the meanest kind of mud. Many threw away their knapsacks, in order to keep up with the regiments, and when the order to halt was given, it was gladly obeyed by all and we were soon lying on the ground, ...sleeping soundly."

The entire army was now reunited on Malvern Hill. McClellan had succeeded in extracting his army from the front door of Richmond to the safety of the James River and the gunboats. As the men of the Philadelphia Brigade climbed the hill they could see the river and the little ships. Thinking that the rebels would not be foolish enough to attack this exceptionally strong position, the men threw down their knapsacks and laid down for a well-deserved rest. It came as quite a surprise when the Confederate artillery began firing at about 7:00 a.m.[21]

Their position high on the hill, well behind the infantry who were posted to repel the Confederate charges, was a good one to watch the battle. It was not too long before the Southern batteries found the range of Sedgwick's division, and shells began raining down on the men, killing two. The men were ordered to lay down, and around noon, they were ordered to march to the extreme right flank of the army, where another attack was expected. About 3:00 p.m., the brigade marched at the "double-quick" to the center of the army, and was met by Generals McClellan and Sumner. The latter ordered them back to their original position, explaining that because of the green flag of the 69th, the brigade had been mistaken for Meagher's Irish Brigade which was needed at the front to help repel a charge. During this period, "...the battle was raging fiercely. The bursting shells, and the cannons spitting fire, and the sharp cracking of the musketry. It was a fearful but splendid sight. Soon after the regiment went on picket where we could plainly hear the rebels giving orders," recorded William Burns in his diary.

At 11:00 that night, the II Corps continued its retreat. The army's destination was Harrison's Landing, a much better site for receiving supplies. This ended the Seven Days' Campaign.[22]

CHAPTER 8

RELIEF OF POPE

The men's spirits soared during the evening of July 1. Assembled at 9:00 p.m., the division began marching on the Malvernton Road *toward* Richmond, not away from it! "The men were in the best of spirits as one said to another, 'we're done retreating, McClellan is going to Richmond!' The desire to advance became contagious," wrote the brigade historian. An officer soon rode up, however, halted the column, and ordered the men to "about face" and march toward the James River. "This disappointment was a sad one, and some of the men could scarcely restrain their tears. After the three-month campaign on the Peninsula with all of its privations, the perils of battle, the wearisome fatigue of the march, to make a retreat when victory seemed within the grasp required all the fortitude of the men to exhibit the obedience of soldiers."

The seven-mile march from Malvern Hill to Harrison's Landing during the early morning hours of July 2 was also difficult because only one road connected these two points. Priority was given to wagons and artillery which could gallop faster than infantry. The troops were marched in the muddy fields on either side of the road, but at times the men attempted to "cheat" by slipping into the road, only to be driven out again by fast-moving teams or cavalry pickets. Because of the frequent delays, the column did not reach Harrison's Landing until after daybreak. Prior to their arrival, it began to rain, further dispiriting the men. William Burns of the 71st wrote, "Arrived at Harrison's Landing in a state of demoralization and very wet. Pitched but what few tents we had in the mud. Passed a miserable cold and wet night but very thankful to be spared."

Upon reaching the landing, Sedgwick's division was ordered to camp in a large muddy wheatfield. Few had tents, so most merely spread straw, and with "perfect indifference to the rain and even to the sound of cannon fire," laid down and went to sleep.[1]

Although the Philadelphia Brigade's losses of 404 (40 killed, 192 wounded, and 172 missing) ranked second lowest of the II Corps' brigades, it fought in three battles (Peach Orchard, Savage Station, and Glendale) and several skirmishes. With losses numbering 159, the 72nd suffered the most heavily, particularly because of its actions at Savage Station. The other regiments' losses were much lighter by comparison (69th=81; 71st=91; 106th=73.)[2]

Illness also reduced the number of men in the ranks. Lieutenant John Lynch of the 106th wrote, "Our regiment do not, I think, now number over 400 men. When we left Camp Observation we had over 800. This is the result of sickness, loss in battle and others which cannot be accounted for. Out of 33 officers which we had, there is only 10 reporting for duty."[3]

Upon arriving at Harrison's Landing, rations of coffee, sugar, and crackers were liberally distributed. The following day, July 3, the troops moved to the banks of a large creek that was not as muddy, and the following day moved again, this time to the vicinity of a mill.

The Fourth of July was appropriately celebrated by the men. Bands commenced playing at noon, and the artillery fired salutes to the nation's independence. "The bands are playing and artillery making all the noise they know how to do. All is noise and bustle," wrote John Lynch. The men were reviewed by General McClellan, who rode past in full uniform. He also left an order to be read to the men, commending their actions during the recent campaign. Joseph Elliott of the 71st wrote, "This being the anniversary of our Nation's Birth, the shipping in the River made a display of their buntings. The regimental bands played the national airs and salutes were fired by the batteries in honor of the day. Gen. McClellan reviewed the different divisions under his command today and was received, as no other commander could be under the circumstances." Some men were bored. One wrote, "The fourth of July was extremely dull—nothing going on except a salute of artillery, which has got to be an 'old tune' to us," wrote one.[4]

General Burns' wound had become infected, so he left for medical treatment. His place was temporarily taken by Colonel Baxter of the 72nd. Before he left around July 8, Burns issued the following order for his men:

> ...the strongest ties have grown around our hearts. I have twice had occasion to report to superior authority the conduct of my brigade in battle. At Fair Oaks I said, 'I am satisfied with my brigade; it has been christened under fire, and will do what is required of it.' You have borne me out in my proud assertion; I say in my report of the recent hard fought battles, 'I repeat my assertion at Fair Oaks—I am satisfied with the conduct of my brigade, none will gainsay it.' You have, indeed, won a proud distinction. Your banners have floated on the hardest fought fields—and in every scene they waved there after the enemy had left. I thank you! I am proud of you—I love you. Good Bye.[5]

The men would miss Burns. After an inauspicious start, they came to realize that his tough training and steadying influence had forged them into a tough-fighting unit which had performed admirably during the past campaign. One wrote, "He had made himself popular with his command, who admired him not only for his personal bravery, and devotion to duty, but for his thorough soldierly training, that taught both officers and men the full duty of a soldier. His loss was deeply regretted."

When Burns finally returned on October 9, it was for only a few days. He had impressed his superiors during the recent campaign, and was recommended for promotion. General Sedgwick wrote to General Sumner, "...call especial attention of the General commanding the Corps to the gallantry of Brigadier General Burns, and respectfully submit that a grade is but a small recompense for his services..." Both Sumner and McClellan agreed, the latter adding, "The conduct of General Burns...was something more than that display of gallantry which every brigade commander ought to possess..." Burns never received a second star, but he did receive a division.

Other changes occurred in the brigade. Several formerly wounded officers and men, including Colonel Wistar and Lieutenant Colonel Markoe of the 71st, returned to their units during the stay at Harrison's Landing. Non-commissioned officer slots were filled. The greatest change occurred in the 71st, which was officially reduced to ten companies through consolidation. The extra officers were mustered out, among them was Major Robert Parrish who led the Second Battalion. Other officers were less than honorably discharged, including Major James DeWitt of the 72nd.[6]

While here, the men returned to their long-neglected drills and inspections. Many could not believe that it had merely been six months since they had last drilled on a regular basis at Camp Observation. Reflecting on

Colonel DeWitt Baxter *(seated)* and staff, 72nd Pennsylvania

their past experiences, many probably would have much preferred the drudgery of camp to the recent experiences of the march and battle. The men also went on fatigue duty and built breastworks that were never used.

On the whole, the men enjoyed their stay here. "But there is one objection and that is we are too much cramped up," wrote Lt. John Lynch. "There is too many regiments in the field which we are in and this forces us to take as little room as possible. I suppose you know that we move always by divisions and encamp in the same way. Always obliged to be together."

On August 15, the men were drawn up to witness the punishment of Private John Mansfield of Company B, 106th, who had been found guilty of desertion. His head was shaved, branded with the letter "D", and he was drummed out of camp. He was sent to Fort Wool, opposite Fortress Monroe, for the remainder of his enlistment. Put to hard labor, a 24-pound ball was attached to his leg by a three and one-half foot chain. All pay and bounties were also forfeited. The sentence was a harsh one, and was intended to act as a deterrent to the other men.[7]

The troops experienced a strange mix of emotions while camped near Harrison's Landing. Upon their arrival, the men retained the hope that the army would regain the offensive. "The army is in good spirits and confident of final success," a soldier from the 106th wrote home. But as time passed, the men grew to realize that the campaign had ended in miserable failure. Many were depressed about the "inglorious termination" of the advance on Richmond, but there was a "feeling of congratulation among them on the bearing of the army during the movements." Many rationalized that the army's failure was due to the enemy's overwhelming numbers and knew that if it were not for the gunboats the army would have been destroyed.

Many distinguished visitors toured the camps during this period, including President Lincoln and some members of his cabinet on July 8. One soldier from the 106th wrote, "President Lincoln has also favored us with a visit, and reviewed all of the troops. He was saluted by artillery, and greeted with deafening cheers, as he passed along. Old Abe is very popular with the boys."[8]

Sumner ordered a "grand" review of the II Corps on July 22. The regimental historian of the 106th recalled,

> Brigades were formed in column of regiments, making each brigade four or five lines deep... about twenty paces between the lines, the artillery drawn up in the rear; the whole line extending over a mile. As General Sumner appeared, a salute of thirteen guns was fired by the artillery; after he rode down the line, the corps passed in review, division front, and all returned to camp in time for dinner.

The camp's location near a swiftly running creek helped satisfy the men's growing urge to clean up. After a week of constant marching and fighting, they were filthy. "One great luxury we have is the river, which is to the nearest point to us, 3/4 of a mile off where we have delightful bathing and fishing," wrote John Lynch to his wife. So strong was the urge, that some bathed twice a day. This impulse may have also resulted from the excessive heat and for the men to rid themselves of the noxious insects. One soldier later wrote, "...innumerable quantities of flies and various kinds, and other insects, annoyed us by day, and mosquitoes by night..." Sickness and disease soon followed these insects. "...fevers, scurvy, and diarrhea prevailed to an alarming extent." Many died within a few days of falling ill. Fortunately, medical supplies and personnel were nearby. The steamer *John Brooke* was pressed into service between the landing and Washington, carrying supplies and the sick and wounded. The Sanitary Commission had become effectively organized by this time.[9]

The steamers also replenished the men's worn clothes, and equipment that were lost or discarded. Particularly needy were the men of the 69th, who had been ordered to toss their knapsacks in a pile in the woods before entering the battle of Savage Station. Unable to retrieve their belongings, the men had only the clothes on their backs. While grateful to finally get additional clothes and supplies, the regimental historian wrote that the "...Government in this case treated the men very meanly by charging them for the clothing they had drawn that so lost."

Orders were received to prepare for a march on July 30 and again on August 2, when the men were issued three days' rations and forty to sixty rounds of ammunition. Neither march occurred. During the latter day, the march was to begin at 3:00 a.m., but the orders were countermanded a half hour earlier.

The men were again ordered to prepare for a march on August 4 with two days' rations and blankets. This was not a false alarm, and Sedgwick's entire division left camp at six o'clock that night and headed toward Malvern Hill. Hooker's division, supported by Sedgwick's, was to cut off and capture the enemy advance guard. Sedgwick's division marched until 1:30 a.m., when it rested on the road. Roused at daylight on August 5, the men were soon on their way. The rebels had, however, learned of their approach and taken flight. Although a few prisoners were taken, the mission was a failure. Remaining on the battlefield for another day, the division began its return trek to Harrison's Landing at 3:00 a.m. on August 7 with the Philadelphia Brigade bringing up the rear.[10]

The brigade was told to be ready to break camp on short notice on August 10. These orders were reiterated on the 11th, 12th, 14th, and then the 15th. They came as no surprise to the men, as the sick and wounded had been evacuated since August 4. Finally, at 5:30 p.m. on August 15, the order came to leave camp with two days' rations in their haversacks and six in the wagons. Few regretted the order. "No matter what uncertainty might hang over the future, there was none among the command who looked upon the place on leaving it with cheerful eyes," wrote the brigade historian. Light marching gear was ordered, so the wagons carried all but the men's arms, accoutrements, rubber blankets, and haversacks.

Upon arriving at division headquarters, the men found the single road clogged with wagons, so they rested by the side of the road. They unsuccessfully tried the road again at 2:00 a.m. After breakfasting at five o'clock that morning, they were formed into line at 7:00 a.m., but stayed here for another hour. Many grumbled that the officers should have known about the wagon train and planned accordingly, rather than forcing the men to wait fifteen hours to finally get under way.[11]

Momentous events were occurring around Washington. Losing confidence in McClellan's ability to take Richmond, Lincoln created a new army on June 26, the 51,000-man Army of Virginia, commanded by General John Pope. The new army was composed of the I Corps, and units from the Shenandoah Valley that had been defeated by Stonewall Jackson. Pope's first communication took a swipe at McClellan and the Army of the Potomac, "I have come to you from the West, where we have always seen the backs of our enemies; from an army whose business it has been to seek the adversary and to beat him when he was found; whose policy has been attack and not defense..."

Pope was to venture south and threaten the Virginia Central Railroad, Richmond's vital link to the Shenandoah Valley. Lee would be forced to detach troops to meet this threat, making it easier for McClellan to take Richmond. The Seven Days' battles began soon after, destroying the plan. After repeated dispatches from McClellan indicating that he would only resume the offensive if he received reinforcements, the Army of the Potomac was recalled to Alexandria on August 4. In the meantime, Lee sent Stonewall Jackson northward to face Pope's threat, and ordered the remainder of his army north on August 13 when he realized that McClellan was removing his troops from the Peninsula.[12]

The Army of the Potomac would leave the Peninsula the same way it had come—by ship from Fortress Monroe. No leisurely marches would characterize this trip, however, as Lincoln desperately needed the men to blunt Lee's new threat. The Philadelphia Brigade's first march from Harrison's Landing took twelve hours on roads so dusty that the men could not see further than ten yards around them. "We eat dust, drink dust, breathe dust, and are thoroughly filled and covered with it from head to foot. It will take us about a week to get clean after our march," wrote George Beidelman.

The brigade camped at 3:30 that afternoon and took up its march at 6:30 the next morning, August 17. Passing through Charles City Court House, they stopped for two hours to rest at 9:00 a.m., then continued. Finding the road again clogged with wagons and artillery, the men thought they would again have the luxury of a rest, but time was short and the men were ordered to march in the fields along the side of the road. The march continued for another eleven hours, when the men finally reached the Chickahominy River, between nine and ten o'clock that night.

Finding only a single pontoon bridge for the entire army, the brigade waited its turn to cross. It came at five o'clock the next morning (August 18), and the last of the brigade crossed a half hour later. The men were now permitted to wash in the river. At eleven o'clock that morning, they marched another five miles before camping for the night.

The brigade was up early the next day, August 19, and on the road by 6:30 a.m. Reaching the outskirts of Williamsburg at 10:00 a.m., they halted outside the town for about two hours. With colors flying and bands playing, the brigade marched through the town. Continuing the march, the brigade camped for the night at 3:00 p.m., having marched fifteen miles that day. The men were again under way at eight o'clock on the morning of August 20, and camped a few miles from Yorktown. As soon as the men were dismissed, they ran for the York River, where they washed their clothes and bodies, and hunted for oysters and crabs.[13]

During the march south, the men were delighted by the number of cornfields they passed with sweet roasting corn. Few ears escaped being "impounded" by the Union army. The brigade historian wrote, "All through the cultivated sections of this country, the citizens appeared to have adopted the advice of Jefferson Davis, 'to anticipate a long war, and plant instead of tobacco, corn and wheat.' For this unintentional hospitality they had the thanks of the Philadelphia Brigade, and after its visitation they no doubt realized the truth of the saying 'one sowth and another reapth.'" In one instance, the division stopped to camp in front of a large cornfield surrounded by a fence. As soon as the arms were stacked, the men rushed to gather the corn. Some of the men were enterprising enough to form details: one group collected the corn and another tore down fences and built fires to roast the corn. In a remarkably short time, not a stalk remained, nor any indication of a fence.[14]

Reveille sounded at 3:00 a.m. on the 21st, but the men were not ordered to fall in for another four hours. Yorktown was reached at about 8:00 a.m., and marching on, they reached Big Bethel at four o'clock that afternoon, and camped for the night. Twenty miles were covered that day, in what many considered to be the toughest march of this part of the campaign. Awakened at 2:00 a.m. on August 22, they were pressed forward again, reaching the fork of the Hampton and Newport News Roads at 7:00 a.m. After resting for half an hour, they resumed their march to Newport News, arriving there at 9:30 a.m. in a heavy thunderstorm. Camping on the James River about two miles from the town, they awaited transportation. William Burns wrote, "Got plenty of apples on the march. Rained very hard during the day and night. Everything on me soaking wet."

The men broke camp on August 25 at 7:00 a.m. and marched to the wharf at Newport News, and boarded the small steamer, *Hero*, which took the men out to the middle of the bay where the large oceanic steamer, *Baltic*, and the smaller *Knickerbocker* awaited them. The *Baltic* was large enough to accommodate all of the troops, except the 71st, which boarded the *Knickerbocker*. Since it took the better part of the day to load the men, the ships remained at anchor until the next day, sailing at 5:00 a.m. As the *Baltic* got under way on August 26, it towed another large ship, *The Planter*, of New York, filled with cavalrymen and their horses. About twelve hours later, the ship entered the Potomac River and anchored at 9:00 p.m. Getting underway at six o'clock on the morning of August 27, the ship continued to make good progress until it ran aground about noon. The steamer, *Nellie Baker*, was returning to Newport News to pick up another load of passengers, when it happened on the scene, and was ordered to take off the men of the 106th. Other boats picked up the remaining men. The regiments were landed at Aquia Creek, Virginia, at about 4:00 p.m., and the men marched two miles inland and prepared to camp for the evening.

Sumner's corps was the last to leave the Peninsula. As the men of the Philadelphia Brigade climbed aboard the transports, the events farther north looked ominous. Jackson had moved around Pope's right flank and into the Federal rear. Realizing the danger, Pope pulled his command back toward Manassas Junction to protect both his supplies and the capital.

No sooner had the men of the Philadelphia Brigade gotten comfortable in their camp near Aquia Creek, that they were ordered back to the wharf, where they embarked on the steamers, *Canoniers*, *City of Norwich*, and the *Alice Price* at six o'clock that night. William Burns aboard the latter ship, wrote in his diary, "She was very crowded. No sleeping room. On board all night. Sailed for Alexandria." On board the *City of Norwich* was General Oliver Otis Howard, their new brigade commander. General Howard had lost an arm at Fair Oaks, and was only now returning to the field.

General Oliver O. Howard, third commander of the Philadelphia Brigade

Massachusetts Commandery Military Order of the Loyal Legion and the USAMHI

Howard was a devout Christian. While many of the men had misgivings about Howard's religious intensity, others were encouraged. "[Howard]...is a very good and brave man and we approve of him much more than our old commander [Burns] on account of his high religious *principles*," John Lynch wrote several months later. Similarly, the deeply religious George Beidelman considered Howard to be an "excellent man and soldier."[15]

Because of Jackson's threat to Washington, Sumner's orders to march eastward from Aquia to support Pope's left flank were countermanded. Instead, Sumner was ordered to land at

Alexandria. The ship left Aquia Creek at seven o'clock that night, and reached Alexandria at 10:00 p.m. After spending the night on board, the men disembarked around 5:00 a.m. on August 28, marched through the city, and camped at the foot of a large hill four miles beyond it. The corps next moved to the Chain Bridge to protect Washington. Upon arriving at Alexandria, the brigade was rejoined by Colonel Isaac Wistar, who had been home recuperating from a bout with typhoid fever. "He was never liked by the men, but this time met with a very cordial and hearty reception, which seemed to be, not because they loved Wistar more, but Jones [temporary commander of the 71st PA] the less...," wrote George Beidelman.[16]

As Sumner's and Franklin's corps moved toward the Potomac, on August 28, Jackson furiously attacked Pope at Groveton, opening the battle of Second Manassas. To beat off these attacks, Pope brought reinforcements from other parts of his line, and from the Army of the Potomac. While Pope shored up his beleaguered right flank, Lee eyed his enemy's now weakened left flank. As Pope launched an attack with the troops on his right flank on August 30, Longstreet fell on his left flank, and pushed it back. The retreat soon became a rout, almost as chaotic as the one the year before on the same battlefield.

Sedgwick's division left Alexandria at 5:00 p.m. on August 29, and marched eighteen miles in seven hours. The following day, they reached Fort Ethan Allen, which the brigade had helped build the year before. Resting here until 3:00 p.m., the brigade was ordered to march another eighteen miles, arriving at Centreville on September 1, the area that Pope selected to reform his troops.[17]

Alternating between depression and hopeless optimism, Pope settled on a unrealistic plan to renew the fight against Lee. Unfortunately, he did not know Lee's position, so on September 1, Howard was ordered to take the Philadelphia Brigade on a reconnaissance along the Little River Turnpike to see what Jackson was up to. Howard described what happened next,

> We marched rapidly until we roused Lee's pickets...When we had pressed them more closely we succeeded in drawing the fire of their noisy batteries. My purpose was now gained, and I fell back slowly and steadily to my place in the general lines. We had found that Lee's army, or a part of it, was out on the Little River Turnpike between Aldie and Fairfax C.H.

This was bad news for Pope. Finally realizing that Jackson was moving around his right flank along the Little River Turnpike to get between the Union army and Washington, Pope sent the IX Corps marching down the turnpike to halt Jackson's advance. Colliding with Jackson at Chantilly, the two forces fought a short, but intense battle here until nightfall.[18]

With Pope's army now in full retreat toward the defenses of Washington on September 2, Sedgwick's division was ordered to act as the rear guard. Their retreat was continually harassed by the enemy. At one point,

Sedgwick deployed his entire division as a skirmish line about a mile and a half from Fairfax Court House, and ordered his men forward. The rebels, seeing this strong line approaching, thought there must be an even stronger force behind it, so they stopped their advance, and prepared to meet this new threat. During the next two hours, the division was exposed to artillery fire, but no infantry attacks. Falling back about a mile to Flint Hill, the division was again overtaken by the enemy, whose cannon fired shot, shell, and railroad iron. Two members of the 106th were wounded.

Later in the day, the Philadelphia Brigade was again assigned the position of honor—rear of the rear guard. Rear guard duty was anything but easy during this retreat. In addition to the constant thrusts by Jackson's men, the rear guard had to cope with the disorganized men in front of them. Col. Isaac Wistar recalled,

> The road was a narrow cart way through a dense and dark pine...forest, crowded by thousands of disorganized troops and fragments of commands; disorderly wagon trains; guns without officers; caissons without guns; and in short, a hopeless and irredeemable mob...it fell to the latter [the Brigade] to keep order by any means however summary; shove the wagons; push the mob; drive up the stragglers; and protect the whole by showing a firm face in the pursuit...[19]

Just before sunset on September 2, Colonel Alfred Sully of the First Minnesota decided to discourage these continual attacks by drawing on his experience fighting Indians. Using the Philadelphia Brigade as a decoy, he hid the First Minnesota and a battery of artillery from view in a closed thicket at the edge of a woods. When the rebels took the bait, Sully's men opened fire, driving them from the field."[20]

Although now dark, the division pushed on toward the Chain Bridge. They reached Langley about midnight, and pushed on until 1:30 a.m., when the officers realized that the men were too exhausted to go any farther. Some of the men marched while almost asleep, while others were giddy from their lack of rest and food. Realizing that the men could not withstand much more of this treatment, the order was reluctantly given to break ranks and permit the men to rest. That night a tragedy occurred that was reminiscent of what happened at Munson's Hill the year before. A wagon broke down, and its horses became unmanageable, running away in a mad dash down the road. The exhausted men of the Philadelphia Brigade, dozing by the side of the road, were awoken to the yells that the enemy's cavalry were upon them. Shots rang out in the night. "Men running in every direction through the woods, many of them were easily detected the next morning as they were minus their caps," wrote the 69th's historian. Eight men were killed and another twenty wounded from the brigade. Private William Burns of the 71st wrote, "Panic caused by some of the teams running away. There was great excitement at the time. We all thought the rebels were on top of us." Many men would never forget that miserable night. Among them was General O. O. Howard, who later wrote, "Who will forget the straggling, the mud, the rain, the terrible panic and loss of life from random firing and the hopeless feeling—almost despair—of that dreadful night march!"

The troops crossed the Chain Bridge the next morning, September 3, and marched to Tenallytown. Pope's campaign was now over. Although the brigade had only formed the rear guard during a portion of the campaign, they, and the remainder of the II Corps, materially assisted in preventing the destruction of Pope's army.

The men were completely exhausted, having marched over 50 miles between August 29 and September 3 with little rest or food. John Lynch wrote home on this day, "We have not had a change of clothing since we left Harrison's Landing over three weeks ago. Living on hard crackers and coffee." They were cheered, however, by the news that Pope was out and McClellan again led the army.[21]

CHAPTER 9

THE ANTIETAM CAMPAIGN

Upon reaching Tenallytown, Maryland, Sedgwick's division was permitted to rest. The past seventeen days had been filled with long, tiring marches in the summer heat. Here the men were issued fresh bread, new clothes, and pay, and their officers promised them plenty of rest. Howard rode to each regiment of the brigade, complimenting the men on their conduct during the recent campaign. He also reminded them that they were among friends in Maryland, and that property rights must be respected. The men cheered at the close of each speech. Good news also reached the ranks—McClellan was restored to command. Realizing that the army's morale had sunk to new lows, Lincoln was forced to swallow his pride and ask McClellan to whip the army into shape.

Additional troops were added to the ranks, and many wounded and captured comrades returned. Promotions in rank were also made. All in all, the brigade was in fairly good shape, although somewhat pessimistic about the future. Many a soldier could not help but contemplate how rapidly the tides of war had changed. Not that long ago, "...the armies of the Union were threatening Lee from different points and he [Lee] was the defender of the Confederate capital. Today the same armies were crouching under the guns of the defenses of Washington; one of them foiled in its advance and the other disastrously defeated," wrote the Brigade historian.[1]

An ominous rumor circulated around the camps within two days of the men's arrival —the rebels were in Maryland. Lee's past aggressive actions in the face of tall odds made the rumor plausible. The men remained in camp for three days, primarily resting and drilling. After completing the third day of drills, they received orders to strike tents and march toward Rockville, Maryland—confirming the rumors. The men resumed their march on September 5, and after ten miles, the brigade camped within a mile of Rockville. William Burns recorded in his diary, "...very pretty girls and full of patriotism." The men marched through the town next day, and after going two additional miles, were halted during late afternoon, and ordered to form a line of battle. They were then ordered to stack arms and bivouack for the night. Remaining here on September 8, the men broke camp the following day and marched seven miles, where they camped in a large field near a creek. The fields were loaded with corn and potatoes, and the men helped themselves to these delicacies. On September 10, the men marched four miles, passed through Mill Creek, stopping for the night near Parksburg. The next day they passed through Clarksburg, and halted at noon on a hill overlooking Hyattstown after a nine-mile march.[2]

The town was occupied by a small force of rebels, so Sedgwick, whose division was leading the II Corps' column, threw out the 71st as skirmishers. After descending a hill and fording a river, Wistar left half the regiment to guard the crossroads, and moved the remaining five companies forward, pushing the enemy skirmishers back before them. Wistar did not see any of the town's residents—the Union batteries throwing shells over the town toward the rebels, had driven them to their basements. The Union artillery suddenly stopped firing, which suggested to Wistar that either the rebels had retired, or that his men were close to them. Sending back for the men left at the crossroads, Wistar slowly moved his regiment through a tall cornfield. It was a tense moment as the men did not know what was in front of them. Leaving the cornfield, they literally bumped into a rebel cavalry unit that had recently arrived to halt the Union advance. Both sides were momentarily stunned to see the other. Wistar weighed his two options— form a square and await their attack or attack them. He decided on the latter because he realized that the cavalry had recently arrived and was somewhat disorganized. As his men dashed forward, the cavalry fled in some disorder. Prisoners informed Wistar that he was up against a full brigade of Southern cavalry. With night approaching, Wistar was joined by the First Minnesota and two cannon. The First's commander, Colonel Sully, brought orders to "hold the ground, but make no such aggressive movement as it might bring on an engagement too big for us to manage." The men were aware that additional Union troops were at least three miles away, and that rebel infantry and cavalry were near. To make matters worse, it began to rain. The two colonels now had a friendly debate over who would command this forward outpost. Each was aware of the dangers involved, and what a defeat would do to his reputation. Wistar later wrote, "I proposed to Sully to take command, on his rank as an officer of the regular army. He however insisted that I possessed the oldest commission, which I could not deny, and after some friendly sparring we agreed to share the command between us..." Since night had fallen, the two units bivouacked. Wistar and Sully spent a miserable night sitting on the ground under a dripping tree, holding the reins of their horses, constantly being jolted awake by the frequent collisions of the opposing pickets.

During the morning, the men captured the rebel cavalry commander's black servant, who accidently entered their lines while searching for a lost horse. Unwilling to talk, the men placed him on a horse with a noose around his neck, which convinced him to tell them all that he knew. Soon after, the men were relieved to see Sumner's long column moving toward them.[3]

The march was not without dissension in the command. As the column approached Frederick, Howard placed Wistar under arrest for not obeying orders. Wistar had refused to consolidate his battered drum corps with the corps of another regiment that had never seen action. Although it seems petty, Wistar considered it to be an affront his regiment's honor. Wistar's offer of his sword was rejected by Howard, but he nevertheless took his place at the rear of the regiment as it continued its march.

After an exchange of notes, Howard finally called Wistar to his tent to discuss the matter. Howard began the discussion by saying, "Sir, I consider your communication insulting, and manifestly intended to be so." When he received no answer from Wistar, he continued, "When you receive an official order, it should be at once obeyed and explanations asked afterwards." Still Wistar would not respond, so Howard continued, "Will you obey the order now?" To this Wistar blurted out, "No, sir, never." The dialogue continued in this vein until Howard admitted that Sedgwick had discouraged taking further action, as the orders may have been misunderstood. Wistar now took the offensive, "...this is not a military order; it refers simply to regimental pageantry. General Sedwick knows me and my regiment well, and we know him, and would obey without question any order whatever from him, knowing he had some good reason." Realizing that he had no support from Sedgwick, Howard swallowed the insults and released Wistar from arrest. The idea for the change, it was later learned, came not from Howard, but from Sumner, who was merely attempting to consolidate the drum corps of the regiments for their march into Frederick. As a result of not communicating this background information, Sumner unnecessarily raised Wistar's hackles.[4]

After leaving Hyattsville on September 12, the column continued its march for seven miles, camping at Urbana for the night. The march continued at daylight on the next day, September 13, and the column finally reached Frederick. If the men had any misgivings about the loyalty of the local population, they were quickly squelched. The brigade historian wrote that the reception was, "handsome as it was unexpected. Flags that had been concealed while the enemy held possession, now decorated the dwellings and were waving along with the emblem that made Barbara Frietchie historical." Another soldier wrote, "The whole population turned out to cheer us on our way, men giving ice-water and milk to all who were thirsty, and the women and children supplying us with pies, cakes, and bread, waving their handkerchiefs and flags as we passed; all manifesting the greatest joy on their release from the presence of the enemy." William Burns wrote, "The Union sentiments are very strong (the women full of patriotism and very handsomely dressed)." The "patriotic manifestations" were not confined to the city—all along the line of march, citizens lined the road with pails of milk or water dispensed with a word of thanks and encouragement.[5]

The corps camped outside the town that night. If the welcome was warm for the II Corps, it was ecstatic for McClellan. "Upon his entrance into Frederick the people were almost wild; they blocked the streets, almost covering him and his horse with flags, as many as could shaking him by the hand, and all cheering him as long as he was in sight," wrote one observer. The march continued the next day, September 14, but did not make much progress as the officers realized they had taken the wrong road, and the column was forced to backtrack. The men could hear the boom of artillery in the distance—the battles of South Mountain were under way. Sumner, always anxious to be at the scene of a battle, hurried his men forward. The footsore men grumbled that the old cavalryman had forgotten his troops were not mounted.

After a long sixteen-mile march, the men were permitted to bivouac for the night after dark. The men could not believe their ears when assembly sounded between 11 p.m. and midnight, and they were shuffled off on a six-mile march through fields and streams until mercifully permitted to rest at 3:00 a.m. It was not until daylight that the men realized that they had camped on a battlefield near Fox's Gap. Wistar later recalled a Confederate field hospital in a blacksmith shop, where the amputated limbs were thrown through the window, "where they still lay in a blue festering heap that would have filled two or three army wagons." The men could also see 400 rebel prisoners in a nearby field. This intense fight threw Lee's troops out of the South Mountain passes with heavy losses, but bought time for the invaders to get their wagon train to safety and capture the large Federal garrison at Harpers Ferry.

As a result of the hard marching, the "sick, lame, and lazy" could not keep up with the column and were weeded out. One soldier wrote soon after the battle, "...so that we entered into the battle with hardly half our original strength in numbers, yet the effective force was in larger proportion than ever before. The mass was homogenous; they were all hardened veterans, who grumbled at having to fight, as all old soldiers will..." As they marched northward, many harbored concerns about their leadership. Lt. John Lynch of the 106th wrote, "I have become somewhat disgusted with how things are going on. Not that I have lost confidence in the bravery of the men of our army, far from it...but it is this constant mismanagement and blundering which at times makes me think that we will not be successful in quelling this rebellion."

After being permitted to rest for only four hours, the men were ordered back into column, then crossed Boonsboro Gap, and finally reached Keedysville on the evening of September 15. Marching a mile beyond the town, the troops bivouacked for the evening, having travelled about thirteen miles. The roughness of the road and the extreme fatigue made this

march especially difficult. The problem was compounded by their overzeal-
ous corps commander, who wanted to ensure that his troops got into the
fray.[6]

The morning of September 16 passed quietly as both armies assembled on either side of the Antietam Creek. Sedwick's men watched as
a battery galloped up and took position on a small ridge in front of them and
unlimbered for action. Almost as soon as the Union guns opened, they
evoked a response from a rebel battery across the creek. Most of the shells
flew over the battery, however, and landed in the compact body of
Sedgwick's men. One shot fell in the midst of the 71st, who were using
their stacked muskets to stretch their shelter tents to provide shade. Wistar
observed that, "Muskets, blankets, knapsacks, and shelter-tents flew into
the air, and any spectator must have been shocked at what seemed terrible havoc of a single shot." Because the shell entered the ground without
bursting, only one man was injured. The 106th Pennsylvania was not so
lucky. It lost one killed and four wounded. Sedgwick ended the drama by
ordering the battery to move to another spot.[7]

That afternoon, McClellan sent General Joseph Hooker's I Corps
across the creek near the Upper Bridge to attack the Confederate left flank.
Night put an end to the hostilities. General Joseph Mansfield's XII Corps
crossed the creek that night, and Sumner received orders to prepare to
cross in the morning. The men were issued eighty rounds of ammunition—
a sure sign that heavy fighting was anticipated. Showers fell that night, and
Wistar and Howard slept together under a few propped-up fence rails that
were partially covered by cornstalks.[8]

The men were roused at 2:00 a.m. to check their cartridge boxes,
and again at 4:00 a.m. for coffee. Knapsacks were piled in heaps, and
everything but the accouterments of battle were left behind. Sounds of
battle could clearly be heard around daybreak as Hooker resumed his operations against the Confederate left. Sumner anxiously waited for orders
to cross the creek and enter the fray, and when they did not come, he rode
over to McClellan's headquarters. McClellan would not see him, so he returned to his men, anxiously pacing back and forth. Sumner could not understand why McClellan was feeding the three corps into the battle in a
piecemeal manner, rather than as a solid mass of 31,000 that could clear
anything in its path.[9]

After initial successes, Hooker was pushed back with heavy losses.
Mansfield's XII Corps now entered the fray, and within minutes, its commander was mortally wounded, and his men fleeing after being exposed to
a murderous fire.

Finally, at about 7:20 a.m., Sumner received orders to cross the creek
and engage the enemy. Actually, only Sedgwick's and French's divisions
were permitted to move forward; Richardson's division was ordered to remain behind until Morell's division of Porter's corps could take its place in

reserve along the creek. Although Morell's division was only a mile to the rear, it took over ninety minutes for it to arrive at the creek. Sumner entered the battle with little information about what had transpired before his arrival, and only at two-thirds strength.

Sedgwick's division moved to the right, marched through some woods, down a hill, and finally forded the creek below the bridge used by Hooker and Mansfield's men the day before. The ground here was very irregular. One soldier from the Philadelphia Brigade characterized it as "like wheeling a wheelbarrow over a mile of heaped up cobblestones, just as regular and just as easy."

Sedgwick's three brigades began their march in three parallel columns—Gorman's on the left, Howard's on the right, and Dana's in the center. Since the men were carrying additional ammunition in their pockets, they had trouble keeping it dry as the fast-moving creek came up to their knees. Moving forward, they passed through woods, across fences, and farms. The division presented an imposing sight, as thousands of rifle barrels and bayonets glistened in the sun. One Federal staff officer wrote, "With flags flying and the long unfaltering lines rising and falling as they crossed the rolling fields, it looked as though nothing could stop them."

Others also watched the 5,000-man division. Lee's outward calm belied his inner turmoil as he watched the column intently through his field glasses. Only a portion of his army stood on the banks of the creek—the remainder were still marching from the recently captured Harpers Ferry.[10]

Sumner personally led the division forward. So intent was he on finding and engaging the enemy, that he completely forgot about French's division, which, was marching about twenty minutes behind Sedgwick's, and without orders, began to drift to the south. Sedgwick's division advanced on its own through the now quiet battlefield. A shell from Jeb Stuart's artillery at the Nicodemus House could soon be seen arcing over the column, harmlessly exploding in the rear. Then another and another, each getting closer to the division, until they found their mark. The division never faltered, continuing onward.

The men passed through an irresistible apple orchard, "the trees of which were fairly bending to the ground with their loads of ripe, delicious fruit, and the men actually under fire, with shot and shell screaming around and among them, their line dressed as on parade, with arms "right shoulder shift" went on at a 'quick step' eating apples," wrote a soldier from the 72nd Pennsylvania.[11]

The division now entered the East Woods from the south, then wheeled to the left to face west. The movement put the division into three parallel lines of battle, each composed of a brigade in two ranks that extended for 500 yards. Gorman's brigade led the division, followed by Dana's, and Howard's Philadelphia Brigade brought up the rear. The Philadelphia Brigade was deployed from left to right: 72nd, 69th, 106th, and 71st.

Sumner briefly halted the division here to take stock of the situation. General Alpheus Williams, who now commanded the XII Corps, tried to explain the situation to Sumner, but the "Bull" refused to listen. His men were up; the enemy was ahead of him, that was all he needed to know. Williams later wrote about "generals who would come up with their commands and pitch in at the first point without consultation with those who knew the ground or without reconnoitering or looking for the effective points of attack." Sumner believed that he was beyond the enemy's left flank, so all that was required was a forward march, followed by a wheel to the left, which would put him behind the rebels. It never occurred to Sumner to send out a reconnaissance party to ascertain the exact location of the enemy, or to bring up French's division to support Sedgwick's. Williams was not the only one who considered Sumner's actions foolhardy—many officers and men did not like the way they were being marched forward, unsupported. Colonel Palfrey of the 20th Massachusetts later wrote, "The total disregard of all ordinary military precaution in their swift and solitary advance was so manifest that it was observed and criticized as the devoted band moved on." Palfrey was particularly concerned about the flanks, "A single regiment in column on both flanks of the rear brigade might have been worth hundreds of men a few minutes later."[12]

In front of them lie Miller's cornfield that had been so hotly contested during the early morning fighting. The division stopped long enough for some men to pull down the fence along the field's eastern side, before entering this terrible field. One soldier from the brigade recalled, "...whole rows of men in blue lay still and cold in death, some clutching their muskets as if in the act of loading, while rested as if fallen...the enemy lie side by side with the Union troops, with all the rigor of agony pictured on their faces. Some of the men had died just as they were climbing the fence which stood in their paths and there they rested with hands and feet on the rails." Colonel Wistar later wrote, "...death and mutilation in shocking forms covered the ground on every side." The wounded men screamed out to avoid being stepped on by the men and horses moving through the stalks of corn. Climbing the fences on both sides of the Hagerstown Road, the line of battle entered the open field beyond it—the Dunker Church was near the left of the line. Howard now detached the 71st to support the XII Corps on the right. The regiment returned within a short time, and the advance continued at the "double-time."

As the men passed through some of Mansfield's units, one Fire Zouave recalled, "Here we passed Geary's 28th Pennsylvania lying in support or reserve, who gave us three hearty cheers as we pressed on, and above the din and roar of the battle, we distinctly heard them give, 'three more for Phila.' You cannot conceive our joy and excitement, the mention of our dear home had some a time created. It electrified the men and the answering shouts that went up from us from enthusiastic beyond description."

Sumner still led the advance, his hat off and white hair streaming in the wind. Shells continued to fall upon the ranks, as Stuart had moved his guns to a point just beyond the West Woods. The divisions' three lines were, unfortunately, a mere fifty to seventy feet apart, permitting enhanced destruction by the rebel artillery. Sometimes a single cannonball tore holes in all three lines; other times, "The projectile that went over the heads of the first line was likely to find its billet in the second or third," wrote Palfrey. The men were veterans though, bowing their heads as though in a hailstorm, and merely closing ranks and continuing on. Howard rode behind his men, offering words of encouragement.[13]

Gorman's brigade, forming the first line, now entered the West Woods. Because of the irregularities of the ground, the brigade was at an oblique angle with the remainder of the division, with its right flank toward the northwest and its left flank to the southeast. This caused its left to touch the left flank of Dana's brigade, while at the opposite end of the line, about 100 feet separated the two commands. Within the West Woods were boulders and limestone ledges that protected the men.[14]

The situation looked dismal to Confederate General Jubal Early. He had seen several Confederate divisions literally cut to pieces during their fight with Hooker's and Mansfield's men and now he could see a large body of troops approaching the West Woods in front of him. His own brigade was just to the south of the West Woods, perpendicular to the Hagerstown Pike. Facing the West Woods from the west, was what was left of the Stonewall Brigade under Colonel Andrew Grigsby. Realizing that it was just a matter of time before these outnumbered troops were swept from the field, Early pleaded for help. He was told that assistance was on the way, but was not reassured until he spied the head of General Lafayette McLaw's division marching rapidly in his direction. The units were exhausted from their fourteen-mile march from Harpers Ferry, but they were ready to fight.

Although not planned, the Confederates now had a sizable force in front and on the left flank of Sedgwick's division, which did not seem to be aware of their danger. What surprised the Confederates most was that the unit was boldly advancing without the benefit of skirmishers in its front, and with both flanks vulnerable to attack.[15]

Ten Confederate brigades quickly took position to fall on the Sedgwick's three unsuspecting brigades. As Gorman's line emerged from the West Woods at 9 a.m., they came under small arms fire from some Confederates at the Poffenberger Farm buildings. Dana's men came up to support Gorman, as did Howard's, although the latter was more concerned about the rattle of small arms fire coming from his left. The firing from the enemy troops in front became heavy, and Gorman's men began to waver. Because of the uneven nature of the ground, the men still could not see the growing number of Confederate units taking position around them. Howard later wrote, "Our three lines, each in two ranks were so near together that a rifle bullet would often cross them all and disable four or five men at a time."

Riding ahead, Sumner was shocked to see long lines of Confederates moving in the direction of his vulnerable left flank. Crying out, "By God, we must get out of this!" he took off in the direction of his troops. Galloping to the division's left flank, he came upon Dana's and Howard's men leaning on their rifles or lying down, their officers smoking their pipes as they awaited orders. The noise was deafening, and wildly gesturing, he cried out to his men, but they could not hear him. Thinking he was ordering them to finally charge, they fixed bayonets. Finally, they could hear him scream, "Fall back; you are in a bad position." Howard later recalled, "He approached from the rear riding rapidly...The noise of the firing was confusing. He was without his hat and with his arms outstretched motioning violently. His orders were not then intelligible; ...'Howard, you must get out of here' or 'Howard, you must face about!'"[16]

It was too late. Three Confederate brigades under Early, Barksdale, and Ransom sliced through the uneven ground, and hit the Philadelphia Brigade squarely on its left flank and rear. Volley after volley was fired into the unsuspecting troops. At the same time, another brigade under General Semmes hit Gorman directly in the front. Nearly 2,000 men were disabled in a matter of minutes. Dana's and Howard's lines fell like dominos, from left to right. The 72nd on the left flank of the brigade, literally dissolved, could not be found until later in the day. The corps' historian later wrote that the 72nd was crushed by the "first fearful blow dealt it, and is driven out in disorder." Almost half of the men present were killed or wounded within a matter of minutes.

Howard valiantly tried to get the brigade to change front to face the enemy. "With troops that I had commanded longer I could have changed front... [but] quicker than I can write the words, my men faced about and took the backtrack. Dana's line soon followed mine and then Gorman's." Howard clearly overestimates his abilities—no commander, no matter how much time he had to drill his troops, could have performed such a maneuver under these circumstances. Sumner's ineptitude had sacrificed the division, and all that could be done was to flee to the rear. This was the first time that Sedgwick's division was driven back in such disorder.[17]

Looking back upon the events of that eventful autumn morning, some brigade veterans recalled that the withdrawal was orderly, and the men fired as they fell back. The veterans of the Philadelphia Brigade were therefore furious when they read Palfrey's account of the battle in 1882: "The third line, the Philadelphia brigade, so called, was the first to go. Sumner tried to face it about preparatory to a change in front, but under the fire from its left, it moved off in a body to the right in spite of all efforts to restrain it. The first and second lines held on a little longer, but their left soon crumbled away, and then the whole of the two brigades moved off to their right, where

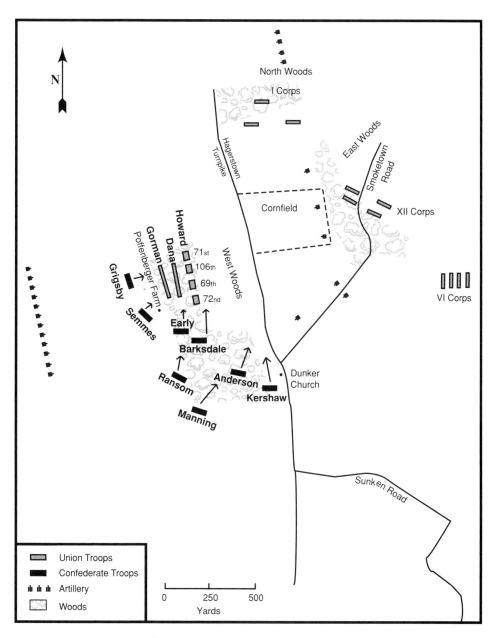

Battle of Antietam (September 17, 1862)

a new line was presently formed." Although the Philadelphians did not know it, Palfrey was simply paraphrasing Sumner's after-battle report.

Howard's after-battle report told a slightly different story:

> ...the left of our division had been completely turned by the enemy, and the order was given by General Sumner in person to change the position of the third line. He afterward indicated to me the point where the stand was to be made, where he wished to repel a force of the enemy already in our rear...The troops were hastily faced about, and moved toward the rear and right in considerable confusion, but at about 100 yards from the right of where the first line was engaged, and nearly perpendicular to the turnpike, a portion of General Gorman's brigade, with one regiment of Dana's brigade, was first halted in line, and by a sharp fire repulsed the enemy advancing at that point.

Howard's report suggests that Sumner wished to rally his troops, not at the point of contact, but to the north. Gorman's report supports this idea, "...I heard Major General Sumner directing the third line to face about, in order to repel the enemy, which had broken our left, supposing the design to be to take up a better position than the one just previously occupied..."

Colonel Owen's report also corroborates Howard's:

> The panic which I had observed on the left ultimately spread along the line, and the impetuous advance of the enemy's column threatened to turn our left flank...Sumner appeared in person in the midst of a most deadly shower of shot and shell, and an order was received to fall back. With some confusion upon the left, the brigade retired.

Chaos reigned for several minutes. Howard later recalled, "When we reached the open ground Sumner himself and every other officer of courage and nerve were exerting themselves to the utmost to rally the men, turn them back, and make head against the advancing enemy, but it was simply impossible til we had traversed those cleared fields; for we had now the enemy's infantry and artillery in rear and on our flank against our broken brigades, pelting with rapid and deadly volleys."[18]

Not all of Sedgwick's division immediately fell back. Gorman's brigade and the right of Dana's held their ground. So too did the 71st, which was on the extreme right of the brigade, separated from it by a limestone ledge. These Union troops were now attacked on three sides by the Confederate infantry, and were exposed to canister from Stuart's artillery. No troops could have long weathered this storm, and Gorman's brigade was forced back throwing Dana's brigade into disorder. The two lines made their way to the rear as best they could.

Up to this point, the 71st's soldiers were unable to discharge their weapons because of the Union troops in front of them. The Philadelphians now rose, and fired a destructive volley into the oncoming Confederate infantry. Knowing that his men could not hold out much longer without support,

Wistar finally ordered his men to retire. He had not gone far before he was hit in his good arm. One of his officers tied a tourniquet to his arm and carried his sword to safety. A long line of Confederate infantry appeared, and one of their officers stopped Wistar and demanded his sword. When told that he did not have it, he demanded his parole. After rejecting this demand as well, Wistar was able to attract the attention of a member of Jeb Stuart's staff, who interceded on Wistar's behalf and ordered the persistent Southern officer back to his regiment. The staff officer proved to be John Mosby, who later become a thorn in the Union's side as a guerilla in the Shenandoah Valley. Mosby gave Wistar water and adjusted his tourniquet, before rejoining the group. Wistar ultimately reached safety.

During the retreat, Colonel Morehead's horse was shot from under him, pinning him to the ground. Assisted by some of his men, Morehead was able to extract himself and limp to the rear. Realizing that he had left his sword behind with his dead horse, he walked back to retrieve it, despite the entreaties of his men. Yelling, "Yes I will, that sword was given to me by my men, and I told them I would protect it with my life and never see it dishonored, and I am not going to let them damned rebels get it." Although fired upon by the enemy, Morehead returned safety with his prized possession.

The men realized that safety could only be found by running northward, where Sumner and his officers were rounding up units to make a stand. Some regiments retained good order during their retreat; others were disorganized masses. This seemed to be related to where the units were originally deployed—those on the left were more disorganized than those on the right. Colonel Owen wrote in his after-battle report, "The Sixty–ninth, One hundred and sixth, and Seventy–first Pennsylvania Volunteers retired in good order; the Seventy–second Regiment Pennsylvania Volunteers, however, being on the extreme left...did not retire in the same good order as the other three regiments, nor was it reformed, nor did it rejoin the brigade until a late hour in the afternoon."[19]

As the men fled for safety, they periodically turned and delivered volleys into the enemy, before continuing their retreat. The 106th made their first stop along a fence that ran at right angles to the Hagerstown Pike, just north of the Dunker Church. Color Sergeant Benjamin Sloanacker planted his colors on the fence and yelled to "rally on the colors." They were joined by men from other units, and after firing several volleys, were able to temporarily halt the rebel advance, but not before a third of the regiment went down. The 106th made another stand just to the north, where they were joined by part of the 15th Massachussetts. Finally reaching the North Woods, and the safety of the I Corps and a number of batteries, the brigade was ordered to halt and reform. The brigade was later moved to the East Woods to support other batteries.

Sedgwick was severely wounded in several places during the battle. Being the senior brigadier, Howard was thrust in charge of the division, and

Joshua Owen took his place in command of the Philadelphia Brigade. Colonel Baxter was actually the next senior officer of the brigade, but he, and the rest of the 72nd, could not be found.

Although not known as an inspirational leader, Howard rushed about trying to get the men of the division to safety. He first helped to stabilize the line, then began an orderly withdrawal by slow stages under the intense enemy barrage. One of his biographers wrote, "How he survived meets the standards of that much overworked term, 'miraculous.'"[20]

Sumner sent a stream of pleas for support to McClellan. He also sought reinforcements from General Williams, whose advice he would not earlier heed, and from the remaining two divisions of his corps. The latter could not to provide any assistance as they had their hands full fighting the center of the Confederate army. To those around him, Sumner seemed dazed and in shock.

There was not much sympathy for Sumner. Palfrey wrote later, "What General Sumner may have expected or even hoped to accomplish by his rash advance, it is difficult to conjecture..." Colonel Owen summed up the problem well, when he wrote in his report that the disaster that befell the brigade was "attributable to its having been placed in too great proximity to the other two lines, and thus, while intended to act as a reserve, subjected to as deadly a fire as those it was intended to support."

Except for artillery shells thrown at them, which tore chunks out of the trees, ricocheted off of rocks, and killed the wounded, the battle in this sector was now over.[21]

The losses were stunning. Sedgwick lost about 2,300 men, most within ten minutes of the start of the attack. The Confederate losses in this sector were less than 1,000. The toll on officers was especially great. In addition to Sedgwick and Wistar, Colonel Morehead was injured when his horse fell on him.

The heaviest losses (902) were sustained by the Dana's brigade, which occupied the middle line. Gorman's losses were only slightly less, 758. The Philadelphia Brigade's move to the right apparently helped to reduce its losses to "only" 568. Most of these losses occurred within a ten-minute span.

One of those killed was Private Edmund Collier. A native of England, Collier was visiting the U.S. when the war broke out. Bitten by martial fever, he enlisted in the 72nd and fought in all of its engagements. Another casualty was William Burns, whose diary accurately chronicled the activities of the 71st. Burns recorded in his diary, "...a shell burst near me and one of the pieces hit me in the foot. It knocked me down and swole [sic] my foot so that I could not walk. While laying here the shells from the rebels and our own batteries fell so near me, I had to get up and hobble away the best I could."

In revisiting Palfrey's assertion that the Philadelphia Brigade was the "first to go," it appears that he is only partially correct. The left side of *both*

Howard's and Dana's brigades did initially break under the pressure exerted by the three Confederate brigades. However, over on the right, the 71st was actually the "last to go," as it remained in position after Gorman's and Dana's troops were driven from their positions. Wistar later wrote, "I personally saw the second line [Dana's] break before the wild rush of fugitives from the front line [Gorman's], and for a few minutes my greatest difficulty was from these fugitives, since they masked the fire of the 71st."[22]

The brigade, along with the remainder of the II Corps, moved back to the East Woods at the edge of the cornfield on September 19, and changed their position again on September 21. "We changed our position yesterday afternoon, about 500 yards to a fine strip of woods, which furnishes good shade and a very strong smell," wrote George Beidelman. The men could not bury the dead fast enough because the decaying bodies "impregnated the whole atmosphere with foul odors arising from their fast decomposing bodies," wrote one member of the brigade. The Federal corpses were buried first, leaving the Confederates to rot in the hot sun. As a result, their bodies swelled and turned black. The men were nauseated by the foul environment, and few could eat.

Finally, at 5:30 a.m. of September 22, the men were ordered to move out. Marching through the town of Sharpsburg, the men saw the havoc wrecked on the small town. Virtually every house bore some sign of the battle. Crammed into many were wounded men. Cannons and wagons were also on every street, which hindered the infantry's march.[23]

CHAPTER 10

FREDERICKSBURG CAMPAIGN

The II Corps began its fourteen-mile march to Harpers Ferry at daylight on September 22, 1862. The hilly terrain made the march especially difficult. Upon reaching the Potomac, the men found that the rebels had burned the pontoon and railroad bridges, forcing them to ford the waist-deep river. The 106th, as it had seven months earlier, led the brigade across the river. Completing the crossing by 1:30 that afternoon, the men marched through town and climbed Bolivar Heights. Here they were joined by Dana's brigade and a battery. All were grateful when the orders to "fall out" rang through the column. The brigade would remain here until October 30.

This was a time for drilling, resting, and refitting. The men grumbled about the former, for after the arduous campaign they would have preferred twenty-four hours of rest each day. They appreciated that McClellan, always the organizer, was able to unloosen a river of supplies. Since no clothing had been issued since the men left Harrison's Landing, the men were in a deplorable condition. "I would be ashamed to be seen in respectable society now: plastered and spotted with grease and dirt of every kind almost; unmentionables given away in a very important place...," wrote George Beidelman of the 71st. Bartram Ashmead of the 72nd provided this accounting of his wardrobe:

> One pair of worn-out shoes;
>
> One cap—Faded from blue to dingy gray;
>
> One blouse—color unknown;
>
> One pair of pantaloons—ragged and soiled;
>
> One pair of suspenders—blank from wear

The men did not grumble about their condition for they knew that the enemy had even fewer supplies. Before long, every soldier received a new uniform.[1]

Monotony eventually set in. "We have little else to do to-day except to cook and eat our rations (which are none the plentiest, by the way)," wrote

Beidelman. He also complained about the water, which "is a little inconvenient too: most of the boys go all the way to the Potomac or Shenandoah rivers, about equidistant from here, say 3/4 mile to either."

Beidelman humorously related how the men were roused each morning:

> First the bugles break the stillness of the morn, those of the artillery arm taking the lead; then the cavalry, ...while the infantry lazily brings up the rear, and the discord commences...probably one half of the players only amateurs (their worthy predecessors having been killed or wounded in battles) and the rattling and clattering of a hundred drums, whose owners have caught the spirit of the grand medley, commence with their accompanying and awfully shrill fifes...[2]

President Lincoln arrived on October 1 to review the troops. As the entourage slowly rode along the lines, the men responded with cheers and the artillery boomed out a twenty-one-gun salute. Some who observed Lincoln thought that he looked "careworn and anxious, and in his whole manner seemed to say, 'Why does McClellan allow the best month of the fall to pass...[without fighting] the army of General Lee?'"

The brigade finally broke camp on October 7, and marched about 300 yards. Here the column was halted and informed that this would be their new camp. Two days later, October 9, the brigade was again assembled to welcome back its old commander, General Burns, who had finally recovered from his wounds. George Beidelman wrote home, "The boys had almost a jubilee over his reception, and the gratification was no doubt mutual." So overcome by emotion was Burns, that he could only utter, "How do you do, men?" The reunion was a short one, however, for within a few weeks, Burns was given command of the First Division of the IX Corps. Drawn up behind their stacked rifles on November 3, the men said goodbye to their beloved leader. After giving him three cheers, the following message was read to the men:

> The order has been received which separates us...In bidding you a final adieu, I cannot refrain from asking you...to pay rigid regard to discipline. Without discipline the bravest must yield to the basest. General Washington wept tears of blood over this great want in his army. You know the necessity now. I beg you will remember me in your determination to do your duty, and I will always feel proud of the victories you will win. Good bless you.

The men were proud of Burns' advancement, but they were also concerned about his replacement. They did not have long to wait. With Howard commanding the division, Joshua Owen of the 69th was promoted to brigadier general and given permanent command of the brigade. Around the same time, John Markoe of the 71st was promoted to colonel, and took command of the regiment.[3]

General Joshua Owen,
fourth commander of the
Philadelphia Brigade

Prior to Owen's advancement to brigade command, his simmering ill-feelings toward Lieutenant Colonel Dennis O'Kane of the 69th boiled over. Accusing O'Kane of being absent from his post, intoxication, and fighting with his superior, he was court-martialed. The latter charge arose during a visit by O'Kane's wife and daughter. Owen was apparently drunk, and rode his horse into the team of horses pulling O'Kane's carriage. Despite pleas from O'Kane, Owen repeated this maneuver several times, calling his subordinate a son of a bitch. Having enough of this treatment, O'Kane pulled Owen from his horse and a fight ensued. O'Kane was eventually found innocent of the charges, partly because of his character witnesses—General Howard, and Colonels Morehead and Baxter.

Soon after arriving at Harpers Ferry, a report was sent to Washington showing that the brigade's paper strength was 3,482, but only 2,169 (62%) were present. The breakdown by regiment (total:present) was: 69th (737:486); 71st (820:510); 72nd (1,197:681); and 106th (728:492).

The brigade's losses from March 30 through September 30 was 1,455 men, or a full one-third in the short span of six months. The brigade had fought in several battles (e.g., Fair Oaks, Peach Orchard, Savage Station, Glendale, and Antietam) and a number of skirmishes during this period. Of this number, seven-eighths were either killed or wounded, most at Antietam.

The routine was broken on October 16, when the division was ordered to make a reconnaissance in force to Charlestown to probe Stonewall Jackson's corps in the Shenandoah Valley. Leaving camp at daybreak and marching down the Charlestown Pike, the men could hear skirmishing and heavy cannonading in the distance. They came under fire of a rebel battery when within one mile of Halltown, killing one soldier and wounding five others from the 71st. Deploying on both sides of the road, the men continued toward Charlestown, where they were ordered to support a battery. Seeing no immediate threat, they stacked arms and rested. The return to Harpers Ferry began on the evening of October 17—the column got as far as Halltown before going into bivouac. Many did not sleep, as the night was very cold, and many had not brought their overcoats or blankets.

Because rebels were feared to be nearby, no fires could be lit, so the men walked back and forth all night to keep warm. The sight of their campground on Bolivar Heights was greeted most enthusiastically later that morning.[4]

The brigade also received a welcomed visit from the paymaster, whom it had not seen for four months. While the government had freely distributed clothing, food, and other essentials, the men did not have access to the desired "extras." As always, the sutlers followed the paymaster. "The town then began to be temporarily filled by that throng of vultures which follow the trail of the paymaster, to extort from the soldiers their pay for the few things they really needed, or felt they needed... they had to pay two or three [times higher] prices," wrote the historian of the 106th. Some received permission to set up shop in abandoned stores in the town, but despite strict orders to the contrary, whiskey continued to be smuggled across the river and sold to the men. The penalties for possessing whiskey were severe. After a warning, the sutler's wares were confiscated and the owner put to work constructing fortifications on Loudoun Heights.

The army's refitting ended on October 26, when McClellan issued orders to move south. Lee had split his army—Jackson's corps was in the Shenandoah Valley, while Longstreet's was at Culpeper. McClellan planned to attack each separately and destroy them. The II Corps began moving out on October 29. The Philadelphia Brigade left the next day, marching first to Harpers Ferry, crossing the Shenandoah River on a pontoon bridge, and marching south for nine miles before camping for the night. On November 1, the brigade moved to Snickersville. During this march many of "Paddy Owen's Regulars" of the 69th had gained access to whiskey, and considerable disruption occurred. Few men reached the bivouac area, as most were unable keep up, and those who did were more disheveled than usual.[5]

The brigade continued its march south on November 2 when it reached Snicker's Gap and continued on for nine more miles before camping for the night. The following afternoon, the men broke camp at one o'clock and marched about five miles, stopping in the vicinity of Upperville. The march continued again at noon on November 4, passing through Upperville, Paris, and Ashby's Gap. Here they spent two days guarding the mountain pass.

On November 6, the brigade retraced its steps to Paris, and camped at about 1 p.m. at Goose Creek after an eight-mile march. The following day, the first snow of the season covered the ground to a depth of two inches. The men had only their small shelter tents to protect them. "They are only made of heavy muslin, and serve merely to keep the storm off our backs without keeping out the cold. As a consequence the fence-rails have to suffer," wrote George Beidelman. The men were cheered when they heard that they would not break camp, but could spend the day resting. The bright sun melted the snow on November 8 as the brigade left camp and marched to Salem. The following day, the column marched eight miles and arrived at Warrenton, the army's assembling point, in the late morning.[6]

November 10 was a memorable day. Lincoln continued to expect that McClellan would launch another campaign against Richmond while the weather was still favorable. McClellan disagreed. First, he argued that the army needed refitting. Next, he needed reinforcements to take on the "large" rebel army, which was actually smaller than McClellan's. Not able to wait any longer, Lincoln again removed McClellan from command and replaced him with General Ambrose Burnside.

With men drawn up on either side of the Warrenton Road, "Little Mac" rode slowly down the line. A thirteen-gun salute rang out as the General approached, and the men presented arms. The historian of the 106th wrote,

> ...to see the sad expression on the faces of the men, tears stealing their way down the bronzed cheeks of the veterans who knew not fear...some left the ranks, rushed into the road and begged him to stay, even seizing his horse. The General was deeply affected; he said, 'I wish you to stand by General Burnside as you have stood by me, and all will be well. Good-bye,' and rode on. The men returned to camp greatly depressed, feeling keenly their loss...

Most men regretted to see McClellan leave. William Lynch of the 106th wrote, "...I really believe if he had asked us to follow him to Washington and kick out of office all those miserable thieves, which hold the high offices, we should have gone with a loud shout and glad hearts for then we could see some prospects of the conclusion of this war..." This feeling was not universal, however. George Beidelman, contrasting the new army commander with McClellan, wrote that Burnside "seems more decided, and certain to accomplish greater results."[7]

The following evening, November 11, the brigade changed its camp again, this time to higher ground. "I know not how to interpret this move, unless it means that we will stay here yet a few days until things get straightened out incident to the change of commander," wrote George Beidelman. The following days were spent discussing the merits of McClellan over Burnside, resting, drilling, and parading.

General Ambrose Burnside, who had successfully invaded North Carolina, was a disappointment during the Antietam Campaign. If he had forced his way across Antietam Creek earlier in the day, Lee's army would have been crushed. After the battle, McClellan wrote to his wife, "He is very slow; is not fit to command more than a regiment." Now Burnside was offered command of the entire Army of the Potomac. Burnside knew his limitations, and twice turned down Lincoln's invitation, vehemently saying that he did not have the capacity to command such a large army and he did not want the headaches involved.

Burnside inherited a splendid army of over 120,000 men, which he divided into three "grand divisions." The II and IX Corps formed the Right Grand Division, commanded by Sumner; the III and V Corps, commanded by Hooker, formed the Center Grand Division; and the I and VI Corps formed the Left Grand Division, commanded by Franklin. Within the Philadelphia

Brigade, the regimental leadership remained fairly stable. Baxter commanded the 72nd, and Morehead commanded the 106th. Lieutenant Colonel Markoe commanded the 71st, and Lt. Col. Dennis O'Kane received command of the 69th when Owen was given the brigade.[8]

Burnside's strategy was to feint a move toward Culpeper, and while freezing Lee's men there, rapidly march his army to Fredericksburg. From there he would strike south and capture Richmond. The plan required quick action once implemented, but this was not to be the case. The army remained in the vicinity of Warrenton until November 15, when it began the long march to Falmouth, opposite Fredericksburg on the Rappahannock River. In 2½ days, the army marched almost forty miles. Many men complained of the harshness of this march. George Beidelman complained to his father,

> Our Generals don't give us enough rest on the march. I would much prefer starting an hour earlier in the morning, and march an hour later at night, in order to get a good rest every couple of miles. The way it is we sometimes march 4 or 5 miles over all sorts of roads, and as fast as we can go down to it, before we halt; and then one is nearly done for. No wonder men straggle...O what deep and heartfelt curses did I repeatedly hear heaped upon the generals, the war, the country, the rebels, and everything else.

Upon arriving at Falmouth, the men went into camp, but had not settled in when artillery shells from a rebel battery across the river filled the air. Pettit's battery immediately galloped up, and after some accurate shooting, drove the rebels from the hill.[9]

Realizing that the heights behind Fredericksburg were weakly held, Sumner petitioned Burnside to allow him to cross the river and take them. Sumner's request was denied, as Burnside wanted to wait until the entire army, and the pontoon boats arrived. This was the first mistake in a campaign filled with many miscues. When the pontoon bridges finally arrived on November 25, Lee's army had shifted to Fredericksburg and was strongly entrenched on the heights overlooking the city.

Burnside's plan was fairly straightforward. The Union army would cross the Rappahannock in two places—Hooker's and Sumner's Grand Divisions opposite the city; Franklin's about two miles south. After crossing, the latter force would sweep north on the newly built military road, and catch Longstreet's corps in the flank while Sumner and Hooker hit him in the front.[10]

Many men were anxious to engage the enemy, because they felt a decisive defeat of Lee could end the war. Private Jacob Pyewell predicted that a fight would be waged at Fredericksburg, and wrote, "I think we will give them the jessie this time. I hope so, anyhow, I don't want to see any more retreats. I want to see this war come to a close as it has lasted too long already and I think that we have got the man at our head that will shove things, Burnside." Some felt like William Myers, also of the 106th, when he wrote, "I do not believe that the rebs will make a stand there. If they do we will have the advantage of them." As events unfolded, Private Myers would realize how wrong he was.

The engineers immediately set to work when the pontoon boats finally arrived. Initially working under the cover of darkness, they were later protected by a thick blanket of fog. As the engineers worked on the bridge, the infantry prepared for their part of the fight. Darius Couch, now commanding the II Corps, was roused at 3 a.m. on December 11 and ordered to prepare for the day's fight. At about 6:30 a.m. the men marched the two miles from camp to the bank of the river, where they were ordered to stack arms and await orders to cross. When all but the last few boats were set in place, the fog burned off, exposing the engineers to highly accurate sharpshooter fire from the town, driving them off the bridge.[11]

A concentrated artillery fire was ordered to clear the town, and thirty-six cannon on Stafford Heights opened on the all-but abandoned city. After several hours, the cannonading ceased, and the engineers returned to work, only to find that the sharpshooters remained in the town. Burnside now ordered all 183 of his artillery pieces to open fire on the city. One historian called it "...the most concentrated bombardment of such a small target ever to be made in the United States." Fires broke out, and some men amused themselves by trying to catch the burning embers floating across the river. After two hours, the firing stopped, but the sharpshooters from Barksdale's brigade remained.

Another strategy was needed, and by 3 p.m. the 7th Michigan was rapidly rowing across the river in pontoon boats. Despite the sniper fire, the Michiganders swarmed up the bank and gained a toehold on the town. Other units from Hall's brigade now crossed, and the part of the town facing the river was finally cleared of sharpshooters. The losses were heavy. The pontoon bridge was now quickly completed, and at 4:00 p.m. the Philadelphia Brigade rushed across under artillery and small arms fire to help clear the town. Forming in line of battle on the riverbank to the left of the bridge, Hall's brigade assembled on their right. Detachments from each regiment were sent toward the left to drive out the remaining rebels.

Owen recalled the dangerous situation in his after-battle report: "The streets perpendicular to my line were enfiladed by squads of sharpshooters and the enemy's batteries located upon the hill. The houses and churches contiguous to my route were filled with sharpshooters, which rendered great caution necessary." Darkness hampered the operation, but the flanking movement from the left helped push the last of the enemy out of the town. By 10:00 p.m., the town was secured and the men permitted to rest on their arms. The brigade captured about twenty-one prisoners, primarily from the 21st Mississippi. As one was marched to the rear past Colonel Morehead, he cried out, "Old man, I see you are alive yet. I had four good shots at you and don't see how it is I did not hit you." Morehead merely growled, "You scoundrel, you," as the man was marched to the rear.[12]

Now that the threat of snipers had passed, the men could see the destructive results of the massed artillery. John Lynch of the 106th wrote home, "We are in this *almost destroyed* city...my heart almost bled to see the wanton destruction of property here in this place. The house which I am now writing this letter in has 20 cannon balls and shells passed through it, making the house a complete wreck. All the nice furniture scattered about in the mutilated confusion, there is hardly a house in the place which is not riddled by shells."

After the Confederates were routed from the town, many of the Union troops went on a looting rampage. Some looked for whiskey, wine, tobacco, and food. William Burns recorded in his diary, "Scrounging for what I could get. Plenty of tobacco, wine, segars [sic], fresh pork, flour, sweet meats, and a music box and handkerchief." George Beidelman of the same regiment added, "We lived high on slapjacks, jam, potatoes, preserves..." Others simply destroyed furniture and personal belongings. By nightfall, all manner of household items, most destroyed in some fashion, were strewn through the streets of the city. The historian of the 106th later wrote in disgust, "No effort seemed to be made to arrest this wholesale destruction until the destroyers seemed tired of their own wantonness." Not all of the troops participated in this destructive behavior, and some even tried to assume a positive role. Such was the case of the 72nd, whose men toiled long into the night trying to extinguish the fires that had been set by the fierce cannonading. The men delighted in having a opportunity to ply their former trade.[13]

Only Sumner's Grand Division had crossed the Rappahannock River that night, December 11—the remainder remained on the northern bank until the next day. As the remaining troops crossed, the Philadelphia Brigade, with the 71st thrown out as skirmishers, advanced through the city. The brigade moved from one position to another during the day, taking care to keep under cover from the heavy artillery fire being thrown into the town by the Confederate batteries on the heights.

If Burnside had a choice, he probably would not have attacked the strongly entrenched Confederate position, but Lincoln had made it very clear that he wanted him to engage Lee's army before the year ended. There were few options. To withdraw now would be tantamount to defeat. Yet, to attack the strongly entrenched Confederate position on Marye's Heights was the height of folly, as the position was all but impregnable.[14]

Sumner's Grand Division was ordered to attack Marye's Heights on December 13, but only after Franklin's Grand Division had successfully attacked the enemy's right flank, and was advancing on the right and rear of the heights. Although the attack was to be launched early in the morning, 10:30 a.m. came and went, and Burnside became increasingly impatient. Believing that he could wait no longer for Franklin, Sumner was ordered to launch his frontal attack. French's division of the II Corps would attack in column of brigades, each separated by an interval of about 200 yards.

General Nathan Kimball's brigade formed the first line. Immediately upon leaving the protection of the city, the men were exposed to an intense artillery fire. Undeterred, they ran forward across the open ground, men constantly falling. When within 100 yards of the stone wall at the base of Marye's Heights, a line of infantry suddenly rose up from behind it and poured sheets of flames into them. The blast was so strong that the survivors threw themselves down on the ground. Some returned the fire, others merely clawed the ground for protection. About a quarter of Kimball's men lie dead and wounded after an assault that lasted but a few minutes.[15]

The second assault line, composed of Colonel John Andrews' brigade, was now launched, but it faltered at about the same place as Kimball's. Colonel Oliver Palmer's brigade now took up the attack, and it suffered the same fate as the first two. French's division lost about 1,000 men in a matter of minutes. Hancock's division was now moved forward to take the heights. Its first brigade, under Colonel Samuel Zook, attacked at about 12:30 p.m., and was immediately hit by the deadly cannon fire. But this brigade was not to be stopped. Sweeping over French's men, they continued toward the stone wall. Fresh rebel regiments were rushed to the stone wall, to form four rows behind the barricade. When within twenty-five yards of the wall, Zook's line could go no farther, and his men fell to the ground for protection. Believing that the rebels could not allow this strong force to remain so close, they grimly fixed bayonets and awaited the Confederate counterattack.

The Irish Brigade now moved forward, but they too were repulsed. Before long, small knots of men from the two divisions began making their way back toward the safety of the town. Into this confusion, advanced Hancock's third brigade, under General John Caldwell, which shared the same fate as the other brigades.[16]

Two divisions had tried to capture the stone wall without success, so Couch committed his last division, Oliver Howard's, which had been resting in the northern half of the city. Howard's orders were to move forward "and support the remaining men of the two shattered divisions." The Philadelphia Brigade had been waiting in line for the order to advance since 10 a.m. During this time, they were joined by the 127th Pennsylvania, which had recently joined the army, but was unattached. The wait was over at 12:20 p.m., when orders to advance finally arrived. Owen moved the brigade, minus the 71st, which was still on picket duty, by the left flank along Hanover Street. As it left the city, the brigade was immediately hit by fierce artillery fire from the cannon positioned on the heights. The line of attack was the 127th Pennsylvania on the left, the 72nd and 106th in the center, and the 69th on the right. As the line moved forward, Kirby's battery galloped up and unlimbered. Owen reported, "The support of this battery highly elated the officers and men, and they moved forward with spirit and confidence, notwithstanding the terrible fire to which they were subjected." It

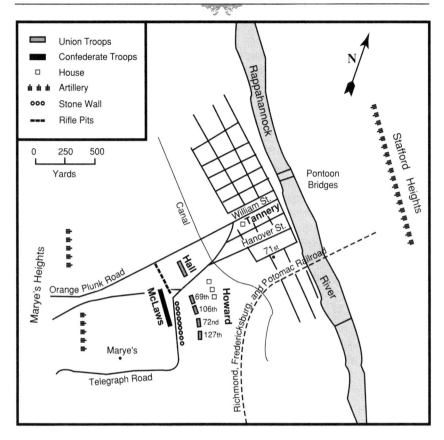

Battle of Fredericksburg (December 13, 1862)

was just after 1:00 p.m. when Owen gave the order, "Forward, double-quick, march—guide center" and the brigade moved smartly forward to the left of Hanover Street, about 400 yards from the rebel's first line of defense.

Almost immediately, Owen's horse was shot in the shoulder, forcing him to dismount and lead his men on foot. Drawing his sword, he yelled for his men to follow him. Owen reported, "...when, from behind a stone wall at the base of the steep declivity; from rifle-pits on the face of the hill; from two batteries on either side of a large brick house at the top of a hill; from traverses on the right and left flanks of my line, and from a line of infantry drawn up on top of the hill, a most terrific fire was opened upon us." The losses mounted, but finally the brigade reached the area that should have contained the remnants of French's and Hancock's divisions. When within about eighty yards of the stone wall, Owen finally realized that there were no men to support. He now faced a dilemma—continue the attack, which would lead to senseless slaughter, or retreat, which would be dishonorable. Choosing the middle ground, he ordered his men to "halt and lay down." In addition to the Confederate batteries in position on the heights and the infantry behind the stone wall, the men could see another line of Southern infantry farther up the hill. Rebel sharpshooters could also be seen resting their rifles on the sills of every window of the Marye Mansion. They seemed particularly interested in the officers. Although Owen's position was somewhat protected by a small wooden fence, any soldier trying to rise up and fire was hit by a hail of bullets. To pour fire into the batteries and infantry behind the stone wall, Owen dispatched three companies to the houses on the right of his line to act as sharpshooters. Each man fired about seventy rounds during his tenure here. So effective was this fire, that some of the artillery diverted their attention to these houses, demolishing at least one of them. Some of the shells being fired from the Federal batteries behind the prone men exploded prematurely, causing shrapnel to fall among them. Owen dispatched a staff officer to inform Howard of the strength of the rebel position and the impossibility of carrying them with the troops at his disposal. Howard's orders were, "hold what he had got, and to push forward the first opportunity, and not to fire, except when he had something to fire at." Reinforcements were also promised.[17]

The historian of the 106th graphically described what it was like for the men of the brigade to be pinned down so close to the enemy's lines:

> ...nothing tested the courage of men more than to be placed in such a position, with shot and shell from both directions, in front and rear, screaming and tearing over our heads or plowing up the ground in our midst, killing and mangling men at our side, the terrible showers of bullets from the many men that filled their two lines of works...Yet there we stayed, compelled to remain inactive, lying flat on the cold ground...with no chance to move sufficiently to circulate the blood enough to keep warm, as the slightest movement but brought on the deadly fire of their sharpshooters; many were killed or wounded by just raising their head from the ground...

Hall's brigade now emerged to their right to attack the rifle pits next to the stone wall. About halfway to the enemy's position, two of Hall's regiments broke to the rear, unable to sustain the rain of destruction. The brigade was subsequently reformed, and its advance continued. When they finally reached the right of the Philadelphia Brigade, Hall ordered his men to lie down, and at the same time, sent a message to Couch saying that he could hold his position, but an advance would be futile. Howard's third brigade under General Alfred never entered the fray as a unit as it was broken up, and its regiments sent to those parts of the field that needed reinforcements.[18]

Soon after the battle, Couch described what occurred to his division on the plains of Fredericksburg:

> There was no cheering on the part of the men, but a stubborn determination to obey orders and do their duty. I don't think there

was much feeling of success. As they charged the artillery fire would break their formation, and they would get mixed; then they would close up, go forward, receive the withering infantry fire, and those who were able would run to the houses and fight as best they could; and then the next brigade coming up in succession would do its duty and melt like snow coming down on warm ground.

Hooker's corps now moved to the II Corps' aid. At about 4:00 p.m., Owen's men watched as Allabach's brigade of Humphreys' division formed behind them. Owen ordered his men to prepare to advance, but before it could, Humphreys' line "staggered, reeled, and fell back in confusion under the awful fire which was poured in up it." Hazard's battery dashed up and deployed as Tyler's brigade was ordered forward. Owen once again ordered his men to rise and charge the heights, but this time, the new troops partially overlapped the brigade and actually fired into them. By the time the confusion ended, the attack had been repulsed. As Humphreys' men fell back in disorder, the 127th Pennsylvania, temporarily assigned to the brigade, also broke for the rear. Over 1,700 men fell in these last two futile attacks. It was later learned that Humphreys' men—inexperienced men—had been ordered to move forward with bayonets fixed on unloaded guns.[19]

Controversy again visited the Philadelphia Brigade during this battle. As Humphreys led his division up the hill, he thought Owen's prone men were skulkers and the historian of the Philadelphia Brigade wrote, "...in commanding tones ordered our brigade to join his column. Being convinced of his error, in a moment he moved on, and we rose to our feet to see the result." The historian of the 106th added that Humphreys "accused us of cowardice in not very flattering terms, and ordered us to join his command in their advance; this General Owen refused to do, knowing from experience what the result would be..."

In his after-battle report, General Humphreys did not hide his disdain for the Philadelphia Brigade. "...one of the greatest obstacles to my success was the mass of troops lying on our front line. They ought to have been withdrawn before mine advanced ...they disordered my lines and were greatly in the way when I wished to bring the brigade to a charge." Most damning was the rest of his report,

> The troops I was to support...were sheltering themselves by lying on the ground. This example Colonel Allabach's brigade immediately followed, in spite of an effort to prevent it, and opened a fire upon the enemy. A part only of his men were able to reach the front rank, owing to the numbers already occupying the ground. The continued presence of the troops I was to support or relieve proved a serious obstacle to my success...I directed them to disregard these men entirely, and to pass over them....As the brigade reached the masses of men referred to, every effort was made by the latter to prevent our advance. They called to our men not to go forward, and

some attempted to prevent by force their doing so. The effect upon my command was what I apprehended—the line was somewhat disordered, and, in part, forced to form into a column, but still advanced rapidly.[20]

The criticism of the Philadelphia Brigade was unfounded. Howard had ordered them, along with Hall's brigade on their right, to lie down and hold their positions. This unquestionably impeded Humphreys' inexperienced troops, but was not the fault of the Philadelphians. That some of the men lying prone may have yelled out warnings not to go forward is indeed a breach of military etiquette. But the prone men of the Philadelphia Brigade knew that any frontal assault was doomed, and they tried to save their comrades from the ineptitude of their leaders. Eight times fresh units had charged the heights, and eight times they were driven back with heavy losses. Humphreys, a professional soldier, was fooling himself if he believed his inexperienced men could do what more experienced troops could not.

The historian of the II Corps came to the Philadelphia Brigade's defense when he wrote about the obstacles posed by prone bodies, "...but it would have been as reasonable to quarrel with the corpses of French's and Hancock's men who had been killed in the charge, as with the bodies of their living companions who had clung to the ground, when the attack failed, deeming that it was their duty to hold what they had gained..."

The Philadelphia Brigade held its position as night ended the slaughter. Owen threw out pickets and waited to be relieved. The moans and screams of wounded comrades in the no-man's-land in front of them were heartrendering. Initial attempts to assist these unfortunates failed when rebel sharpshooters fired at the torches. Finally, Owen's men screamed for the wounded to groan loudly and continually, so they could be found in the dark. The brigade remained in this position until it was relieved by the 2nd U.S. Infantry. So close and vigilant was the enemy, that prior to moving out, the men were ordered to arrange their equipment to avoid making noises which would give away their movement and cause a deadly volley to be fired into their ranks.[21]

Although Burnside considered renewing the attack the following day, cooler heads prevailed, and he decided to withdraw instead. While most of the Philadelphia Brigade rested in and around the town on December 14, the 71st, now under Colonel Markoe since Wistar had been promoted to brigadier general and brigade command, remained near a tannery, only fifty yards from the rebel position. Here they were exposed to rebel sniper fire. What happened at about noon is described in William Burns' diary:

> Saw rebels throwing up breastworks. Did not dare stand up. If you did you would hear a bullet whistle past you. So there we had to lay very still. Soon after the rebels got a battery to bear on us. When our Lt. Col. [Markoe] told the men to save themselves. There was

some tall running at this time. The shells were bursting all around us and many a poor fellow went down...

On December 15, the Philadelphia Brigade was ordered to the left, where it formed on the right of the IX Corps. At 6 p.m., the brigade was ordered to help construct a redoubt. The men had barely gotten under way when the order was countermanded, and at 8:00 p.m., Owen received orders to recross the river and return to his old camp, which he reached at midnight. The brigade historian recalled that the men did not return to their old camps "with mortification over a defeat, but rather with sorrow over the useless death of comrades." William Burns disagreed—"The men were completely disheartened and demoralized with our defeat." Quartermaster Joseph Elliott, also of the 71st, wrote in his diary on December 16, "Defeated. Disgusted. Disheartened."[22]

Despite the intense cannon and small arms fire they were exposed to, Owen reported that the Philadelphia Brigade's losses were relatively low: 27 killed, 209 wounded, and 29 missing for a total of 265. However, even this figure may be high. Only the 69th and 106th losses have been reported, and collectively number only 131. If the 72nd losses are considered to be the average of the two regiments listed, they would number only 66. William Burns recorded in his diary that the 71st lost 46 men. Therefore, the brigade's losses were probably closer to 245.

These losses compare with 515 for Hall's brigade, which charged the heights several times, and 122 for Sully's brigade, which merely supported other units. At the divisional level, Hancock's division lost 2,032, French lost 1,160, and Howard lost 914.

Howard singled out Owen for special recognition in his after-battle report writing, "Colonel Owen, Sixty–ninth Pennsylvania, commanding the Second Brigade, has been warmly recommended by General Sedgwick and myself. Again let me show him as a man who cannot be outdone on the battle-field. His horse was killed under him." He also recommended the promotion of Colonels Owen and Morehead in this report.[23]

CHAPTER 11

WINTER QUARTERS AND CHANCELLORSVILLE

As the days stretched into weeks, morale plummeted, because of the disastrous defeat at Fredericksburg, and the high command's seeming lack of plans. The men had lost hope in Burnside, although they admired his willingness to take responsibility for his reverses, unlike prior commanders. Straggling and desertions rose—almost 200 men left the army daily. Families sent civilian clothes to soldiers who donned them when on picket duty, and then escaped from the army. The next day, only discarded uniforms marked a man's post. In an attempt to stem the wholesale degeneration of the army, men were executed in unprecedented numbers.[1]

Several officers tried to raise the men's spirits. Division commander Oliver Howard held a regimental inspection for the 106th soon after the men returned to camp. Thanking them for their recent actions, Howard told them to continue to prove themselves as "good soldiers," defending the constitution and laws of the country. He closed his speech by proposing three cheers for the Union, to which the men responded with gusto. Colonel Morehead asked for three more for Howard and the men also responded. General Sumner arrived a few days later to inspect the men.[2]

Reduced spirituality accompanied the poor morale. George Beidelman of the 71st wrote, "No one seems to take an interest in the moral and spiritual well-being of the men." Only one-third of the regiments had chaplains, and those that were present were seldom at their posts. Beidelman also complained about the large amount of "fire-water" being sold by the sutlers. "In the evening the throng of purchasers was so great that a guard had to be placed around the tent."

The losses from the battle of Fredericksburg, coupled with illness and desertions, dramatically reduced the brigade's strength. Only 1,639 of the 2,874 men on the rolls were present for roll call on December 31, 1862— just 60%. The total:present breakdown was: 69th (390:204); 71st (367:282); 72nd (524:468); and 106th (359:280). Again, the 72nd had the highest percentage missing; the 69th had the lowest.[3]

New Year's Day was not enjoyed by the men. William Burns recorded in his diary, "A very poor new year's day for the boys. Nothing to eat except hard tack and coffee." When President Lincoln issued the Emancipation Proclamation on January 1, morale continued to fall. Many in the ranks complained that they had not enlisted to free the slaves, and some said that they would not have enlisted had they known what Lincoln had in mind.

Burnside reviewed the entire army on January 17. As he rode past the Philadelphia Brigade, Howard rode up and asked for three cheers for their commander. Not a man complied. The historian of the 106th wrote later, "They were in no humor for cheers, there was no enthusiasm; they did what their duty required of them but no more.[4]

Soon after the battle of Fredericksburg, the men settled in for the winter around Falmouth. Comfortable huts were built of logs plastered with mud. Many contained fireplaces, but wood was becoming scarce, so details were sent out on a regular basis to haul it back to camp. Vegetables were served for the first time in months, and the paymaster appeared during the last week in January. Picket duty was performed on a rotational scheme by companies of each regiment, and drills and reviews became commonplace. Most importantly, ten-day leaves were issued to the men— two men out of each 100 were permitted to be gone at a given time. When they returned, other men took their places on the trains heading back home to Philadelphia.

George Beidelman related how inspections were conducted in a letter to his father:

> We fall in, and manoeuvre to the proper position...First... a minute inspection of every piece-musket and rifle, and of the personal appearance of each soldier...arms are stacked, and knapsacks unslung and unpacked for inspection...The officer passes through the centre of the line, and I doubt not but he often uses extra efforts to suppress a smile at some of the sights which greet his visuals...We repack and sling our knapsacks, close orders, take arms, and march off to our quarters...

Excitement swept through the troops on January 20, 1862, when Burnside's orders were read at the conclusion of a parade. As a result of "brilliant" Federal victories elsewhere, Lee's army had been weakened, and it was now time for the Army of the Potomac to strike a "death blow to the rebellion." Despite their low morale, the men actually welcomed an opportunity to engage the rebels again, if it meant that they could return home.[5]

Lieutenant William Lynch wrote home that day, "We have been expecting to receive orders to move every day. In fact we have gotten orders to hold ourselves ready to march at a moment's notice... we have all sorts of rumors, (or what they call chin music) but I think it is very doubtful that there will be another attempt to cross the river and take the heights." Lynch later wrote, "I daresay Burnside is trying to do something without having the rebs advised as to the details before hand."[6]

This was easier said than done, as Lee had placed troops at all the fords that Burnside could possibly use. The day before Burnside gave his speech to the men, January 19, Sigel's XI Corps and part of General Couch's II Corps made a feint below the Fredericksburg. The next day, the main strike force, Hooker's and Franklin's Grand Divisions, moved northward to Banks' Ford on the Rappahannock River. Their goal was to cross the river and attack Lee's left flank and rear. That evening a winter nor'easter hit the area bringing heavy rains and high winds for forty-eight hours. The ground first thawed, then became engorged with water, then when it couldn't hold any more, flooding occurred. The storm wreaked havoc on the movement. The mules and their wagons became hopelessly mired in the mud, and no amount of pulling or pushing could extract them. The men were miserable—cold, soaked to the skin, and covered in mud from head to foot. Realizing the impossibility of the task, Burnside reluctantly aborted the mission and ordered the men back to camp. So ended Burnside's "Mud March." Many observers thought that the army was on the verge of mutiny.[7]

The Philadelphia Brigade was spared the ordeal of this march because the II Corps' camps were visible to the enemy, and any movement to join the columns, moving northward, would have warned the rebels. Instead, the men remained in their camps, trying as best they could to remain warm and dry. As the troops returned, the men were turned out to assist in pulling the wagons back into their camps. The rebels across the river taunted them. One perched a door upright against a tree on which was written in large letters, "Burnside stuck in the mud."

Many general officers now openly expressed their concerns about Burnside's ability to lead the army, and the men's morale continued to sink. The 69th's historian wrote, "It [the army] was little better than an armed, disagreeable mob; all confidence in the leaders was destroyed, and murmurings were loud and frequent against everyone in authority, and our highest commanders were treated with contempt."

Several generals covertly plotted against Burnside. Lincoln could not permit this to continue, so on January 25 he finally accepted Burnside's resignation. General Hooker, one of the major conspirators against Burnside, was now placed in command. The same order also announced that Edwin Sumner had resigned as well. Sumner was an old man, and the ordeal of a field command had taken its toll. Simply worn out, Sumner was also disgusted with the constant "croaking" of his colleagues. Although the men knew Sumner's shortcomings, they nevertheless still considered him to be a father figure.

One of Hooker's first acts was to reorganize the army. Corps, each with two divisions, replaced the Grand Divisions, which Hooker believed to be too large and unwieldy, "impeding rather than facilitating" army business. The II Corps continued to be commanded by General Darius Couch.[8]

A West Point graduate, Couch saw service in the Mexican War. Resigning after the war, he entered his wife's family's copper fabricating business in Massachusetts, and when the war broke out was appointed colonel of the 7th Massachusetts. Like Burns, he was a protégé of McClellan, and promotions came rapidly. By the Peninsula campaign, Couch commanded a division in Keyes' IV Corps. He fought with distinction at Fair Oaks and Antietam. When he tried to resign his commission because of poor health, McClellan would hear nothing of it. He took over the II Corps during the Fredericksburg campaign when Sumner was elevated to a Grand Division command.

Hooker implemented other changes. Building on the system devised by General Phil Kearney before he was killed, Hooker ordered the men to wear a badge designating his corps and division. For the men of the Philadelphia Brigade, it was a white trefoil to symbolize the Second Division of the II Corps.[9]

Hooker quickly realized that the army must return to its former level of discipline. One of his first acts was to withhold furloughs and other privileges until the inspector's report certified a unit's adequate level of discipline. As one might expect, these inspectors were not the most popular men in the army. The 69th's historian wrote, "...on some occasions, these inspectors were hooted from the regiment and brigade camps, and on one occasion,...was snowballed away." This occurred for good reason—on March 3, all furloughs were denied the 69th because of severe lapses in discipline and appearance. This sanction brought a rapid improvement, for furloughs were restored on March 14.

Court-martials were commonplace, and Hooker ordered every regiment to provide a description of its deserters, so they could be identified and rounded up. The number of desertions fell precipitously, until on March 31, they had fallen to 4% of the absences from the army, compared with 30% back in January. Aside from the furloughs, nothing seemed to perk up morale as much as the fresh bread that Hooker ordered for the men on a regular basis. Eventually, discipline was fully restored.[10]

During this time, other activities were undertaken, particularly picket duty and drills. After one tour of picket duty, Lt. Richard Lynch wrote home about the activities of the Confederate troops on the other side of the river,

> Not one moment of time do they rest, but are making the vicinity of Fredericksburg impregnable. Every crest of the hill which may command any point whatever in our front is now fortified and here we are looking over at them almost under their noses, laughing at them. Nothing being done to interrupt their work...Here we are looking with amusement at the very things being constructed for our destruction. What a queer world this is.

Many units again took up collections to purchase swords for their officers. On February 7, the non-commissioned officers and enlisted men of the 72nd collected over $600 for a magnificent sword, sash, and belt for General Burns. General Owen also received a set on April 7.[11]

All military actions were now halted for the winter. Except, that is, for the Philadelphia Brigade. Its turn to make a miserable march came on the evening of February 25, when it was sent after enemy cavalry who had crossed the river and were threatening the army's right flank. The ground was initially covered with about seven inches of snow as the men trudged out of camp. To the west, the men could see the familiar ominous clouds of a brewing storm. After marching about four miles toward Hartwood Church, the men were halted and permitted to rest. Because of the presumed proximity of the enemy, no fires were allowed, so the men resorted to stomping their feet on the ground to try to stay warm. The men were angry about this state of affairs, but Colonel Baxter, who was leading the brigade in the absence of General Owen, could merely say that he was following orders.

The rains started about midnight, and descended in torrents, turning the snow into slush, and the ground into mud. As the morning dawned, the men scattered in all directions to find fence rails to make fires. Nothing escaped the frozen and numb fingers of the men, including outbuildings and wagons. At 8:00 a.m., orders to move out were received, but now the men realized how much the rain, which continued to fall, had changed the hard road into a muddy one. It came up to the tops of their shoes, making marching exceedingly difficult. In fact, after an hour, the brigade had only travelled a mile. After two more miles, the men were ordered to halt and await the arrival of two wagons that carried their breakfasts. Their expectations turned to anger when, at noon, the wagons arrived, carrying only hardtack. The wagons also contained whiskey, which was liberally distributed to the men, "...which they gladly accepted, being greatly in need of some such stimulant; almost wet to the skin, our feet completely soaked, the snow-water penetrating our shoes as though they were made of so much paper," wrote the historian of the 106th.

An aide arrived at 2 p.m. with orders to return to camp. Despite mud that reached over the men's knees in some places, the march was now much more rapid as the men anticipated the delights of dry clothing and blazing campfires. The exhausted men finally reached their camps at about 5 o'clock that night and were immediately permitted to fall out. This was among the worst marches that the men had ever experienced, although they had only travelled ten miles that day. Many angrily discussed the stupidity of their officers. "A fruitless march of a brigade of infantry after a body of cavalry well mounted, that had at least twelve hours the start, and were no doubt safely across the river and in their camp before we started," wrote the historian of the 106th.[12]

March 23rd brought sad news—General Sumner had died at Syracuse, New York. Despite his lapses in command, the men still idolized him. "He had won the hearts of his men; his age and genial disposition had won for him the paternal name of 'Pop Sumner,' and his 'children' were always ready to obey his slightest command, and to follow wherever he led. He shared all the dangers of his men, and never seemed so happy as when with them hotly engaged with the enemy. He never considered his own personal safety," wrote the 106th's historian.

Many men tried to find ways of breaking the camp monotony. Chaplains provided religious instruction. Games were played, and the more enterprising began a barter system. This was especially true of some of the New England men, who took to making candles, which they exchanged for other items. When the supply of wicks and wax was depleted, the men turned to baking cakes and pies. St. Patrick's Day brought a welcome change for the men. The Irish Brigade organized a series of hurdle-races, pole-climbing competitions, and a variety of other sports, to the glee of the men from the other units. Tables were piled high with cakes, and liquor was much in evidence. William Burns recorded in his diary, "St. Patrick's day. The Irish Brigade full of fun. Whisky and horseracing." Two weeks later, Burns recorded, "April Fool's Day- Fun in camp. Weather pleasant." Ever the word-thrift, Burns unfortunately did not describe what form the "fun" took.[13]

An army camped for a prolonged time in an area took its toll. "This country so rough and woody three months ago, when we came here, is now all clear; we have to go about two miles to cut good oak wood, which is hauled to us by the brigade wagons," wrote George Beidelman of the 71st.

On April 8, the men were visited by President Lincoln, accompanied by his wife and two sons. Hooker had done much to improve the morale of the men, and they were ready for another fight with Lee's "mob." John Lynch wrote home, "Still, since Gen. Hooker has become commander there has been a great change. Gen. Hooker is garnering the esteem of the men regarding the pressing affairs. We feel that there is an energy for us..."[14]

On April 11, the Second Division received a new commander, Brigadier General John Gibbon. A Philadelphian by birth, Gibbon grew up in Charlotte, North Carolina, and graduated from West Point. At the outbreak of the war, he threw his lot with the North, although his three brothers fought for the South. Gibbon was well known as the commander of the famed "Iron Brigade," which he led until early November 1862, when he was given a division in General John Reynolds' I Corps. Wounded at the battle of Fredericksburg, he lost command of the division during his three-month convalescent period. Upon his return to the army in April, he was assigned the Second Division of the II Corps.

The men received orders on April 14 to turn over all extra clothing and supplies to the quartermaster. Each was entitled to retain an extra shirt, pair of underwear, and socks. The men were also issued five days' rations in their haversacks that included coffee, sugar, crackers, salt, and salt pork, with meat "on the hoof." Tents were returned, and the men received forty rounds of ammunition. Time for action was at hand.[15]

Hooker's plan was a bold one. Dividing his army, Hooker sent 40,000 men comprising the V, XI, and XII Corps stealthily northward to Kelly's

Ford on the Rappahannock River, about twenty-seven miles above Fredericksburg. After crossing the river they would be on Lee's left flank and rear. At the same time, the I, III, and VI Corps, all under Sedgwick's command, were to drive past the Confederate forces at Fredericksburg, and hit Lee's rear at Chancellorsville.

Gibbon's division was sent to Sedgwick—the other two divisions of the II Corps marched to the United States Ford. Actually, Sedgwick only retained the First and Third Brigades of the Second Division—the Philadelphia Brigade was dispatched to guard Banks' Ford, about midway up the river between the United States Ford and Fredericksburg.

Facing Sedgwick's force of 27,000 men and 66 guns was Jubal Early's division along with some brigades from Anderson's and McLaw's division, totalling in all almost 13,000 men and forty-six guns. Early had a six-mile front to defend, so he decided to concentrate most of his units south of Marye's Heights. Only 1,200 infantry and eight guns protected the heights, as Early did not think that Sedgwick would be foolhardy enough to repeat the slaughter of the past December.

After the last of Sedgwick's men crossed the river, one of the bridges was disassembled and transported to Banks' Ford, where it was to be reassembled. Chief engineer General Henry Benham was placed in charge of this operation. Starting off on the wrong foot, Benham was roaring drunk, making a fool of himself. But his subordinates were experienced enough to carry out the operation until Benham dried out.

The Philadelphia Brigade was awakened at about 2 a.m. on May 1, and ordered to leave all of their equipment and arms in camp and assist the pontoon train over the rough and hilly roads to Banks' Ford. The task was completed at 8 o'clock that morning, when the entire brigade was ordered back to its camps at Falmouth. The 69th Pennsylvania was left behind to guard the crossing and support the engineers. Upon reaching their camp at Falmouth, the 106th was immediately ordered to collect its equipment and return to the ford to relieve the 69th. These men arrived back at the ford at about 4 p.m., exhausted from their eighteen-mile excursion. The remainder of the brigade was permitted to rest until midnight, when they too were put back on the road to Banks' Ford, arriving there at about 2 a.m. on May 2. Later that morning, the 72nd relieved the 106th at the bridgehead. Looking across the river, the men could plainly see the rebel pickets and farther back, their fortifications held by General Cadmus Wilcox's Alabama brigade.[16]

Wilcox's men on the other side of the river prevented the engineers from laying the bridge, so a detachment from the 71st under Lieutenant Seabury was sent across on the morning of May 3. Although fording the river at this point was difficult, the men succeeded in capturing some of the enemy pickets and driving away the rest. Although no one admitted it, only fifty rebels remained in the rifle pits at this time—Wilcox had withdrawn the rest of his brigade to deal with Sedgwick's threat to the south. With the aid of sixty pieces of artillery, the detachment of the 71st on the south side, and the remainder of the brigade on the north, the engineers quickly completed the pontoon bridges by three o'clock that afternoon.[17]

Sedgwick sent his troops across the river at sunrise on May 3, and the first assault on Marye's Heights began at 10:00 a.m. Units from Burnham's and Newton's divisions ran forward, took the infamous stone wall, and swept up the hill where they captured several guns of the famed Washington Artillery. Hooker was unable to savor the moment, as he had his hands full trying to fend off a full-scale Confederate attack at Chancellorsville. Sedgwick now began his eleven-mile march to attack Lee from the rear.

Despite the fighting raging to their south and west, the day was relatively peaceful for the Philadelphia Brigade at Banks' Ford. William Burns recorded in his diary, "All quiet with us. The battle raging very fiercely on the other side of the river. Felt very contented where I was stationed. Could hear the battle very plainly but could not see it."

Sedgwick now realized that he was between Lee's main force at Chancellorsville to his west, and Early's reassembling troops to the southeast. Caught between these two pincers, he could be destroyed. Deciding to push on to Chancellorsville, the column had progressed two miles along the Plank Road by noon. Not certain about his authority over Gibbon's two brigades, Sedgwick left them north of Fredericksburg to guard the bridges.

During this time, Wilcox's brigade, which had contested the bridge construction at Banks' Ford, rushed south to block Sedgwick's advance at Salem Church. Wilcox wrote in his official report, "Having visited my line of pickets on the morning of the 3d instant, I found that the enemy had reduced very much (apparently) his force. The sentinels on post had their haversacks on, a thing unusual. This induced me to believe that much of the force from Banks' Ford had been sent to Chancellorsville..." These sentinels were undoubtedly from the Philadelphia Brigade.

Although Sedgwick saw Wilcox's brigade deployed across his front, he did not see that McLaw's division had rushed up and had formed on both sides of Wilcox. Sedgwick attacked Wilcox's troops with some success, but eventually the enemy line held, and the Union troops were forced to break off the advance for the night.[18]

After Wilcox left the bridgehead, the Philadelphia Brigade, with the 71st in the van, crossed the pontoon bridge to provide support. Upon arriving on the opposite bank, Owen deployed the 71st as skirmishers and positioned the remaining three regiments to protect the bridge from attack, for this was to be Sedgwick's escape route, if needed. General Hunt, commander of the artillery reserve, rode up to Owen and ordered him to connect with Sedgwick's right flank, which was soon accomplished.

Hooker had been knocked out during the fighting at Chancellorsville, so General Gouverneur Warren of his staff ordered Sedgwick to hold his

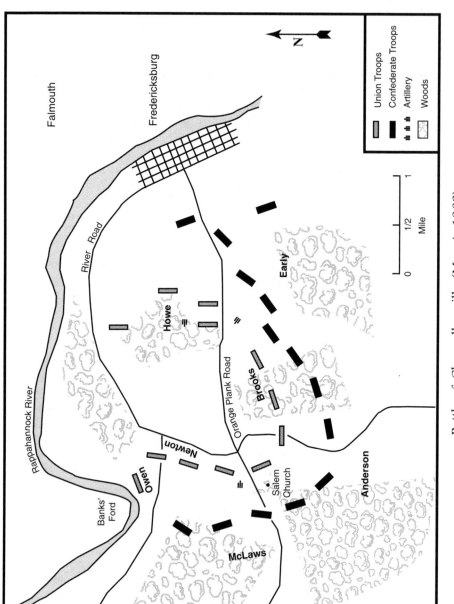

Battle of Chancellorsville (May 4, 1863)

communications with the bridges at Fredericksburg or Banks' Ford and to cross to safety at the most desirable place. Neither man knew that Lee had already sent orders to Early to crush Sedgwick at first light. While some of Early's division marched north to recapture Marye's Heights, brigades from McLaw's and Anderson's divisions linked with the left of Early's division. In all, 23,000 veterans were moving into position to crush Sedgwick.

While the 71st was left on the south side of the river, the remainder of the brigade recrossed the pontoon bridge on May 4. Private Burns of the 71st wrote in his diary, "Just before daylight heard that the brigade had crossed the bridge back again and left us to our fate. Then we got orders to not fire if the rebs attacked us. A very pleasant situation to be in I thought." Less than half a mile away was Mahone's brigade of Anderson's division, which occupied the Confederate left flank.

What Burns did not know was that Sedgwick's men were close to the bridgehead, so the Philadelphia Brigade was no longer needed on the southern bank. During the late afternoon of May 4, Early's division, which occupied the right of the Confederate line, launched its attack against Sedgwick's left flank. Instead of being driven back, the Union regiments held their ground and repulsed Early's determined attacks. Evening brought a welcome end to the hostilities. Realizing that Sedgwick's men would entrench if given the chance, Lee contemplated a night attack. Common sense prevailed, however, and Lee permitted his infantry to rest for the night.[19]

Hooker received a message from Sedgwick that evening, describing his desperate situation. His response was: "Dispatch this moment received. Withdraw. Cover the river, and prevent any force crossing." Receiving this order at 2 a.m. on May 5, Sedgwick immediately put his corps in motion toward Banks' Ford.

Later that day, Burns recorded in his diary, "Fell back slowly from our positions as pickets and got over the river in safety. They had been shelling the bridge where they thought we would cross but we had another one laid and everybody got over safe. One shot after we left came near hitting the left our regiment (but nears don't count). Arrived in camp and put up our tents."

The last of Sedgwick's men trudged over the bridges at Banks' Ford by 4 a.m., and the engineers cut the cables on the south bank. The current pushed the bridges to the north bank, where they were disassembled. By nine o'clock that night, the bridges were secured on the wagons and moving south toward Falmouth. During this long day, the men of the Philadelphia Brigade again assisted the engineers in their work.

That day, Hooker's thoroughly defeated wing also recrossed the Rappahannock River at the United States Ford and trudged back to Falmouth. As the Philadelphia Brigade returned to camp, an old message from Hooker awaited them that read, "Soldiers,—The events of the last three days prove that the enemy must either ingloriously fell, or come out from behind the defenses and give us battle on his own ground, where certain destruction awaits him." No one missed the irony of this message.[20]

The historian of the Philadelphia Brigade accurately summed up the unit's role during the Chancellorsville campaign, when he wrote,

> ... the part, however important, that was assigned the Philadelphia Brigade did not give an opportunity to gather glory of any kind; but instead it offered at one period of the movement a full share of the risk and toil, with no possibility of gaining distinction by the service.

Some of the men of the Philadelphia Brigade apparently had a hard time stomaching their minor role, so they embellished their activities to the folks back home. For example, Lt. William Lynch of the 106th wrote home on May 17, "I think I did not mention in my former letters to you that our brigade covered the retreat of Gen. Sedgwick's corps across the river. We had indeed a very critical post. We had just gotten to the bridge when we heard the firing of the rebel's advancing skirmishers. Had they been a little slower in approaching, we should have had a pleasant trip to Richmond which might have been life for us, but see Darling, the hands of Providence." While the letter is accurate, it overplays the seriousness of the danger. Individual soldiers were not the only ones to embellish the story. The historian of the 69th wrote, "During this time some of the pickets from the regiments of the brigade went across the river and were involved with the engagement at Marye's Heights and assisting in the capture of the rebel battery known as the Washington Artillery." None of this actually occurred.[21]

At the other extreme was General Joshua Owen, who filed perhaps the shortest report of any brigade commander who participated in the campaign:

> ...I have the honor to report that there are no killed, wounded, and missing to account for in my brigade...The only property captured was a black horse, by Lieutenant Seabury, one of my aides. No property of any description was lost by my command.

Because the Philadelphia Brigade played only a supporting role in this campaign, it sustained no losses.[22]

CHAPTER 12

THE MARCH TO GETTYSBURG

The brigade settled back into camp after returning from Banks' Ford. On May 9, they packed up their belongings, took down their tents, and moved to a new location. William Burns recorded in his diary, "Moved our camp to a better place. Put up our tents and made ourselves quiet comfortable." Despite the severe loss at Chancellorsville, the army did not sink back into the depths of depression. The men were, however, disillusioned over Hooker's leadership. Many felt that at least Burnside had the courtesy to take responsibility for the loss. Hooker was not about to make such an admission.

Not being able to stomach Hooker any longer, General Darius Couch resigned as commander of the II Corps on May 22. He was quickly replaced by General Winfield Hancock, who was elevated from command of the First Division of the II Corps. Hancock's distinguished record and fine military bearing was well known to the men of the Philadelphia Brigade, and they were proud to serve under him.

Immediately after the battle of Chancellorsville, the brigade's "paper" strength was 2,021, but only 1,606 were actually present. A number of leadership changes were made during this period. With Owen permanently assigned to brigade command, Colonel Dennis O'Kane assumed leadership of the 69th, and Adjutant Martin Tschudy was elevated to lieutenant colonel. Twice wounded, Lieutenant Colonel John Markoe of the 71st resigned from the army because of ill health, and Major R. Penn Smith was promoted to colonel and assumed command. Captain Charles Kochersperger was promoted to lieutenant colonel of the regiment. Colonel Morehead of the 106th was placed in temporary command of the division's First Brigade, as its commander, Alfred Sully was arrested for not halting a mutiny by one of his regiments. In Morehead's absence, Lieutenant Colonel Curry was temporarily assigned to command the 106th. Changes involving the officers of lower rank were also made.[1]

147

During the month of May, the men drilled, were reviewed several times, and received a number of new recruits. The monotony of the camp was broken on May 27, when, during an altercation, Captain Bernard McMahon of the 71st shot and killed Captain Andrew McManus of the 69th. William Burns recorded in his diary, "Great excitement in camp. Sgt. of the Guard had Captain McMahon under close arrest with orders to shoot him if he attempted to escape or if any of the 69th attempted to molest him..."[2]

During the early part of June, the men could detect subtle changes in the rebel's behavior on the opposite side of the Rappahannock River. They were more active, and the pickets more "bold and insolent." Despite reconnaissances in force in early June, Hooker was unaware of Lee's intention to invade the North, nor was he aware of the Confederate army's initial movements into the Shenandoah Valley.

As time went on, Hooker and his men's expectations for a new campaign grew. William Burns recorded in his diary on June 13, "All quiet with us. Expecting a move. Went on picket." The following day, Burns related some interesting occurrences in the brigade, when he wrote, "Relieved of picket. Preparing to move. Fun in camp after taps. Left camp and marched about two miles and about faced and marched back to camp and went to sleep. Some of the men got drunk on mincemeat." Unfortunately, Burns did not elaborate on the "fun in camp" or the aborted march. Details of the latter event were provided by the historian of the 106th, who wrote that the men were ordered to pack up all the belongings they could carry and destroy everything else. To prevent the enemy across the river from seeing that they were breaking camp, the men were ordered to quietly cut, tear, and break all unneeded items. No fires were permitted. The tents were left standing until after dark, when they too were taken down and thrown into waiting wagons. Many men amused themselves by making "dummies" with old uniforms, and attaching old guns to them, so they resembled Federal soldiers. At 9 p.m., the men were ordered into line and marched three miles. At one point, they crossed a wet, mucky swamp, which soaked the men to their knees. Suddenly, at 11 p.m., the men were halted and ordered to return to their camps, without explanation. Like so many times during the war, the men were left wondering about the competence of their officers. Dropping down to rest, the men were roused at 3 a.m., ordered back into line and marched to division headquarters. Remaining here until daybreak, they continued the march, and reached Stafford Court House at about 10 a.m., when they were permitted to rest after their ten-mile march.

At about 11:30 a.m., the weary men were again formed into line and marched another eight miles. The day was oppressively hot, and many men in their woolen uniforms, loaded down with full accoutrements, three days' rations and extra ammunition, could not keep up, and eventually fell from the ranks. Some, like Joseph Ward of the 106th, experienced heatstroke. He described these experiences in the third person:

Without a moment's notice as he was marching at the head of the Regiment, he dropped in his tracks as though shot down, and unconscious was lifted to one side of the road, placed in the shade, and left. How long he remained there he knew not, but late in the afternoon he regained consciousness and realizing his danger of capture, was not a vestige of our troops were in sight, so gathering up his remaining strength he started after the retreating column.

The Philadelphia Brigade, with the rest of the II Corps, camped that night about a mile beyond Aquia Creek. It must have felt like an exceptionally short rest, and it was, for at 2 a.m. on June 15, they continued the march. With the 72nd in the lead, the brigade led the II Corps' advance. The column reached Dumfries at 7 o'clock that morning, where the men halted for two hours to rest and have breakfast. The march then continued until 3 p.m., when the men were permitted to rest for half an hour, before pushing on and reaching Wolf Run Shoals on the Opequon Creek at 4 p.m.[3]

The following day was also very hot, and the men suffered. William Burns recorded in his diary, "A very warm day. Men dying very fast with the heat. Had to be left behind as all the ambulances were full of officers. The poor bucks had to walk or remain behind and be captured."

Those who made it to the Opequon Creek were permitted the luxury of bathing and swimming in its clear, cool waters, which had the effect of revitalizing the men. The soldiers of the 71st had an extra treat—they were rewarded by General Gibbons for having the least number of stragglers in the division during the march.[4]

The next day's march did not begin until 8 a.m. The column marched eight miles to Sangster's Station on the Orange and Alexandria Railroad, where it formed into line of battle to await a Confederate attack, which never came. The corps remained here through the afternoon of June 19, when the march continued to Centreville, which was reached at 5 p.m. After a leisurely night and morning, the men left their bivouac area, marched through Centreville and passed over the Bull Run battlefields. The men were distressed to see knees, heads, and arms sticking out from the shallow graves. The 106th historian commented, "It seemed hard to give one's life for their country and harder yet, so long after the battle, not to be decently buried, or at least have dirt enough to cover one's bones." The army's pioneer corps were detailed to fall out and rebury the bodies.

The small hamlet of Gainesville was reached about dark, and the men began to harbor thoughts of a quiet evening. This was not to be, for while the rest of the II Corps camped at Haymarket, the brigade pressed on, passing through Haymarket at 8 p.m., and finally reaching Thoroughfare Gap at 11 o'clock that night. The Philadelphia Brigade had marched a total of twenty-one miles that day in rain that lasted from the afternoon through the evening. The march in the dark from Haymarket was particularly difficult, as the road contained large stones, which many men tripped over, and depressions, which caused several twisted ankles. Upon reaching Thoroughfare Gap, the thoroughly exhausted and famished men threw themselves down to rest for the night. Many doubted whether any troops could have gone much farther. The men were thankful when they were not ordered to resume the march at daybreak on June 21. Although the brigade remained here until June 25, they were not idle. For example, fearing a rebel cavalry attack on their camps, the 71st was marched out of camp on June 21 and deployed to ambush any enemy that was foolhardy enough to approach. When no Confederates materialized, the regiment returned to its camp. The next day, the regiment moved out again, this time to support pioneers who were blocking a side path over the mountains, so the rebels could not steal a march on the Federal troops.

During this period, the brigade defended the right side of the Gap, facing south. The 72nd was deployed on the right, with the 106th on its left. In their rear was a battery, the 69th and the 71st.

All was relatively peaceful until the morning of the 25th, when at daylight the pickets were attacked, and the 71st and the 69th were rushed forward. Nothing more materialized, so after three hours, the 72nd and 106th were permitted to have breakfast, then moved up to relieve their sister regiments. The men were now ordered into line for the march back to Haymarket to rejoin the rest of the II Corps. Suddenly halted, they were formed into line of battle, but when no rebel troops appeared, the march continued. About a mile of Haymarket, a Confederate battery hastily took position on a slight rise about 400 yards to the right of the road, and opened fire. The initial shots were well aimed, wounding five men of the 106th. Subsequent shots knocked over two caissons—one was righted, the other was severely damaged and left behind. A Federal battery galloped up and unlimbered, dismounting one of the rebel guns and forcing the others to beat a hasty retreat.

The column finally reached Haymarket, and after a short rest, moved with the rest of the corps to Gum Springs at 9 p.m. The men thankfully camped here for the night, for it had been another long day. They had made a difficult march of about twenty-three miles in a light rain which muddied the roads.[5]

The men were already on the march at 6 a.m. on June 26, and after travelling twelve miles, reached Edward's Ferry, where the men were permitted to rest until dark. Marching down to the Potomac River, the men could see that the pontoon bridges were congested with troops, wagons, and artillery, so they waited until 10 p.m. that night, when they finally crossed into Maryland. Marching a mile, they camped near General Hancock's headquarters.

The men were again pleased when they were not ordered into line at dawn on June 27. While waiting, the men rested, mended worn clothing, and pursued other needed activities. The march began at 2 p.m., passing through Poolesville two hours later, and Barnsville late that night. After marching two more miles, the men were ordered to fall out and bivouac for the night, after the sixteen-mile march.

The brigade left camp at 9 a.m. on June 28 and by noon, had reached Urbana. At nightfall, the corps reached Frederick, the army's assembly point during its march after Lee's army, which was already in Pennsylvania. General Joe Hooker decided to quit that day, and in his place, Philadelphian, General George Meade, received command of the army. The news was received with great surprise, for while the men had lost faith in Hooker, they did not think it wise to replace an army commander in the middle of a campaign, when the enemy was well into Northern territory.

The day also brought another change that directly affected the Philadelphia Brigade—its commander, General Joshua Owen, was arrested and temporarily replaced by General Alexander Webb. None of the primary sources explain why this change occurred. One historian wrote, "Just what was Owen's offense is uncertain; being Irish, he may have taken a drop too much at the wrong time." William Burns, may have supported this idea, writing on this day in his diary, "General O. H. laying in the woods drunk." While it is conceivable that Burns was referring to General Oliver Howard, the XI Corps was not in the vicinity, and Howard was a fervent Christian, who abhorred the use of alcohol. Although only one letter of the initials is correct, it could have been a transcriptional error, or Burns' way of disguising whom he meant. Lapses in discipline may have also contributed to Owen's downfall.[6]

General Alexander Webb, fifth commander of the Philadelphia Brigade

Massachusetts Commandery Military Order of the Loyal Legion and the USAMHI

Webb's army service had not been auspicious. Graduating from West Point in 1855, he fought the Seminole Indians the following year. At the outbreak of the war he commanded a battery. After First Bull Run, Webb accepted a staff position with General W. F. Barry, the army's artillery chief. Webb became the V Corps' chief of staff, serving under Meade, during the invasion of Maryland in 1862. Following the battle, Webb returned to Washington to serve as an artillery inspector in an instructional camp. He returned to the V Corps in January 1863, to become the inspector general of Meade's V Corps. Meade must have been impressed with Webb's potential, for when Paddy Owen got into trouble during the march to Gettysburg, he apparently replaced him with Webb without hesitation.

Owen was very popular with the men, so they could not have been happy over the change in command. They did not know Webb, and what little they did, they did not like. Particularly distressing was the fact that he was both a New Yorker, and a Regular Army officer. They viewed him as a "young whipper-snapper, and scented dandyism in his spit-and polish staff-officer's uniform." Webb's first acts only reinforced this first impression. Issuing an officers' call on June 29, he cast a disapproving eye on the assemblage. After what seemed to be an eternity to the officers, Webb said, "I presume you are officers since you attend the Call. There are but few of you whom I am able to recognize as officers as you have no insignia of officer except your swords." The men had long put away their shoulder straps as it called undue attention from the enemy. He later told his officers that there was too much straggling, and if it continued, the offenders were to be brought to him, and he would "shoot them like dogs." This certainly did not endear him to the men, but it was effective—the next day the number of stragglers numbered less than twelve men for the entire brigade.[7]

That day, the men could only wonder at the reason why the rest of the corps had moved out, while they remained in camp. Rumors flew, including one that had them being detached to guard Frederick. An aide soon galloped into camp looking for General Webb, and shortly thereafter, the bugles sounded assembly, and the column rushed after the long-departed II Corps. The change in command apparently resulted in some confusion, so Webb never received orders to move out with the rest of the corps.

Bringing up the rear, the brigade crossed the Monocacy Creek, and passed by Frederick. Here the brigade parted company with the remainder of the corps. Webb was acutely aware that because of the misunderstanding regarding the orders, his brigade had lost its position at the forefront of the corps. This was only his second day in command, and Webb was not about to have his reputation sullied. He decided to make a wide loop and regain his place at the head of the corps, even if it meant a longer march with fewer rest stops.

Webb ordered the brigade to make a detour, where they were again forced to cross the Monocacy. However, unlike before, no bridges were available, so the men were required to ford the knee-deep creek. Before plunging into the water, the men stopped to remove their shoes and socks, and roll up their pant legs. Webb, however, had been told by Gibbon to "ride the brigade" as discipline under Owen had declined, and besides, he had no time for this delay, so he ordered the men to forego this practice and wade into the creek. To set an example, Webb dismounted in the center of the creek to both encourage and drive on the men. Many men loudly muttered about this "harsh" treatment by their new commander. One

Irishman was not reluctant to say to Webb as he passed, "Sure its no wonder ye can stand there when ye are leather up to your waist." Although Webb glared at the soldier, he said nothing. Looking over in the distance, Webb spied Captain Breitenbach of the 106th trying to cross the creek on a fallen log. Webb quickly put him under arrest, and ordered him to turn around and cross the creek like the other men. The ingenious officer later asked a doctor for a document certifying a pre-disposition to rheumatism that would be aggravated by wading the stream. Webb accepted the certificate, but first lectured Breitenbach on the importance of following orders. When the last man had finally crossed, Webb mounted his horse and rode to the head of the column.

The detour added another three miles to the brigade's march, and because Webb hoped to get in front of the corps, he marched the men at "quick time" without any breaks. Just as the brigade reached the road on which Hancock's column was marching, the head of the column entered the intersection. Because Webb could not break into the column, he was forced to wait until the entire corps passed. Despite all of the additional exertions, the brigade finally joined the column in the identical place it would have occupied if Webb had done nothing. It was certainly not an auspicious introduction to the new brigade commander.

The column reached Liberty at noon, when a rest was ordered. Webb was so intent on regaining his place at the head of the line that he pushed the brigade on without a rest. The brigade finally reached the head of the column, but to do so it had marched nineteen miles without a rest, and the men were in foul humor. Fortunately, as the column moved through Johnsville and Union Bridge, the women supplied the men with cool water, milk, pies, bread, and butter. Being at the front of the column finally yielded some rewards, for the men got first crack at these luxuries. The brigade reached Uniontown at nine o'clock that night, and went into camp a mile beyond. This was the longest march the brigade had ever made—thirty-five miles in fourteen hours. Many were unable to maintain this pace, and fell out. One was William Burns of the 71st, who was so fatigued that he could go no farther, and went to sleep in a field by the side of the road. The next day he caught up with the brigade outside of Uniontown.

June 30 brought a double treat. Not only were the men permitted to remain in camp, they received two months' pay. Although exhausted from their long marches in the blazing heat, some of the men felt well enough to visit the town of Uniontown.[8] On June 30, General Webb filed a report of his brigade's numbers listing a paper total of 2,219, and an actual strength of 1,553 (or 70%). The breakdown by regiment (total:present) was: 69th (459:344); 71st (538:393); 72nd (745:473); and 106th (477:343).[9]

The column was put in motion again at 7 a.m. on July 1, and passed through Uniontown. Taneytown was reached at eleven o'clock that morning, and the men rested here until 3 p.m. By now the battle of Gettysburg was well under way, and the II Corps was pushed forward. At five o'clock they crossed the Pennsylvania state line. Unlike the Pennsylvania Reserves of the V Corps, whose commander stopped the march here to give the men an inspiring speech about defending their beloved state, the II Corps was rushed toward the battlefield. As they approached, they could hear the dull booming of cannon in the distance. Continuing on they passed a long line of wounded soldiers, signalling the fact that they would soon be engaged.

Marching on the Taneytown Road, the brigade finally reached its bivouac point between Little Round Top and the road at 9 p.m. The division was posted "to cover the retreat of the First Army Corps, should that be ordered."

The brigade had now completed still another strenuous march—this one eighteen miles. William Burns recorded in his diary that night, "Orders not to make large fires as the rebs were near us and could see them." This was not quite true, as the only Confederate troops on the field at this point were in position well to the north and northwest.[10]

The first day's fight had not gone well for the Federals. Although Reynold's I Corps had valiantly battled overwhelming odds west of town during the morning and afternoon, it sustained heavy losses and was finally forced to retreat to the heights south of the town of Gettysburg. Howard's XI Corps had occupied a position north of town, but it too was forced to retreat, actually flee, despite outnumbering the Confederates in this sector. When the II Corps arrived on the battlefield, the I and XI Corps were entrenching on Cemetery Hill. The XII and III Corps had already arrived and the V Corps was close to the battlefield.

CHAPTER 13

GETTYSBURG–THE SECOND DAY

The exhausted troops were awakened at 3 a.m. on July 2. Never had they been asked to march as many miles in such a short time. Now that they had reached their destination, their soreness began to subside with the knowledge that the enemy was within a few miles of them, and they would be engaged before the sun set that day.

The men were ordered into column and moved rapidly along the Taneytown Road toward the town of Gettysburg. After two miles, the brigade was halted and massed in a field just to the right of the road. General Webb slowly rode by, quietly eyeing the brigade. Finally stopping, he addressed the men. The men knew very little of Webb during the three days he commanded them, except that he was an unreasonable taskmaster. While his actual remarks are lost in history, the historian of the 106th recalled that Webb told them that,

> ...they would now be called upon to defend their own state by hard fighting, that it would require each man to do his full duty to defeat the elated enemy...and then told them that any one found shirking it in the slightest degree would be severely dealt with, that he would shoot any one leaving the line, and called on any man to do the same to him if he failed in his duty, told them that they had a commander that would not fail in his duty nor allow the men to fail theirs.

The men were now permitted to rest and have breakfast of hardtack and coffee. The adjutant of each regiment counted the men and reported this number to General Webb's adjutant. To Webb's delight, only thirteen men were absent from the time that he had first taken command of the brigade, three days before. But the men never had such a great motivation—Lee was on their soil and if not defeated, could move on Philadelphia.[1]

At six o'clock that morning, Gibbon's division was ordered back into line and marched northward toward Cemetery Hill. Wheeling to the left (west), the division now took up positions on Cemetery Ridge. General

Alexander Hays' Third Division formed to their right and General John Caldwell's First Division formed on their left. To Caldwell's left was General Andrew Humphrey's Division of General Daniel Sickles' III Corps.

The Philadelphia Brigade occupied the extreme right of Gibbon's division, in the area of a triangular clump of trees. The remainder of the division formed on their left. Posted nearby were Lt. Alonzo Cushing's 4th U.S. Artillery and Lt. Fred Brown's Battery B, 1st Rhode Island Artillery.

Only the 69th moved down the slope facing the rebels on Seminary Ridge, to take a position behind a low stone wall in front of the clump of trees. Forming a double line of battle, its front extended for 250 feet. The regiment's color company (C) took their position of honor in the center of the line. The remaining three regiments rested on the opposite side of the ridge, hidden from the rebels. As the men of the 69th looked out across the 3/4 wide expanse between the two ridges, they must have considered the difficulty of crossing it under hostile fire and hoped that their side would not be taking the offensive.[2]

Each regiment was ordered to send out skirmishers between the two hostile lines. No sooner had these men crossed the Emmitsburg Road and deployed, that the rebel artillery on Seminary Ridge opened fire on them. Cushing's and Brown's batteries returned the fire. The distance was great, and the accuracy low, so few casualties were sustained during this period.

Later that morning, General Meade rode up to the Philadelphia Brigade, wishing to know the position and strength of the Confederates in front of them. Ever anxious to please, Webb quickly volunteered to advance his entire brigade toward Seminary Ridge to ascertain this information. Meade could not have been happy with his new brigade commander who seemed more interested in gaining a reputation than in exercising good judgement. Known for his irritability, Meade probably held his tongue because he was fond of Webb, and calmly told him that such an advance could be construed as an attack on the enemy's position, and this might elicit a counterattack against Cemetery Ridge. Knowing that two of his corps had not yet arrived, Meade was not anxious to bring on any engagement at this time. Instead, he suggested that Webb send out Company B of the 106th, which was on skirmish reserve, just west of Emmitsburg Road. Upon receiving these orders, Captain James Lynch cautiously advanced his men across the fields toward Seminary Ridge. Finally reaching the woods marking Seminary Ridge, Lynch ordered his men to enter them. They had not gone far when they ran into masses of Confederate soldiers. After looking all around, Lynch and his men beat a hasty retreat, and provided Meade with some of the information he desired.[3]

Lynch's heroics were not yet done for the day. Later that afternoon, men from Posey's Confederate brigade advanced to the Bliss House, midway between the two contesting lines, where it dislodged the First Delaware. As they retired, the right flank of Company A of the 106th was exposed, forcing it to fall back as well. Both lieutenants from the company were

69th Pennsylvania's monument behind the low stone
wall in front of the copse of trees

Position of the 69th Pennsylvania on July 2 and 3, 1863. The men crouched behind the low stone wall when repelling Wright's Charge on July 2 and Pickett's Charge on July 3. The upright markers on either side of the monument indicate the positions of the regiment's companies. The 106th Pennsylvania's monument, which can be seen at the crest of Cemetery Ridge, to the left of the copse of trees, shows where the regiment fired its fatal volley into the 48th Georgia on July 2.

Author's Collection

wounded. Captain Lynch's Company B was now sent forward to drive the rebels from the farmyard. Initially thinking that he was merely facing a small force of skirmishers, Lynch quickly realized that he was really up against the entire 16th Mississippi. The error cost him a lieutenant and eleven men. Sending back for reinforcements, General Alexander Hays rushed four companies of the 12th New Jersey to Lynch's aid, and together, they drove the rebels from the farm buildings.

That afternoon, the men watched in consternation as Sickles moved his entire III Corps off Cemetery Ridge to a forward position on high ground between the two ridges. Prior to this movement, three powerful Confederate divisions took their positions on Seminary Ridge, opposite the II and III Corps.

Lee's plan was for each brigade to attack the Federal left and center *en echelon*. Beginning with the Confederate right-most brigade, each would attack in turn, similar to the toppling of a line of dominos. This movement is intended to both freeze reinforcements from being taken from one part of the line to support another, and at the same time, exploit any weaknesses in the line. Unfortunately for the Confederates, because the brigades were lined up abreast of each other, there are no troops forming a second line to exploit breaches made in the enemy lines.

The attack began at 4 p.m., when General John Hood's right brigade moved forward toward the Round Tops. Over the next hour, the remainder of Hood's brigades entered the fray. Next, General Lafayette McLaw's division was next launched by brigades. Intense fighting developed at Little Round Top, Devil's Den, the Wheatfield, and the Peach Orchard, as Longstreet's two divisions smashed into Sickles' exposed position.

Desperately needing reinforcements, Meade sent Caldwell's division to the Wheatfield, creating a half-mile gap on the left of Gibbon's division, to the great concern of Colonel Norman Hall, commanding the third brigade. Earlier that afternoon, Gibbon had moved two small regiments from Harrow's reserve brigade off the ridge to the Emmitsburg Road, to try to maintain at least some communication with Humphrey's advanced division. Brown's battery was also moved up to try to pour a more effective fire against the rebel batteries on Seminary Ridge.[4]

Having launched Longstreet's two divisions, it was now time for General Richard Anderson's division to begin its attack against Cemetery Ridge. Two of Anderson's brigades attacked Humphrey's division in its front, while another from McLaw's division hit its left flank, causing the Union soldiers to flee for safety after sustaining heavy casualties. Seeing that Cemetery Ridge was about to be taken, General Hancock threw available troops against the on-rushing Confederates, halting their advance and sending them back to Seminary Ridge.

The 69th, occupying the west-facing side of Cemetery Ridge, warily watched the tide of battle roll in their direction. Looking to their left, they could see the 59th New York and the 7th Michigan of Hall's brigade also crouching behind the low stone wall. To their right, a gap existed that was partially closed by Arnold's battery. Behind them, on the opposite side of the ridge, was the remainder of the Philadelphia Brigade, arranged in the following order from top of the ridge to its base: 71st, 72nd, 106th.

Rebel artillery now found the 69th's position, forcing the men to dive for cover. Even the remaining three regiments on the opposite side of the ridge were not immune to this cannonade—the 106th lost one officer and several men wounded from this fire. About 6:30 the men could see long, well-dressed lines of infantry moving in their direction. Initially thinking (or perhaps hoping) that they were merely a part of Humphrey's division that was pulling back toward Cemetery Ridge, the men watched and fingered their weapons nervously. As the line swept forward, their worst fears were realized—a powerful Confederate brigade was moving against their position. This was Brigadier General Ambrose Wright's brigade of Georgians. Fourteen hundred men strong, it was a veteran unit that had won its share of laurels. Corporal John Buckley of the 69th recalled after the war that these men were "the best clothed soldiers that we had ever come across on their side." This probably made their charge seem even more fearsome.[5]

In their path were the 600 men of the 15th Massachusetts and 82nd New York deployed along the Emmitsburg Road. Tall grass blocked their view of the formidable line of approaching rebels, otherwise, they probably would have bolted for the safety of the rear. Earlier that day, their brigade commander, General William Harrow, had pulled out his gun and told them that he would shoot any man who ran to the rear. Realizing they were in for perhaps the fight of their lives, the worried men of these two veteran regiments did their best to build breastworks that were flimsy at best.

Hearing the dreaded rebel yell and realizing that the enemy were closing in on their positions, the men were ordered to open fire. One private wrote, "With a shout we sprang up on our knees and resting our muskets over the rails, we gave them one of the most destructive volleys I ever witnessed... They hesitated, then reeled, they staggered and wavered slightly, yet there was no panic." Instead, Wright's men pressed on. Harrow's men were furious when they realized that many of the artillery rounds that were supposed to be thwarting the rebel charge, were actually falling short, killing and wounding many Union soldiers.

The 82nd New York on the right of the line crumbled first, and the 15th Massachusetts was ordered to retreat and seek safety on Cemetery Ridge. What began as an organized retreat, soon became a stampede. A footrace now ensued between the yanks trying to flee for safety and the rebs, trying to add them to the growing ranks of prisoners. Many Federal soldiers realized that it was foolhardy to try to escape, and threw down their rifles and raised their arms to surrender. To their surprise, their offer was not taken up by the advancing rebels. A Union soldier wrote, "They spoke not a word to me but passed over and on, every reb's eye seemed to be fixed on our artillery wich [sic] they were after."[6]

The left of Wright's line now cast their attention on Lt. Fred Brown's six-rifled cannon. When Wright's line of attack burst out of the woods on Seminary Ridge, it progressed so quickly that Brown was only able to bring to bear four guns on the oncoming rebels. The position of the remaining two guns on the right of the battery could not be changed fast enough, so they continued to lob shells into the woods. The battery held its ground despite the fleeing Federal troops around them. Initially, the guns opened with spherical case shells whose fuses were cut to explode in four seconds. Filled with 70 leaden balls, they wrecked havoc on Wright's troops. Still they advanced, and "our fuses were cut at 3, 2, and one second, and then canister at point-blank range, and finally double charges were used," wrote the battery's historian. But Wright's men continued on. One wrote that "shells around us tore our bleeding ranks with ghastly gaps...we pressed on, knowing that the front was safer now than to turn our backs..."

Taking fearful losses from the onrushing Confederates, Brown realized the hopelessness of the situation, and ordered his guns to the rear.

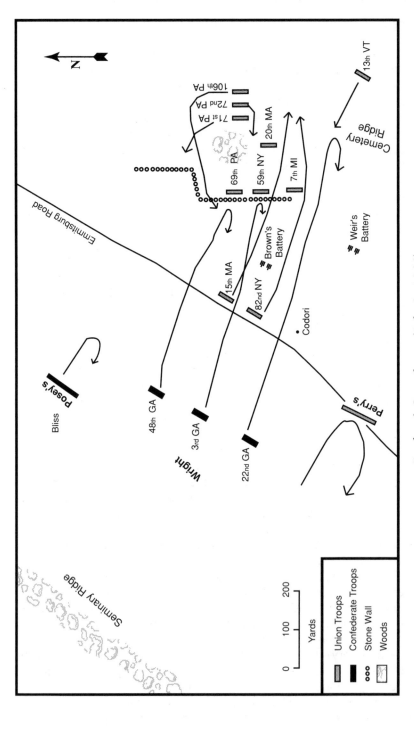

Battle of Gettysburg (July 2, 1863)

N

106th PA
71st PA
72nd PA
69th PA
59th NY
20th MA
7th MI

Emmitsburg Road

15th MA

82nd NY

Brown's Battery

Cemetery Ridge

13th VT

Weir's Battery

Codori

48th GA

3rd GA

Wright

22nd GA

Posey's

Bliss

Seminary Ridge

Perry's

0   100   200

Yards

Union Troops
Confederate Troops
Stone Wall
Woods

Sergeant Albert Straight, who commanded one gun, ordered it to be loaded and fired one last time, however. During this short interval, two of his horses went down, and the gun had to be abandoned. A second cannon was abandoned. One of Wright's men later wrote, "With a mighty yell, we threw ourselves upon the batteries and passed them, still reeking hot."[7]

As Wright's men continued their advance, the men of the 69th were ordered to prepare to fire. They were prevented from firing because Brown's retreating four guns were between them and the rebels. Making for a gap in the stone wall within the 69th's position, one gun got through, but then two tried to gallop through at the same time, creating quite a mess. The fourth gun had no choice but to wait until the passageway was clear. However, as Wright's men closed to within fifty feet of the wall, the Irishmen could wait no longer. As the colorbearer of the regiment calmly shook the folds out of the green flag, the grim veterans opened fire, forcing the gunners of the fourth gun to hug the ground for cover. Looking up, the cannoneers could see a "vivid flame sending messengers of death to the foe."

When a rebel officer mounted one of the abandoned cannon to encourage his men, Captain Michael Duffy of the 69th became so enraged, that he screamed to his men to "knock that d-d officer off the gun." The officer soon crumbled to the ground. Duffy also fell soon after with a serious wound. Despite the tremendous pounding that Wright's men had taken from Brown's guns and now the intense small arms fire from the 69th, the 48th Georgia on the left of the Confederate line continued to rush forward. Not one Pennsylvanian ran for the rear. The historian of the 69th recalled,

Still came on the mad Georgians until they reach point-blank range of our rifles. We met their charge with such a destroying fire that they were forced back in confusion. They rally again and make a second effort and again are their lines broken and thinned as we pour volley upon volley into their disordered rank, until they finally retire a dispirited mob...

No one could have survived such a firestorm, but the gallant men of the 48th Georgia pressed on.[8]

While the men of the 69th were blazing away at the onrushing Southerners, Generals Hancock and Webb ordered the remaining three regiments of the Philadelphia Brigade forward. The 71st was ordered to take position behind a low stone fence to the right of the copse of trees, about 200 feet behind the 69th, with its right connecting with Arnold's Company A, 1st Rhode Island Light Artillery. In front of the 71st was Cushing's Company A, 4th U.S. Artillery. Behind the left flank of the 69th, was the 20th Massachusetts, and behind it were the remnants of Brown's Battery. Hancock ordered the 72nd to rush to the left of the copse of trees. The 106th was also brought forward, just to the right of the copse of trees. Colonel Curry of the 106th described what happened next,

I advanced the regiment to the crest of the hill, and opened fire upon the enemy. After several volleys, perceiving that we checked his advance, and seeing his lines waver, I ordered bayonets fixed and a charge to be made, which movement resulted in a complete success, the enemy retiring in confusion to his original position in the woods.

After taking horrific losses during their advance, and now seeing the men of the 106th jumping over the low stone fence and rushing toward their flank, cheering at the top of their lungs, the men of the 48th Georgia realized that there were just too few of them left to handle this situation, and turned around to begin their retreat to the safety of Seminary Ridge. Seven times their flag had fallen during the charge—six times it was picked up, but after the seventh, there was no one left to pick it up, and it was captured by the victorious Philadelphia Brigade. The 48th Georgia lost about 57% during this charge.[9]

While the Philadelphia Brigade had steadfastly repelled the Confederates, the same was not true on its left. Here, Wright's men saw the gap in the Federal line to the left of the 7th Michigan, and drove through it to reach the crest of the ridge. Just as the men of the 22nd Georgia gained the top of the ridge, they were hit by a savage counterattack by part of the 13th Vermont of General George Stannard's brigade that had been rushed to this area from the vicinity of Cemetery Hill. The fighting was short, but intense, and the rebels were finally forced back the way they came.[10]

On the opposite side of the line, the 106th continued its charge, and with the 71st, recaptured Brown's lost guns. The 72nd also rushed forward, and while the 71st remained with the cannon, the 106th and 72nd followed the rebels to the Emmitsburg Road. What happened now is the subject of debate. According to the historian of the 106th, the regiment spied a Confederate officer waving a white handkerchief as they approached the Codori Farm buildings. Captain Ford was ordered forward to investigate, so he affixed an old newspaper to one of the men's bayonet, and cautiously advanced. There he purportedly met Captain Snead of the 48th Georgia, who informed him that his regimental commander, Colonel William Gibson, was seriously wounded and needed immediate medical attention. Standing by Colonel Gibson in the farmyard were the remnants of his regiment. Ford surveyed the situation and replied that he would be pleased to honor the request, but not before the unit had surrendered. Captain Snead strenuously objected, saying that he wished to return with his men to his lines, as they had only intended to remain with their stricken leader. Ford persisted, and finally Captain Snead complied. Returning to Colonel Curry with arms loaded down with officers' swords, Captain Ford led the captured men of the 48th Georgia back to the Union lines. Besides Colonel Gibson, the historian wrote that the unit had bagged five captains, fifteen lieutenants, and about 250 enlisted men. The story is corroborated by General Webb's after-battle report.[11]

A close examination of the facts cast suspicion on this story. The brigade historian, whose book was published well before the history of the

106th, mentions the capture of Colonel Gibson and a captain tending to him, but nothing about large numbers of men remaining in the farmyard. If the capture of almost half a regiment had occurred, one would think that the event would have been highlighted in the brigade history. It is also difficult to believe that the men of the 48th Georgia, after so gallantly storming Cemetery Ridge, would remain in such an exposed position with their commanding officer. Likewise, why would the Confederates request medical attention, when they could have carried Gibson back to Seminary Ridge? A recent analysis of the unit's losses found that only fifty-seven men were missing. While it is plausible that Colonel Gibson was laying in the farmyard and that some of his men were with him, the actual numbers are probably much smaller and less dramatic that what has been represented by the 106th's historian.[12]

As the men searched the buildings, they found a "large number of officers and men" in the cellar of the Codori barn. Colonel Birkett Fry of the 13th Alabama was supposedly captured by Captain John Lynch of Company B. This was probably another distortion by the 106th's historian, as Colonel Fry led Archer's brigade on July 3, when he was wounded twice and captured during the Pickett's Charge.

The tale continued when the historian of the 106th wrote that the regiment crossed the road and took possession of four cannon abandoned by the enemy. Having no means of bringing the guns off the field, they had been left behind. Unfortunately, no rebel battery ever reached this advanced point during the day—again a fabrication.[13]

Realizing their advanced position made his command vulnerable, Colonel Curry threw out a line of skirmishers and sent back for support. When the aid did not materialize, Curry turned the command over to Major Stover and rode over the General Webb. Realizing that nothing was to be gained from the 106th's advanced position, Webb ordered Curry to return his command to the safety of the ridge.

As daylight faded into darkness the men could see the fields dotted with dead and wounded. Many walked about to see which of their comrades had been killed or wounded. Losses to Wright's brigade were exceptionally heavy. Taking just over 1,400 men into battle, the unit lost almost 700 or about half of its men. Losses to the Philadelphia Brigade were much lighter, only 127 men or 10.5%. The breakdown by regiment was: 69th=45; 71st=14; 72nd=4; and 106th=64. The losses reflect the activities of each regiment. The units playing a supporting role (71st and 72nd) sustained the lowest number of casualties. Although the 69th bore the brunt of the 48th Georgia's attack, the low stone wall apparently prevented it from sustaining heavy losses. The highest losses were sustained by the 106th, whose charge threw back the Georgia regiment. Colonel Baxter, commanding the 72nd, went down with a wound as he moved his men into position to the left of the copse of trees, and Lieutenant Colonel Theodore Hesser assumed command.[14]

About ten minutes after the 106th reached the safety of Cemetery Ridge, an aide rode up to Colonel Curry with orders to move the regiment rapidly to Cemetery Hill. In the gathering darkness, General Richard Ewell had finally unleashed his attack on the Federal right flank. Two brigades of General Jubal Early's division moved out of the town and into the intense storm of lead being thrown at them. As they pushed their way forward, General Oliver Howard's men of the XI Corps fled from their breastworks. The triumphant rebels now had a clear path to the top of the hill, as the fleeing troops did not permit the cannon on the hill to fire. The men of Rickett's battery subsequently refused to budge, and fought their attackers with swabs and rammers. Other units from the XI Corps converged on the area, as did General Carroll's brigade of Hayes' division.

Prior to this final dramatic struggle for the crest of Cemetery Hill, Howard sent an urgent plea for reinforcements. According to the historian of the 106th, he specifically asked for the 106th, as he was aware of its fighting prowess. Leaving behind the battered Companies A and B that had been on skirmish duty prior to Wright's charge, Curry rushed the remainder of the regiment toward Cemetery Hill. What probably happened was that Hancock, upon hearing the firing on Cemetery Hill took it upon himself to order the 106th forward. It arrived just as Carroll's brigade had pushed the last of Early's Confederates from the crest of the hill. Howard personally deployed the 106th in a position to support the artillery. As he did so, he is purported to have said to the commander of his artillery, "Major, your batteries may be withdrawn when that regiment runs away." The regiment remained here on Cemetery Hill for the remainder of the battle under artillery fire from at least three Confederate batteries.[15]

At the same time that the 106th was dispatched to Cemetery Hill, Hancock ordered the 71st to reinforce the army's extreme right flank. Formerly held by two divisions of General Howard Slocum's XII Corps, all but one brigade was rushed to the left flank where Longstreet's attacks were making headway. The brigade left behind was commanded by General George "Pap" Greene—the oldest general officer on the field that day. Greene was ordered to hold the position formerly held by 10,000 men. As evening descended, General Edward Johnson's Confederate division launched several against Greene's position.

Greene needed help, and the 71st was sent to shore up his unsteady line. The men had great difficulty moving over the rough terrain in the darkness, and did not know where to go. Forunately, they were met by Captain Craig Wadsworth of Wadsworth's division, which was occupying the western slope of Culp's Hill, and led to the right. Here they were turned over to Captain Charles Horton, Greene's adjutant, who led them to their assigned position on the right of the 137th New York. As they took their positions on the east slope of Culp's Hill, the Pennsylvanians gave three loud cheers, presumably to announce their arrival to the beleaguered men of Greene's brigade. This also served to announce their presence to the Confederates, who opened fire.

No sooner had the men of the 71st settled in on the right of the Federal line, than Steuart's brigade attacked their front and flank. To the amazement of the men of the 137th New York, the Pennsylvanians rose, left their breastworks, and filed to the rear. No panic or disorder was evident. William Burns recorded in his diary that night, "It was a blunder on the part of our officers and came near costing us dear. It was the heaviest and wickedest musketry fire for about half an hour that ever I lay under. We lost 15 men and four officers."

Colonel Smith described the incident in his after-battle report:

> An adjutant-general directed me to proceed to the front, assuring me that all was safe on either flank. Arriving at the front, I became engaged with the enemy on the front. At the same time he attacked me on my right and rear. I immediately ordered my command to retire to the road in my rear, when I returned to camp against orders. During the engagement, I lost 3 commissioned officers and 11 enlisted men.

As Colonel Smith moved his command back in the direction they had come, Captain Horton rushed up and demanded to know what he was doing. Smith angrily replied that he would not have his men murdered in such a fashion, and besides, he had orders to return to his former position. General John Geary, commanding a division in this sector wrote, "...they soon fell back and were withdrawn—the commanding officer saying that he had received orders from his commanding general to retire...placed the right of Greene's brigade in a critical position. General Webb's did not support his subordinate's claim, writing tersely in his official report, "It [71st] returned at about 12 o'clock without orders." This was echoed by Hancock in his report.

In recalling this event Horton wrote that the men of the 71st appeared mortified by the actions of their commanding officer.

After the war, the brigade historian attempted to cast the incident in a positive light by changing some of the facts:

Colonel Richard Penn Smith,
71st Pennsylvania

By some misunderstanding, Colonel Smith, in attempting to go into position, found himself in the presence of a strong force of enemy, and owing to the darkness and want of familiarity with the ground...[two officers] and sixteen of the men acting as skirmishers, were taken prisoners. After this, Colonel Smith assumed the responsibility of rejoining his brigade...

This theme was picked up later by the historian of the 106th who wrote that because of the darkness and removal of Geary's division, the 71st "moved too far to the right...and ran into Johnson's men, then occupying Geary's works, came near being all captured."

Smith's official report never mentioned losing any men as prisoners, and it appears that his regiment was already *in position* when the attack commenced. Stumbling into an unfamiliar position in the dark and being immediately attacked, one can empathize with Smith's decision, particularly because this was his first battle in command of the regiment.

With the 71st gone, the Confederates attacked the 137th New York in the front, flank, and rear, forcing it backward after sustaining heavy losses. Before long, the rebels were successfully established in some of the abandoned breastworks. It is difficult to understand Colonel Smith's behavior, especially given its subsequent impact. There is no record of any disciplinary action taken against him as a result of his actions on the evening of July 2. The regiment subsequently returned to its original position on Cemetery Ridge, stacked arms and went to sleep.[16]

Despite the fact that he had been removed from command of the Philadelphia Brigade prior to the battle, General Joshua Owen was apparently on the field. Leading his XII Corps division south on the afternoon of July 2 to reinforce the Federal left flank, General Alpheus Williams met General Owen at the George Weikert House. Williams was disappointed when Owen "could give me very little information about anything." According to Williams, Owen had been released from arrest, but was given no formal unit to command during the battle. Instead, he had a "roving commission." Williams described Owen as being "in not a very clear state of mind."[17]

CHAPTER 14

GETTYSBURG–THE THIRD DAY

During the quiet morning hours of July 3, the men could easily see the aftermath of Wright's charge, and ponder what the day might bring. The hot sun had caused the bodies to begin decomposing, and the smell was becoming sickening. All were hungry, as they had not eaten for more than twenty-four hours. Joseph McKeever of the 69th was able to beg some hardtack from the men of Cushing's battery.

The quiet unnerved many of the men, as related by the historian of the 69th, who later wrote, "About noon a still reined that was death-like and unusual at such a time; and anxious looks could clearly be seen on the faces of the men, and feelings of mingled dread and determination pervaded the minds..."[1]

During the morning, Lee cast about for a plan to drive the Federals from their positions. Recalling Wright's success the day before, Lee decided to repeat the charge against the Union center. This time Longstreet would make the charge, not with one brigade, but with about 13,000 men in eleven brigades from four divisions. Pickett's newly arrived division would spearhead the charge. His target would be the clump of trees and the Philadelphia Brigade.

Just after 1:00 p.m., a single Confederate cannon fired and soon 140 rebel cannon were belching smoke and fire along a three-mile front. Their objective was to smash the Union center. About eighty Union guns replied. So began the greatest artillery barrage on American soil. Lee's orders were to wait until the cannon fire had annihilated the infantry and artillery in the center of the Union line before launching the attack.

The maelstrom created by the cannonade was described by the historian of the 69th,

> The air is filling with the whirling, shrieking, hissing sound of the solid shot and bursting shell; all throw themselves flat upon the ground, behind the little stone wall; nearly 150 guns belched forth messengers of destruction, sometimes in volleys, again in irregular, but continuous sounds, traveling through the air, high above

us, or striking the ground in front and ricochetting over us, to be imbedded in some object to the rear...

Joseph McKeever of the same regiment added, "After the cannonading began, we were all hugging the earth and we would have liked to get into it if we could."[2]

The Federal generals handled the cannonade differently. Division commander Gibbon felt that he had proven himself on too many fields to risk exposure, so he sat down on the opposite side of the ridge, probably not far from the 71st and 72nd. Newly appointed Alexander Webb felt that his men needed to see that their new commander was unaffected by the storm around him. Standing in the most exposed place he could find, he leaned on his sword and calmly puffed on a cigar. Despite his men's pleas, "he stood like a statue watching the movement of the enemy."

After about an hour, Gibbon realized that many of the shots were falling closer to him, and that the side of the ridge facing the rebels appeared to be taking fewer hits. He therefore walked to the crest of the ridge, then down the other side. Passing the copse of trees, he made his way to the 69th's position. In response to Gibbon's casual remark, "What do you think of this," he received a number of replies, such as "O, [sic] this is bully," "We are getting to like it," "O, [sic] we don't mind this." Continuing on about 200 yards into the no-man's-land between the two armies, Gibbon found a place to sit under some trees. Hearing an explosion, he looked back and saw that a rebel shell had struck a section of the 69th's breastwork. Soon several men joined their division commander in an area they thought was safer than their own. Gibbon gently sent them back saying that they were in God's hands and nothing they did could change that.[3]

Cushing's and Brown's batteries were badly shattered during the cannonade, and the casualties among the men and horses were high. "...caissons exploding, battery wagons, forges, literally swept away, shattered into splinters, horses disemboweled, their flesh and entrails scattered, men beheaded, limbs torn, and bodies most horribly mangled into shapeless and unrecognizable masses of human flesh," wrote the 69th's historian. With all of the officers down, and too few gunners to work the cannons, Brown was ordered to move his three remaining guns to safety. Early in the cannonade, three of Cushing's ammunition chests had exploded, killing and maiming a number of his men. He too had only three cannon remaining.[4]

Suddenly the cannonade stopped, and an unsettling lull prevailed. Surprisingly, the brigade sustained only about fifty casualties during this massive display of firepower. The lull permitted the Federal officers to prepare their men. Some, like Colonel Dennis O'Kane of the 69th, offered inspirational speeches and encouragement to the men. He ordered his men to conserve their ammunition until they could see the "whites of their eyes" and reminded them that they were defending their beloved state. He concluded his remarks with, "and let your work this day be for victory to the death." Webb, standing by the left of the line, also addressed the troops, telling them not to fire until the enemy had crossed the Emmitsburg Road, and concluded his remarks with "if you do as well today as you did yesterday, I will be satisfied."[5]

Webb also used the lull to reposition the brigade. Since Cushing's depleted battery was not replaced, Webb brought up the 71st from its reserve position to the stone wall and formed them to the right of the battery. This was the same stone wall that sheltered the 69th to the left. Colonel Smith realized that the stone wall in this sector did not extend far enough to deploy his entire regiment, so he sent his remaining two companies to take position behind another stone wall, about 200 feet in the rear. An historian later noted, "By this shift at a critical moment, most of the regiment was sent into a position with which it was unfamiliar. In such a situation, troops are likely to be nervous."

Colonel Dennis O'Kane,
69th Pennsylvania
Civil War Library and Museum

Webb's front line now consisted of the 69th in front of the copse of trees, and to its right, eight companies of the 71st. Cushing's remaining guns occupied a small gap between the two regiments. An officer later recalled the stone fence in front of these two regiments—"...infantry at the wall had very slight protection...certainly not over two feet high...There was not enough soil there to strengthen the wall and raise it higher." The 72nd remained behind the copse of trees. Webb also sent a small detail of forty-five men under the command of a captain to stand behind the brigade with orders to shoot any man that tried to get past them. The 106th, with the exception of Companies A and B, remained on Cemetery Hill with the XI Corps.[6]

Because Cushing's battery did not have enough men still standing to service the guns, several volunteers from the 71st were enlisted. Some of the cannon were now rolled down the slope to fill the gap between the 69th and 71st. Because they were so close to the right flank of the 69th, two of their privates had their heads blown off when the guns opened with canister.[7]

Concerned about the condition of Brown's and Cushing's batteries, Webb sent an aide galloping toward Cemetery Hill for a fresh battery. Finding Captain Andrew Cowan, the aide asked him to move his battery south to the copse of trees. While Cowan was sympathetic to Webb's plight, his battery was a part of the I Corps, and he therefore could not obey the orders of an officer from another corps. However, when he saw Webb frantically waving his hat, he decided to throw caution to the wind, and ordered his cannon rushed toward the clump of trees. While one gun unlimbered to the north of it, the remaining five took position near Brown's battery's former position just to the south of the trees. Even as the guns were being unlimbered in their new positions, fuses were cut, and in a matter of moments, the guns were in action.

The heat and humidity were sweltering—approaching eighty-seven degrees and percent. The Union soldiers did not have long to think about the weather, because Pickett's division emerged from the cover of Seminary Ridge at about 3 p.m. Marching in two lines, Kemper's and Garnett's brigades moved forward. Behind them was Pickett's third brigade under General Lewis Armistead—the understrengthed Philadelphia Brigade would soon be facing most of Pickett's division.[8]

The first interaction between the two opposing forces occurred when the Philadelphia Brigade's skirmishers stubbornly held their ground against Garnett's approaching brigade. So tenacious was this resistance, that Garnett was forced to halt the brigade to fire a volley into the line of skirmishers. Some of the Confederates confused this line of skirmishers with the Federal's first line of defense. Realizing that they could do no more, the skirmishers ran back to their lines on Cemetery Ridge at full speed. The two isolated companies of the 106th, which formed part of the skirmish line, took position on the left of the 72nd. Captain James Lynch wrote later, "We never received any orders from General Webb or anybody else, but it was one of those actions in which every soldier felt that his duty was to be in the fight..."[9]

When Garnett's brigade was within 250 feet of the stone wall, some of the 69th on the left flank opened fire. Most waited until the enemy were within fifty feet, when they sprung up on their knees and opened fire. Cushing's cannons were also firing, but they had expended their ammunition, so the men fired stones, broken shells, and even bayonets. The smoke from the initial volley enveloped the Virginians, and when it cleared, many fewer men were left standing. Half the battle flags went down, only to be quickly picked up by other men, who invariably were also shot down. As they looked toward the Union line, all they could see was the Philadelphia Brigade's flags, the glitter of the sun on the rifle barrels, and the red flashes sending a hailstorm of lead into their ranks.

The initial firing of the 69th and 71st were unusually intense, and probably suggested stronger units defending the area around the clump of trees. Prior to the charge, the men had been ordered to scour the area for the guns lying on the ground. Now each man had between two and five loaded guns that were used in quick succession. Many of the men were using twelve buckshots in each load. The regiment therefore delivered

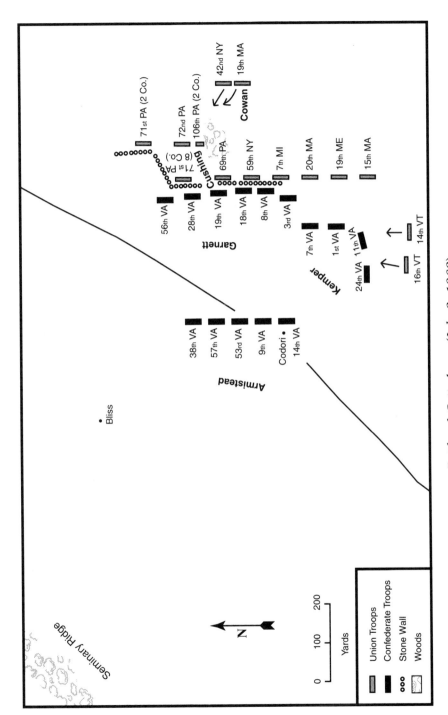

Battle of Gettysburg (July 3, 1863)

Seminary Ridge

71st PA (2 Co.)

72nd PA
106th PA (2 Co.)

42nd NY
19th MA

Cowan

71st PA (8 Co.)
69th PA
59th NY
7th MI

20th MA
19th ME
15th MA

Cushing

56th VA
28th VA
19th VA
18th VA
8th VA
3rd VA

Garnett

7th VA
1st VA
11th VA
14th VT

24th VA
16th VT

Kemper

38th VA
57th VA
53rd VA
9th VA
Codori •
14th VA

Armistead

• Bliss

N

Yards

0   100   200

Union Troops
Confederate Troops
Stone Wall
Woods

between 700 and 1,000 rounds into Pickett's men in the initial minute of the contest.[10]

Through the smoke and ear-splitting noise, the two Pennsylvania regiments and the 59th New York to their left could probably make out ten Confederate regimental battle flags crammed into their narrow front. Defending this 500-foot sector were less than 400 infantry and six guns that had all but expended their ammunition, and three that were out of action. To make matters worse, the gap between the 69th and 71st loomed invitingly to the onrushing Confederates. Another gap existed between the left of the 69th and the right of the 59th New York that was created to provide a space through which Cowan's guns could fire.

While several hundred rebels from Kemper's brigade opened fire on the left of the 69th while lying prone in a brushy area, Garnett's regiments in front of the 69th briefly halted and returned the fire while standing. To the right of the 69th, the 28th and 56th Virginia, and part of the 19th Virginia, approached the gap and the 71st. Surging forward, they were hit by canister from Cushing's guns. But it was simply a case of too few against too many, and the battery was overwhelmed and the men of the 71st were forced to flee for their lives. William Burns recorded in his diary, "The fight soon became awful. We mowed the rebs right and left but still they came on. We had to retreat." Garnett's men now rushed for the stone fence and crossed it.[11]

Looking to their right, the victorious Southerners could see the 69th, and the small regiments to its left, gallantly holding its position against the 19th, 18th, and 8th Virginia regiments of Garnett's brigade and at least part of the 3rd Virginia of Kemper's brigade. In front of Garnett's men, beyond the fleeing Yankees of the 71st, a large mass of Federal infantry suddenly materialized. Prior to Garnett's men reaching Emmitsburg Road, Webb realized that it was time to bring up the 72nd to plug the gap between the 69th and 71st. John Reed testified, "After the firing had got pretty well advanced, General Webb made a whole lot of motions, or sword motions, and we advanced then to our right. That would be towards the 71st, and then as soon as we advanced along to the 71st, he commenced to pull his sword this way. He may have said something but it would be very hard for anybody to hear what he did say. He may have said a great many things, but I can't tell what he said." The move had been made from behind the copse of trees by a "right oblique" to a position parallel, but about twenty to thirty feet below the stone fence that protected the two right companies of the 71st. About halfway down the ridge to the left, the line extended to the copse of trees. No sooner had they reached this position, that they were ordered to fire a volley into Garnett's troops which had now claimed the stone fence previously held by the 71st.

George Finley of the 56th Virginia vividly remembered the scene,

> At that instant, suddenly a terrific fire burst upon us from our front, and looking around I saw close to us, just on the crest of the ridge, a

fresh line of Federals attempting to drive us from the stone fence, but after exchanging a few rounds with us they fell back behind the crest, leaving us still in possession of the stone wall. Under this fire, as I immediately learned, General Garnett had fallen dead.

With Garnett killed by the 72nd's first volley, most of the Southerners remained at the wall, waiting for Armistead's men to arrive before making a final charge. While waiting, they continued to exchange fire with the 72nd holding its position near the crest of the ridge. As the men of the 71st surged to the rear, they were stopped by Webb and reformed behind the 72nd. William Burns of the 71st recorded in his diary, "I thought it was all up with us when our general (Webb) rallied the men."[12]

While Garnett's men gathered at the wall, Webb realized that a charge by the 72nd could drive the Southerners back to Seminary Ridge. Standing by the copse of trees on the regiment's left, Webb called for the men to charge. The men later testified that the roar of battle was so intense, that Webb could not be heard beyond ten feet. Realizing this, Webb moved forward to personally lead the charge. Webb recounted what happened next: "The color bearer and myself stood together, I holding onto the staff and he did not move forward with me. I ordered him forward; this was the color bearer of the 72nd regiment. I know of no words said when I ordered him forward, he moved in his place but did not carry the colors out of the regimental line." The flag bearer, Sergeant William Finecy, would soon be lying dead on the battlefield with anywhere from six to thirteen bullet holes in him. Part of the reason for the 72nd's hesitancy to attack may have been that Webb was so new to the brigade that the men did not recognize him. Indeed, he admitted that he personally gave the orders to attack, rather than transmitting them through Lieutenant Colonel Hesser or any of the other regimental officers.

Seeing the 71st flee, and now unable to move the 72nd forward, Webb's spirits sank. He fully realized the magnitude of his error of not re-placing Cushing's battery with the 72nd at the start of the battle. A few days after the battle, he wrote to his wife, "When they came over the fences, the Army of the Potomac was nearer being whipped than it was at any time of the battle. When my men fell back I almost wished to get killed." Webb may now have indeed tried to get himself killed, as he walked down to the right of the 69th, which was under heavy attack at this time.[13]

While waiting for Armistead, many of Garnett's men dropped down behind the stone fence and fired at the 72nd, exposed on the ridge. Webb never intended for them to occupy this vulnerable position—they were to have moved down to the wall. The Fire Zouaves were dropping in two's and three's, but they stood their ground and returned the fire. They may not have charged, but they were not about to leave the fight. A stalemate now developed, as Garnett's leaderless men knew that they did not have the numbers to dislodge the 72nd in front of them, and the 72nd would not charge. Garnett's brigade's error was a costly one, because while it waited for Armistead, Colonel Norman Hall moved two of his regiments from the left of the clump of trees toward the scene of the fighting in this sector.

Garnett's men did not have to wait long, however, as Armistead's brigade, which was behind Garnett's and Kemper's during the charge, now arrived. Seeing the 69th intact, but Garnett's men holding the wall to the left, Armistead led his men in that direction, weathering a terrific flank fire from the 69th. Leaping upon the wall, Armistead surveyed the scene. Realizing that he could not remain in this vulnerable position, he cried to his men, "Come on, boys, give them the cold steel! Who will follow me?" Climbing over the wall, they overwhelmed the right of the 69th and drove for the 72nd. As Armistead's men rushed for the gap in the line, the right companies of the 69th were ordered to refuse the line to now face to the right and rear, where the enemy were pouring through the wall. The right-most company, Company I, received and obeyed the order, as did the next one, Company A. However, the captain of the next company (F) was shot just as he was about to give the order, and as a result, the company held its position facing Seminary Ridge. Within a few moments, it was overwhelmed by Armistead's men—those who were not killed or wounded were sent toward Seminary Ridge with the other prisoners.

With a gap in the right of the line, the 69th faced destruction. Before it could be exploited, Company D, which was on the left of the stricken Company F, turned and drove to the right. Led by Captain Patrick Tinen, the men took on the Confederates in desperate hand-to-hand fighting. One giant of a man, Hugh Bradley, took on several Confederates before being struck down. After several minutes of the most savage fighting, the breach was finally sealed. The 69th's seven left and center companies fell back slightly, but still faced the wall, while its two remaining companies formed at a right angle to them, facing the direction of the 72nd.[14]

The 69th's left flank was also under attack by some of Kemper's regiments. Cowen's battery belched canister at the oncoming rebels, but some of the balls bowled over the 69th's men instead. Many were also hit with stones dislodged as the canister hit the ground. Some of the rebels actually jumped over the crouched men of the 69th at the wall and ran for Cowen's guns. At least one band, led by a major, came close to capturing Cowen's guns, but they were blown away by double canister at almost point-blank range. The regiment tried to hold its position, but was slowly forced back toward the clump of trees. Both flanks now bent back to try to stem the flank attacks. Despite these attacks on both flanks and center, the gallant regiment's Stars and Stripes and its green flag still waved proudly. Colonel O'Kane was killed and Lieutenant Colonel Martin Tschudy went down with a mortal wound. The command now fell to Major James Duffy, who was also wounded at the height of the action. Captain William Davis now took command of the regiment.

Joseph McKeever of the 69th recalled that "We all fell back just as they were coming in to the inside of the trees and they made a rally, and then they were coming in all around, but how they fired without killing all our men I do not know." At this point, all order had been lost, and the regiment, and Pickett's attacking units could only be called a "mob." Still they fought on.[15]

As Webb walked toward the front, Confederate officers pointed him out as a target for their men. A bullet subsequently grazed his thigh, but the wound was not severe enough for him to leave the field. As he walked toward the 69th, he probably passed within ten or fifteen feet of General Armistead. Finally reaching the right flank of the 69th, Webb did what he could to encourage the regiment to hold its position. One soldier wrote, "We thought we were all gone."

Just as Armistead, with his black hat perched on his sword held aloft like a torch, touched one of Cushing's now abandoned cannons, he fell mortally wounded. The 72nd had again brought down one of Pickett's brigade commanders. This took the heart out of some of Armistead's men— while several continued to fire into the backs of the 69th and into the 72nd, others threw down their weapons and surrendered.

Just to the south of this bitter fighting, Colonel Arthur Devereux, of the 19th Massachusetts of Hall's brigade, moved his regiment and the 42nd New York toward the heaviest fighting, smashed into the disordered mass of Confederates, and closed the gap on the right of the 69th. An officer from the 19th Massachusetts later complimented the 69th when he wrote, "They were doing some pretty good fighting. They did not yield one inch, and the enemy swarmed right over them, but whenever they got a chance to get in a shot here and there they let the enemy have it." Anthony McDermott of the 69th returned the compliment when he wrote that the regiment "never could have withstood all this force if it had not been for the shifting to our aid of Hall's men and the 72nd Penna to the crest of the ridge."

Pandemonium reined. Captain Cowan later wrote, "The 69th Pa. Regt. was before our guns, but I do not think...there was such a thing as regiments. The men were fighting pretty much at will..." All order was lost, as individual fights broke out between the men on both sides. This was a desperate time for the Confederates, as each man had to make the decision about whether to turn his back to the enemy and retreat, and face death, or to remain at the wall, and also face death. When the Union soldiers called for the rebels to surrender and save themselves, hundreds threw up their hands.[16]

After being in their exposed position for about twenty minutes, the 72nd finally charged the rebels who were advancing from the stone fence. Major Samuel Roberts recalled, "The color bearer, seizing the stump of the staff of the colors, whirling his hat around his head, moved with the regiment down to the wall; many of our men being wounded or killed in the

advance and the men behind that wall, besides men out in the field surrendered; the men out in the field throwing up their hands and shouting 'Don't
shoot.'" The color bearer, Sergeant Thomas Murphy, was at least the seventh that had carried the regiment's flag that day. All of the rest lie dead or
wounded.[17]

Frank Haskell, one of Gibbon's aides, told a different story. Riding to
the remnants of the 71st which had formed behind the 72nd, he called out
to a major, "lead your men over the crest, they will follow." When he refused, he found Captain Sapler of the same regiment, who also refused to
lead the attack. Haskell claimed that he now rode over to the 72nd and
finally got it to charge. The regiment's assistant adjutant testified after the
war that Haskell's horse was "crowding" the left part of the line, so it appears he was nearby. Others believe that the 72nd finally charged the enemy when they saw the two regiments from Hall's brigade advancing to
provide support. It is also possible that the 72nd's officers, oblivious to
Webb's earlier attempts to get the regiment to charge, finally gave the
order. Either way, charge they did, without any special formation. The en-
suing fight was short-lived but desperate, as the last of Pickett's men were
either killed, wounded, captured, or fled to the rear. Most appeared to realize that flight was foolhardy, and threw up handkerchiefs and other garments in surrender. According to Sergeant William Burns, the 71st also
participated in the charge, which he said was led by Webb. "He went right
in front of us and led us when we gave a yell and charged on them and
drove them back with great slaughter." The 71st captured two flags in the
hand-to-hand fighting; a third was picked up after the battle.[18]

Soon after the repulse, the men roamed the area, looking for their
missing comrades. All around them were massive numbers of dead and
wounded. Literally thousands of Confederates had simply given up and
surrendered. So overburdened were the men that the rebels were often
sent to the rear without guards. Rifles and accoutrements were everywhere.

Later, those regiments that captured Confederate regimental flags
received the most recognition. In reality, many of the flags were merely
lying on the ground. Despite the ferocity of its defense, and the fact that at
least eight battle flags were lying all around them, the 69th did not pick up
any of them. According to one veteran, the men were too busy tending to
the wounded and trying to recover from the shock of the assault to pick up
any of the flags.[19]

A special bond formed between the men of Pickett's division and the
Philadelphia Brigade after the war. The Philadelphians were entertained in
Richmond, and the courtesy was returned when the Virginians were invited to Gettysburg. During the reunions, the old soldiers often repeated
the charge, and on at least one occasion, things got a bit hot, and a battle
involving walking sticks broke out. The fiftieth reunion was most remembered, when the 120 survivors of Pickett's division re-enacted their charge

against the 180 survivors of the Philadelphia Brigade. When the Southerners reached the wall, the two sides shook hands, much to the delight of the
photographers. During the ceremonies that followed, the members of the
Philadelphia Brigade presented a flag to Pickett's survivors.[20]

A number of "disagreements" developed after the war about the Phila-
delphia Brigade's actions during Pickett's Charge. One was waged over
General Abner Doubleday's assertion that Hall's regiments went through
Webb's brigade to repulse Pickett's men. The veterans of the Philadelphia
Brigade took this as an assertion that they were not performing their duty.
Regimental historian Joseph Ward, wrote, "At no time was Webb's line
passed over, or through, by any of our troops, from the time his command
was placed in position...Webb yielded his position to no one... and with his
own brigade, Webb cleared his own front, though ably assisted by the
brave troops on his right and left." Hall's regiments apparently approached
the wall from the left of the 72nd, and did not move through the ranks of
any regiment in the Philadelphia Brigade.[21]

The most intense disagreement involved the 72nd. The controversy
erupted when the Gettysburg Battlefield Memorial Association rejected the
72nd's claim that its monument occupy a position near the stone fence,
between the 69th and 71st memorials. The association instead believed
that the memorial should be placed almost 300 feet farther up the ridge,
where the 72nd had formed its line of battle and delivered its initial volley
that killed General Garnett. It took a court case to decide where the monument would be placed. While the association admitted that parts of the
72nd had indeed moved forward to the stone fence, it was not as an organized unit. A series of witnesses took the witness stand, each often giving
conflicting testimony. In the end, the Court of Common Pleas of Adams
County sided with the association in 1889, and the 72nd's monument was
to be placed farther up the ridge. An appeal was filed, and the Pennsylvania Supreme Court overturned the original verdict in 1890, saying that the
regiment did its greatest fighting within twenty feet of the stone fence. The
monument, which shows a zouave holding the barrel of his musket upright
to hit an unseen enemy, now stands close to the stone fence.

Several years after the battle, Colonel Devereux of the 19th Massachusetts recalled Webb saying immediately after the repulse that the 72nd
would receive a "severe scolding" for its behavior. Given Webb's admitted
difficulty in getting the 72nd to charge the enemy at the stone fence, and his
anger expressed after the battle, some statements in his official report are
curious: "The Seventy–second Pennsylvania Volunteers were ordered up to
hold the crest, and advanced to within 40 paces of the enemy's line." Later in
the report, he complimented the regiment by writing, "The Seventy–second
Pennsylvania Volunteers fought steadily and persistently..." After the war,
Webb tried to amend his statement by adding, "the portion of the 72nd volunteers near me remained steadily in their position, a little retired from the

Philadelphia Brigade head-
quarter's flag flown during
the battle of Gettysburg.

Archives of the Union
League of Philadelphia

crest, and fired at the advancing enemy." This too does not truly convey the strong feelings of frustration that he described during his court testimony. Toward the end of his testimony, he was asked by the lawyers for the 72nd, if he had "ever seen anything that approached cowardism in this regiment?" Obviously flabbergasted at the question, Webb, bluntly testified, "I have nothing in my mind that would question their bravery and I never have had." Parts of his testimony suggest otherwise.[22]

In addition to speaking positively about the 72nd in his after-battle report, Webb tried to put a positive face on other individuals and units whose behavior could have been criticized. For example, in describing Colonel Smith's actions on July 3, he never mentioned the regiment leaving the stone fence but instead wrote, "This disposition of his troops was most important. Colonel Smith showed true military intelligence on the field." No one could have criticized the actions of the 69th, but just in case someone tried, he wrote, "The cover in its front was not well built, and it lost many men lying on the ground; still, I saw none retire from the fence.[23]

Two weeks after the battle, Webb continued to sing the praises of the 69th. In a letter to his father on July 17, 1863, he wrote, "The 69th lost all its field officers. It obeyed orders. After the Rebs were inside the fence I went to them and told them to fire to front and rear and to a man they replied that I could count on them." The euphoria began to wane the following month, when Webb wrote to Pennsylvania Governor Curtin, "...it is impossible to govern 'Irish Regiments' when the Officers do not belong to a more intelligent class..."

Webb emerged as one of the heroes of the battle, ultimately receiving the Congressional Medal of Honor for his feats. Yet, two weeks after the battle, Webb's insecurities were evident when he wrote to his father that because of his actions, he had finally won the confidence of his men. He also boasted that men never fought better than his.

The repulse came at a very high cost to the Philadelphia Brigade. The brigade, which numbered about 862 men (without the 106th) lost 418 men or 49%. The specific breakdown was: 69th=121; 71st=100; and 72nd=197. A loss of almost 50% is tremendous, but when added to the second day's losses, the brigade's totals for the battle were 121 killed, 383 wounded, and 41 captured for a total of 545 or a total of 45% of the brigade's effectives. The brigade was now a mere skeleton of its former self, numbering only 660 men. The bruised, but not beaten, 69th could only muster 115 men after the battle.[24]

Despite their high losses, the men realized the magnitude of the victory and those who were not killed or wounded gave thanks for their good fortune. John Lynch of the 106th wrote home on July 5, "With what gratitude I feel towards All Mighty God for his marvelous protecting care which he has shown toward me in this last engagement. It seems almost incredible after going through with what I have in the last two days that I am yet spared—not a scratch..."[25]

That night, the men were issued three days' rations. About midnight, a drenching rain fell that continued for several days. Not only did it saturate the men, it also reduced the hardtack to a pulpy consistency that even the hungriest of men would not eat. Each man slept that night with several loaded guns by his side. The following day, the brigade continued burying the dead. Sergeant William Burns, a veteran of many battles, merely wrote, "Shocking sights." On July 5, the men heard the welcome news that Lee had begun his retreat back toward Virginia. Ordered into line, the pursuit began.

Leaving the battlefield was a relief because, as one man wrote, the "stench was awful and sickening." After marching three miles, the column halted for the night at Two Taverns. The men remained here on the 6th, and the march continued the following morning at 5 a.m. No food was available, so when the column reached Taneytown, Maryland, they were permitted to forage. William Burns reported in his diary, "Plenty to eat. Fresh bread, shortcake, eggs, butter, and plenty of meat. Lived like a fighting cock."

The II Corps left camp between 4 and 5 a.m. on July 8 and marched five miles in a heavy rain toward Frederick. During one of the rest stops, General Webb informed the men of the fall of Vicksburg. Despite the fact that they were wet and muddy, cheering erupted from the ranks. Sergeant Burns recorded in his diary, "Cheered for the first time in a year." The march seemed a bit easier now, as the prospects for victory seemed bright. With the torrential rains, the roads were rapidly becoming impassable, so the column was ordered to march through the fields, which soon became almost as bad as the road. The route took them through Bruceville, Pine Creek, and Woodsboro, that day. The rain finally stopped in the afternoon, and the column halted for the night at 4 p.m. near Walkersville on the banks of the Monocacy River. While the twenty-mile march that day had exhausted the men, many could not resist the temptation of a cleansing bath in the river to rid themselves of the dirt, grim, and lice that plagued them. The march began the next day, July 9, at 6 a.m. and the column reached Frederick two hours later. Making themselves as presentable as possible, the column marched through the town with bands playing and flags waving. Sergeant Burns recorded in his diary that night, "...full of pretty well dressed girls who seem to like the soldiers. Had a pie." After a continuous march, which took them through Jefferson and Burkittville, they stopped to camp for the night at 5 p.m. Actually, their leaders had other plans for them, for after about an hour of preparing their fires and beds, orders were issued to reform the column and continue the march. After crossing the South Mountain passes at Turner's Gap, they finally camped for the night near Rohrersville, after a march of twenty-two miles.

A number of men experienced difficulty keeping up during these long marches in extreme heat. The move south continued the next day, July 10, at 5 a.m. as the troops marched through Locust Grove and Keedysville. The column stopped for the night near Tilghman, after "only" a twelve-mile march.

Soon after striking out toward Williamsport on July 11, the column ran into some rebels, so the brigade formed into line of battle on the left of the V Corps. The 72nd was sent forward to support the skirmishers, but nothing developed. The brigade remained here with the rest of the division until sometime between 11 p.m. and midnight, when they were rushed to a position two miles away, and reformed in line of battle. They remained here until daylight, when they were moved back about a mile. Despite the torrential rains that began that afternoon, the brigade was ordered to change its position three additional times before they finally went into camp for the night. The II Corps' First Division was now on their left and the Third Division on their right. Skirmish fire could be heard throughout the day. On the evening of July 12, breastworks were dug and occupied on the evening of July 13. But the next day they were ordered forward about three miles toward Falling Waters, where the rebel rear guard was stationed. Along with their normal rations, the men were issued whiskey which helped them to forget how wet, muddy, and miserable they were.[26]

Heavy rains had swelled the Potomac River, preventing Lee from crossing. In an unenviable position with his back to the river, he ordered his men to construct breastworks and waited for the river to fall. Back in Washington, Lincoln was furious with Meade. A great victory had been won at Gettysburg, Vicksburg had fallen, and now a swift move by Meade could end the war. But Meade did not attack Lee, and the war dragged on for almost two additional years.

On July 14, Sergeant Burns recorded in his diary, "Heard that the rebs skedaddle. After them on the double quick." The Philadelphia Brigade, along with the rest of the II Corps, advanced that day to near Williamsport, and the next day, they marched seventeen miles through Downsville, Bakersville, Sharpsburg, and camped within three miles of Sandy Hook. That day, the men had the opportunity to observe the now abandoned rebel breastworks. Burns wrote disparagingly, "They were poor affairs and could have been easily taken."

The march began the next day at 7 a.m., and after marching four miles, the column came within sight of Harper's Ferry. Clothes were issued to the men while they camped here. The 17th brought a welcome reprieve from the long marches, as the men were permitted to remain in camp. The unrelenting rain continued to make life miserable, however. Perhaps realizing that they had erred in "wasting" a day, the officers ordered the men up at 2 a.m. on July 18, but orders to begin the march did not arrive until 6 a.m. Passing through Sandy Hook, they crossed the Potomac and Shenandoah Rivers and entered the Shenandoah Valley, camping near Hillsboro at 2 p.m.

Realizing that Lee had successfully made his escape, the Union leaders eased up on the men. Except for July 20, when they guarded a wagon train and marched fifteen miles, most of the marches were now fairly short (July 19, five miles; July 21, rested; July 22, ten miles). This changed on July 23, when they were roused before daylight, left camp at 4 a.m., and rushed fifteen miles toward Manassas Gap to support the III Corps which was skirmishing with the enemy. The 71st led the II Corps. After the threat was over, some of the men stealthily left their units to forage. Sergeant Burns noted, "Had a bully supper of ham, mutton, and butter. Nearly dead carrying it!" However, some were caught with their illegal bounty. "Five men of Co. H were drummed around camp for getting caught by the Provost Guard for killing pigs, sheep and chickens. Our colonel let the men keep what they brought into camp," Burns wrote. After returning to their original positions on July 24, the corps marched nineteen miles to White Plains on July 25, and reached within three miles of Warrenton Junction the next day, after a twenty-mile march. The heat continued unabated. Sergeant Burns recorded in his diary, "Fifteen men died on this march from the heat. General Hays under arrest for overmarching the men when there was no occasion for it. Damn him."[27]

Because of the heat, and the fact that Lee had gotten away, the II Corps remained here until 5 p.m. on July 30, when they made a ten-mile march to Elk Run, which they reached at about 11 p.m. Except for a six-mile march on July 31, and a shift of camp on August 4, the troops spent almost the entire month of August near Morrisville, about six miles from Kelly's Ford, on the Rappahannock River. From the time the troops left Falmouth on June 15, until July 31, the Philadelphia Brigade had marched over 450 miles.[28]

Alexander Webb's headquarters after the battle of Gettysburg. Webb is purported to be standing in the left of the picture.

Photographic History of the Civil War

CHAPTER 15

THE FALL 1863 CAMPAIGNS AND WINTER QUARTERS

Because of the losses at Gettysburg, General Webb temporarily commanded the Second Division and Lieutenant Colonel William Curry of the 106th commanded the Philadelphia Brigade. The 69th was commanded by Captain Thomas Kelly, the 71st by Lieutenant Colonel Charles Kochersperger, the 72nd by Major Samuel Roberts, and the 106th by Captain John Breidenbach.[1]

The brigade rested during the month of August 1863. The men were exhausted. The 106th's historian wrote, "...for over seventy days had we been marching day after day, with hardly any rest, on short rations, scarcely any clothes; some in our brigade actually marching in their undershirt and drawers, many barefoot or with only an apology for a shoe..."

It was also a time when the officers strived to re-instill discipline. Increasingly concerned about the amount of unauthorized foraging, Webb ordered assembly sounded on August 1, and had the men "stand on their arms" until the absentees returned from their foraging trips. On August 21, the entire division was assembled to witness the execution of a deserter from the 71st. Sergeant Burns of the 71st recorded in his diary, "He was not killed at the first volley. When two of the firing party advanced right over him and put him out of his misery. He bore himself bravely and died like a soldier."

August 31 brought an end to this period of inactivity. Leaving their camp near Kelly's Ford at 4 a.m., the division marched for about twelve hours, covering nineteen miles. Passing through Grove Church, and Hartwood Church on its way to Banks' Ford, the brigade was ordered to resist a crossing of the river by rebel cavalry. The report was false, but the troops remained here until September 3, when at 5 o'clock, they were ordered to return to Kelly's Ford, arriving there at 1:00 a.m. the next day. Stuart's rebel cavalry were active during this period, as were local guerrillas. Sergeant Burns of the 71st wrote disparagingly in his diary, "All the deadbeats in camp doing guard duty for fear of the guerrillas by order of our brave quartermaster."[2]

The brigade was back on the march on September 12, when it left camp at 11 a.m. and marched in a drenching rain to Rappahannock Station, arriving there at 4 p.m. The intent of this march was to support a cavalry movement against Stuart's troopers. At six o'clock the next morning, the corps began its march to Brandy Station, arriving before noon. The next three days the brigade performed provost duty in Culpeper.

Leaving town on September 17, the brigade marched to Raccoon Ford on the Rapidan River, where they relieved Kilpatrick's cavalry division on the picket line. The Philadelphians were outraged when they were fired on by the opposing pickets, thus breaking the unwritten truce. They soon learned, however, that Kilpatrick's cavalrymen had been issued new Sharp's repeating carbines, and the troopers had used the Confederates across the river for target practice. The rebs returned the favor. When the Philadelphia Brigade arrived, they heard the rebels on the other side of the river yell out to them, "Lay down Yanks; we are going to fire on the cavalry as they are relieved." With the offending cavalry gone, the peace typically associated with the picket lines was restored.

A considerable number of new replacements arrived, but they proved to be of little help in restoring the numbers of the army. Many promptly deserted, and most of those remaining were medically unfit for army service. The executions for desertion continued. William Burns recorded in his diary on October 9, "One of the 59th New York was shot for desertion. While they were digging his grave his pardon arrived." Not all deserters were shot, however. The hair on half the head of one deserter was shaved off, his head was branded with the letter "D," and he was marched through the camp between two guards while the drum corps walked behind him playing the "Rogue's March."

Relieved by units of the VI Corps on October 5, the division marched back to Culpeper the next morning. Reveille was sounded early on October 11, and by 3 a.m. the brigade was on the road for the eighteen-mile march to Bealton Station. Lee had crossed the Rapidan and in response, the cautious Meade pulled the army back behind the Rappahannock. Reconsidering his actions, Meade recrossed his troops to face Lee. The Philadelphia Brigade crossed about noon on October 12, and formed a line of battle as it advanced toward Brandy Station with the remainder of the II Corps. When within about a mile and a half of Brandy Station, the men were ordered to bivouac for the night. At least, that's what the men thought, but at 11 p.m. that night, they were roused and ordered back into line. Ascertaining that Lee had again slipped passed his right flank in a maneuver similar to the one that resulted in the Union fiasco at Second Bull Run, Meade quickly ordered a move north to protect Washington. Retracing its steps, the column arrived at Sulphur Springs about sunrise, where it stopped for breakfast. After the short break, the march continued to Warrenton Junction, where the men were given a much-needed rest for the night. The march of twenty-three miles had taken them about nineteen hours because of delays in front of them.[3]

The march resumed the next day, October 14, at 5 a.m. Reaching Catlett's Station, the division formed into line of battle. Spying the Philadelphia Brigade, which was now commanded by Colonel Baxter, Meade ordered it to escort the ammunition train to Centreville. While detailing the 106th and 72nd to guard the flanks, Baxter ordered the other two regiments to march with the trains.

As a result of being detached, the Philadelphia Brigade missed the sharp and highly decisive battle at Bristoe Station. General Gouverneur K. Warren, who was in command of the II Corps in Hancock's absence, wrote in his report, "Where these divisions (the Second and Third) halted, the trains passed on to the rear toward Centreville, our appointed place of concentration, guarded by the Second Brigade, Second Division, under Colonel Baxter, which was thus thrown out of the more brilliant operations which closed the day at Bristoe."

The battle developed when Confederate commander A. P. Hill, seeing Meade retreating across the river, threw several brigades against the bridgehead without first reconnoitering. He did not see the strongly placed II Corps, which administered a swift and decisive repulse of Hill's men.[4]

As the rear guard fight at Bristoe Station was raging, Meade concentrated the rest of his troops at Centreville. Realizing that he had lost the race, Lee slipped southward, tearing up the Orange and Alexandria Railroad, which was so critical to Meade's army. The Philadelphia Brigade rejoined the division near Bull Run on October 15. While Baxter continued to command the Philadelphia Brigade during this period, Joshua Owen, the brigade's former commander, received command of the Third Division's, Third Brigade, and Colonel Morehead of the 106th temporarily commanded the Division's Third Brigade.

The Second Corps, and the rest of Meade's army remained quietly camped around Centreville until October 19, when it was finally ordered after Lee's army. The division reached Manassas Junction by the end of the day, and Auburn the following day, going into camp at about 11 p.m., after a sixteen-mile march. After a rest on the 21st and 22nd, the column marched eight miles to Warrenton Junction, and remained here until November 7 while the Orange and Alexandria Railroad was repaired. Up at 5 a.m. and leaving camp two hours later on November 7, the corps marched along the railroad to Bealton, then marched overland toward the Rappahannock River, camping about half a mile from it.

Taking position behind the Rappahannock River, Lee grimly waited for Meade to take the offensive. For his part, Meade was content to merely go into winter quarters now that October was coming to a close. Lincoln, however, had other ideas. Increasingly frustrated with Meade's seeming disinterest in engaging and destroying Lee's army, he compared the army's movements immediately after Gettysburg to "an old woman shooing geese across a creek." Lincoln insisted that Meade launch another offensive campaign before the onset of winter. In response, Meade developed a plan similar to Hooker's, about six months earlier—cross the Rappahannock and crush Lee's right flank. While sending his left column toward Kelly's Ford, Meade sent his right to capture the bridgehead at Rappahannock Station. On November 7, his right column, under Sedgwick, virtually destroyed two Confederate brigades, and crossed the river.[5]

Realizing the vulnerability of his position, Lee pulled his army behind the Rapidan River on November 8. That same day, the Second Division crossed Kelly's Ford, formed line of battle and advanced—but the Confederates had already left the area and their winter quarters. William Burns wrote in his diary, "Halted where the rebels had been building their winter quarters. They must have left in a hurry for there was a good deal property left behind. Got some fresh beef." The huts were log cabin affairs that measured fourteen feet by six feet, each with a fireplace. It was clear that the rebels had left in a hurry, as the members of the Philadelphia Brigade helped themselves to the griddle cakes in the skillets, and the personal possessions left behind.

The march after Lee's army resumed about 2 p.m. that afternoon. The II Corps reached Brandy Station on November 10, and remained there until November 26. Thinking that this would be their winter quarters, the men began erecting their own log huts. Disciplining of deserters continued. William Burns recorded in his diary on November 23, "One of Baxter's men—72nd PA—had his head shaved and drummed around the camp and to serve four years on the public works for desertion. Since been pardoned and returned to his company."

On November 24, the men were awakened at 4 a.m. and ordered to break camp. After marching about a quarter of a mile through a driving rainstorm, they were stopped and ordered to about-face and return to camp. Sergeant Burns angrily wrote in his diary, "Everything wet. Meade stuck in the mud." Thanksgiving was spent in camp. The meal included, "Pork- raw; crackers- very hard; coffee- good," according to Burns.[6]

The men were again roused at 4 a.m. on November 26, and told to strike their tents. Leaving camp at 6:30 a.m., the column stopped after an hour, and the men had breakfast. The men reached the Rapidan River at Germanna Ford later that morning, but did not cross until about 4 p.m. Marching another four miles, or a total of thirteen for the day, the brigade went into bivouac. Because Colonel Baxter was away, Colonel Arthur Devereux of the 19th Massachusetts temporarily commanded the brigade.

The march along the Orange Plank Road continued early the next morning. General Hays' division struck the enemy near Robertson's Tavern, and at 11:30 a.m., the Philadelphia Brigade, which was leading the Second Division, was ordered to enter the woods on the right of the road and capture a ridge. Knowing that rebel troops were just ahead, Devereux threw the 72nd, led by Lieutenant Colonel Hesser, forward as skirmishers. Behind the 72nd, marched the rest of the brigade in line of battle. Reaching their destination, the men were ordered to lie down in the cold underbrush. As the 72nd continued forward, firing broke out. Initially, the Pennsylvanians were successful in pushing back General Harry Hays' Louisiana Tigers, but some confusion occurred in the ranks, possibly because of the dense woods. Seeing his men about to break for the rear, Hesser drew his sword and was in the process of ordering them to charge, when he was shot through the head, probably dying instantly. Realizing the seriousness of the situation, Webb rushed the 106th to the aid of the 72nd. Rebel troops could be seen on the left of the road, so Webb quickly sent the 71st across the road to confront this threat. At the same time, Webb sent the 69th to the right to stabilize that part of the line. The firing continued to intensify along the right of the line, forcing Webb to bring up three regiments from the First Brigade to reinforce the line held by the 69th, 72nd, and 106th. These reinforcements helped shore up the line, and

Lieutenant Colonel Theodore Hesser, 72nd Pennsylvania, killed during the Mine Run campaign, 1863

Massachusetts Commandery Military Order of the Loyal Legion and USAMHI

only sporadic firing occurred during the remainder of the afternoon. Nevertheless, the situation did not look promising as the III Corps had not yet arrived to support them. Webb paid homage to Hesser and praised his regiment when he wrote in his report, "...Lieutenant-Colonel Hesser, a brave and efficient officer of the Seventy-second Pennsylvania, was killed while leading his regiment. Credit is due the Seventy-second for the manner in which they held a long skirmish line."

The brigade held this line until 6 p.m., when it was finally relieved. The men moved to the rear, stacked arms, and after a cold supper, went to sleep. According to William Burns, the Union troops fraternized with the enemy, who were still nearby. "Rebs and us talking. Wanting each other to come from behind the trees. Men crowing and making all kinds of noises."[7]

The men were awakened and ordered to form into line of battle at 5 a.m. on November 28. Three corps, I, II, and VI, slowly advanced, expecting to encounter Confederate troops. Instead, they found the rebel's abandoned works. Advancing almost two miles through dense woods, the Union line finally encountered rebel skirmishers near Mine Run. It did not take a trained military eye to realize that the rebel fortifications, 3/4 of a mile behind the skirmish line, were too strong for a frontal attack. In his after-battle report, Meade described the appearance of the western bank of Mine Run as being "crowned with infantry parapets, abatis and epaulements for bat-teries." To the men, it looked like Fredericksburg all over again, only worse.

General Warren suggested a new idea to Meade—permit him to take his corps on a long detour around the enemy's right flank, and attack his flank and rear. Meade readily accepted his subordinate's idea, and sent him a division from the VI Corps. Warren began the move at daybreak on November 29, with the Second Division bringing up the rear. The troops arrived on the enemy's flank about two hours before dark, after marching fifteen miles that day. During the march, the men passed a dead guerilla along the road, and farther along, Sergeant Burns saw signs of a fight. "Saw two of our men dead and stripped naked," which was probably the work of some desperate Confederates needing clothing.

Realizing that an immediate attack could be successful, Warren be-gan making preparations. Colonel Francis Walker, II Corps' historian wrote that the Confederate works were "slight and thinly occupied...success seemed to be within our grasp, and so it would have been but for one circumstance—the day was nearly spent." Warren was thus forced to bide his time until the morning. Confederate reinforcements poured into the works in the darkness, and the Union soldiers could hear the Confederates hard at work strengthening their fortifications. Warren ordered his men to make extra campfires, "my object being to make a demonstration of heavy force."[8]

Meade's new plan was to attack both of Lee's flanks simultaneously. Warren's attack on Lee's right was to begin at 8 a.m. and Sedgwick's at-tack on the left, an hour later. Warren ordered his men awakened at 2 a.m. on November 30, marched about two miles at the double-quick, and formed into line of battle. In addition to his own three divisions, Warren had two divi-sions from the III Corps, and a division from the VI Corps, or a total of 28,000 men. Warily watching these preparations from behind the breastworks, about 600 yards away, were about the same number of Confederates.

Lying in line of battle in front of the Confederate works, the tempera-ture fell below zero, chilling the men to the bone as no campfires were permitted. Water froze solid in the canteens, and the pickets had to be relieved every half hour to prevent them from freezing to death.

Webb's attack was to be made in two lines—the Philadelphia Brigade was in the first. When the attack was ordered at 8 a.m., they were not to fire until told to do so. Each man was to carry a blanket with him, and if shot, he was to wrap himself in it to keep from freezing to death until help arrived. Any unwounded man going to the rear was to be shot. These were certainly not reassuring words.[9]

When the dawn finally broke, the veterans of two and a half years of war knew they would never see home again. John Burns wrote, "It would have been a desperate undertaking." However, a hopeful rumor now made the rounds, as related by Burns, "...the rebs in front of us were North Caro-lina troops and that when we charged on them they would surrender." Few probably believed this rumor, because the brigade historian wrote that,

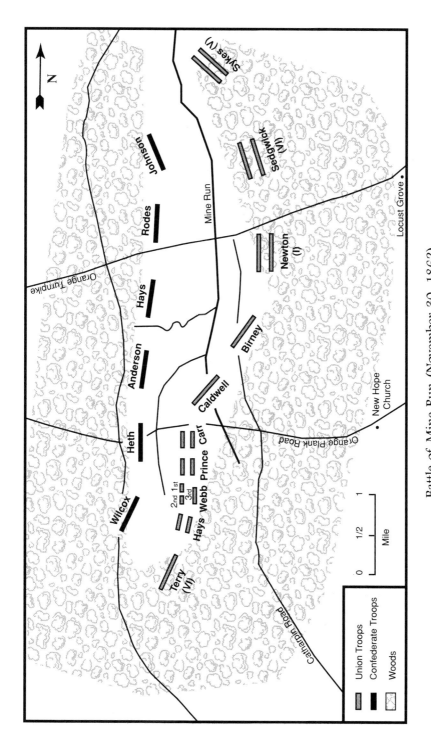

Battle of Mine Run (November 30, 1862)

Union Troops
Confederate Troops
Woods

Mile
0   1/2   1

Many had written their names on pieces of paper and fastened them to their garments; others had torn strips of underclothing to be used for bandages, and some, with a semi-ludicrous thoughtfulness, had filled their pockets with hard-tack, so that for a time at least they would not suffer with hunger if wounded or captured.

The men could see at least sixteen guns in place, and rebel infantry were well positioned to pour a frontal and flank fire on the attackers. A 400-yard-wide open plain in front of the Confederate works made survival doubtful.

With his preparations completed, Warren sat in front of a campfire, musing on the future, and finally told his aides, "If I succeed to-day I shall be the greatest man in the army; if I don't, all my sins will be remembered." Warren closely examined the Confederate works just after dawn. Calculating the strength fortifications and the fact that it would take at least eight minutes for his men to cross the open space, he realized that the attack had virtually no chance of succeeding. Too far from Meade's headquarters to seek advice, and almost eight o'clock, he took it upon himself to cancel the attack.

When Meade heard the cannonade begin, but no subsequent small arms fire, he suspected that something was wrong. A courier galloping into his camp carried the news from Warren, "[The enemy's] position and strength seem so formidable in my present front that I advise against making the attack here. The full light of the sun shows me that I cannot succeed." Clearly disappointed, Meade halted all offensive actions.[10]

No one told the men that the attack had been canceled, so they remained in position for most of the day, dreading what was in store for them. A great sense of relief flooded over them when they finally learned that the charge was canceled. William Burns wrote, "Felt very thankful that we did not charge. If we had it would have been the last day of the Second Division." About dark, the brigade was moved back about 300 yards to a large, dense woods, where they were finally permitted to make fires. Remaining here all of December 1, they began constructing their own breastworks in the afternoon. Just as they were making themselves comfortable at about 9 o'clock that night, they received orders to pull back. "Everything was muffled, and in order to still further conceal our movement from the enemy, it was necessary that two men from each regiment should remain behind to keep up the fires...," wrote the 106th's historian.

After considering several options, Meade decided it was best to conclude offensive operations for the year, and go into winter quarters. The army reached the Rapidan River on December 2, and crossed at Culpeper Ford. After a brief break for breakfast, the army continued its march back to its old camps. Burns recorded in his diary, "Put up tents and went to sleep. Men completely used up on the march. 23 hours."

So ended the Mine Run campaign. The Philadelphia Brigade's losses during this campaign were light, 21 officers and men (69th=7; 71st=3; 72nd=10; and 106th=1).[11]

The Philadelphia Brigade spent the next three and a half months near Stevensburg. Profiting from two years of experience, the men made themselves comfortable by constructing cabins. A sawmill nearby was kept in continual operation to provide boards for the men. After completing their huts, the men built a large building near General Warren's headquarters, which the officers used for large parties, and the men used for plays and concerts. The building was the site of a large ball held in honor of Washington's Birthday.

On Christmas Day, the men of the Philadelphia Brigade were invited to their headquarters, where much-welcomed whiskey was served in large quantities. Before long, fights broke out among the troops. Most of the men were content to watch, pleased that the camp monotony was broken, even for a day. The day after Christmas, the 106th received a new silk national flag that replaced the torn and tattered one they had carried since entering the war. The regiment's historian wrote, "During the two years and our months of its service, it never drooped before the enemy, except when its bearer was shot down, and then to be quickly held aloft by the next man..."[12]

While in camp, the 72nd lost another commander when Lieutenant Colonel Henry Cook was arrested for "between the hours of taps and reveille, permit and encourage an assemblage of officers and enlisted men in and around his tent...carousing, shouting, cheering, and singing...disturbing the quietness of the camp and vicinity, to the prejudice of good order and military discipline." The court found him guilty and he received a dishonorable discharge.

The quiet of winter camp was abruptly broken at 4:30 a.m. on February 6, when the men were roused and told that they would leave camp at 7 o'clock that morning. Marching to Morton's Ford, the division, with the Philadelphia Brigade in the lead, crossed the Rapidan, driving the enemy's pickets before them. The Philadelphia Brigade led the advance. The division halted a short distance beyond the ford and remained here during the night, returning to camp the next day. The men later learned that the movement was merely a feint to help distract attention from General Ben Butler's movements on the Peninsula.

Not wishing to lose the veterans whose terms of enlistment were about to expire, the government began offering incentives for the men to re-enlist for another three years. Each would receive a $625 bounty and a month's furlough. Many men from the 69th and 106th took advantage of this offer, and on March 14, left for a late-winter reprieve from army life, returning a month later. Most of the men of the 69th re-enlisted, and out of the 229 men present in the 106th, 104 re-enlisted (45%). During their visit to Philadelphia, the green flag of the 69th was retired and a new one replaced it.

St. Patrick's Day brought the usual fun and games, including horse races and hurdle jumping competitions. Several changes occurred during this period. Back home in Philadelphia, the 69th marched as a unit to mass, hoping that this display would encourage their countrymen to enlist in the unit. Few did.

Second State Color of the 69th Pennsylvania carried
from November 1863 through the end of the war in 1865.

A new regiment, the 152nd New York, was added to the brigade on March 26. While swelling the brigade by an additional 500 men, it was not from Philadelphia, or even Pennsylvania, for that matter. General Gibbon returned from his convalescent leave on April 6 to resume command of his division. His temporary replacement, Alexander Webb, was assigned command of the First Brigade, much to the dismay of the Philadelphia Brigade who had come to respect him. Their old commander, Joshua Owen, who had been commanding the Third Brigade, would return to command the brigade. Many men were not overjoyed to welcome him back.

One of the founding regimental commanders, Colonel Turner Morehead of the 106th, tendered his resignation from the army during the early spring. Although he had temporarily commanded the Third Brigade during the Mine Run campaign, he was again passed over for permanent brigade command. Feeling unappreciated, and angry over his treatment, he felt it best to leave the army and return to Philadelphia. The historian of the regiment recalled the parting, "The men were drawn up in line without arms and he attempted to address them, but succeeded in saying only a few words, being overcome by his feelings in parting with his men; the men gave him three hearty cheers, and, shaking hands with the officers and some of the men, he left." On April 14, Major John Stover was promoted to the rank of colonel and assigned command of the 106th. Captain William Davis of the 69th was similarly promoted and assigned to command that regiment.

While these changes were important to the men of the Philadelphia Brigade, a more important change was made on March 10, when President Lincoln assigned General U. S. Grant to command of all of the Union's armies. He arrived at the army's winter quarters in late March, and held a grand view of the entire army on April 22.

On April 30, the brigade filed a report listing a paper strength of 2,509, but 1,568 or 63% actually present. The breakdown by regiment was (total:present): 69th (342:324); 71st (589:316); 72nd (631:295); 106th (429:238); and 152nd New York (518:385). The brigade would start the new campaigning season with four veteran regiments and a raw one, at a strength it had not seen for over a year.

In preparation for the campaign, the men of the 152nd New York received new accoutrements that replaced their old ones marked with the letters, "I.C.," which the men translated to mean "I'm condemned."[13]

CHAPTER 16

THE WILDERNESS AND SPOTSYLVANIA

Like his predecessors, Grant requested additional troops to defeat Lee. Lincoln responded by sending additional units which swelled the army to over 120,000 men. Lee could muster but 65,000 men against Grant.

A reorganization of the army added a division to the II Corps: Francis Barlow commanded the First, John Gibbon the Second, David Birney the Third, and George Mott the Fourth. The Second Division retained its three brigades: Alexander Webb commanded the First, Joshua Owen commanded the Philadelphia Brigade, and Samuel Carroll commanded the Third.

Grant planned to move the army south in two columns. Crossing the Rapidan River at Germanna Ford, the V and VI Corps would march southward along the Orange Turnpike. The II Corps' route was longer—after crossing the river at Ely's Ford, it would march along the Pamunky Road, south of, and parallel to, the other two corps. Caught between these two pincers, Lee would be destroyed. To achieve its goal, the army had to first traverse the "Wilderness," which extended for five miles. The brigade's historian described the area as a "labyrinth of forests, in many places filled with tangled underbrush, penetrated by few roads, and these for the most part narrow and easily obstructed."

Recalling the Mine Run campaign, when it took nearly thirty hours for Lee to concentrate his forces, Meade was confident that his army could clear the Wilderness without tangling with the enemy. Meade's officers were not so sure. Gibbon ordered the train to be in front of the column and "at every halt troops will be massed."[1]

Just before midnight on May 3, Hancock's men broke camp and began their spring campaign. Each man had been issued eight days of rations and was ordered to fill his canteen. An air of confidence permeated the army, as well as a knowledge that their enlistments would soon expire. For the 71st, this would come as early as June; the 106th would leave in September. It was with mixed emotions that the men left their winter quarters, which they had occupied for the longest period of the war.

Hancock's infantry column, preceded by John Gregg's cavalry division, reached Ely's Ford the next morning, and found the engineers putting the finishing touches on a pontoon bridge. Crossing at 9 a.m., they pushed ahead into the foreboding Wilderness. The day was hot, and the men's four months of inactivity took its toll. Soon a trail of overcoats, blankets, and other personal belongings could be seen strewn along the road as the men attempted to lighten their loads. Knowing the desperate condition of Lee's army, the men took special care to tear these items into shreds to make them unusable by the enemy.

Hancock's column reached the Chancellorsville House at about three o'clock that afternoon, and camped for the night. Some of the units had marched twenty-five miles from their winter camp, and the men were exhausted. All around them were reminders of the horrific battle of Chancellorsville that had taken place here the year before.

Signals from Confederate observation posts told the Union high command that Lee was aware of their movements. Still, they remained confident of victory. Although thwarted during his summer and fall campaigns, the men knew that Lee had plenty of fight left in him. Realizing the odds against him, Lee decided the best way to neutralize Grant was to engage him in the Wilderness. Ewell's corps was quickly sent marching up the Orange Turnpike—the same road being used by the V and VI Corps. Hill's corps took the parallel Orange Plank Road. Lee's Third Corps, under James Longstreet, was far behind in Gordonsville, and would need time to reach the Wilderness.[2]

The Philadelphia Brigade arose at about 4 a.m. on May 5, and quickly gobbled down a breakfast of raw pork, hardtack, and coffee. The 106th led the brigade down the Catharpin Road, with one company thrown forward as an advance guard, and another deployed as flankers. Halting at Todd's Tavern at 9 a.m., the brigade was ordered into the woods on the left of the road where it remained for two hours. Vigilance was required because rebels were in the area. While waiting at the tavern, the II Corps was fired on several times, but no losses were incurred by the brigade.

To the south, the lead elements of Hill's corps were only a mile from the Brock and Orange Plank crossroads when Hancock realized that his troops would lose the race to this vital intersection. In response to this information, Meade dispatched George Getty's division of Sedgwick's corps to the crossroads, beating the Confederates by a short margin. At 11:30 a.m., Hancock ordered his troops rushed to the vital intersection to support Getty's troops who were now skirmishing with the enemy. He was also to capture Parker's Store, where he would link up with Warren's corps. Unfortunately, Hancock's men were still several hours away.

While drafting Hancock's orders at about 10:30 a.m., Meade also decided to launch an attack by his right wing, composed of Warren's and Sedgwick's corps. Several of Warren's officers balked at attacking until all of the divisions were deployed, and Sedgwick's men were up. Unable to wait any longer, the attack was finally made at about 1 p.m. Warren's divisions that made the attack were easily repelled by Ewell's corps with heavy losses. When Sedgwick's men finally arrived, they too were ordered to attack's Ewell's troops with similar results.[3]

Hancock's lead division, under General David Birney, arrived at the crossroads first, and began constructing breastworks. Right behind was Mott's division, kicking up dust as it marched along the dry roads. Despite the fact that only two of his divisions had arrived, Meade ordered Hancock to immediately attack. Getty strongly believed that it was prudent to wait until the remaining two divisions of the II Corps arrived. But he obeyed his orders to attack on both sides of the Orange Plank Road.

Facing Hancock's 17,000 men was Harry Heth's 6,500 men. Rushing forward, Getty's men were hit by a tremendous small arms fire, and driven back. The opposing forces could scarcely see each other through the smoke and dense thickets. Mott's division came up on their left, but they too were greeted by a hail of lead, and broke for the rear. One of its brigade commanders, in a broad understatement, wrote that, "Our division did not do well." Birney's division now advanced as well.

An impatient Hancock sat at the intersection of the Orange Plank and Brock Roads, trying to ascertain what was happening in his front. Soon, a throng of Mott's men stormed past, and it was all that he could do to get them to stop and reform. An officer from Getty's command informed him that the men were being hard-pressed, and almost out of ammunition. It was now 3 p.m., and it appeared that the critical crossroads would be lost. Looking frantically to the rear, he was overjoyed to see Gibbon's lead brigade swing into view. Gibbon wrote in his report of the battle,

> As the head of Webb's brigade came in sight of the firing, the enemy was close to the Brock road, firing rapidly upon our disordered troops. We were marching left in front, but there was no time to change the formation. The file closers were shifted to the right flank, and as the leading regiments came up they were faced to the left, and by their fire soon drove the enemy back, took possession of the road, and held it. As Owen's brigade arrived upon the ground it was posted on Webb's right.

Because Birney had a good grasp of the situation, Gibbon's division was temporarily put under his command. The continued resistance of Heth's division was rapidly wearing down the Federal troops, and the rebels were approaching the Brock Road. While Webb's brigade was left behind to continue strengthening the breastworks, Carroll's brigade was deployed north of the Orange Plank Road and the Philadelphia Brigade advanced to the south of it. Pushing slowly through the thickets, the two brigades passed remnants of other Federal units. Soon they could see the Confederates through the dense underbrush, and poured a destructive fire into them, halting their advance. The fighting now became confused, as the thickets and dense smoke prevented the antagonists from seeing each other. While his men were holding their own, Hancock did not think that they could push the rebels back. Around this time, Wilcox's Confederate division arrived to bolster Heth's line, and Barlow's division also entered the fray. Slowly, the Federal line pushed the Confederates back.

The historian of the 152nd New York, described what happened during the regiment's baptism of fire:

> We entered the woods, passing over the bodies of those who had fallen before. We forced a passage through the thick undergrowth, becoming separated and considerably mixed up...A sharp crackling of musketry and the whizzing of many bullets caused the men to stagger and fall. The attack was so sudden that it caused the line to waver...Instantly recovering, we began to fire at will, and poured volley after volley in the darkness of night. We fell back a few paces and formed the picket line.

The regiment lost a captain and five men in this short action.[4]

Nightfall brought an end to the hostilities. The II Corps had successfully defended the crossroads, but with their superior numbers, there should never have been a doubt. Other Federal units were arriving, and soon Hancock would have 33,000 men to throw against Hill's thin line.

Both Grant and Meade realized that better coordinated attacks would have spelled doom to Lee's army, and vowed that the next day would be different—four powerful Union corps would strike Lee's line simultaneously.

The night was long and horrific. Thousands of wounded men cried out in the darkness, but the opposing lines were so close to each other and the thickets so dense, that they could not be aided. The whippoorwills called out constantly, and the men interpreted the sound as "Grant will whip, Grant will whip." "It had the effect of instilling in the hearts of the men a confidence in our Great Commander, and a firm belief that a heavenly choir had been sent to cheer us on," wrote the 152nd New York's historian.

Hancock was too busy planning the next day's attack to interpret the whippoorwills around him. Four divisions in three parallel lines would move against Hill at first light. Birney's brigades, and one from Mott's division, formed the first line; Getty's division, and a second brigade from Mott's division, formed the second line; and Gibbon's division formed the third. Carroll's brigade occupied the north side of the Orange Plank Road; Owen's formed on the south side; and Webb's brigade formed the reserve behind them. To the right and almost perpendicular to Hancock was Wadsworth's four brigades, which were poised to hit Hill's flank while Hancock attacked its front.[5]

A signal gun sounded at 5 a.m. on May 6, and the attack columns surged forward. Incredibly, Hill and his division commanders had done nothing to re-form their lines or construct breastworks. The men were just too exhausted from fighting off overwhelming numbers of yankees the day before. Caught between two powerful wings, Hill's line was crushed and the survivors stampeded wildly for the rear. Because the Philadelphia Brigade was in the third line, it did not see much action, only dead and dazed rebels. As it moved forward, the men in Hancock's front lines also had difficulty seeing the Confederates, but they continued throwing volleys into the thickets as they moved forward. Reaching a small creek, the Union line was halted and men reformed.

As Hancock's men continued their advance, they were met by a heavy small arms fire. Confused by this sudden resistance, they pressed on, only to be stopped in their tracks by a series of tremendous volleys. Word passed from mouth to mouth that Longstreet's corps had now arrived and was in front of them. Hancock's first line melted away, and part of Getty's division in the second line tried to halt the Confederate advance. Outnumbered and about to be overrun, they were reinforced by Owen's and Carroll's brigades. The latter had already been roughed up in the initial attack, but had reformed. Throwing up makeshift breastworks, they were joined by the remnants of Mott's and Birney's divisions.

Despite the protection of the breastworks, the Philadelphia Brigade began sustaining casualties, including Lt. Col. Charles Kochersperger commanding the 71st and Colonel DeWitt Baxter of the 72nd. Other troops on both sides entered the fray. The brigade historian described the fighting during the morning hours:

> At no time...could there be seen a body of the enemy numbering fifty men, and yet heavy volleys of musketry sent the balls flying into and about our ranks. The line of fire in response to these attacks was indicated only by the direction which the shots were received.

About 10 a.m., the firing ceased. No additional reinforcements were available to either side, so the opposing forces were content with a stalemate.[6]

The quiet was soon broken when "without any apparent cause that could be seen from the position of the brigade, the troops on our left began to give way, and commenced falling back towards the Brock Road" wrote the brigade's historian. Unbeknownst to the Philadelphians, four Confederate brigades had stealthily marched along an unfinished railroad cut and fell on Hancock's unsuspecting left flank. Continuing, the historian wrote, "Those pressing past...did not seem to be demoralized in manner, nor did they present the appearance of soldiers moving under orders, but rather of a throng of armed men who were returning dissatisfied from a muster."

Realizing their danger, Owen's men joined the rearward movement, finally stopping when they reached the breastworks along Brock Road. Here they joined a sea of blue-uniformed soldiers, still full of fight. So jumbled were the units, that soldiers from Robertson's division of the V Corps formed on the brigade's right and units from Getty's division of the VI Corps formed on their left. The Philadelphia Brigade's historian wrote, "The color-sergeants, as they arrived, placed their flags on the defenses, while the men, with faces begrimed with powder, but showing no anxiety for the result of the coming attack, calmly fell into their places and awaited the enemy." Before long, Longstreet's men appeared, but did not mount a serious attack.

Just after 4 p.m., Lee foolishly launched a frontal assault against the Federal breastworks. "Our men were but little exposed, and their position gave them an opportunity to repay the severe handling they had received

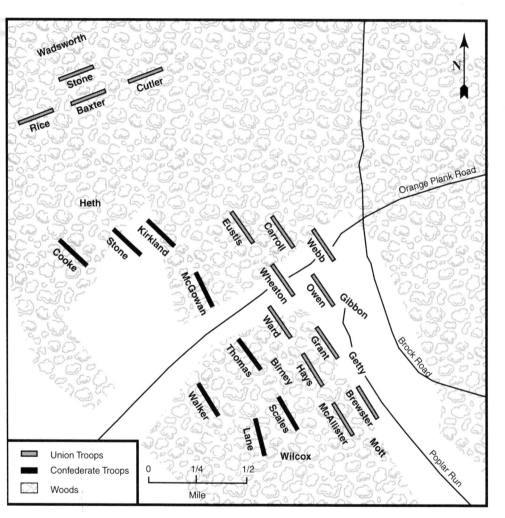

Battle of the Wilderness (May 6, 1864, 4:30 a.m.)

in the early morning," wrote one of the men of the Philadelphia Brigade. The assault was repelled with heavy losses to the attackers. However, the woods to the left of the brigade caught on fire and spread to the breast-works, forcing the Federal troops to pull back from them. The Confeder-ates were quick to take advantage of this opportunity—some South Carolinians literally jumped through the flames to attack the retreating Fed-eral line. The Federal artillery which, up to this time, had played only a minor role in the battle, now opened on the Southern troops, sweeping them from the breastworks. The Union infantry also turned back toward the Confederates and drove them from the burning breastworks, ending the bloody battle of the Wilderness on the Union left.

The losses were high. Meade lost in excess of 17,500 men, while Lee lost at least 11,000 irreplaceable men. The Philadelphia Brigade lost 229 men. The breakdown by regiment was: 69th=19; 71st=44; 72nd=57; 106th=58; and 152nd New York=51. Compared to Webb's First Brigade's losses of 460 and Carroll's Third Brigade's losses of 559, the Philadelphia Brigade's losses were fairly modest, and reflect the fact that they fought in a reserve role for much of the battle, often behind breastworks.[7]

The opposing sides warily watched each other the following day, Sat-urday, May 7. Realizing that nothing could be gained by renewing the ac-tion against Lee in the Wilderness, Grant ordered Meade to move his army around the right flank of his opponent. This would put the army between Lee and Richmond, forcing an engagement at a place of Grant's choos-ing—Spotsylvania Court House. Orders were issued for Warren's V Corps to move south at 8:30 p.m. that night along the Brock Road, while Sedgwick's VI Corps moved along the Orange Turnpike. Hancock would follow Warren's men southward. Realizing that something was afoot, Lee ordered his I Corps to move south to block any Federal advance.

Warren's delays prevented Hancock's men from beginning their march until after daylight on May 8. Barlow's division led the march, followed by Gibbon's and then Birney's division. One of Gibbon's men recalled that they began the move at 7 a.m. Todd's Tavern was reached at about 10 a.m., where the corps was halted and deployed. About 2 p.m., Gibbon's division was detached and sent to join Warren's corps which had encoun-tered rebel troops near Spotsylvania. When Gibbon arrived, he deployed his men on Warren's right flank—Carroll's brigade connected with Warren, next came Owen's, and Webb's First Brigade formed on the right of the division. Hancock's remaining divisions arrived the following day, and formed on Gibbon's right flank.[8]

While visiting Gibbon's position at about 3 p.m. on May 9, Grant and Meade spied what appeared to be an unprotected Confederate wagon train on the opposite side of the Po River, and ordered its capture. Crossing the river during the early evening hours, the II Corps drove away the Confeder-ate pickets. But night was rapidly descending, so Hancock decided to break off the pursuit. When dawn broke on May 10, the wagon train had already reached the safety of the Confederate lines. Gibbon's and Birney's divisions recrossed the Po at about ten o'clock that morning, and eventually returned to their old positions. Owen was ordered to leave behind two regiments, the 69th and 72nd, both under the command of Major William Davis, to guard a bridge over the Ta River.

Later that day, Davis was alarmed to learn that the First Division had crossed the river, and enemy troops were advancing on his right and rear. Realizing the danger, Davis ordered his men to double-quick three miles back to the Po River, where they crossed the river to safety. Unfortunately, part of one company of the 72nd lost its way, and was gobbled up by the advancing enemy.

Major (later Lieutenant Colonel) William Davis, 69th Pennsylvania
Donald Enders Collection, USAMHI

The other three regiments of the Philadelphia Brigade, along with the remainder of Gibbon's division, warily examined strongly defended Laurel Hill in front of them. Earthworks with an abatis of timber with sharpened branches had been constructed that were guarded by well-deployed cannon. Directly in front of them was a belt of dead cedars, which Gibbon described as, "filled with dead cedar trees, whose hard dry branches, projecting like so many bayonets from the stem, rendered the movement of a line of battle in any sort of order utterly impracticable."

The V Corps had been ordered to capture the works, but realizing that he could not carry them alone, Warren called for reinforcements, and Gibbon's division was sent. Carroll's brigade was on the left of the line, Webb's on the right, and the Philadelphia Brigade formed the reserve.

The attack began at about 5 p.m. that night, and was met by a terrific Confederate small arms and artillery fire. While a few of Carroll's men came close to the Confederate works, most never got very far before pulling back. Their commander described the fire from the two lines of Confederates behind the breastworks as "murderous." Webb wrote in his after battle report,

> This could hardly be termed a charge. Orders were sent to the brigade to cheer when the division on my right, under General Crawford, did so, and to charge at once. The men had had time to examine the enemy's line. They had found it necessary to hug the ground very

closely for some hours, since the firing was severe. They had convinced themselves that the enemy was too strongly positioned to be driven out by assault, and this was evident in the attempt at a charge.

Incredibly, the Union high command ordered another attack at 7 p.m. This time, the Philadelphia Brigade, minus the 69th and 72nd, which had not yet returned from the Po River, took the place of Carroll's brigade. As the three regiments finally reached the open fields in front of the rebel works, their lines were blown apart by heavy artillery fire, and the men quickly withdrew. The Philadelphia Brigade's historian, later wrote in disgust,

> No officer of higher rank than a brigade commander had examined the approaches to the enemy's works on our front...The men had weighed the probabilities of success and decided that the attempt was hopeless. The advance along the line was made without enthusiasm, and it continued only a short distance, when a halt was made and firing commenced and continued for a brief period, when the while force fell back as suddenly as before.

Even after the war, the historian was frustrated and embarrassed by the day's events. "Some of the best troops...not only retired without any real attempt to carry the enemy's works, but actually retreated in confusion to a point far to the rear of the original line..." Gibbon admitted in his official report, "The only result of the two assaults was to kill and wound a large number of men, many of whom were burnt to death by the fierce conflagration which raged in the dry timber."[9]

The men strengthened their breastworks the next day, May 11. Occupying an exposed position, a number of men were killed by snipers, including Colonel William Curry of the 106th, who fell mortally wounded, and died in Washington on July 7. These sharpshooters had already deprived the army of one of its most beloved leaders, "Uncle John" Sedgwick, who was killed on May 8 after he had chided his men about hiding from unseen rebels.

Finally realizing that the attacks had no probability of succeeding, Grant tried a new strategy, moving the II Corps from its position on the right of the Federal line, to the left. To prevent Lee's men from learning of this movement, which began between ten and eleven o'clock that night, the men were ordered to keep their canteens, cups and accoutrements quiet. Although only a distance of three miles, the rain, mud, darkness and road obstructions slowed the march, and they did not reach the left of the VI Corps until just before sunrise.

According to Grant's plan, the 19,000 man II Corps would attack the vulnerable "Mule Shoe" position held by Ewell's corps at first light. Barlow's division was on the left of the first line and Birney's on its right. Mott's and Gibbon's divisions formed behind them. A cool rain fell, and when it hit the ground, a fog formed that restricted visibility to less than fifty yards. "A funeral silence pervades the assembly, and like spectres the men in blue await the order to attack," wrote the 152nd New York's historian.

The advance began at about 4:30 a.m. on May 12. The onrushing yanks gobbled up some of the rebel pickets and kept moving forward. Fearing problems with Barlow's exposed left flank, Hancock ordered Gibbon to send troops to extend the line. Gibbon responded by sending the Philadelphia Brigade and Carroll's brigade. The troops could hear Owen's loud voice screaming, "Attention! Second Brigade, Fix Bayonets! Forward! Guide! Center! Charge!" Barlow's troops were moving so fast, that Gibbon's men had to double-quick to keep up with them. Seeing what they thought were the rebel works on an elevation, thousands of voices let out a yell. Rushing

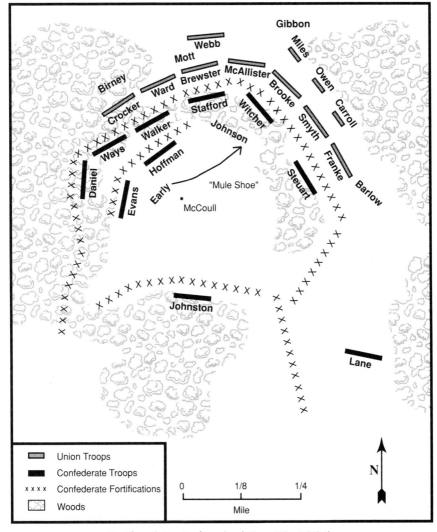

Battle of Spotsylvania (May 12, 1864)

forward to capture them, the men were dismayed to learn that the rebel works were still 200 yards ahead.

The half asleep, but now alerted Confederates of Steuart's brigade, poured an effective fire into Gibbon's line. Realizing that success was theirs if only they could push on a few more yards, a loud cheer again echoed down the line, as the men closed on the works. The two sides fought hand-to-hand, but the heavily outnumbered Confederates realized that the situation was hopeless, and threw down their weapons; others scampered for the rear.

As a result of this unexpected attack, General Edward Johnson and almost his entire Confederate division were captured. Four thousand Confederates, twenty cannon and thirty battle flags were also captured in one of the great charges of the war. Some of the men tried to turn the guns on their former owners. One Irishman who was trying to fire one of the guns whose barrel was at a 45° angle was told that he would have better luck if he depressed the barrel. The soldier replied, "Niver fare: it's bound to come down on somebody's head." General Owen sent back for some artillerymen, who effectively serviced the guns.

By this time, Brooke's, Owen's, and Carroll's brigades were hopelessly mixed. One historian later called it a "disorganized mass intermingled without regard for unit integrity." Without orders, the mass lurched forward to complete their route of the rebels, as their officers yelled, "To the interior line! We have them now! Up men and at them! The union forever!" As this mass advanced, it gained the rear of Lane's North Carolina Brigade, forcing fifty to sixty tarheels to surrender.[10]

It was only a bit past 5 a.m. Sensing a great victory and perhaps even the destruction of Lee's army, Hancock's men looked south to where the remnants of the Johnson's division had taken refuge. They knew they should attack this line before reinforcements arrived to plug the hole, but the mass of Federals was so confused, that no coherent actions could occur.

Still, the crush of men forged on for about a half a mile until they approached a secondary line of works. Seeing some rebels in front of them, they opened fire. These troops were from battle-toughened Evans' and Hoffman's brigades, and after withstanding the Federal's volley, sent their own into the mass of blue-clad soldiers in front of them, which "mowed down the boys like grain on the bloody field." The Confederates then charged with their harrowing rebel yell. Flushed with victory, the disorganized Federal troops refused to withdraw, and hand-to-hand fighting resulted. Realizing that there was little to be gained by trying to fight this obviously large and determined force, the Union troops backtracked toward the original breach in the Southern line. Before long, the Confederates attacked again, but were repulsed.

The brigade historian called the rest of the day as the "most sanguinary and deadly fight of this campaign." The fight for the ramparts lasted all day, with each side taking turns driving the other back. Battle flags of both armies were perched on opposite sides of the breastworks, not more than a few feet apart. Grabbing a rebel flag, Captain Charles McNally of the 69th struggled with the flagbearer. After a few moments, the captain struck down the Confederate soldier, and seized the flag. Seeing other enemy soldiers dashing toward him, he threw the flag behind him. "The flag was picked up by someone in the rear (who no doubt wears a medal), while no report of Captain McNally's struggle for its possession was ever noted—another instance of the heedlessness of the men of the 69th to seek rewards for their special acts," wrote a bitter Anthony McDermott after the war.

By the end of this long and bloody day, the bodies lay in heaps. Heavy skirmishing continued throughout the night. The Federal forces lost approximately 7,000 men; the Confederates, about 6,000. Among the seriously wounded was the Philadelphia Brigade's former commander, Alexander Webb. Grant and Meade anxiously awaited the daylight on May 13 to learn if Lee had retreated southward. A strong reconnaissance in force was ordered by Gibbon, who selected the Philadelphia Brigade to move forward to see if it drew fire from the Confederate line. Curiously, the movement was made under the direction of General Carroll of the Third Brigade, not under Owen. As the troops moved out, with the 69th and part of the 72nd on the skirmish line, a Minie ball slammed into Carroll's arm, shattering the bone. Entering the Confederate salient, the men drove away the pickets, but found no other troops there. Moving cautiously forward, they saw strongly defended earthworks in front of them. Lee had abandoned the vulnerable salient, but had consolidated his lines behind it, and was there in force. Having successfully completed its mission, the brigade quickly returned to its lines.[11]

During the pre-dawn hours of May 14, preparations were made for a continuation of the fight—Warren's V Corps and Wright's VI Corps were to attack the rebel lines, while Hancock was in reserve. This attack was never launched.

Details were assembled during the pre-dawn hours of May 15, to collect and bury all of the arms that could not be carried away, to prevent them from falling into Lee's hands. About 5 a.m. the division withdrew from the captured Confederate works, moved toward the left of the Union line, and crossed the Ny River. Taking position behind the right flank of the IX Corps, about five miles from the rebel works, they felt safe for the first time in days. That afternoon they were moved to the right of Burnside's corps and threw out skirmishers—they were back on the front lines.

The division moved again on May 16. This time two miles to the right, to assist in the evacuation of a II and V Corps hospital. General Thomas Rosser's Confederate cavalry had captured the hospital, and removed not only the wounded Confederate prisoners who were able to walk, but all of the Union personnel not sporting medical badges on their uniforms. Although driven off by Carroll's 12th New Jersey, the rest of Gibbon's division was ordered to the area to prevent a return visit by the rebel cavalry. The 700 Federal and Confederate wounded were loaded into 200 empty wagons the division brought with it, and transported to safety. The division then returned to its position adjacent to the IX Corps.

The II Corps moved back to its original position in front of the Confederate salient to the left of the VI Corps just after dark on May 17. A new attack to capture the works was to be made by the II and VI Corps at about 4 a.m. on May 18. If successful, Burnside's IX Corps would join in as well. Since May 13, Ewell's corps had had little to do, except strengthen their works behind the salient area, making them all but impregnable.

Difficulties in properly aligning the troops prevented the attack from commencing until 4:30 a.m. Hancock's assault force was composed of two divisions—Gibbon's on the right and Barlow's on the left. The VI Corps formed on Gibbon's right. Gibbon placed the newly arrived Irish or Corcoran Legion and Webb's brigade (now commanded by H. Boyd McKeen) on the first line and Carroll's (now commanded by Thomas Smyth) and Owen's brigades on the second line.[12]

As with the successful attack on May 12, the strike force moved forward through a heavy ground fog. When they came to the salient area, the four brigades in Hancock's front line climbed into the abandoned rebel works and continued forward, while the four brigades in the second line waited here until needed. As the first line advanced, they came under heavy and accurate artillery fire. The supporting brigades were now ordered forward in support. As the first line advanced, it could see the abatis in front of them, in some places, over 100 yards in depth. It was now about 5:30 a.m., and the officers, realizing the impossibility of the task ahead, ordered their men to lie down.

Webb's brigade on the right side of the division's first line began to give way, so Gibbon ordered Owen to bring forward the Philadelphia Brigade to fill the gap. Owen obeyed the order, but as his men moved forward, rebel canister blew large gaps in his ranks, and men and body parts flew in all directions. Realizing the folly of this charge, Owen called a halt, and ordered his men to return to the safety of the works. He had disobeyed a direct order from his commander. These actions were negatively described by General Gibbon in his after-battle report,

> During the action...Brigadier-General Owen's brigade instead of moving forward as directed in support of the first line, had fallen back into a line of works into its rear. An investigation into the facts proved the correctness of the report. The brigade had not at all supported the attack made by the front line.

Other units began to fall back, and by 8:30 a.m., Hancock reported that the attack had failed. Meade called off the attack, but not before hundreds of men were senselessly killed and wounded in an attack that should never have been made. Again, plans had been made without first conducting a careful reconnaissance. So powerful was the Confederate artillery response, that the Union soldiers never came close enough for the rebel infantry to enter the fray. After the Federals had returned to their lines, the victorious Confederates saw just how destructive their fire had been—gruesome sights of bodies blown apart or crushed into pulp by the pounding.[13]

Grant finally realized that he could not pry Lee from his strong breastworks, so he ordered another sliding movement to the left of Lee's army to force his opponent out of the works and into the open. The II Corps pulled out of its position that night, thus ending the battle of Spotsylvania Court House.

The losses to the Philadelphia Brigade were again moderate in relation to the other two brigades. While the Philadelphia Brigade lost 271 men in this campaign (69th=38; 71st=76; 72nd=39; 106th=48; and 152nd New York=70), Webb's brigade lost 430 and Carroll's brigade lost 653 men.[14]

CHAPTER 17

NORTH ANNA, TOTOPOTOMOY, AND COLD HARBOR

Deciding to use the II Corps as bait to draw Lee out of his Spotsylvania entrenchments and into the open, Grant sent Hancock's men south to the North Anna River. Slipping out of their trenches on May 18 at 9 p.m., the men marched toward the army's left flank. Crossing the Ny River, the column finally reached Anderson's Mills at 2 a.m. on May 19. The men remained here until 11 p.m. that night, when they were ordered back into column, but the orders were countermanded, and the men returned to their slumber. The cause for the delay was concern over the nature of Ewell's troop movements to their right. Although not mentioned in any first-person accounts, the men must have relished this, their first reprieve from fighting since the campaign began in early May.

Hancock's men remained here until 11 p.m. on May 20, when they continued their march south, passing through Bowling Green. Arriving at Milford Station at 4 a.m. on May 21, the men were permitted to rest for a few hours after the twenty-mile march. Soldiers disliked these night marches because lurking enemy soldiers could not be seen, nor could they see the cause of delays. Many had developed an ability to doze while marching, and when halts were made, they could flop down and instantly fall into a deeper sleep.

The column crossed the Mattapony River about 11 a.m. on May 21, and formed into line of battle because rebel troops were in the vicinity. The troops were now in an area that had been untouched by the ravages of war. It did not take long for the soldiers to end this reprieve. Soon after their arrival, the troops were ordered to entrench. The men had become proficient diggers during the past few weeks, and often dug shelters without orders. The brigade historian wrote, "When the enemy were in front and an attack was probable, rife-pits were dug as soon as a halt was made, often times before the soldiers had partaken of their hardtack and coffee." Entrenching tools were kept in the ammunition wagons, but when they were not available, the men used bayonets, tin cups, and utensils. If given enough time, these earthworks were topped off with wooden planks from slaves' huts and outbuildings.[1]

Lee did not take Hancock's bait, but the effect was the same as he pulled his troops back again between Grant and Richmond, this time to the south side of the North Anna River. The II Corps remained near Milford Station on May 22. The march after Lee began the following morning at 7 o'clock. Arriving at the North Anna River at 3 p.m., they found two entrenched Confederate divisions defending the Chesterfield Bridge and a railroad bridge over the river. The II Corps formed the left flank of the army— to their right was Burnside's IX Corps at Ox Ford. Warren's V Corps was about four miles upstream at Jericho Mills, and Wright's VI Corps formed the army's right flank.[2]

Birney's division of the II Corps assaulted Chesterfield bridge just before dark on May 23, and successfully drove Henagan's brigade across the river with heavy losses. After darkness put an end to the hostilities, Gibbon moved his division up to support Birney with orders to cross the river at 8 o'clock the next morning. Unfortunately, the Confederates burned the bridge that night, making the crossing more difficult. Birney's men again led the attack, and gained a foothold on the opposite side of the river. Two pontoon bridges were quickly laid, and by noon, the rest of the II Corps had crossed. Grant's army was vulnerable during this period, as it was split into three separate segments by the bends of the North Anna River.[3]

After crossing the river, Birney again successfully drove the enemy backward, until his men came to well-defended earthworks. Encountering an effective small arms and artillery fire, Birney ordered his men to entrench. Hancock had stepped into a hornet's nest—in front of him was the Confederate II Corps, and to his right was the I Corps.

Not aware of the disposition or strength of the enemy, Smyth's brigade was ordered forward to the left (east) of the Richmond, Fredericksburg, and Potomac Railroad to make a reconnaissance at 3 p.m. When they encountered heavy resistance, the Philadelphia Brigade and H. Boyd McKeen's brigade were moved up to form a second line of attack. Behind them was Colonel James McIvor's inexperienced brigade.

Strongly entrenched rebel troops were encountered at about 4 p.m., and an attack was quickly ordered. The rebels were initially driven from their rifle pits, but reinforcements arrived, and a savage counterattack pushed Smyth's men slowly backward. The 152nd New York from the Philadelphia Brigade, and other units from McIvor's brigade were now rushed forward. The New Yorkers replaced the 7th West Virginia, which had expended its ammunition. Gibbon also brought up the rest of his division and fed them into the battle. Because of the limited visibility of the forest, each regiment slugged it out alone with the partially seen enemy. Hancock now ordered Barlow's division into the fight to Smyth's right, but it encountered heavy small arms fire and several of its units were forced to retire.[4]

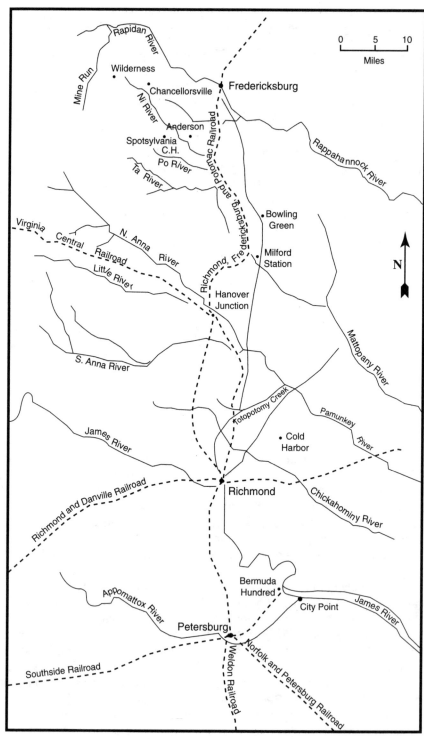

0 5 10
Miles

Rapidan River

Mine Run

Wilderness

Chancellorsville

Fredericksburg

Ni River

Anderson

Spotsylvania
C.H.

Po River

Ta River

Rappahannock River

Richmond, Fredericksburg and Potomac Railroad

Bowling
Green

Milford
Station

Virginia

Central Railroad

N. Anna River

Little River

Hanover
Junction

N

S. Anna River

Mattopany River

Totopotomy Creek

James River

Cold
Harbor

Pamunkey River

Richmond and Danville Railroad

Richmond

Chickahominy River

Appomattox River

Bermuda
Hundred

City Point

James River

Petersburg

Southside Railroad

Weldon Railroad

Norfolk and Petersburg Railroad

From the Wilderness to Petersburg (May–June 1864)

Smyth's line continued to barely hold its own. One soldier recalled that the men would "summon up all our courage, and occasionally without any orders would charge with a cheer...the Confederates would rally and in turn would force us back over the ground we had just won." The level of firing was tremendous. The 152nd New York expended all fifty rounds of their ammunition, but refused to withdraw, and held its position with bayonets.

Storm clouds gathered during the fight and a wet, drenching rain commenced. "There we stood, our line and that of the enemy, poised for another deadly blow and looking at one another without firing, fearful our ammunition would be soaked in the rain," wrote one of the participants. The battle resumed when the rain ended.

The Confederates now launched a counterattack on the Federal lines. Seeing the rebels moving around their left flank, the 69th was rushed to this sector. It was a case of too many against too few, and the 69th along with the remainder of Smyth's line, were finally shoved backward. The troops rallied in the rear, and nightfall did what the Union troops could not—put an end to the Confederate advance.

This ended the battle of the North Anna, in which the Confederates defeated Grant's men on all fronts. The defeat could have been more decisive had Lee not been incapacitated by a severe case of diarrhea. The North lost just under 2,000 men; the South slightly more.

On May 25 and 26 the two sides warily watched each other from behind their respective defensive works. Sharpshooters continued their grisly work, causing additional names to be added to the casualty lists.[5]

Only twenty-one miles separated the army from Richmond, and after considering his options, Grant again decided to slide around Lee's right flank. A rebel salient on the right of the Confederate line had to be neutralized before the movement could begin. At about 5 p.m. on May 26, Smyth was ordered to take several regiments, including the 69th, to drive the rebels out of this stronghold, which he successfully accomplished, after a sharp skirmish.

A subtle change had occurred in the army. Having grown tired of Grant's form of warfare, which showed little concern for the lives of the men, the veterans warily approached each attack. Writing of one attack, the brigade historian wrote, "The moment Gibbon's line...emerged from the woods, the veterans began to calculate, as they moved forward, the possibility of success, while the [new troops] only considered how they could get into the works." General Gibbon also wrote, "Immense numbers of men would quit the ranks upon the slightest pretext or none at all, leaving the more faithful to do the fighting." The number of these men reached alarming proportions.

As the army pulled out, the II Corps formed the rear guard. Gibbon's division, which brought up the rear, did not begin its move until 10:30 p.m. on May 26. Crossing the North Anna, the men were permitted to rest until 10 o'clock the next morning. All through that day and evening the men trudged first east, and then south, literally dropping in their tracks from exhaustion during the few rest stops. During one such stop, the last brigade in Gibbon's line did not receive orders to continue, and it was not until the rest of the division was several miles down the road that Gibbon learned that he had "lost" a brigade. Orderlies galloped back to rouse the men, who soon caught up with the remainder of the division. Gibbon later remarked, "When the halt was made, every member of the brigade from the commander down had sunk into deep sleep from which they did not awake until all the rest of the division was far on the road!"[6]

At midnight, the troops were three miles from the Pamunkey River, and they were finally permitted to camp for the night. The march began again at daylight the next morning, May 28, when the column crossed the river at Nelson's or Huntley's Ford at 7 a.m. Marching another mile and a half, the men were halted and ordered to form into line of battle. Entrenching began immediately. Having safely crossed the Pamunkey River, Grant positioned his army for a new thrust against Lee. The Federal line from right to left was the: VI Corps, II Corps, V Corps, and the IX Corps formed the reserve.

Not knowing the whereabouts of Lee's army, Grant ordered each corps' commander to reconnoitre his front with a division on the morning of May 29. Hancock chose Barlow's division, and after encountering stubborn Confederate defense along the Totopotomy Creek, the remainder of the corps moved up in support. Birney formed on Barlow's right and Gibbon's division took position on Barlow's left. After driving the rebel pickets back toward the river, Hancock's men entrenched in front of the Confederate works.[7]

The following morning, May 30, both Barlow and Gibbon sent heavy skirmish lines to push the rebels back to the north side of the creek. After meeting with some success, Brooke's brigade was relieved by the Philadelphia Brigade, which continued to push the rebels down the road toward the creek. During the day, two additional corps came to Hancock's aid.

Meade ordered a general advance along all points of his line on May 31, and Barlow's troops met with initial success, driving the rebels across the creek. Following the Confederates across the river, Barlow's men attacked the enemy works. In the meantime, Birney's and Gibbon's divisions also crossed. The Philadelphia Brigade which was deployed from right to left, 106th, 69th, 71st, 72nd, moved forward with McKeen's brigade, while Smyth's brought up the rear. They too pushed the rebel pickets back into their works.

During the day, Confederate sharpshooters concealed in a small wooden church between the lines racked up casualties among the Philadelphia Brigade. Having enough of this, Owen asked for volunteers who crept forward and set the house on fire.[8]

The Confederates launched a blistering attack against Warren's position that afternoon. Meade considered launching a counterattack by Hancock's troops, but after inspecting the strong Confederate lines, Barlow told Hancock that an attack was foolhardy. Joshua Owen reported at about 3 p.m. that the "enemy is still moving to the right, apparently in great haste," so Hancock now considered an attack by Gibbon's division along A. P. Hill's weakened front.

At about 4 p.m., fifty men selected from each regiment joined the skirmish line, and inched forward toward the strong Confederate fortifications. Few came close to them, and those who did, were captured. Unbeknownst to the men, Meade was drafting an order for their withdrawal at the very moment their futile attack was launched.[9]

Grant's army was swelled by 16,000 muskets on June 1 by the temporary addition of Baldy Smith's XVIII Corps, from Ben Butler's Army of the James. No sooner had they arrived that Grant launched these new troops, along with Wright's corps, against the Confederate breastworks. The attack staggered the Confederate line, but did not break it, and the Union troops fell back. One brigade commander bitterly wrote in his after-battle report, "...our loss was very heavy, and to no purpose." Realizing that he could not extract Lee from his trenches, Grant decided on another slide to his left, thus ending the Totopotomoy campaign.

The brigade's losses during the North Anna and Totopotomoy campaigns were only 37 (69th=6; 71st=7; 72nd=5; 106th=3; and 152nd NY=16), which were again the lightest losses of the division. The First Brigade (McKeen's) lost 284, most during the charge at Totopotomoy. Smyth's Third Brigade lost 73 men.[10]

Thinking that the Confederate right was weak, Grant moved the II Corps from the army's right flank to its left during the evening of June 1. Marching orders were issued at 6:40 p.m., and Gibbon's division recrossed the Totopotomy Creek at 9 p.m. that night. After marching all night to the left flank of the army, Cold Harbor was reached at eight o'clock the next morning. The corps was delayed, so the attack planned for first light was postponed, and the men were put to work erecting earthworks.

Heavy skirmishing occurred for most of June 2. A Federal attack, scheduled for 5 p.m. that evening, was canceled by heavy rains and hail. The men lay on the wet ground that night, using knapsacks or cartridge boxes for pillows, covering their faces from the hail. Their spirits were further dampened by the news that they would assault Lee's strong breastworks the next morning.[11]

While still dark, the officers prepared their men for an advance that was to be similar to the successful one at Spotsylvania the month before. This time, the entire Union army would attack at once. The II Corps' assault would be made by Barlow on the left and Gibbon on the right, with Birney's division in reserve. Gibbon's division was ordered to attack on a two division front. Smyth formed on the left of the first line, and Tyler on the right. Behind Smyth was the Philadelphia Brigade, which had been reinforced by the 184th Pennsylvania, and behind Tyler was McKeen's brigade.

In front of them was General Breckinridge's strongly entrenched division. To complicate matters, the ground between the two lines was swampy. At 4:30 a.m., Gibbon ordered one cannon to fire to signal the assault. One man later wrote, that after the gun fired, "hell broke loose." So began the bloody battle of Cold Harbor.

Part of Barlow's line easily punched through the Confederate defenses not protected by earthworks, but was savagely counterattacked while waiting for their supports to arrive. The cause for the delay was that the Philadelphia Brigade was not ready to advance at the appointed time, and this permitted A. P. Hill to pull troops from Gibbon's front to reinforce his right flank. Gibbon wrote in his official report, "At daylight I rode to the line and found Owen's brigade not even under arms, and, of course, not in the advanced position I had assigned it the day before. As soon as it was put in position the signal was given and the troops moved to the attack." This caused at least a fifteen-minute delay, and when the attack was finally launched, it ran into immediate difficulty because of a swamp between the two lines, which Gibbon and Hancock apparently had not properly reconnoitered.

The swamp formed a triangle in front of Gibbon's position—as his men advanced, it widened, forcing each flank to move in opposite directions. Smyth's brigade and two of Tyler's regiments moved left; the remainder of Tyler's men veered to the right. One wrote, "We felt it was murder, not war, or at best that a very serious mistake had been made."[12]

While parts of the two brigades did reach and capture parts of the works, most of the men never got within 100 yards of them. The fire was so deadly that Smyth ordered his men to lie down and entrench. General Tyler and many of his men were already killed or wounded.

The 164th New York of Tyler's was successful in capturing a portion of the rebel works. Now its men waited expectantly for support from the Philadelphia Brigade. Encountering the same swamp, Owen angled farther to the left than Smyth, and this brought him far to the left of the 164th New York. Reaching a point within seventy-five yards of the Confederate works, and seeing Barlow's men falling back on his left, General Owen ordered his men to protect themselves by lying down and entrenching. The men used their bayonets, knives, and tin cups to scrape away some dirt.

The historian of the 69th vividly remembered the advance:

Hurling from the rifles of the men and the cannon of the artillery all the death-dealing missiles of destruction at his command. The discretion and good judgement of our commander, General Owen, saved what might have been almost total destruction by ordering the men to lay down when within a short distance of the [rebel] works.

After the repulse, many Southern soldiers jumped up on their breastworks to fire on the prone men.

The two newest regiments of the brigade, the 184th Pennsylvania and the 152nd New York, were successful in capturing a section of the works. The latter's historian recalled,

> ...the brigade being massed in solid square by order of Gen. Owen, rushed parallel with the enemy's works through the cleared field, which was swept by shot and shell...We turn and rush toward the front, crossing the sunken road and swamp. Ascending the hill, we madly charge across the level space, and are met with a cyclone of bullets. A winrow of the First Division [Barlow's] lie cold in death. Our solid square press on, the 184th Pa. leading, with the 152nd N.Y. We scale the enemy's works and capture three cannon, holding the breach made five minutes. Gen. Finnegan at once rallied his reserves and drove us out, capturing the wounded.[13]

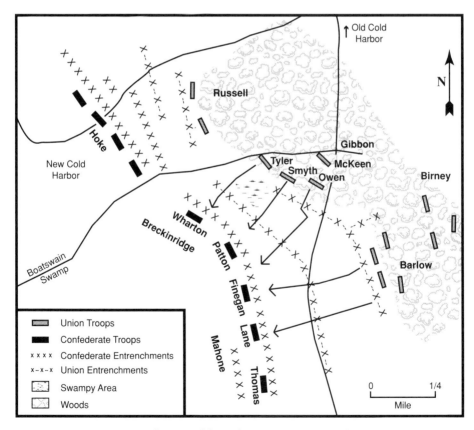

Battle of Cold Harbor (June 3, 1864)

Many criticized the behavior of most of the Philadelphia Brigade. Most damning was General Gibbon, who wrote, "General Owen, instead of pushing forward in column through Smyth's line, deployed on his left as soon as the latter became fully engaged, and thus lost the opportunity of having his brigade well in hand and ready to support the lodgment made by Smyth and the 164th New York. In his memoirs, he further stated that Owen's men "opened fire and did little to support the leading brigade."

A Confederate counterattack swept the 164th New York from the captured works. The regiment's commander, James McMahon, tried to rally his men, taking "the colors in his own hands, and rammed the staff into the earth, and was shouting to his men, only a few whom were near, when he was seen to clap his hand to his side, to walk back a few steps, and then sink to the ground," dead.[14]

The Philadelphia Brigade spent the remainder of the day clinging to its position in front of the rebel works in a manner similar to the battle of Fredericksburg. Just before dark, sounds from the Confederate works suggested that an attack was in the offing. Sweeping out of their works, Finegan's Florida Brigade attacked the prone men. The brigade historian described what happened:

> Soon the commands of their officers were heard, then the well-known yell, and a rush for our line. Now came our turn, but we had not the advantage of strong earthworks. The men rose in their places and poured in heavy volleys of musketry, and for a few moments there was a struggle as severe as in the morning.

The Floridians were driven off with heavy losses, and the Philadelphians returned to strengthening their defenses.

During June 4, 5, and 6, the men strengthened their works and did their best to stay out of the sights of the rebel sharpshooters. "The least exposure of the body was attended with wounding or even death from the fire of sharpshooters, and almost every day closed with an attack or a heavy fusillade," wrote a soldier from the Philadelphia Brigade.

The enemy made a charge on the works at dusk on June 4 and again the following evening. Both were repulsed. The Confederates now used a different strategy. Rather than charging the works and sustaining heavy losses, they stealthily crept up to the defenders, and when close enough, jumped up and tried to use their bayonets against the unsuspecting Union soldiers. "Our men kept quiet and allowed them to get up very close when they opened on them with a well-directed volley that sent them flying back to their works leaving many behind, killed or too badly wounded to get back," wrote the 106th Pennsylvania's historian.[15]

The conditions in the trenches were severe. Gibbon's report perhaps best summarizes the privations:

> ...confined for ten days in narrow trenches with no water to wash with and none to drink except that obtained at the risk of losing life. Unable to obey a call of nature or to stand erect without forming targets

for hostile bullets, and subjected to the heat and dust of midsummer, which soon produced sickness and vermin, the position was indeed a trying one, but all bore it cheerfully and contentedly, constructed covered ways down to the water and to the rear, and joked of the hostile bullets as they whistled over their heads to find perhaps a less protected target far in the rear of the lines. I regard this as having been the most trying period of this most trying campaign.

No truce had been declared, so the wounded lie exposed between the two lines. The dead reeked as they decayed. A truce was finally enacted on June 7, and when the men ventured forward, they found the dead as black as coal. Decomposition was so advanced that the bodies could not be moved, and were buried where they were found. Many of the wounded had also died for lack of medical assistance. The living spent the time walking and stretching—luxuries after the past several days. Bathing was also common. "Members of both sides were washing together in the same small run, and joking each other on the results of the previous days. It seemed very odd to see these men mingling with each other, laughing and joking and very friendly, that only a short time before were watching for an opportunity and trying their best to kill each other, and would so soon be trying it again," wrote the historian of the 106th.[16]

The truce expired the next morning at 11 a.m. At this time, the men of the Philadelphia Brigade heard the Southern officers calling their men back to the breastworks and informing the Yankees, that they had five minutes to return to their lines before the shooting would commence again. True to their word, the firing soon began and continued throughout the day and well into the night.

The brigade remained on the front lines on June 9, 10, and 11. On the latter day, the men grumbled when they saw the First and Third Brigades of the division being pulled back, leaving them and the Fourth Brigade in position. Because of the exposed position of the Philadelphia Brigade, the men suffered from the sun. No shelters were permitted as they would draw the enemy's fire, so they lie there, day after day, exposed to the sun and heat. To compound their misery, water was scarce. A few days after the battle, the Confederates brought up some brass howitzers, whose cannonballs buried themselves when they hit the earth. Several men were killed and wounded each time one exploded; the rest were covered with gritty sand.

Orders were received on June 12 to pull back after dark. After marching awhile, the men were formed into column and marched to the left all night, toward the Chickahominy River.

Grant's plan again had failed. This time, at a great cost. During this, the Cold Harbor campaign, Grant lost over 15,000 men to Lee's 1,400. Particularly distressing were the number of officers killed and wounded, including Tyler and McKeen. Gibbon's losses were heavy during the Cold Harbor campaign—almost 1,600 men.

General John Gibbon,
commander of the Second Division

Massachusetts Commandery Military Order
of the Loyal Legion and the USAMHI

Again, since the 1864 campaign began, the Philadelphia Brigade's 122 casualties (killed=26, wounded=90, missing=6) were fewer than its sister brigades in Gibbon's division. Tyler's Fourth Brigade lost 922, McKeen's First Brigade lost 396, and Smyth's Third lost 227. The brigade's losses were: 69th=21; 71st=16; 72nd=32; 106th=21; and 152nd New York=32).[17]

Unhappy with Owen's leadership during the past several campaigns, Gibbon pressed charges of "disobedience of orders" against him. Three specifications were listed. The first referred to the aborted attack at Spotsylvania Court House on May 18, 1864, when despite an order from Gibbon, "to move his brigade up in support of the front line, then making an attack of the enemy's works, [Owen] did fail to obey said order, and did fall back and occupy a line of rifle-pits in his rear."

The second specifications referred to Cold Harbor. On the afternoon of June 2, Owen was ordered "to mass his brigade in a certain position at daylight the next morning, preparatory to an assault on the enemy's works, did fail and neglect to obey said order. This at or near Cold Harbor, Va., on or about the 3d of June, 1864."

The last specification referred to what transpired on June 3—when Owen was ordered to "assault the enemy's works with his brigade in column in rear of the right of Colonel Smyth's brigade, and not to deploy his column until the head of it reached the enemy's entrenchments, [Owen] did fail to obey said order and did form his brigade in a deployed line before reaching the enemy's works and to the left of Colonel Smyth." One of the Philadelphia Brigade officers, Captain Joseph Lynch of the 106th, who was serving on Gibbon's staff, was listed as a witness to the first two specifications.

General Hancock wrote on June 8 that a "proper" court-martial could not be arranged at this time, so Owen was sent to Fortress Monroe to stand trial by order of Assistant Secretary of War, Charles Dana. On June 27, Grant wrote, "Respectfully forwarded to the Secretary of War, with the recommendation that Brig. Gen. J. T. Owen be mustered out of the service."

The matter came to a quick conclusion on July 16, 1864, in the hands of the Secretary of War and the President:

> "Respectfully referred to the President."
> EDWIN STANTON,
> Secretary of War.
> "Recommendation of General Grant approved."
> A. LINCOLN.

So ended the military career of Brigadier General Joshua Owen, who formed and led the 69th before being named the fourth commander of the Philadelphia Brigade.[18]

Before the troops filed out of their trenches, the 71st's term of service expired, and the men who had not re-enlisted, went home. The 106th's historian wrote:

> It was a sad and yet a joyous parting; sad to us remaining behind, for it was like taking part of our body from us, and joyous to those going, having the consciousness of duty well done, and crowned with the laurels of many hard-fought battles, victories won, and faithful services rendered; and yet sad to them, that so few were left to go.[19]

The 69th's historian added,

> While we regretted parting with so gallant a regiment, yet we felt rejoiced that there were a few at least who could return to the embraces of parents, wives, children, and no doubt to receive the welcoming smiles of sweethearts.

The 71st, Baker's First California, finally marched into history, after it was mustered out in Philadelphia on July 2, 1864. Those men who re-enlisted were added to the rolls of the 69th, swelling its ranks by almost 150 men.[20]

CHAPTER 18

PETERSBURG AND THE DISBANDING OF THE BRIGADE

Finally realizing that any attempt to take Richmond from the east would fail, Grant decided on a move on the capital from the south. He would cross the James River and link up with Ben Butler's Army of the James to take Petersburg, a vital railroad center. If he moved quickly, he could then drive north and take Richmond before Lee's army arrived. All that stood between Grant and Petersburg was a small force under General Gustave Beauregard.

Gibbon's division began its march on the evening of June 12. Marching all night, it crossed the Chickahominy River at 11 a.m. the next morning. Charles City Court House was reached at about 6 p.m. that night. The march continued, until the column reached within a half mile of the James River, when the men were permitted to rest for the night after their long thirty-mile trek.

The men could not help but think back to the time, two years ago, when McClellan led them over this same ground. In comparing the two periods, the brigade historian wrote, "Now the troops appeared cheerful and full of hope for the future, giving evidence, in their bronzed faces flushed with health and in their firm step, of ability to make still greater sacrifices." Written after the war, the passage confirms how memories fade. This was not a positive time for the men—they had fought and marched non-stop for almost six weeks. They had seen their ranks grow progressively smaller, as Grant launched ill-conceived attacks on the strongly entrenched rebel lines. None of the regimental commanders from the Peninsula campaign were with their units, and rare was the company that possessed the same commander. Many of the new officers had begun their service as enlisted men, and in one case, one of them actually led a regiment.[1]

Crossing the James River between Wilcox Landing and Windmill Point, the following day (June 14), was a formidable task. Steamers ferried the troops because the river was over 2,000 feet wide and 84 feet deep here. It was a slow process. The II Corps began crossing in the morning, but the

Second Division did not cross until about five o'clock that night, and it was not until 10 p.m. that the entire corps had crossed.

The brigade bivouacked about two miles from the river. "Light haversacks and light stomachs was the order of the day," wrote Henry Roback of the 152nd New York. Butler had been ordered to provide 60,000 rations to Hancock's corps after they crossed the river, but they never arrived. After several hours, Hancock decided he could wait no longer, and continued the march toward Petersburg at 10:30 a.m. on June 15.

As the II Corps made its way toward Petersburg, General William "Baldy" Smith's XVIII Corps, which had returned to the Army of the James, attacked the thinly manned Confederate works. The attack occurred too late in the day, so nightfall put an end to the successful attack on Petersburg's outer works.

While Smith's corps was preparing to attack, Meade ordered the II Corps to move up in support. Marching on Prince George Road, about six miles from Petersburg, Gibbon's division found a country road, and hastened to the front. "The road was covered with clouds of dust, and but little water was found on the route, causing severe suffering among the men," recalled Hancock. Arriving well after dark, Gibbon's division relieved Smith's victorious troops. Still having nothing to eat, Gibbon's men begged Smith's troops for food, and each man was given seven pieces of hardtack.[2]

That night, the advance units of Lee's army began arriving, and were immediately put to work strengthening the works. By the time the sun rose on June 16, the opportunity to easily take Petersburg had passed. Realizing that every hour brought additional rebel units, Hancock decided to press the attack. Just before dawn, skirmishers moved forward and pushed their rebel counterparts back into their fortifications. The all-out assault began at about 6 a.m. by Hancock's entire corps. Despite the fact that the attack was made with "considerable spirit," it failed to dislodge the entrenched Confederates. Another attack was made at 6 p.m., this time with the addition of two brigades from the IX Corps and an equal number from the XVIII Corps. Charging together, the Philadelphia Brigade (from right to left: 106th, 69th, 72nd) and the Fourth Brigade successfully captured a line of rifle pits, and then continued forward toward Harrison's Creek. Here they found still another well-defended Confederate fortification. Realizing that Birney's division was not advancing on his right, Gibbon halted the attack, and ordered his men to entrench. Some of the units were a mere thirty yards from the rebel works, when the halt was ordered.[3]

June 17 brought continued attacks on the rebel works. During this advance, which involved the entire II and IX Corps, parts of the rebel lines were captured, including Hare Hill, upon which Fort Stedman was later built. Ordered to continue the advance later that day, Barlow's troops suffered a severe repulse.

The hammering continued on June 18, when Hancock received orders for an early morning attack. Placed under arms at 2 a.m., the men caught whatever sleep they could muster. A heavy cannonading began just before dawn, and at 6 a.m., the infantry stepped off. The First Brigade, under Colonel B. Pierce, and the Philadelphia Brigade, under Colonel John Fraser of the 140th Pennsylvania, formed the first line on the right of Prince George Court House Road. They were supported by Smyth's Third Brigade, and Frank's Brigade of Mott's division. To the relief of the men, they found that the rebel works in front of them were abandoned.

The advance continued until the attack column came to an occupied breastwork. Gibbon brought up Smyth's brigade on the right, and ordered at attack at about noon. As the line moved forward, they were hit by a terrific fire along their front and flank. Two attempts were made to carry the position, but both were repulsed.

The men relaxed as best they could through the afternoon, but at 5 p.m. they were ordered to reform for another attack. This one would be made with nine lines of battle, each line representing a brigade. The Philadelphia Brigade occupied the fourth line. The column moved forward to within 150 feet of the rebel works, when the enemy opened fire with their artillery. The shells soon fell among the men and sliced off parts of young pine trees, showering the men with these sharpened missiles. The order was now given to charge. After taking no more than ten paces, the enemy opened on them with small arms fire. The "murderous fire, resembling a violent tornado or rushing wind...the front line recoiled, leaving half their number dead and wounded on the field," reported Henry Roback. Realizing the hopelessness of this attack, Birney, now temporarily in charge of the corps, pulled the men back to safety.[4]

For the first time in several days, the II Corps was permitted to rest and build earthworks on June 19 and 20. The reprieve did not last long, for on the night of the 20th, Gibbon's division was relieved by Neil's division of the VI Corps, and marched away, camping near the Blackwater. On the 21st, the movement to the left continued, until the column reached the Jerusalem Plank Road. The vital Weldon Railroad loomed in front of the corps' position. The division formed on the left of the road, while the V Corps formed on the right of it. On Gibbon's left were Mott's division, and on his left, Barlow's. The corps was again ordered to entrench. The brigade, now under Major O'Brien, of the 152nd New York, formed on the left side of the first line, disposed in the following manner from left to right: 106th, 72nd, and 69th. The 152nd formed the reserve. Pierce's First Brigade was on its right. Between these two brigades was McKnight's battery. Smyth's Third Brigade and Blaisell's Fourth Brigade formed the second line.

The almost continual fighting was taking its toll on the men. They were rarely more than 100 feet from the enemy when in position. Writing of this period, the historian of the 152nd New York wrote, "...a spirit of demoralization came slowly creeping upon all, who were exhausted from want of sleep, and forced marches. The chances of life were unfavorable...if not by the bullet or shell, then by sheer fatigue."

The rebels opened an artillery barrage during the late morning of June 22, and several rebel attacks were made on the First Brigade and the Philadelphia Brigade, but they were repulsed.[5]

Barlow's and Mott's divisions on the left of Gibbon's division were now ordered to attack. As they moved forward, they were to swing to the right—a "right half-wheel," using Gibbon's division as the pivot. The movement never occurred as planned, and as a result, a growing gap formed between the VI Corps on the left and the two attacking divisions. Seeing this vulnerable spot, General William Mahone attacked with his Confederate division at 3 p.m. Barlow's division tried to resist, but was forced back in disorder. The gray-clad soldiers next turned their attention on Mott's men, and soon they were fleeing for the rear.

While these events were occurring, the rebels continued to attack Gibbon's front. The Confederates, advancing against Gibbon's position, wore dark uniforms, and were assumed to be "friendly." The Philadelphians therefore held their fire, but lingering doubts existed because of their "manner and direction of their formation." Just then, a rebel battery galloped up, unlimbered, and threw canister at the Union line from a short distance. As the 106th continued to fire at the enemy in their front, a volley rang out from their left flank and rear. They were astounded to see Confederates all around them, and before they had a chance to change their positions, the enemy had closed on them, demanding their outright surrender. Major Anderson of the 47th Georgia demanded that Captain Tyler of the 106th surrender his command. Realizing that further resistance was hopeless, Tyler ordered his men to throw down their arms. The men were then hurried to the rebel lines.

Knowing that all was lost, the 106th's color bearer, Corporal John Houghton, quickly ripped the flag from its standard and stuffed it into his blouse. Realizing that he had been seen, he pulled it out again, and, with the help of two or three colleagues, ripped it apart, rather than allow it to fall into the hands of the tattered rebels. The remnants were hidden and the flagstaff was broken in two and thrown over the breastworks.

The defeat was especially surprising to the men of the 106th, because they had successfully repulsed the rebel charges just a few moments before, and heard their officers yelling, "Keep it up, boys, we're driving them." At the end of the engagement, the regiment could muster but one officer and 28 men.[6]

Having disposed of the 106th on the left of the line, the rebels now turned their attention on the 72nd. Fortunately, the remainder of the brigade had already seen what occurred to its sister regiment, and were moving most rapidly toward the right. A large number of men were nevertheless scooped up by the victorious rebels. The 69th lost four companies comprising their left wing. One soldier from the 152nd New York recalled that the brigade's commanding officer ordered the regiment to fall back, "but the confusion was so great, with the shot and shell, and the rebel horde closing around, with furious and exultant yells, that few heard the order." Everyone acted independently, and used their own judgement and legs in getting away. A few ran into the ranks of the enemy amid the blinding smoke, and were captured. So rapid was this Confederate movement that McKnight's battery

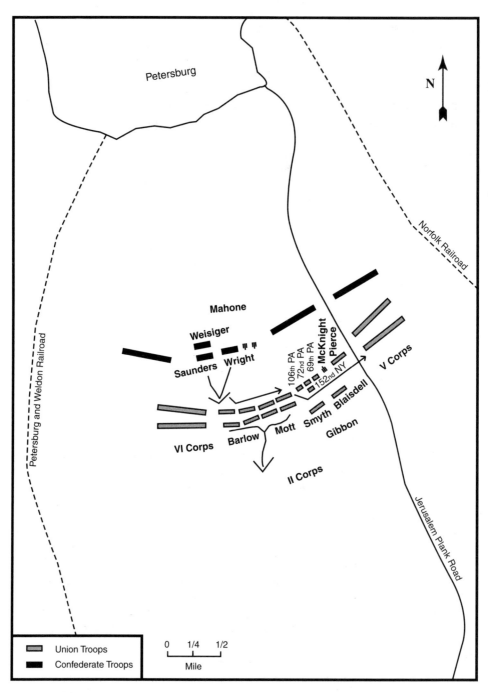

Battle of Jerusalem Plank Road (June 22, 1864)

was overrun after firing only one shot at the approaching enemy. Two of the guns were quickly spiked, but because the horses were so far in the rear, and there were not enough men available to move the guns, they were captured. These were the first guns lost by the II Corps since its formation.

The gray tide continued moving to the Union right, now taking on the First Brigade. Most of five of its regiments, 19th Massachusetts, 42nd New York, 82nd New York, 15th Massachusetts, and 59th New York, were captured.

A fresh brigade from the V Corps arrived to stem the onslaught. What was left of Gibbon's division was reorganized about 250 yards in the rear, and then thrown against the rebels holding their works. The Confederates turned McKnight's guns on the attackers, and with a hail of small arms fire, repulsed every attack aimed at reclaiming the lost works.[7]

Nightfall brought an end to the fiasco along the Jerusalem Plank Road. Gibbon's division lost about 1,700 men, most of them prisoners.

This marked the last engagement of the Philadelphia Brigade. Many compared it to Antietam, as the left flank was crushed by an attack on the front, left, and rear. However, at Antietam, most of the men were able to flee to safety. The differences, according to the brigade historian, were "the apparent absence of skillful and efficient officers in the former [Jerusalem Plank Road], and the presence of "Old Sumner" and his subordinates at the latter." By 1864, most of the most competent officers had either left the army or were promoted to higher posts. Majors commanding brigades and captains commanding regiments were fairly common. Gibbon agreed. "Officers and men who escaped informed me that the presence of one or two good regimental officers would probably have stopped this discreditable affair long before the enemy reached the battery."

The finger pointing began soon after the battle. Gibbon blamed not only the regimental officers, but also the brigade commanders, when he wrote,

> The Second Brigade appears to have given way without an attempt at resistance, and, it is said, by direction of the brigade commander, Major O'Brien, who has been placed in arrest; troops were at once placed at the disposal of General Pierce to retake the battery, but he was so dilatory...

The regimental officers blamed the general officers, as none were present during the fiasco. Others blamed the faulty disposition of the troops and the utter exhaustion of the men. Even if they had more warning, it is doubtful that they could have scrambled to safety.[8]

Some of the men also recalled the similarity with Ball's Bluff, when a large part of the 71st was captured. Now, with the brigade's service drawing to a close, it was the "junior" regiment that sustained the indignation. Similarly, both units' flags were lost, but not to the enemy, allowing the II Corps to continue to brag that it had never lost a standard to the enemy.

An advance the next day by Gibbon's division found that the rebels had abandoned the captured works. The men reoccupied them, and buried the dead.

The fighting between June 15–30 had left Gibbon's division almost 2,300 men weaker. The greatest losses were sustained by the First Brigade, which lost 1,115 men, 816 of which were captured. The Fourth Brigade lost 690, and the Third Brigade lost only 78 men during this period. The Philadelphia Brigade lost 365 (21 killed; 116 wounded; 228 missing). The breakdown by regiment was: 69th=103; 72nd=55; 106th=167; and 152nd=40. As can be expected, the 106th losses were most severe. At the end of the engagement, only thirty men remained of this proud regiment.

The losses were but a continuation of the bloodletting that had begun since Grant took command. The fighting from May 3 through July 30 was endless. General Gibbon wrote in his official report that he began the Wilderness campaign with 11,062 men and lost 5,075 or 46%. His four brigades were led by seventeen different commanders during this three-month period. All four Pennsylvania regiments in the Philadelphia Brigade were commanded by captains at some point during these campaigns.[9]

On June 26, the Philadelphia Brigade was broken up, it's four remaining units barely amounting to a good-sized regiment. The brigade's original regiments were transferred to Smyth's Third Brigade, while the 152nd New York was sent to the First Brigade. The move infuriated the men of the brigade. Not only had they lost their identity, they also relinquished their unit designation, the Second Brigade, Second Division, II Corps to what had been the Fourth Brigade, which had only been in the field since May. Joseph Ward wrote,

> This was a severe blow to our officers and men, one that they keenly felt; and they did not hesitate at all times to give expression to their feelings whenever General Gibbon was around...which the men attributed to his antagonism to General Owen...and now robbed them of their good name and battle-scarred standard, which might have been left to them a few months longer, when their term of service would have expired.

The following day, June 27, the II Corps marched back to Prince George Court House, where enemy cavalry threatened Union trains. Two days later, the corps returned to the front to relieve the VI Corps. They remained in this position until July 2, when they moved to the right.

So cut up was the II Corps that it was pulled back from the front during the early part of July, and the men spent three weeks picketing, guarding trains, and tearing down old rebel fortifications and building new ones.

July 20 brought exciting news—units, such as the 72nd and 106th whose terms of service were to expire within thirty days, were removed from the field and sent to Washington for garrison duty. Left behind were the 69th, whose men had re-enlisted *en masse*, and Companies F, H, and K of the 106th, whose men had entered the service later than their counterparts. The latter companies were formed into the 106th Pennsylvania Battalion under Captain Frank Wessels. Since he was away on staff duty,

Lieutenant John Irwin replaced him. Those men from the 72nd who had re-enlisted were incorporated into Colonel Joseph Lynch's 183rd Pennsylvania.[10]

After bidding farewell to their colleagues, the 72nd and 106th left early on July 21, marched to City Point, and boarded transports. The ships began their journey down the James River toward home that afternoon. Finally disembarking at Washington on July 24, they marched to Arlington Heights, where they were attached to General DeRussey's division. Ironically, they were sent to Fort Ethan Allen, their first position at the front.

The 72nd left the army for home in early August. So excited were the city officials that they ordered a public reception. The entire Philadelphia Fire Department escorted the "Fire Zouaves" in their march through the city. Finally stopping at City Hall, they were met by the mayor of Philadelphia and other city officials. The unit was mustered out on August 24.

The 106th's journey home began on August 28, when they crossed the Long Bridge to Washington, and marched to the "Soldiers' Retreat," which they had visited almost three years earlier when they first arrived in 1861. After having dinner and supper, the regiment embarked on trains at 6 p.m. and arrived in Baltimore at about 10 o'clock that night. Detraining, the regiment marched through the streets to the Philadelphia Depot, and at 11:30 p.m., boarded trains bound for Wilmington, Delaware. They finally arrived in Philadelphia at 8 a.m. on August 29, when they were marched to the Coopershop Refreshment Saloon, cleaned up and sat down to a "real" breakfast—something they hadn't experienced for several years.

Colonel William Davis *(center seated)* and staff,
69th Pennsylvania, June 1865

That afternoon, they marched through the streets of Philadelphia, escorted by the now mustered out men of the 72nd. After a short speech, the men were disbanded, but told to be ready to assemble at a moment's notice to be officially mustered out. After a number of aborted attempts, the unit finally passed into history on September 10, 1864.

Although safely home, these veterans closely followed the exploits of the 69th Pennsylvania and 106th Pennsylvania battalion through the remainder of the war, which included fights at Ream's Station, Deep Bottom, and Hatcher's Run. These units were present at Lee's surrender at Appomattox Court House. The 106th Pennsylvania battalion was finally mustered out on June 30, 1865; the 69th on July 1, 1865. Both marched in the Grand Review through the streets of Washington.

Although the war was over, the battles and marches would live on in the minds of the veterans until they died.[11]

CHAPTER 19

ANALYSIS

Because of Gettysburg, and to a lesser degree, Ball's Bluff, the Philadelphia Brigade occupies a special place in the annals of the Army of the Potomac. Composed primarily of soldiers from a highly urban area, it took longer for them to learn their trade than soldiers hailing from more rural locations.

The history of the brigade is fraught with controversy. It started when Governor Andrew Curtin officially protested the recruitment of Pennsylvanians that were being credited to a distant state. Soon after, a controversy arose over Baker's handling of his troops at Ball's Bluff. The behavior of some of the troops, particularly the 72nd, during the battle of Savage Station was questioned, but it paled in relation to the debate over the brigade's flight at the battle of Antietam. The blame for the dual fiascos at Ball's Bluff and Antietam can probably be laid at the feet of the commanding officers—Baker at the former and Sumner at the latter.

Owen's handling of the brigade further called its effectiveness into question, particularly when he decided not to sacrifice his men on useless charges. At the battle of Fredericksburg, he ordered his men to lie down at the foot at Marye's Hill before the unit was decimated like so many others. Owen repeated this behavior at Spotsylvania Court House and at Cold Harbor. The latter was the final straw for Gibbon, who finally removed Owen from command and subsequently punished the brigade by dispersing them a short time before their terms of service expired.

While Gettysburg was unquestionably the brigade's finest hour, the actions of some of its regiments were called into question. The 71st's withdrawal from Culp's Hill on the evening of July 2, and its retreat from the Angle during Pickett's Charge were harshly criticized. The 72nd's behavior on July 3 is much more enigmatic. While it did move midway down Cemetery Ridge, it apparently refused to advance nor would it fall back, despite taking heavy losses. Its actions, while questionable, did materially assist in repulsing Armistead's and Garnett's brigades.

These lapses could certainly have been due to problems with discipline and morale. In his farewell speech to the brigade, General Burns confirmed that something was not quite right when he said, "In bidding you a final adieu, I cannot refrain from asking you,...to pay rigid regard to discipline."

Although William Fox designated all four regiments as among the "Fighting 200," a hierarchy of effectiveness can be discerned. Few can argue that the 69th activities at Glendale and Gettysburg cause it to be considered the finest fighting unit in the brigade. Next would be the 106th, which fought so well at Gettysburg and acquitted itself well on several other battlefields. Although suffering from poor leadership at times, the 71st was probably the next most effective regiment, and the 72nd was probably the least effective. One private in the division's first brigade wrote that the 72nd, "never was known to stand fire," and a captain wrote that the regiment did all its fighting on the rear of the line.[1]

The Philadelphia Brigade benefitted from a number of effective leaders, particularly early in the war. Among the best were Burns, Howard, and Webb. Although Baker was wanting on the battlefield, he was an outstanding organizer. At one time or another, every one of the original regimental commanders at least temporarily commanded a brigade. In some cases, the temporary nature of the assignments led to disillusionment, and in the case of Colonel Turner Morehead, resignation from the army.

Several Philadelphia Brigade officers were promoted to the rank of general and given their own brigades. However, at least two, Wistar and Owen were found wanting, and forced from the army. Others who attained the rank of general and commanded brigades were Joseph Lynch and Thomas Smyth. In recognition of their service to the army, three others, Baxter, Marcoe, and Morehead also received a star, but no permanent brigade command.

Losses were high, as can be seen from the figures listed below. Over 45% of the men who served in the brigade died or were wounded.

UNIT	SIZE	M. WOUNDED/ KILLED	DISEASE	WOUNDED	TOTAL DEAD
69th	1,715	178	110	431	288
71st	1,655	161	99	383	260
72nd	1,596	193	71	543	264
106th	911	104	93	295 (est.)	197
TOTAL	**5,877**	**636**	**373**	**1,652 (est.)**	**1,009**

Appendix B illustrates the brigade's battle losses, which ranged from none at Chancellorsville to 545 at both Gettysburg and Antietam. Heavy losses were also incurred during the Seven Days' campaign, and during the siege of Petersburg.

Men left the brigade in a variety of ways as can be seen in Appendix C. The greatest percentage, 21% were mustered out, 18% were sent home because of their wounds and health problems, 14% were killed or died of disease, and an equal number deserted.

Despite some lapses, the brigade did what was expected of it. It was usually steady and dependable, and was certainly a credit to the city that provided its name.[2]

APPENDIX A

PHILADELPHIA BRIGADE STRENGTHS AT VARIOUS TIMES DURING THE WAR

	69th P/A*	69th Pt	71st P/A	71st P	72nd P/A	72nd P	106th P/A	106th P	152nd NY P/A	152nd NY P	TOTAL P/A	TOTAL P
Winter 1861–62	981	952	1,155	1,129	1,465	1,415	1,051	1,036	-	-	4,652	4,532
Yorktown	879	726	1,002	904	1,289	1,215	811	779	-	-	3,981	3,624
After Antietam	737	486	820	510	1,197	681	728	492	-	-	3,482	2,169
After Fredericksburg	594	408	649	388	992	545	639	386	-	-	2,874	1,726
Gettysburg	459	344	538	393	745	473	477	343	-	-	2,219	1,553
Winter 1863–64	342	324	589	316	631	296	429	238	518	385	2,509	1,568

* Present and absent
† Present

APPENDIX B

BATTLE LOSSES OF THE PHILADELPHIA BRIGADE

	69th K	W	M	T*	71st K	W	M	T	72nd K	W	M	T	106th K	W	M	T	152nd NY K	W	M	T	TOTAL K	W	M	T
Fair Oaks-																					5	30	0	35
Seven Days	6	31	44	81	9	54	28	91	14	85	60	159	11	22	40	73	-	-	-	-	40	192	172	404
Antietam	19	32	2	53									5	69	4	78	-	-	-	-	93	379	73	545
Fredericksburg								46	?	?	?	66 †					-	-	-	-				243
Gettysburg																								
July 2	17	28	0	45	4	10	0	14 †	1	3	0	4 †	9	54	1	64	-	-	-	-	31	95	1	127 †
July 3	32	71	18	121	22	59	19	100	36	158	3	197					-	-	-	-	90	288	40	418
Mine Run				7				3				10				1				-				21
Wilderness	3	11	5	19	3	33	8	44	4	40	13	57	10	43	5	58	9	37	5	51	29	164	36	229
Spotsylvania	3	29	6	38	8	60	8	76	4	22	3	39	13	32	3	48	9	52	9	70	37	195	39	271
N. Anna				6				7				5				3				16				37
C. Harbor	7	14	0	21	4	12	0	16	5	25	2	32	4	16	1	21	6	23	3	32	26	90	6	122
Petersburg	10	20	73	103	-	-	-	-	6	11	38	55	5	77	85	167	0	8	32	40	21	116	228	365

* K= killed; W= wounded; M= missing/captured; T= total

† Estimated

APPENDIX C

STATUS OF THE MEN IN THE PHILADELPHIA BRIGADE
WHEN THE REGIMENTS WERE MUSTERED OUT
(IN PERCENTAGES)

	69th	71st	72nd	106th	Total
Killed/mortally wounded	7.1%	7.5%	8.2%	6.8%	7.5%
Died	7.2%	5.9%	6.2%	7.9%	6.7%
Deserted	14.0%	19.2%	12.2%	10.1%	14.3%
Discharged before end of enlistment	22.5%	24.4%	25.2%	33.1%	24.9%
Wounded at end of term of enlistment	9.1%	1.5%	0.6%	2.5%	3.7%
In prison at time of end of term of enlistment	1.9%	0.1%	0.0%	1.1%	0.8%
Missing	0.2%	0.6%	1.4%	1.1%	0.8%
Transferred to another unit	3.1%	2.9%	5.5%	5.2%	4.0%
Transferred to another unit when unit mustered out	–	23.0%	15.2%	–	10.5%
Mustered out with unit	24.9%	13.6%	19.9%	31.4%	21.4%
Other	9.9%	1.3%	5.6%	0.8%	5.0%

234

APPENDIX D

FATES OF MEN WRITING LETTERS
AND DIARIES DURING THE WAR

George Beidelman: Wounded at Gettysburg, he died of disease on March 14, 1864.

William Burns: Survived the war and was mustered out at the expiration of his three-year term of service.

Frank Donaldson: After being wounded at Fair Oaks, he returned as captain of the 118th Pennsylvania.

Joseph Elliott: The 71st Pennsylvania's quartermaster was mustered out at the expiration of his three-year term of service.

John Lynch: Discouraged by not being promoted, he was discharged on September 7, 1863.

William Manley: Died on June 27, 1862 of the wounds he received at the battle of Fair Oaks.

Richard Margerum: Promoted to corporal on February 14, 1863, he was absent when the regiment was mustered out.

William Myers: Promoted to corporal on May 13, 1864, he was mustered out at the end of his three-year term of service.

Jacob Pyewell: Transferred to Veteran Reserve Corps, December 15, 1863.

William Townsend: Died of wounds on May 30, 1864, sustained at the battle of the Wilderness.

James Welch: Deserted on July 4, 1862.

Alfred Wheeler: Discharged on a surgeon's certificate, September 1862.

NOTES

CHAPTER 1

1. Isaac Jones Wistar, *Autobiography of Isaac Jones Wistar, 1827–1905* (Philadelphia: The Wistar Institute of Anatomy and Biology, 1937), pp. 353–55.

2. Anthony McDermott and John Reilly, *A Brief History of the 69th Regiment, Pennsylvania Veteran Volunteers* (Philadelphia: D. J. Gallagher and Company Printers, 1889), pp. 5–7 (hereafter, "McDermott and Reilly"); Samuel Bates, *History of Pennsylvania Volunteers, 1861–65* (Harrisburg: D. Singerly, State Printer, 1969), 2:218–19; Joshua Owen letter, June 3, 1861 (69th Pennsylvania Re-enactors' Archives, hereafter, "69th Archives"); John Nicholson, *Pennsylvania at Gettysburg—Ceremonies at the Dedication of the Monuments* (Harrisburg, Pa.: William Stanley Ray, State Printer, 1904), 1:402.

   McDermott and Reilly offered a different account—the regiment volunteered to stay on to help General Patterson, but this offer was not accepted.

3. Joseph Ward, *History of the One Hundred and Sixth Regiment, Pennsylvania Volunteers* (Philadelphia: Grant, Faires, and Rogers, 1883), p. 1 (hereafter, "Ward"); Bates, *Pennsylvania Volunteers,* 1: 201–2; Joseph Elliott diary, May 21, 1861 entry, U.S. Army Military History Institute (hereafter, "USAMHI").

4. Charles Banes, *History of the Philadelphia Brigade* (Philadelphia: Butternut Press, 1984), pp. 7–9 (hereafter, "Banes"); Wistar, *Autobiography,* p. 355; Stewart Sifakis, *Who Was Who in the Civil War* (New York: Facts on File, 1988), pp. 27–28; Ezra Warner, *Generals in Blue* (Baton Rouge: LSU Press, 1964), p. 16.

5. Bruce Catton, *Mr. Lincoln's Army* (Garden City, N.Y.: Doubleday, 1951), p. 74; Shelby Foote, *The Civil War—A Narrative* (New York: Vintage Books, 1986), 1:105; Carl Sandburg, *Abraham Lincoln—The War Years,* vol. 1 (New York: Harcourt, Brace, and World, 1939), pp. 300, 324; Richard Irwin "Ball's Bluff and the Arrest of General Stone," *Battles & Leaders of the Civil War* (New York: The Century Company, 1887), 2:126; Wistar, *Autobiography,* p. 355.

   Baker was offered a promotion to brigadier general on August 6, 1861, to rank from May 17, 1861, but he declined on August 31. His commission to the rank of major general was dated September 21, 1861, but at the time of his death on October 21, 1861, he had neither accepted nor declined with appointment.

6. Harry Blair and Rebecca Tarshis, *Colonel Edward D. Baker, Lincoln's Constant Ally* (Portland: Oregon Historical Society, 1960), pp. 124–25.

7. Frank Taylor, *Philadelphia in the Civil War, 1861–65* (Philadelphia: Dunlap Printing Company, 1913), p. 85.

8. Wistar, *Autobiography*, p. 355; Banes, p. 9.

    Another acquaintance from California, James Lingenfelter, would also sign on to become commander of Company B of the California Regiment.

9. Paul Fatout, "The California Regiment, Colonel Baker and Ball's Bluff," *California Historical Society Quarterly*, 31:229–40, 1952; Wistar, *Autobiography,* pp. 356–57; Alfred Wheeler Letter, August 1861, USAMHI.

10. Bell Wiley, *The Life of Billy Yank* (New York: Bobbs-Merrill, 1951), pp. 24–25; Wistar, *Autobiography*, p. 357; John Frazier, "Col. Baker's Regiment, How It Was Raised in Philadelphia by Mr. Wistar," *Philadelphia Weekly Times*, September 20, 1879.

11. *New York Times*, June 12, 1861; *Bucks County Intelligencer*, June 18, 1861; Harry C. Blair and Rebecca Tarshis, *Colonel Edward Baker,* p. 130; Catherine Vanderslice, *The Civil War Letters of George Washington Beidelman* (New York: Vantage Press, 1978), p. 22 (hereafter, "Vanderslice").

12. *Bucks County Intelligencer*, June 25, 1861; Frank Donaldson Letter, May 30, 1861, Civil War Library and Museum (hereafter, "CWLM").

    According to a dubious story by Taylor (*Philadelphia in the Civil War,* p. 86), the First California received grey uniforms that had been confiscated in New York when about to be shipped to a Confederate artillery regiment.

13. Wiley, *Billy Yank,* pp. 24–25; *New York Evening Post,* June 24, 1861; Wistar, *Autobiography*, p. 357; Donaldson letter, June 9, 1861 (CWLM).

14. Frazier, *Philadelphia Weekly Times*, September 20, 1879.

15. *Sacramento Union Supplement*, November 18, 1861; Blair and Tarshis, *Colonel Edward Baker,* pp. 130–31.

16. Ward, p. 1; Vanderslice, p. 21.

17. O.R., series 3, vol. 1, pp. 526–27, 541.

    According to Bates (*Pennsylvania Volunteers,* 1:788), the regiment was "not recognized by either Pennsylvania or New York" and was therefore treated as belonging to the Regular Army.

18. *New York Times*, June 29, 1861.

19. *Bucks County Intelligencer*, July 16, 1861; Banes, pp. 9–10; Wistar, *Autobiography*, p. 358.

20. *Philadelphia Public Ledger*, July 1, 1861; Richard Sauers, "*Advance the Colors—Pennsylvania Civil War Battle Flags* (Harrisburg: Capitol Preservation Committee, Commonwealth of Pennsylvania, 1987), 1:193.

21. O.R., vol. 3, pp. 763–64; Vanderslice, p. 26.

22. *Philadelphia Inquirer*, July 9 and 16, 1861.

23. Frank Donaldson letter, July 9, 1861, CWLM; *Bucks County Intelligencer,* July 16 and 30, 1861; Alfred Wheeler letter, August 1861, USAMHI; Wistar, *Autobiography*, p. 358.

24. Donaldson letters, June 6 and July 26, 1861, CWLM; Vanderslice, pp. 29, 41; *Bucks County Intelligencer*, August 6, 1861; Richard Margerum letter, August 10, 1861, Pennsylvania Historical Society (hereafter, "PHS"); Blair and Tarshis, *Colonel Edward Baker,* p. 134; Banes, p. 10; Ward, p. 6.

25. *Bucks County Intelligencer*, August 27 and September 3, 1861; Vanderslice, pp. 30, 39; *Philadelphia Bulletin*, August 23, 1861.

CHAPTER 2

1. Banes, pp. 10–15; Ward, p. 2; Bates 2:697; Warner, *Generals in Blue,* pp. 353–54; Sifakis, *Who Was Who,* p. 482.

    Confusion exists over the identity of the Second California. While recruiting posters and early reports from the 69th Pennsylvania refers to the regiment as the Second California. The brigade and regimental histories use the designation for the 72nd Pennsylvania. This convention is followed in this book.

2. Taylor, *Philadelphia,* p. 86; Ward, p. 3.

   The problems with Company K did not stop here. Captain William Doyle, who had expected to command the company, was rejected, and one of the lieutenants, Theodore Fimple, was left behind in Philadelphia to recruit additional men. Arriving at Harpers Ferry, he was dismayed to learn that Captain Martin Frost of the 69th Pennsylvania had been assigned to command the company.

3. Banes, pp. 14–16; Ward, p. 2.

4. William Manley letter, August 29, 1861, PSH; Banes, pp. 13, 15; James Wilson testimony, *Survivors of the Seventy-second Regiment of Pennsylvania Volunteers, Plaintiffs vs. Gettysburg Battlefield Memorial Association,* p. 141 (hereafter, "Trial"); Ward, p. 2.

5. Banes, p. 61; Wiley, *Billy Yank,* p. 27.

6. Sauers, *Advance The Colors,* 1:188, 195, 197, 354.

7. Sauers, *Advance The Colors,* 1:189, 355; Banes, p. 13; Ward, p. 5; Joseph Elliott diary, September 15, 1862 entry, USAMHI.

   The Third California was ordered to the front on September 17 (Bates, *Pennsylvania Volunteers,* 2:697).

8. Banes, p. 13; Ward, pp. 5–6; Nicholson, *Pennsylvania at Gettysburg,* 1:401.

9. Ward, pp. 5–7.

10. Banes, p. 17.

11. William Manley letter, September 23, 1861, PSH; William Burns' diary, October 20, 1861 entry, USAMHI.

12. Richard Margerum letter, October 18, 1861, PHS; Alfred Wheeler letter, September 19, 1861, USAMHI; Vanderslice, pp. 35–37; Frank Donaldson letters, August 11 and September 16, 1861, CWLM.

13. Banes, pp. 18–20; *Philadelphia Evening Bulletin,* October 21, 1911; Frank Donaldson letter, August 15, 1861, CWLM; William Manley letter, September 23, 1861, PHS; *Bucks County Intelligencer,* August 27, 1861.

14. Frank Donaldson letter, September 16, 1861, CWLM; *Bucks County Intelligencer,* October 1, 1861; William Manley letter, September, 23, 1861, PHS; O.R., vol. 5, pp. 168–69, 183–84, 215–16.

    General Smith's name came from his thinning hair during his West Point days.

15. O.R., vol. 5, pp. 215–17; McDermott and Reilly, p. 7; *Bucks County Intelligencer,* October 1, 1861; Frank Donaldson letter, October 15, 1861, CWLM; Wistar, *Autobiography,* p. 359; Alfred Wheeler letter, September 26, 1861, USAMHI.

16. Foote, *The Civil War,* vol. 1, p. 103; Wistar, *Autobiography,* pp. 359–60; O.R., vol. 5, p. 218; Banes, p. 20; *Philadelphia Weekly Press,* October 1, 1861; Charles Bombaugh journal (69th Archives).

    There is some confusion over these early events. Lieutenant Colonel Wistar reported that the troops left camp at 9:30 p.m.; Banes, 10:00 p.m., Surgeon Charles Bombaugh 10:30 p.m.; and Lieutenant Colonel O'Kane reported it was just before midnight. Only O'Kane's report discussed the confusion over orders and the officers' trepidation of moving forward without knowing their destination. Wistar's report omits these details—not surprising given his reprimand by Smith. Surgeon Bombaugh also recalled that a staff officer rode into camp, not General Smith.

17. O.R., vol. 5, pp. 218–20; McDermott and Reilly, p. 8; Banes, pp. 21–22; John Baltz letter, February 5, 1887, CWLM; *Bucks County Intelligencer,* September 17, 1861; Charles Bombaugh journal (69th Archives).

    Frank Donaldson (October 15, 1861 letter) reported that several men broke for the rear and climbed over a worm fence prior to the first volley. The "phantom" force doing the firing has been hypothesized to be either the Fourth Michigan or Berdan's Sharpshooters.

18. *Lebanon Courier,* October 3, 1861; Joseph Johnston, *Narrative of Military Operations During the Civil War* (New York: Da Capo, 1990), p. 74; Banes, p. 22; Frank Donaldson letter, October 15, 1861, CWLM; Wistar, *Autobiography,* p. 360.

General Smith's star rose during the early part of the war, and he eventually commanded a corps. After several poor judgements, the Senate failed to confirm his promotion to the rank of major general and he lost his command. His friendship with General U. S. Grant gained him another chance to command a corps, but he performed poorly at the battle of Bermuda Hundred and again lost his command (Sifakis, *Who Was Who,* pp. 608–9).

19. Gregory Coco, *From Ball's Bluff to Gettysburg...and Beyond* (Gettysburg: Thomas Publications, 1994), p. 16; *Bucks County Intelligencer,* September 17, 1861.

20. Banes, pp. 24–25; McDermott and Reilly, p. 8; Ward, p. 8; Frank Donaldson papers, CWLM.

CHAPTER 3

1. O.R., vol. 5, p. 32; Kim Holien, *Battle of Ball's Bluff* (Orange, Va.: Moss Publications, 1985), pp. 20–23.

2. O.R., vol. 5, pp. 33, 290.

3. O.R., vol. 5, pp. 290, 293.

4. O.R., vol. 5, pp. 291, 309, 327; Coco, *From Ball's Bluff,* p. 40.

   The number of boats actually used has been disputed. For example, one of Baker's staff reported "...two flat-boats of the capacity of 25 to 40 men, and a small skiff, which would carry but 3 or 4 men (O.R., vol. 5, p. 327). Capt. William F. Bartlett, of the 20th Massachusetts, wrote, "...during the morning brought round from the other side of the island a small scow, the only means of transportation excepting the whale-boat, holding 16, and the two skiffs, holding 4 and 5..." (O.R., vol. 5, p. 319).

5. O.R., vol. 5, pp. 293–94, 308.

6. O.R., vol. 5, pp. 294–95, 308, 318, 321, 327–28.

7. Holien, *Ball's Bluff,* p. 27; Banes, pp. 25–26; Ward, pp. 10, 14; William Burns' diary, October 21, 1861, entry, USAMHI; Charles Bombaugh journal (69th Archives).

   The right battalion was composed of Companies A, C, D, G, H, L, N, and P (Bates, *Pennsylvania Volunteers,* 2:789).

8. O.R., vol. 5, p. 296; Catton, *The Army,* p. 75.

9. O.R., vol. 5, pp. 296–97, 309–10, 312, 320.

   According to Devens' official report, the remainder of the regiment was on "detached duty."

10. R. A. Shotwell, "The Battle of Ball's Bluff," *The Philadelphia Weekly Times,* April 6, 1878; Coco, *From Ball's Bluff,* pp. 43–44; Holien, *Ball's Bluff,* p. 42.

11. O.R., vol. 5, p. 321; Catton, *The Army,* p. 75; Foote, *Civil War,* p. 106; Coco, *From Ball's Bluff,* p. 40; *Village Record,* November 9, 1861; Banes, p. 26; *Bucks County Intelligencer,* October 15, 1861.

12. O.R., vol. 5, pp. 238, 239, 310, 321; William Burns' diary, October 21, 1861 entry, USAMHI; Catton, *The Army,* p. 75; Foote, *Civil War,* p. 106.

13. Robert Moore, *A Life for the Confederacy* (Wilmington, N.C.: Broadfoot Publishing, 1991), p. 69; Catton, *The Army,* p. 75; Wistar, *Autobiography,* pp. 364–65.

14. Wistar, *Autobiography,* p. 365; O.R., vol. 5, pp. 297, 310, 319; R. A. Shotwell, "The Battle of Ball's Bluff," *The Philadelphia Weekly Times,* April 6, 1878.

15. Coco, *From Ball's Bluff,* p. 41; Foote, *Civil War,* pp. 106–7; William Harris memoir, Frank Donaldson papers, CWLM; O.R., vol. 5, pp. 310, 319, 321–22, 328; *Bucks County Intelligencer,* November 5, 1861.

16. O.R., vol. 5, pp. 322, 328; William Burns' diary, October 21, 1861 entry, USAMHI; William Harris memoir, Frank Donaldson papers, CWLM; Wistar, *Autobiography,* pp. 376–77; Byron Farwell, *Ball's Bluff* (McLean, Va.: EPM Publications, 1990), pp. 99–103.

17. O.R., vol. 5, pp. 297, 311, 322, 324, 358, 368; Andre E. Ford, *The Story of the Fifteenth Regiment, Massachusetts Volunteer Infantry in the Civil War* (Clinton: Press of W. J. Coulter, 1898), pp. 88–89.

18. Foote, *Civil War*, p. 107; O.R., vol. 5, p. 328; Moore, *A Life*, p. 70; Coco, *From Ball's Bluff*, p. 46; Shotwell, "The Battle of Ball's Bluff," *The Philadelphia Weekly Times*; Francis W. Palfrey, *Memoir of William Francis Bartlett* (Boston: Houghton, Osgood, and Company, 1878), pp. 25–26.

19. O.R., vol. 5, pp. 297, 311, 319, 322; Moore, *A Life*, p. 70; Palfrey, *William Bartlett*, pp. 25–26; William Burns' diary, October 21, 1861 entry, USAMHI.

    The order to throw arms into the river was only partially obeyed. In addition to capturing about 700 men, the Southern troops collected about 1,200 muskets.

20. George Bruce, *The 20th Regiment of Massachusetts Volunteer Infantry* (Boston: Houghton Mifflin, 1906), pp. 53–54; R. A. Shotwell, "The Battle of Ball's Bluff," *The Philadelphia Weekly Times*.

21. Banes, p. 29; Bowen, *From Ball's Bluff*, pp. 49–50; Shotwell, "The Battle of Ball's Bluff," *The Philadelphia Weekly Times; Bucks County Intelligencer*, November 5, 1861; *Village Record*, November 9, 1861; Ward, p. 11.

22. John Lynch letter, October 22, 1861, PHS; O.R., vol. 5, pp. 298, 333.

23. O.R., vol. 5, pp. 307–8; Bates, *Pennsylvania,* vol. 2, p. 790; Sifakis, *Who Was Who*, p. 28; *Battles and Leaders*, vol. 2, pp. 123, 132; Catton, pp. 69–70; John Baltz, *Hon. Edward D. Baker* (Lancaster, Pa.: Inquirer Printing Company, 1888), pp. 53–59.

    Captain Otter may have drowned. Colonel Baker's body was sent to the Pacific Coast for burial. The losses are from the official records of Union losses in the battle. Both Ward (p. 12) and Banes (p. 30) cite the losses as 312 men.

24. O.R., vol. 5, pp. 323–24; Ward, p. 12; William Burns' diary, October 21, 1861 entry, USAMHI.

25. *Philadelphia Evening Bulletin*, December 11, 1861.

CHAPTER 4

1. James Welch letter, December 21, 1861, Pennsylvania State Archives (hereafter, PSA); John Lynch letter, October 30, 1861, PHS; *Bucks County Intelligencer*, March 4, 1862; Ward, pp. 12–15; *Philadelphia Bulletin*, December 11, 1861.

2. William Manley letter, undated, PHS; Warner, *Generals in Blue*, p. 56; Sifakis *Who Was Who*, pp. 92–93.

3. *Philadelphia Inquirer*, February, 10, 1862; *Munsey Luminary*, December 17, 1861; Vanderslice, p. 51; Frank Donaldson papers, CWLM; Wistar, *Autobiography*, p. 383; Ward, p. 15; Banes, p. 34; William Manley letter, November 19, 1861, PHS; *Philadelphia Inquirer*, December, 17, 1861.

4. John Nicholson, *Pennsylvania at Gettysburg*, 1:408–9; Banes, pp. 34–35; Joshua Owen letter, October 21, 1861 (69th Archives).

5. Joshua Owen letter, November 9, 1861 (69th Archives); Ward, p. 16; Frank Donaldson letter, October 15, 1861, CWLM; Nicholson, *Pennsylvania at Gettysburg*, 1:402; *Bucks County Intelligencer*, December 31, 1861; *Munsey Luminary*, January 7, 1862; *Philadelphia Inquirer*, December, 21, 1861, January, 22, 1862.

6. Ward, p. 16; *Philadelphia Inquirer*, January 16, 1862; *Munsey Luminary*, December 17, 1861.

7. Ward, pp. 19–20; *Philadelphia Inquirer*, December 30, 1861; *Munsey Luminary*, January 7, 1862; Alfred Wheeler letter, December 21, 1861, USAMHI.

8. Banes, pp. 35–36; *Munsey Luminary*, December 23, 1861, and January 7, 1862; Alfred Wheeler Letter, December 21, 1861, USAMHI.

9. Vanderslice, p. 54; *Bucks County Intelligencer*, October 1, 1861.

10. *Munsey Luminary*, December 17, 1861; *Bucks County Intelligencer*, October 1, 1861; *Philadelphia Inquirer*, January 16, 1862.

11. Banes, pp. 31, 61; Ward, pp. 16–17; Vanderslice, pp. 52–53; William Lynch Letter, November 20, 1861, and December 2, 1861, PHS; William Burns' diary, January 1, 1862 entry, USAMHI; James Welch letter, December 26, 1861, PSA.

12. James Welch letter, December 26, 1861, PSA; *Bucks County Intelligencer*, January 28, 1862; William Burns' diary entry, November 6, 1861, USAMHI; Alfred Wheeler letter, December 21, 1861, USAMHI.

13. O.R., vol. 5, p. 714; Ward, pp. 19–21; *Philadelphia Inquirer*, January 16, 22, 1862.

14. Ward, pp. 17–19, 22; Banes, p. 33.

15. Ward, pp. 21–22; *Bucks County Intelligencer*, January 28, 1862; Vanderslice, p. 53; Joseph Elliott diary, February 22, 1862, USAMHI; *Munsey Luminary*, December 17 and 23, 1861.

16. *Bucks County Intelligencer*, January 28, 1862, March 4, 1862, and March 25, 1862; *Philadelphia Inquirer*, February 6, 1862; Frank Donaldson letter, March 29, 1862, CWLM; Wistar, *Autobiography*, p. 383.

17. Banes, p. 8; William Lynch letter, January 20, 1862, PHS; *Philadelphia Inquirer*, February 6, 1862.

    The term "Sacred Soil" was commonly used to refer to the state of Virginia.

18. Alfred Wheeler letter, January 28, 1862, USAMHI; *Philadelphia Inquirer,* February 6, 1862; Banes, pp. 37–39; Ward, p. 23.

19. *Munsey Luminary*, March 11, 1862; Ward, p. 23; Banes, p. 39; O.R., vol. 5, pp. 728, 733, 740, 750, 751; Catton, *The Army*, p. 104.

    "Uncle John" Sedgwick was among the most beloved of the Union generals. Prior to the war, Sedgwick served in the Seminole War and the Mexican War (Sifakis, *Who Was Who*, pp. 578–79).

20. Banes, p. 38; Ward, p. 24; William Burns' diary, February 25, and 26, 1862 entry, USAMHI; *Munsey Luminary*, March 11, 1862.

21. Banes, p. 39; William Lynch letter, March 2, 1862, PHS; Ward, p. 25.

22. Frank Donaldson letter, March 12, 1862, CWLM; *Munsey Luminary*, March 11, 1862; William Manley letter, February 28, 1862, PHS; Ward, p. 26.

23. Warner, *Generals in Blue*, pp. 26–27; Ward, p. 30.

24. William Manley letter, March 16, 1862, PHS; William Burns' diary, March 7 and 11, 1862 entries, USAMHI; *Munsey Luminary*, April 1, 1862; Ward, pp. 29–30.

25. Foote, *Civil War*, 1:269; William Manley letter, March 24, 1862, PHS; Banes, p. 43; William Burns' diary, March 15, 17, 23, 25, and 27, 1862 entries, USAMHI.

26. Ward, p. 31.

CHAPTER 5

1. Stephen Sears, *To the Gates of Richmond* (New York: Ficknor and Fields, 1992), pp. 9–23; Catton, *The Army*, pp. 85–110; Foote, *Civil War*, pp. 248–70; O.R. vol. 5, pp. 1079, 1086; Joseph Johnston, *Narrative of Military Operations During the Civil War* (New York: Da Capo Press, 1990), p. 97.

2. O.R., vol. 5, p. 18; Francis Walker, *History of the Second Army Corps* (New York: Charles Scribner's and Sons, 1886), pp. 9–10; Sears, *Gates*, p. 32; *Munsey Luminary*, July 29, 1862.

    Blenker's division was detached to General Charles Fremont's newly formed Mountain Department on March 31 and never joined the II Corps.

3. Frank Donaldson letter, March 24, 1862, CWLM; O.R., vol. 11, pt. 3, p. 53; Banes, p. 34; McDermott and Reilly, p. 10; William Burns' diary, March 25 and 27 entries, USAMHI; John Lynch letter, March 27, 1862, PHS.

4. Banes, pp. 44, 46; Joseph Elliott diary, March 27 entry, USAMHI; William Burns' diary, March 28, 30, 1862 entries, USAMHI; Ward, p. 35; McDermott and Reilly, p. 10; John Lynch letter, March 29, 1862, PHS.

5. McDermott and Reilly, pp. 10–11; Banes, p. 118; Ward, p. 34; Frank Donaldson letter, April 4, 1862; *Bucks County Intelligencer,* October 28, 1862; CWLM; O.R., vol. 4, pp. 569–70; Joseph Elliott diary, March 31, 1862 entry, USAMHI; William Burns' diary, March 30 and 31, 1862 entries, USAMHI.

6. O.R., vol. 11, pt. 3, p. 393; William Manley letter, April 12, 1862, PHS; Ward, p. 36.

7. Ward, p. 36; William Manley letter, April 12, 1862, PHS.

8. Sears, *Gates*, pp. 26, 30–45.

9. Banes, pp. 50–52; William Manley letter, April 12, 1862, PHS; *Munsey Luminary*, April 22, 1862.

10. Ward, pp. 38–39; Banes, pp. 50–52.

11. Banes, pp. 52–54; *Munsey Luminary,* April 22, 1862; William Townsend letter, April 25, 1862, USAMHI.

12. Ward, pp. 39–40; William Manley letter, April 12, 1862, PHS.

13. *Munsey Luminary*, April 22, 1862.

14. Ward, pp. 39–40; Banes, pp. 53–55; Frank Donaldson letter, April 21, 1862, CWLM; William Townsend letter, April 25, 1862, USAMHI.

15. William Manley letter, April 12, 1862, PHS; William Manley letter, April 4, 1862, USAMHI; Banes, pp. 52–54; Ward, pp. 39–40; McDermott and Reilly, p. 11.

16. Frank Donaldson letter, April 24, 1862, CWLM; Ward, p. 52; William Manley letter, April 12, 1862, PHS; Ward, p. 41; Coco, *From Ball's Bluff*, p. 90.

17. Frank Donaldson letter, April 21, 1863, CWLM; Ward, p. 54; Wistar, *Autobiography*, p. 385; Alfred Wheeler letter, May 1, 1862, USAMHI.

18. O.R., vol. 11, pt. 1, pp. 334–35 354–57; William Manley letter, April 12, 1862, PHS; John Lynch letter April 16, 1862, PHS; William Manley letter, April 4, 1862, USAMHI; William Townsend letter, April 25, 1862, USAMHI.

19. Sears, *Gates*, pp. 61–62; Banes, p. 55;

20. O.R., vol. 11, pt. 3, pp. 510–11; Sears, *Gates*, p. 66; Banes, pp. 55–56; William Myers letter, May 13, 1862, USAMHI; William Burns' diary, May 6 entry, USAMHI; Charles Bombaugh journal (69th Archives).

21. Ward, pp. 43–44.

22. Sears, *Gates*, pp. 67–82.

CHAPTER 6

1. Banes, pp. 56–57; Ward, pp. 44–46; Bombaugh journal (69th Archives); *Bucks County Intelligencer,* October 28, 1862.

2. Sears, *Gates*, pp. 85–86; *Battles and Leaders of the Civil War*, vol. 2, p. 276; Banes, p. 59; Ward, p. 47; Frank Donald memoirs, CWLM; Joseph Elliott letter, May 7, 1862, USAMHI.

3. Wistar, *Autobiography,* p. 386; Banes, pp. 59–60.

4. Banes, pp. 58–59, 62–63; Ward, pp. 47–49; Joseph Watt letter, May 30, 1862, USAMHI; Bombaugh journal (69th Archives); William Lynch letter, May 18, 1862, PHS; Aunt and the Soldier Boys from Cross Creek Village, USAMHI; William Burns' diary, June 21, 1862 entry, USAMHI.

5. Ward, pp. 49–50; Foote, *Civil War*, vol. 1, pp. 441–42; Jacob Pyewell letters, May 11 and 18, 1862, USAMHI; Sears, *Gates*, pp. 103–16.

6. Banes, pp. 62–64; Ward, pp. 48–51; Joseph Elliott diary, May 27, 1862 entry, USAMHI; Joseph Watt letter, May 30, 1862; Aunt and the Soldier Boys from Cross Creek Village, USAMHI.

   At the battle of Hanover Court House, General Fitz John Porter manhandled General Lawrence Branch's Confederate brigade.

7. O.R., vol. 11, pt. 1, pp. 896–99, 933–35, 989–90; Frank Donaldson memoirs, CWLM; Walker, *Second Corps,* pp. 22–23; Sears, *Gates,* pp. 120–34; Clifford Dowdey, *The Seven Days: The Emergence of Lee* (Boston: Little, Brown, 1964) pp. 114–16.

   Because of Lincoln's concern over the safety of the capitol, General Irwin McDowell's I Corps was retained near Washington. When it moved south, it would swell McClellan's strength by another 30,000 men.

8. Walker, *Second Corps,* p. 28; Sears, *Gates,* pp. 135–36.

9. Oliver Howard, *Autobiography,* vol. 2, p. 237; Banes, p. 65; Frank Donaldson memoirs, CWLM; Ward, pp. 52–53; William Burns' diary, May 31 entry, USAMHI.

    The gray overcoats may have been retained by some of the men after they had been issued blue-colored uniforms.

10. O.R., vol. 11, pt. 1, pp. 791, 796, 798–801, 806; Nicholson, *Pennsylvania at Gettysburg,* 1:409; Banes, p. 66.

11. O.R., vol. 11, pt. 1, p. 806; Banes, p. 67; John Lynch letter, June 12, 1862, PHS.

12. O.R., vol. 12, pt. 1, pp. 791–92, 806, 990–91; Frank Donaldson memoirs, CWLM.

13. O.R., vol. 11, pt. 1, pp. 791–92, 796; Ward, p. 53; Walker, *Second Corps,* pp. 35–37; Bombaugh journal (69th archives); *Bucks County Intelligencer,* October 28, 1862.

    Captain Kirby's battery was commanded by Captain Ricketts at the battle of First Bull Run. Losing all of their guns and twenty-seven of their gunners at the battle, Kirby and his men were anxious to avenge the loss (O.R., vol. 2, p. 407).

14. Dowdey, *Seven Days,* p. 120; Sears, *Gates,* p. 137; O.R., vol. 11, pt. 1, pp. 990–91; Banes, p. 68.

15. O.R., vol. 11, pt. 1, pp. 806–7; 791–92; Ward, p. 55; Banes, pp. 68–69.

16. Banes, p. 69; O.R., vol. 12, pt. 1, pp. 758, 792, 807.

17. Alfred Wheeler letter, June 10, 1862, USAMHI; Banes, p. 70.

18. Banes, pp. 70–71; Ward, pp. 58–59.

19. William Burns' and Joseph Elliott diaries, USAMHI.

20. O.R., vol. 12, pp. 1065–66; John Lynch letter of June 20, 1862, PHS.

21. O.R., vol. 11, pt. 1, pp. 1065–66; Banes, pp. 71–72; Ward, pp. 58–59; William Burns' diary, June 8 and 13 entries, USAMHI.

CHAPTER 7

1. Banes p. 73; Ward, pp. 61–62.

2. Walker, *Second Corps,* pp. 58–65; Banes, pp. 76–77; Ward, pp. 62–63; Mac Wyckoff, *A History of the 3rd South Carolina Infantry* (Fredericksburg, Va.: Sergeant Kirkland's Museum, 1995), p. 47.

3. Dowdey, *Seven Days,* pp. 261–63; O.R., vol. 11, pt. 2, pp. 90–91; William Burns' diary, June 16, 1862 entry, USAMHI; Bates, *Pennsylvania Reserves,* vol. 1, p. 791.

    Ward (pp. 64–65) stated that the 106th was sent back to destroy supplies and equipment, but there is no evidence to support this claim.

4. Ward, p. 65; O.R., 11, pt. 2, pp. 90–91, 707, 709; Bates, 2:791.

5. *Munsey Luminary,* July 29, 1862; *Bucks County Intelligencer,* November 18, 1862; O.R., vol. 11, pt. 2, pp. 49–50, 56, 77, 90–91; Ward, pp. 64–65; Webb, pp. 137–39; Sears, *Gates,* pp. 265–66; Banes, pp. 78–79.

    Some confusion exists about which Pennsylvania regiment did most of the fighting at Allen's Farm. Both Webb and Walker attribute it to the 53rd Pennsylvania. The members of the Philadelphia Brigade steadfastly claimed that the 71st carried the brunt of the battle, and the relative number of losses in the two regiments support their claim.

6. O.R., vol. 11, pt. 2, pp. 49–50, 89; Walker, *Second Corps,* p. 66; Ward, p. 65; William Burns' diary, June 29, 1862 entry, USAMHI; Ward, p. 66.

7. *Philadelphia Inquirer,* July 11, 1862; O.R., vol. 11, pt. 2, pp. 50–51.

8. Wyckoff, *3rd South Carolina,* pp. 49–50; Banes, pp. 79–80; O.R., vol. 11, pt. 2, p. 91; Walker, *Second Corps,* p. 68.

9. *Philadelphia Inquirer,* July 11, 1862; Augustus Dickert, *History of Kershaw's Brigade* (Newberry, S.C.: Elbert Aull, 1899), p. 129; O.R., vol. 11, pt. 2, p. 91.

    Controversy flared when the *New York Herald* reported that the 106th was "seized with momentary panic," and later, "a regiment of rebel cavalry galloped in and drove the regiment off." This was angrily refuted in a subsequent issue of the *Philadelphia Inquirer* (July 11, 1862).

10. O.R., vol. 11, pt. 2, pp. 73, 91; William Burns' diary, June 29 entry, USAMHI; Richard Moe, *The Last Full Measure* (New York: Avon Books, 1993), pp. 153–54; O.R., vol. 11, pt. 2, p. 91; Wyckoff, *3rd South Carolina*, p. 52.

   Meagher mistakenly reported that General Daniel Butterfield took up the 69th New York's flag. Commanding a brigade in Fitz John Porter's corps, he was not present on the battlefield.

11. McDermott and Reilly, p. 14; O.R., vol. 11, pt. 2, pp. 74, 478–79, 741; Wyckoff, *3rd South Carolina*, p. 54.

12. William Burns' diary, June 29 entry, USAMHI; O.R., vol. 11, pt. 2, p. 91; Banes, p. 81; Ward, pp. 68–69; McDermott and Reilly, p. 14.

13. Walker, *Second Corps*, pp. 68, 70; Dickert, *Kershaw's Brigade*, p. 129; *Bucks County Intelligencer,* November 18, 1862; Banes, pp. 81–82; O.R., vol. 11, pt. 2, pp. 87, 94.

14. Banes, p. 83; William Burns' diary, June 29 entry, USAMHI.

15. Ward, p. 69; Sears, *Gates*, pp. 278–83; Asa Smith diary, *American Heritage*, February 1971, p. 57; Joseph Elliott diary, June 29 entry USAMHI.

16. Edward Alexander, *Military Memoirs of a Confederate* (Dayton: Morningside Books, 1977), p. 107; O.R., vol. 11, pt. 2, pp. 91, 93, 94, 403; Sears, *Gates,* pp. 294–99; Dowdey, *Seven Days,* p. 285.

17. O.R., vol. 11, pt. 2, p. 92; McDermott and Reilly, pp. 14–15.

18. *Lewisburg Chronicle*, November 21, 1896; McDermott and Reilly, pp. 14–16; Banes, pp. 84–85; O.R., vol. 11, pt. 2, pp. 92, 111–12.

19. Ward, pp. 70–71; O.R., vol. 11, pt. 2, pp. 81, 92–93; William Burns' diary, June 30 entry, USMHI.

20. McDermott and Reilly, p. 16; Banes, pp. 86–88.

21. *Munsey Luminary*, July 29, 1862; Banes, pp. 87–88.

22. McDermott and Reilly, pp. 16–17; William Burns' diary, July 1 entry, USAMHI; Walker, *Second Corps*, p. 87.

CHAPTER 8

1. Banes, pp. 89–90; Ward, p. 72; William Burns' diary, July 2, 1862 entry, USAMHI.

2. O.R., vol. 12, pt. 2, pp. 24–26.

3. John Lynch letter, July 4, 1862, PHS.

4. McDermott and Reilly, p. 17; Ward, pp. 72–73; John Lynch letter, July 4, 1862, PHS; William Burns' diary, July 2 and 3 entries, USMHI; Joseph Elliott diary, July 4 entry, USAMHI; *Munsey Luminary*, July 29, 1862.

5. Stackhouse Collection, PSA; Ward, p. 80.

6. Ward, pp. 75–76; Sifakis, *Who Was Who,* pp. 92–93; Banes, p. 96; Walker, *Second Corps*, p. 88.

   DeWitt's horse broke away as the regiment was marching into the battle of Fair Oaks. Rather than sending men after it, DeWitt followed it, and therefore did not participate in the battle. Frank Donaldson, of the 71st, wrote, "To my mind his conduct was anything but dignified—or that of a brave soldier. He escaped the battle-at all events." (Donaldson memoir, CWLM).

7. John Lynch letter, July 13, 1862, PHS; McDermott and Reilly, p. 17; Ward, p. 80.

8. *Munsey Luminary*, July 29, 1862; Banes, pp. 91–93; Lucian Alexander letter, July 16, 1862, PSA; Ward, p. 80.

9. Ward, pp. 79–80; John Lynch letter, July 19, 1862, PHS.

   In a letter to his father in August, George Beidelman wrote that there were no mosquitoes present (Vanderslice, p. 75).

10. William Burns' diary, July 30, and August 7 entries, USAMHI; McDermott and Reilly, p. 8; Walker, *Second Corps,* p. 89.

11. Banes, p. 98; Ward, p. 82; Vanderslice, p. 77.

12. O.R., vol. 12, pt. 3, pp. 428, 448, 473; John Hennessy, *Return to Bull Run* (New York: Simon and Schuster, 1993), pp. 8–30.

13. Ward, pp. 83–84; Vanderslice, p. 80.

14. Banes, pp. 99–100.

15. Abner Doubleday to Samuel P. Bates, October 19, 1875, Bates Collection, Pennsylvania State Archives; John Lynch letter, November 1862, PHS; Vanderslice, pp. 83, 88.

    Because of the severity of Howard's wound, his return to the army was doubtful, so Sumner assigned his brigade to General John Caldwell.

16. Ward, pp. 82–85; William Burns' diary, August 22 and 27 entries, USAMHI; Joseph Elliott diary, August 25 entry, USAMHI; Hennessy, *Second Bull Run*, pp. 96–135; Vanderslice, p. 88.

17. William Burns' diary August 29, 30, and September 1 entries, USAMHI; Hennessy, *Second Bull Run*, p. 439.

18. Wistar, *Autobiography,* pp. 387–88; O. O. Howard, *Autobiography of O.O. Howard* (New York: Baker and Taylor Company, 1907), p. 268; O.R., vol. 12, pt. 2, pp. 17, 414; Hennessy, *Second Bull Run*, pp. 449–50.

19. Ward, pp. 87–88; Banes, pp. 101–4; Wistar, *Autobiography*, pp. 388–89.

20. McDermott and Reilly, p. 18.

21. Ward, p. 88; William Burns' diary, September 2 entry, USAMHI; McDermott and Reilly, pp. 18–19; Howard, *Autobiography,* p. 269; John Lynch letter, September 3, 1862, PHS.

CHAPTER 9

1. William Burns' diary, September 3, entry, USAMHI; Banes, pp. 102–6; Ward, pp. 94–96.

2. Banes, p. 107; William Burns' diary, September 4, 5, 6, 7, 8, 9, 10, 11 entries, USAMHI; Ward, p. 96.

3. Wistar, *Autobiography*, pp. 393–95.

   Wistar believed he faced a brigade of cavalry under "Baker." Colonel L. S. Baker actually commanded the First North Carolina Cavalry, which was acting as the army's rear guard during this time. (O.R., vol. 19, pt. 1, p. 817.)

4. Wistar, *Autobiography*, pp. 395–97.

5. Banes, pp. 107–8; Ward, pp. 96–97; William Burns' diary, September 12, 13 entries, USAMHI.

6. Wistar, *Autobiography*, pp. 398–99; Ward, pp. 97–100; *Philadelphia Inquirer,* October 1, 1862; John Lynch letter, September 20, 1862, PHS; Vanderslice, *Letters,* pp. 100–101.

7. Wistar, *Autobiography*, pp. 399–400; Ward, p. 100.

8. William Burns' diary, September 16 entry, USAMHI; Banes, pp. 109–10; Wistar, *Autobiography*, p. 400.

9. James F. Larkin, "The Last To Go," *Philadelphia Weekly Times*, April 8, 1882; Stephen Sears, *The Landscape Turned Red* (New Haven, Conn.: Ticknor and Fields, 1983), pp. 216–17.

10. Banes, pp. 111–12; James Murfin, *The Gleam of Bayonets* (New York: Thomas Yoseloff, 1965), pp. 227–29; Sears, *Landscape,* p. 218; Wistar, *Autobiography*, p. 403; Ward, p. 104; William Rumkel, "The Philadelphia Brigade. Its Part, Under Sedgwick and Howard, in the Battle of Antietam," *Philadelphia Weekly Times*, April 8, 1882.

11. Sears, *Landscape*, pp. 222–23; Wistar, *Autobiography,* p. 403; Larkin, *Philadelphia Weekly Times*, April 8, 1882.

12. Milo Qualife, *From the Cannon's Mouth: The Civil War Letters of General Alpheus Williams* (Detroit: Wayne State University Press, 1959), p. 135; Sears, *Landscape,* pp. 220–22; Francis Palfrey, *Antietam and Fredericksburg* (New York: Jack Brussel, n.d.), p. 84.

13. O.R., vol. 19, pt. 1, p. 305; Larkin, *Philadelphia Weekly Times*, April 8, 1882; Wistar, p. 403; Rumkel, *Philadelphia Weekly Times*, April 8, 1882; Murfin, *Gleam*, p. 233; Palfrey, *Antietam and Fredericksburg*, pp. 82–84; Sears, *Landscape*, p. 223; Ward, p. 102.

14. Palfrey, *Antietam and Fredericksburg*, pp. 84–85.

15. O.R., vol. 19, pt. 1, pp. 969–72.

16. Howard, *Autobiography*, p. 296; Sears, *Landscape*, p. 226.

17. Sears, *Landscape*, p. 226; Howard, *Autobiography*, p. 297; Walker, *Second Corps*, p. 106; Palfrey, *Antietam and Fredericksburg*, p. 87; Murfin, *Gleam*, p. 239; Bates, 2:851; Rumkel, *Philadelphia Weekly Times*, April 8, 1882.

18. O.R., vol. 19, pt. 1, pp. 276, 306–7, 311, 318; Howard, *Autobiography*, p. 297; Wistar, *Autobiography*, pp. 404–5.

19. O.R., vol. 19, pt. 1, 318; Sears, *Landscape*, pp. 227–28; Wistar, *Autobiography*, pp. 407–9; Ward, p. 105.

20. Ward, pp. 105–6; Gerald Welland, *O. O. Howard, Union General* (Jefferson, N.C.: McFarland & Company, 1995), p. 57; Bates, 2:831.

21. O.R., vol. 19, pt. 1, p. 319; Palfrey, *Antietam and Fredericksburg*, p. 88; Sears, *Landscape*, pp. 229–30; Wistar, *Autobiography*, p. 409.

22. O.R., vol. 19, pt. 1, p. 308; Banes, p. 115–16; William Burns' diary, September 17, USAMHI; Ward, p. 109.

23. Ward, pp. 115–17; Vanderslice, *Letters*, pp. 103–4, 106.

CHAPTER 10

1. Vanderslice, pp. 106–8; Banes, pp. 120–22; Ward, p. 117.

2. Vanderslice, pp. 108, 112.

3. Vanderslice, pp. 113–14, 119, 123–24; Ward, pp. 118–22; Banes, p. 125.

4. Anonymous biographical sketch, 69th Pennsylvania file, Gettysburg Military Library; Frank Boyle, *A Party of Mad Fellows* (Dayton: Morningside Books, 1996), pp. 201–2; Court-martial records of the 69th Pennsylvania, PSA; Banes, p. 118; William Burns' diary, October 14, 15, 16, 17 entries, USAMHI; Vanderslice, pp. 127–30.

5. Banes, pp. 124–25; Ward, pp. 118–20; Vorin Whan, *Fiasco at Fredericksburg* (State College, Pennsylvania: Pennsylvania State University Press, 1961), p. 15; William Burns' diary, October 30 and November 1 entries, USAMHI.

6. Banes, pp. 128–29; Ward, pp. 120–23; William Burns' diary, November 2, 3, 4, 5, 6, 8, and 9 entries, USAMHI; Vanderslice, pp. 140–42.

7. Ward, pp. 123–26; Foote, *Civil War*, pp. 754–57; Catton; Vanderslice, p. 144; William Burns' diary, November 10 entry, USAMHI; William Lynch letter, November 18, 1862, PHS; William Myers' letter, November 20, 1862, USAMHI.

8. Vanderslice, pp. 144–45; Whan, pp. 15–16; Ward, p. 127.

9. Whan, p. 18; Vanderslice, pp. 147–48; Banes, pp. 130–31; Ward, pp. 127–28.

10. Whan, pp. 24–27, 30, 54–55.

11. Jacob Pyewell letter, November 26, 1862, USAMHI; William Myers' letter, November 20, 1862, USAMHI; O.R., vol. 21, p. 277; William Burns' diary, December 11 entry, USAMHI; Ward, pp. 129–30.

12. Whan, pp. 40–43; O.R., vol. 21, pp. 262, 277; Vanderslice, p. 166; Ward, 131.

    Owen reported that the brigade crossed the river at 4:00 p.m.; Colonel Morehead of the 106th recalled that it was at 5:30 p.m.

13. John Lynch letter, December 13, 1862, PHS; Whan, pp. 43–44; William Burns' diary, December 12 entry, USAMHI; Vanderslice, pp. 162–63; Ward, pp. 132–35.

14. McDermott and Reilly, p. 23; O.R., vol. 21, pp. 277–78.

15. Whan, pp. 81–84; *Philadelphia Inquirer*, December 31, 1862.

16. Whan, pp. 84–89.

17. *Philadelphia Inquirer*, December 23, 1862; O.R., vol. 21, pp. 263, 278–79, 281; Whan, pp. 89–90; McDermott and Reilly, p. 24; Banes, pp. 141–42.

18. Ward, p. 139; O.R., vol. 21, pp. 263, 282.

19. Whan, p. 91; O.R., vol. 21, pp. 223, 278–79; Banes, p. 143.

20. Banes, pp. 142–43; Ward, pp. 138–39; O.R., vol. 21, pp. 431–32.

21. Carol Reardon, The Forlorn Hope: Brigadier General Andrew A. Humphreys' Pennsylvania Division at Fredericksburg. In *The Fredericksburg Campaign—Decision on the Rappahannock,* Gary Gallagher, ed. (Durham: Univ. of North Carolina Press, 1995), pp. 103–4; Banes, pp. 143–44; O.R., vol. 21, pp. 278–79; Walker, *Second Corps,* pp. 185–86.

22. Banes, p. 144; Bates, 2:795; William Burns' diary, December 15 entry, USAMHI; Vanderslice, pp. 168–70; O.R., vol. 21, pp. 279, 281; Banes, p. 145; Joseph Elliott diary, December 16 entry, USAMHI.

23. O.R., vol. 21, pp. 129–31, 224, 264, 266, 280; Ward, p. 281; McDermott and Reilly, p. 25. Burnside's after-battle report lists 258 casualties in the brigade.

CHAPTER 11

1. Stephen Sears, *Chancellorsville* (Boston: Houghton, Mifflin Company, 1996), pp. 16–18; Banes, pp. 147–48.

2. Ward, p. 151.

3. Vanderslice, p. 149; Banes, p. 146.

4. Ward, p. 152; Banes, p. 148; William Burns' diary, January 1 entry, USAMHI.

5. Vanderslice, p. 118; Ward, pp. 152–53, 155; Banes, p. 149.

6. William Lynch letters, January 20 and 30, 1863, PHS.

7. Sears, *Chancellorsville*, pp. 19–20.

8. William Marvel, *Burnside* (Durham, N.C.: Univ. of North Carolina Press, 1991), pp. 208–12; Ward, pp. 155–56; Banes, pp. 150–51; McDermott and Reilly, p. 25; Sears, *Chancellorsville*, pp. 58–61, 63.

9. Warner, *Generals in Blue*, p. 95; Ward, p. 159.

10. McDermott and Reilly, p. 25; Boyle, *A Mad Party,* p. 238; Sears, *Chancellorsville,* pp. 70–73.

11. John Lynch letter, February 10, PHS; Ward, pp. 158–60.

12. Banes, pp. 151–52; Ward, pp. 158–60; William Burns' diary, February 25 and 26 entries, USAMHI.

13. Ward, p. 166; Banes, pp. 154–55; William Burns' diary, March 17 and April 1 entries, USAMHI.

14. Vanderslice, p. 176; Ward, p. 160; John Lynch letter, April 2, PHS.

15. Sifakis, *Who Was Who,* pp. 245–46; Warner, *Generals in Blue,* pp. 171–72; Ward, p. 160–61; Banes, pp. 157–58.

16. Sears, *Chancellorsville,* pp. 348–50; Banes, pp. 158–59; Ward; pp. 162–63; Stephen Weld, *War Diary and Letters of Stephen Minot Weld, 1861–1865* (Boston: Massachusetts Historical Society, 1979), pp. 187–90.

17. O.R., vol. 25, pt. 1, p. 855; Ward p. 163; Banes, pp. 161–62.

18. O.R., vol. 25, pt. 1, pp. 396, 855; Sears, *Chancellorsville,* pp. 376–85; Ward, p. 164; Banes, pp. 162–63; William Burns' diary, May 3 entry, USAMHI.

19. O.R., vol. 25, pt. 1, pp. 247–48; Sears, *Chancellorsville,* pp. 396–98, 410–18.

20. O.R., vol. 25, pt. 2, pp. 418–19; William Burns' diary, May 4 and 5 entries, USAMHI; Banes, pp. 164–65.

21. Banes, p. 157; William Lynch letter, May 17, PHS; McDermott and Reilly, p. 26.

22. O.R., vol. 25, pt. 1, p. 357.

CHAPTER 12

1. Sifakis, *Who Was Who,* pp. 146, 279–80; Warner, *Generals in Blue,* pp. 202–3; William Burns' diary, May 9 entry, USAMHI; Banes, pp. 166–67; Ward, pp. 169–70.

   Couch commanded the newly created Department of the Susquehanna during the Gettysburg campaign. A year and a half later, he returned to lead a division in the Army of the Ohio.

2. Banes, p. 170; William Burns' diary, May 27 entry, USAMHI.

   McManus, in writing, and verbally, repeatedly called McMahon a "coward and a loafer." When McManus refused to refrain from calling him these names, McMahon went to his tent and shot him. A court-martial subsequently found McMahon guilty and sentenced him to death by firing squad. The sentence was later commuted (Judge Advocate General's Office Report, August 10, 1863, 69th Archives).

3. Ward, pp. 170–72; William Burns' diary, June 13 and 15 entries, USAMHI.

4. William Burns' diary, June 16 entry, USAMHI; Ward, pp. 171–72.

5. Ward, pp. 172–74; William Burns' diary, June 16, 19, 20, 21, 22, 25 entries, USAMHI.

6. Ward, pp. 175–78; George R. Stewart, *Pickett's Charge* (Cambridge, Mass.: The Riverside Press, 1959), pp. 74–75; William Burns' diary, June 29 entry, USAMHI.

7. Warner, *Generals in Blue,* pp. 544–45; Sikafis, *Who Was Who,* pp. 698–99; Stewart, *Pickett's Charge,* p. 75; Boyle, *A Party,* pp. 258–59.

8. Ward, pp. 179–80; William Burns' diary, June 29, and 30 entries, USAMHI; John Lynch letter, June 30, 1863, PHS; Stewart, *Pickett's Charge,* p. 75.

9. Banes, p. 174.

10. O.R., vol. 27, pt. 1, p. 429; Ward, pp. 181–87; William Burns' diary, July 1 entry, USAMHI.

CHAPTER 13

1. Banes, pp. 178–79; Ward, pp. 187–88.

2. O.R., vol. 27, pt. 1, pp. 430–31; Bradley M. Gottfried, "Wright's Charge on July 2, 1863: "Piercing the Union Line or Inflated Glory?" *Gettysburg Magazine,* vol. 17 (July 1997), pp. 71–72; "It Struck Horror to Us All," *Gettysburg Magazine,* vol. 4 (January 1991), pp. 91–92.

   While one officer reported that the men constructed some breastworks—"we took up our line of position behind a temporary breastwork made of fence rails, strengthened with stone..."—it is doubtful that much effort was expended.

3. Ward, pp. 188–89; Banes, pp. 180–81.

4. Ward, pp. 190–91; O.R., vol. 27, pt. 1, pp. 426, 370; Gottfried, *Gettysburg Magazine,* vol. 17 (July 1997), pp. 71–72.

5. O.R., vol. 27, pt. 1, pp. 427, 434; John Buckley to John Bachelder, in Ladd and Ladd, *Bachelder Papers,* 3:1403.

6. Coco, *From Ball's Bluff,* pp. 196–201; Ford, *Fifteenth Massachusetts,* p. 267; O.R., vol. 27, pt. 1, pp. 419–20, 425–26; Wiley Sword, "Defending the Codori House and Cemetery Ridge: Two Swords with Harrow's Brigade in the Gettysburg Campaign," *Gettysburg Magazine,* no. 13 (July 1995): 46–47; *New York at Gettysburg,* 2:664.

7. John H. Rhodes, *The History of Battery B, First Regiment, Rhode Island Artillery* (Providence: Snow and Farnham, Printers, 1914), pp. 200–202; William Paul, "Severe Experiences at Gettysburg," *Confederate Veteran,* vol. 19 (1912): 85.

8. *Pennsylvania at Gettysburg,* 1:415, 550–51; McDermott and Reilly, p. 28; Rhodes, *The History of Battery B,* pp. 202–3.

9. O.R., vol. 27, pt. 1, pp. 427, 434, 436, 447–48; Ward, pp. 191–92; *Pennsylvania at Gettysburg,* 1:550–51; John Busey and David Martin, *Regimental Strengths and Losses at Gettysburg* (Hightstown, New Jersey: Longstreet House, 1986), p. 294.

10. Ralph O. Sturevant, *Pictorial History, Thirteenth Vermont Volunteers* (Burlington, Vt.: Regimental Association, 1910), pp. 267–69.

11. Ward, p. 193; O.R., vol. 27, pt. 1, p. 427.

12. Paul, *Confederate Veteran*, vol. 19 (1912), p. 85; Busey and Martin, *Regimental Strengths and Losses*, p. 294; Banes, p. 183.

13. George R. Stewart, *Pickett's Charge* (Cambridge, Mass.: The Riverside Press, 1959), pp. 277–78; Ward, p. 193.

    Why the regimental historian added such distortions is not obvious. The 106th was moved to Cemetery Hill during the evening of July 2 and therefore missed Pickett's Charge on July 3.

14. Gottfried, *Gettysburg Magazine*, vol. 17 (July 1997), pp. 81–82; O.R., vol. 27, pt. 1, pp. 424, 432, 433; John Gibbon, *Personal Recollections of the Civil War* (Dayton, Ohio: Morningside Press, 1978), p. 176.

15. Harry W. Pfanz, *Gettysburg—Culp's Hill and Cemetery Hill* (Chapel Hill: University of North Carolina Press, 1993), p. 220; Ward, p. 196; O.R., vol. 27, pt. 1, p. 434.

16. O.R., vol. 27, pt. 1, pp. 427, 432, 826–27, 856; Letter from Charles Horton to John Bachelder, Jan. 23, 1867; William Burns' diary, July 2 entry, USAMHI; Pfanz, *Gettysburg—Culp's Hill and Cemetery Hill*, pp. 221, 443; Banes, p. 186; Ward, p. 196.

17. Pfanz, *Gettysburg—Culp's Hill and Cemetery Hill*, pp. 198–99, 439; Ladd and Ladd, *The Bachelder Papers*, pp. 164, 216.

CHAPTER 14

1. *Gettysburg Compiler*, June 7, 1887; *Trial*, p. 259; Stewart, *Pickett's Charge*, pp. 67–68; McDermott and Reilly, p. 29.

2. McDermott and Reilly, p. 30; *Trial*, p. 266.

3. Frank A. Haskell, *The Battle of Gettysburg*, Volume 43 of the Harvard Classics (New York: P. F. Collier and Sons, 1910), pp. 399–400.

4. John Gibbon, *Personal Recollections of the Civil War* (Dayton: Morningside Books, 1978), pp. 146–59; McDermott and Reilly, p. 30.

   Whether Cushing had two, three, or four functional cannon at this time is subject to debate.

5. O.R., vol. 27, pt. 1, p. 428; McDermott and Reilly, p. 31; Anthony McDermott to John Bachelder, June 2, 1886, in Ladd and Ladd, *Bachelder Papers*, 3:1406; *Trial*, p. 259.

6. Stewart, *Pickett's Charge*, p. 166; Andrew Cowan, "When Cowan's Battery Withstood Pickett's Splendid Charge," *New York Herald*, July 2, 1911.

   Whether the 71st had eight companies at the forward wall and two behind it at the parallel wall or visa versa is contested. Both the commander of the 71st and General Webb recalled that it was the former.

7. O.R., vol. 27, pt. 1, pp. 428, 432; Anthony McDermott, "The 69th at Gettysburg," *Philadelphia Weekly Press*, June 11, 1887.

8. O.R., vol. 27, pt. 1, p. 428; Andrew Cowan to John Bachelder, November 24, 1885, in Ladd and Ladd, *Bachelder Papers*, 2:1146; Stewart, *Pickett's Charge*, p. 181.

9. Stewart, *Pickett's Charge*, p. 197; Samuel Roberts to John Bachelder, August 18, 1883, in Ladd and Ladd, *Bachelder Papers*, 2:967; *Trial*, p. 304.

   The remaining eight companies of the 106th remained with Howard's XI Corps and did not participate in this part of the battle.

10. John Buckley to John Bachelder, in Ladd and Ladd, *Bachelder Papers*, 3:1403; R. Penn Smith, The Battle—The Part Taken by the Philadelphia Brigade in the Battle, *Gettysburg Compiler*, June 7, 1887; Hartwig, *Gettysburg Magazine*, p. 92.

    The 69th received orders to pick up the guns on the night of July 2; the 71st picked up spare guns after Pickett's men emerged from Seminary Ridge.

11. Stewart, *Pickett's Charge*, pp. 206–8; Kathy Harrison and John Busey, *Nothing But Glory* (Gettysburg: Thomas, Inc., 1993), p. 64; George Finley, "The Bloody Angle," *Buffalo Evening News*, May 29, 1894; William Burns' diary, July 3 entry, USAMHI; Smith, *Gettysburg Compiler*, June 7, 1887.

Colonel Smith steadfastly claimed that *he ordered* the 71st to retire when Garnett's men approached, and that it was an orderly move to realign it with his other two companies. However, many observers, including some from the 71st, recalled that the men fled to the rear, only to be halted by Webb. Yet, several years after the battle, Webb wrote that the rebels were defeated by the "stubbornness" of the 69th and 71st Pennsylvania.

12. *Trial*, p. 35; Finley, "The Bloody Angle," *Buffalo Evening News*, May 29, 1894; Stewart, *Pickett's Charge*, pp. 212–13; James Clay, "About the Death of General Garnett, *Confederate Veteran*, XIV (February 1905), p. 81; William Burns' diary, July 3 entry, USAMHI.

13. *Trial*, pp. 99, 160–61, 172, 317; Edwin Coddington, *The Gettysburg Campaign: A Study in Command* (New York: Charles Scribner, 1968), p. 517.

14. Rawley Martin and John Smith, "The Battle of Gettysburg and the Charge of Pickett's Division, *Southern Historical Society Papers*, XXXIX (1904), pp. 186–87; John B. Bachelder, "The Third Day's Battle, *Philadelphia Weekly Times*, December 15, 1877; O.R., vol. 27, pt. 1, p. 431; *Trial*, p. 160; Hartwig, *Gettysburg Magazine*, vol. 4 (1991), p. 98.

15. Report of Charles Morgan, 1362; Anthony McDermott to John Bachelder, in Ladd and Ladd, *Bachelder Papers*, 3:1362, 1648, 1656–57; Stewart, *Pickett's Charge*, pp. 222–23; William Davis letter, July 17, 1863 (69th Archives); Bates, *Pennsylvania Volunteers*, 2:703–4; *Trial*, pp. 135, 260, 267.

The clump of trees contained heavy brush and debris, which restricted movement through parts of it, hence it formed a barrier to the 69th's retreat.

16. Anthony McDermott to John Bachelder, in Ladd and Ladd, *Bachelder Papers*, 3:1655; Stewart, *Pickett's Charge*, pp. 218–19; Harrison and Busey, *Nothing But Glory*, pp. 104, 111; Andrew Cowan to John Bachelder, in Ladd and Ladd, *Bachelder Papers*, 2:1156–57.

Soon after the fighting ended, some men from the 72nd requested, and received, permission to carry Armistead to a hospital in the rear.

17. *Trial*, pp. 56, 86, 150.

18. Gary G. Lash, "The Philadelphia Brigade at Gettysburg," *Gettysburg Magazine*, vol. 7 (July 1992), pp. 97–113; Samuel Roberts letter, August 18, 1888 (69th Archives); p. 110; Ida Johnston, "Over the Wall at Gettysburg," *Confederate Veteran*, XXXI (1914), p. 249; Haskell, *Gettysburg*, pp. 411–12; William Burns' diary, July 3 entry, USAMHI; *Trial*, p. 274; Richard Rollins, *The Damned Red Flags of the Rebellion* (Redondo Beach, Ca.: Rank and File, 1997), pp. 173–76.

19. "Gettysburg Once More," *Philadelphia Weekly Times*, June 4, 1887; "The 69th at Gettysburg," *Philadelphia Weekly Times*, July 11, 1887; Anthony McDermott to John Bachelder, in Ladd and Ladd, *Bachelder Papers*, 3:1414–15.

20. Stewart, *Pickett's Charge*, pp. 290–91; Lewis E. Beitler, *Fiftieth Anniversary of the Battle of Gettysburg* (Harrisburg, Pa.: William Stanley Ray, Printer, 1915), pp. 168–69.

21. Abner Doubleday, *Chancellorsville and Gettysburg* (New York: Charles Scribner's Sons, 1882), p. 195; Ward, p. 202.

22. O.R., vol. 27, pt. 1, p. 428; Stewart, *Pickett's Charge*, pp. 213–14; Lash, *Gettysburg Magazine*, vol. 8, p. 112; Testimony of Charles Banes, in Ladd and Ladd, *Bachelder Papers*, 3:1703–4; *Trial*, pp. 63, 99, 139, 165, 179, 187.

When amending his report long after the war, Webb did not attempt to correct the part about the regiment being ordered to "hold the crest."

23. O.R., vol. 27, pt. 1, p. 428.

24. Alexander Webb letter to father, Webb Collection, Yale University (Copy in 69th Archives); Alexander Webb letter to Governor Curtin, August 11, 1863, 69th Pennsylvania File, PSA; O.R., vol. 27, pt. 1, pp. 432–33; Stewart, *Pickett's Charge*, p. 271.

The losses in the two companies of the 106th are not included because they were never reported. They were probably proportional to those of the 72nd.

25. John Lynch letter, July 5, 1863, PHS.

26. O.R., vol. 27, pt. 1, pp. 430–31; William Burns' diary, July 4, 5, 6, 7, 8, 9, 10, 11 entries, USAMHI; Ward, pp. 213–14.

27. O.R., vol. 27, pt. 1, p. 430; William Burns' diary, entries for July 14, 15, 16, 17, 18, 19, 20, 21, 22, 23, 24, 25, 26, USAMHI.

28. Ward, p. 215.

CHAPTER 15

1. Banes, pp. 198–99.

2. William Burns' diary, August 1, 21, 28, 31, and September 3, 4 entries, USAMHI; Ward, pp. 216–17; McDermott and Reilly, p. 34; Walker, Second Corps, p. 318.

3. Ward, pp. 217–22; William Burns' diary, September 12, 13, 14, 17, and October 9, 11, 12, 13, 14 entries, USAMHI; Banes, pp. 202–4; William D. Henderson, The Road to Bristoe Station (Lynchburg, Va.: H. E. Howard, Inc., 1987), pp. 70–71, 92, 137–38; Walker, Second Corps, p. 324.

4. O.R., vol. 29, pt. 1, p. 241–43, 277–78; Foote, The Civil War, 2:792–93; Henderson, Road, pp. 168–82.

5. Martin Graham and George Skoch, Mine Run: A Campaign of Lost Opportunities (Lynchburg, Va.: H. E. Howard, Inc., 1987), pp. 4–5, 21–29; William Burns' diary, November 7 entry, USAMHI.
The XI and XII Corps had been sent west prior to this campaign.

6. William Burns' diary, November 8, 23, 24, 26 entries, USAMHI; Ward pp. 224–26.

7. O.R., vol. 29, pt. 1, pp. 694–95, 721, 722; William Burns' diary, November 27 and 28 entries, USAMHI; Banes pp. 107–8; Graham and Skoch, Mine Run, pp. 48, 50.
The 69th's historians told a conflicting tale—the regiment formed on the left of the 71st, but seeing the rebels on their flank, formed a new line of battle at right angles with the original one. The rebels drove back Webb's division, but rallying, they recovered their lost ground before nightfall. (McDermott and Reilly, p. 36.)

8. Graham and Skoch, Mine Run, pp. 48, 50, 59, 69–71; O.R., vol. 29, pt. 1, pp. 16–17, 696–97; Walker, Second Corps, p. 379; Ward, pp. 226–27; William Burns' diary, November 29 entry, USAMHI.

9. O.R., vol. 29, pt. 1, pp. 16–17; Graham and Skoch, Mine Run, pp. 73–74.

10. William Burns' diary, November 30 entry, USAMHI; Banes, p. 209; Graham and Skoch, Mine Run, pp. 75–79; Thomas Livermore, Days and Events, 1860–1866 (Boston: Houghton Mifflin Co., 1920), p. 301.

11. William Burns' diary, November 30, December 1 and 2 entries, USAMHI; Graham and Skoch, Mine Run, pp. 80–81; Ward, pp. 227–28; O.R., vol. 29, pt. 1, p. 680.

12. Banes, pp. 212–13; Ward, pp. 231–32; Sauers, Advance The Colors, p. 354.

13. Court-martial proceedings, 72nd Pennsylvania file, GNMP; McDermott and Reilly, p. 38; Ward, pp. 233–35; Banes, pp. 214–15; Boyle, Party of Mad, p. 311; Sauers, Advance The Colors, p. 189; Henry Roback, The Veteran Volunteers of Herkemer and Oswego Counties in the War of the Rebellion (Utica, N.Y.: L. C. Childs, 1888), p. 65 (hereafter, "Roback.")

CHAPTER 16

1. Gordon C. Rhea, The Battle of the Wilderness (Baton Rouge, La.: Louisiana State University Press, 1994), pp. 34, 51–54; Ward, pp. 237–39; Banes, pp. 216–22; O.R., vol. 33, pt. 1, p. 1036.

2. Ward, p. 239; O.R., vol. 36, pt. 1, p. 442; Rhea, Wilderness Campaign, pp. 76, 83; Roback, p. 65.

3. Rhea, Wilderness Campaign, pp. 133, 141–72, 180–84, 188–89; O.R., vol. 36, pt. 1, pp. 442, 676; O.R., vol. 36, pt. 2, pp. 403–7; Roback, p. 65.

4. O.R., vol. 36, pt. 1, pp. 429–30, 437, 443, 676–77; Rhea, Wilderness Campaign, pp. 190–206; James I. Robertson, ed., The Civil War Letters of General Robert McAllister

(New Brunswick, N.J.: Rutgers University Press, 1965), p. 416; Banes, pp. 227–28; Robach, pp. 67–68.

5. Horace Porter, *Campaigning with Grant* (New York: Century Company, 1897), pp. 53–54; O.R., vol. 36, pt. 1, pp. 321, 430.

6. Roback, pp. 68–69; Banes, pp. 228–31; Rhea, *Wilderness Campaign*, pp. 283–343.

7. Rhea, *Wilderness Campaign*, pp. 351–78, 390–95, 435–36, 440; Banes, pp. 231–33; O.R., vol. 36, pt. 1, p. 121.

8. O.R., vol. 36, pt. 2, pp. 483–84, 495–96, 566–67; Banes, p. 237; Ward, p. 245; Gibbon, *Recollections,* p. 217.

9. O.R., vol. 36, pt. 1, pp. 430, 439, 445, 447–49; Gibbon, *Recollections,* p. 218; Banes, 243–44.

10. Ward, p. 247; Banes, pp. 244–47; Roback, p. 77; O.R., vol. 36, pt. 1, p. 445; pt. 2, p. 629; William D. Matters, *If It Takes All Summer* (Chapel Hill, N.C.: University of North Carolina Press, 1988), pp. 101, 189, 196.

11. Ward, pp. 248–49; Roback, pp. 78–79; Matter, *Takes All Summer,* pp. 202–4, 267, 272; Banes, pp. 247–48; O.R., vol. 36, pt. 1, pp. 446, 449; McDermott and Reilly, p. 40.

    In his report, Lieutenant Colonel Davis of the 69th stated that he was in temporary command of the Philadelphia Brigade on May 13, but was operating under General Carroll's direction. Curiously, the two most definitive histories of the unit do not mention the reconnaissance.

12. O.R., vol. 36, pt. 1, pp. 232, 338, 361; pt. 2, pp. 700, 711–12, 752, 844; Ward, p. 254.

13. O.R., vol. 36, pt. 1, pp. 431–32, 459; pt. 2, pp. 868–69, 878; Matter, *Takes All Summer,* pp. 308–12.

14. O.R., vol. 36, pt. 2, pp. 864–65, 869, 872; pt. 1, pp. 38–39.

CHAPTER 17

1. Matter, *If It Takes All Summer,* pp. 312–13, 331–32; O.R., vol. 36, pt. 1, pp. 432, 803, 910; Banes, pp. 252, 255–56; Ward, pp. 255, 258.

2. J. Michael Miller, *The North Anna Campaign* (Lynchburg, Va.: H. E. Howard, Inc., 1989), pp. 1–7.

3. Miller, *North Anna Campaign,* pp. 56–59; O.R., vol. 36, pt. 1, pp. 311, 432, 450, 482; pt. 3, pp. 147–48, 157, 161–62.

4. O.R., vol. 36, pt. 1, pp. 412, 417, 432, 443, 450–51, 500; Miller, *North Anna Campaign,* pp. 110–13; Roback, p. 87.

5. Thomas F. Gallwey, *Valiant Hours* (Harrisburg, Pa.: Stackpole and Company, 1961), p. 225; Roback, p. 87; Miller, *North Anna Campaign,* pp. 114–26, 132; O.R., vol. 36, pt. 1, pp. 241, 250–51.

6. O.R., vol. 36, pt. 1, p. 451; Banes, p. 266; O.R., vol. 36, pt. 1, p. 432; Ward, pp. 259–60; Gibbon, *Recollections,* pp. 223, 225–26.

7. Banes, pp. 262–63; Ward, pp. 259; O.R., vol. 36, pt. 1, pp. 343, 364, 432; pt. 3, pp. 305, 847; John W. Haley, *The Rebel Yell and the Yankee Hurrah; The Civil War Journal of a Maine Volunteer* (Camden, Maine: Down East Books, 1985), p. 164.

8. O.R., vol. 36, pt. 1, pp. 432, 452; pt. 3, p. 306; pt. 2, p. 968; Ward, pp. 260–61; McDermott and Reilly, p. 42.

9. O.R., vol. 36, pt. 1, p. 443; pt. 3, pp. 437–39, 444–45; Ward, p. 261; Banes, pp. 265–66.

10. O.R., vol. 36, pt. 1, pp. 154–55; Peter S. Michie, *The Life and Letters of Emory Upton* (New York: D. Appleton and Company, 1885), p. 109.

11. O.R., vol. 36, pt. 1, pp. 244, 452; pt. 3, pp. 432–33, 440–43; Ward, pp. 263–64; Banes, pp. 268–69.

12. Louis J. Baltz, *The Battle of Cold Harbor* (Lynchburg, Va.: H. E. Howard, 1994), pp. 137–42; Ward, p. 265; O.R., vol. 36, pt. 1, p. 433.

None of the accounts written by the men of the Philadelphia Brigade mention this delay or its cause.

13. O.R., vol. 36, pt. 1, p. 452; Banes, p. 271; Ward, pp. 264–66; Baltz, *Battle of Cold Harbor,* pp. 142–43; McDermott and Reilly, p. 43; Roback, pp. 91–92.
14. O.R., vol. 36, pt. 1, p. 433; Gibbon, p. 233; John Jones, "From North Anna to Cold Harbor," *Sketches of War History*, vol. 4, Ohio Commandery MOLLUS, p. 164; *New York Tribune*, June 7, 1864.
15. Baltz, *Battle of Cold Harbor,* p. 207; Banes, pp. 273–74; Ward, p. 268.
16. Baltz, *Battle of Cold Harbor*, pp. 179–92; O.R., vol. 36, pt. 1, p. 434; pt. 3, pp. 598–99; Ward, p. 268.
17. O.R., vol. 36, pt. 1, pp. 167–68.
18. O.R., vol. 36, pt. 1, pp. 96, 435–36.

Two other general officers were also having their problems. One of them, General Eustis, was relieved of his command on charges of neglect of duty and general inefficiency because "He is said to eat opium."

19. Ward, pp. 268–71; Banes, p. 275.
20. O.R., vol. 36, pt. 1, p. 434; McDermott and Reilly, pp. 44–45; Bates, 2:705.

CHAPTER 18

1. Banes, p. 278.
2. Roback, p. 99; O.R., vol. 40, pp. 282, 303–4, 366.
3. Ward, p. 274; O.R., vol. 40, pp. 305–6, 377; McDermott and Reilly, pp. 44–45.
4. O.R., vol. 40, pp. 307, 366, 377–78.
5. O.R., vol. 40, pp. 366, 382; Ward, p. 276; Roback, 102.

According to McDermott and Reilly (p. 45) the 69th was on the left of the line, but this could not have been the case.

6. Ward, pp. 276–77; Banes, pp. 283–84; McDermott and Reilly, p. 45.
7. Roback, p. 104; O.R., vol. 40, pp. 386–88; McDermott and Reilly, p. 46.
8. Banes, pp. 285–86; O.R., vol. 40, pp. 371, 376, 385, 386–87.

Hancock blamed Gibbon for the fiasco, and suggested that his subordinate tender his resignation (Gibbon, *Recollections*, pp. 248–51).

9. O.R., vol. 36, pt. 1, p. 434; vol. 40, pp. 220–21; Ward pp. 279–80.
10. Ward, pp. 279–78, 287; Banes, p. 287; O.R., vol. 40, pp. 366, 383.

Joseph Lynch had been an officer in the 106th Pennsylvania, and after Gettysburg, served on Gibbon's staff.

11. Bates, 2:705–6, 801, 833, 854; Banes, pp. 290–93; Ward, pp. 284–85.

CHAPTER 19

1. Ward, p. 121; Stewart, *Pickett's Charge,* pp. 59–60.
2. William Fox, *Regimental Losses in the American Civil War* (Albany: Albany Publishing Company, 1889), pp. 119, 277–79.

Percentages are calculated from muster rolls in Bates.

BIBLIOGRAPHY

Alexander, Edward. *Military Memoirs of a Confederate.* Dayton, Ohio: Morningside Books, 1977.

Bachelder, John B. "The Third Day's Battle, *Philadelphia Weekly Times*, December 15, 1877.

Baltz, John D. *Hon. Edward D. Baker.* Lancaster, Pa.: Inquirer Printing Company, 1888.

Baltz, Louis J. *The Battle of Cold Harbor.* Lynchburg, Va.: H. E. Howard, 1994.

Banes, Charles H. *History of the Philadelphia Brigade.* Philadelphia: Butternut Press, 1984.

Bates, Samuel. *History of Pennsylvania Volunteers, 1861–65.* Harrisburg: D. Singerly, State Printer, 1869.

Beitler, Lewis E. *Fiftieth Anniversary of the Battle of Gettysburg.* Harrisburg, Pa.: William Stanley Ray, Printer, 1915.

Benedict, George G. *Army Life in Virginia.* Burlington, Vt.: Free Press Association, 1895.

Blair, Harry C., and Rebecca Tarshis. *Colonel Edward D. Baker: Lincoln's Constant Ally.* Portland: Oregon Historical Society, 1960.

Boyle, Frank. *A Party of Mad Fellows.* Dayton: Morningside Books, 1996.

Bruce, George A. *The Twentieth Regiment of Massachussets Volunteers, 1861–1865.* Boston: Houghton Mifflin Co., 1966.

Busey, John W., and David G. Martin. *Regimental Strengths and Losses at Gettysburg.* Hightstown, New Jersey: Longstreet House, 1986.

Catton, Bruce. *Mr. Lincoln's Army.* Garden City, N.Y.: Doubleday, 1951.

Clay, James. "About the Death of General Garnett." *Confederate Veteran* 14 (February 1905).

Coco, Gregory A., ed. *From Ball's Bluff to Gettysburg... And Beyond: The Civil War Letters of Private Roland E. Bowen, 15th Massachusetts Infantry 1861–1864.* Gettysburg: Thomas Publications, 1994.

Coddington, Edwin B. *The Gettysburg Campaign: A Study in Command.* New York: Charles Scribner, 1968.

Cowan, Andrew. "When Cowan's Battery Withstood Pickett's Splendid Charge." *New York Herald*, July 2, 1911.

Devine, John, et al. *Loudoun County and the Civil War.* Leesburg: Loudoun County Civil War Centennial Commission, 1961.

Dickert, Augustus. *History of Kershaw's Brigade.* Newberry, S.C.: Elbert Aull, 1899.

Doubleday, Abner. *Chancellorsville and Gettysburg.* New York: Charles Scribner's Sons, 1882.

Dowdey, Clifford. *The Seven Days: The Emergence of Lee.* Boston: Little, Brown and Company, 1964.

Evans, Clement A., ed. *Confederate Military History: A Library of Confederate States History.* Atlanta, Georgia: Confederate Publishing Company, 1889.

Farwell, Byron. *Ball's Bluff.* McLean, Va.: EPM Publications, 1990.

Fatout, Paul. "The California Regiment, Colonel Baker and Ball's Bluff." *California Historical Society Quarterly* 31 (1952): 229–240.

Finley, George. "The Bloody Angle," *Buffalo Evening News,* May 29, 1894.

Foote, Shelby. *The Civil War—A Narrative.* New York: Vintage Books, 1986.

Ford, Andrew E. *The Story of the Fifteenth Regiment, Massachusetts Volunteer Infantry in the Civil War.* Clinton: Press of W. J. Coulter, 1898.

Fox, William. *Regimental Losses in the American Civil War.* Albany: Albany Publishing Company, 1889.

Frazier, John W. "Col. Baker's Regiment, how it was raised in Philadelphia by Mr. Wistar." *Philadelphia Weekly Times* (September 20, 1879).

Gallwey, Thomas F. *Valiant Hours.* Harrisburg, Pa.: Stackpole and Company, 1961.

Gibbon, John. *Personal Recollections of the Civil War.* Dayton, Ohio: Morningside Press, 1978.

Gottfried, Bradley M. "Wright's Charge on July 2, 1863: Piercing the Union Line or Inflated Glory?" *Gettysburg Magazine,* vol. 17 (July 1997): 70–82.

Graham, Martin F., and George F. Skoch. *Mine Run: A Campaign of Lost Opportunities.* Lynchburg, Va.: H. E. Howard, Inc., 1987.

Haley, John W. *The Rebel Yell and the Yankee Hurrah: The Civil War Journal of a Maine Volunteer.* Camden, Maine: Down East Books, 1985.

Harrison Kathy G., and John W. Busey. *Nothing But Glory.* Gettysburg: Thomas, Inc., 1903.

Hartwig, Scott. "It Struck Horror To Us All." *Gettysburg Magazine,* vol. 4 (1991): 89–100.

Haskell, Frank A. *The Battle of Gettysburg.* Vol. 43 of the Harvard Classics. New York: P. F. Collier and Sons, 1910.

Henderson, William D. *The Road to Bristoe Station.* Lynchburg, Va.: H. E. Howard, Inc., 1987.

Hennessey, John. *Return to Bull Run.* New York: Simon and Shuster, 1993.

Holien, Kim B. *Battle of Ball's Bluff.* Orange, Va.: Moss Publications, 1985.

Howard, Oliver. *Autobiography of O. O. Howard.* New York: Baker and Taylor Company, 1907.

Johnston, Ida. "Over the Wall at Gettysburg." *Confederate Veteran* 31 (1914): 248–49.

Johnston, Joseph E. *Narrative of Military Operations During the Civil War.* New York: Da Capo Press, 1990.

Johnson, Robert, and Clarence Buel. *Battles & Leaders of the Civil War.* New York: The Century Company, 1887.

Jones, John. "From North Anna to Cold Harbor," *Sketches of War History.* Vol. 4, Ohio Commandery MOLLUS.

Lang David. Letter to General Edward A. Perry, 19 July 1863. *Southern Historical Society Papers* 27 (1899): 192–205.

Larkin, James, R. "The Last To Go." *Philadelphia Weekly Times,* April 8, 1882.

Lash, Gary G. "The Philadelphia Brigade at Gettysburg." *The Gettysburg Magazine* 7 (July 1992): 97–113.

Livermore, Thomas L. *Days and Events, 1860–1866.* Boston: Houghton Mifflin, Co., 1920.

McDermott, Anthony W., and John E. Reilly. *A Brief History of the 69th Regiment, Pennsylvania Veteran Volunteers.* Philadelphia: D. J. Gallagher and Company Printers, 1889.

Martin Rawley W., and John H. Smith. "The Battle of Gettysburg and the Charge of Pickett's Division." *Southern Historical Society Papers* 39 (1904), pp. 186–87.

Marvel, William. *Burnside.* Durham, N.C.: University of North Carolina Press, 1991.

Matters, William D. *If It Takes All Summer.* Chapel Hill, N.C.: University of North Carolina Press, 1988.

Michie, Peter S. *The Life and Letters of Emory Upton.* New York: D. Appleton and Company, 1885.

Miller, J. Michael. *The North Anna Campaign.* Lynchburg, Va.: H. E. Howard, Inc., 1989.

Moe, Richard. *The Last Full Measure.* New York: Avon Books, 1993.

Murfin, James. *The Gleam of Bayonets*. New York: Thomas Yoseloff, 1965.

New York Monuments Commission for Battlefields of Gettysburg and Chattanooga, *Final Report on the Battlefield of Gettysburg*. 3 vols. Albany: J. B. Lyon Company, Printers, 1900.

Paul, William. "Severe Experiences at Gettysburg." *Confederate Veteran* 19 (1912): 85.

Pennsylvania Gettysburg Battlefield Commission, *Pennsylvania at Gettysburg: Ceremonies at the Dedication of Monuments to Mark the Positions of the Pennsylvania Commands Engaged in the Battle*. Edited by John P. Nicholson, 2 vols., rev. ed. Harrisburg, Pennsylvania: William Stanley Ray, State Printer, 1904.

Palfrey, Francis W. *Antietam and Fredericksburg*. New York: Jack Brussel, n.d.

Palfrey, Francis W. *Memoir of William Francis Bartlett*. Boston: Houghton, Osgood, and Company, 1878.

Paul, William. "Severe Experiences at Gettysburg." *Confederate Veteran* vol. 19 (1912): 85.

Perry, Milton F. *Infernal Machines: The Story of Confederate Submarine and Mine Warfare*. Baton Rouge: Louisiana State University Press, 1965.

Pfanz, Harry W. *Gettysburg: The Second Day*. Chapel Hill: University of North Carolina Press, 1987.

Pfanz, Harry W. *Gettysburg: Culp's Hill and Cemetery Hill*. Chapel Hill: University of North Carolina Press, 1993.

Porter, Horace. *Campaigning with Grant*. New York: Century Company, 1897.

Qualife, Milo. *From the Cannon's Mouth: The Civil War Letters of General Alpheus Williams*. Detroit: Wayne State University Press, 1959.

Reardon, Carol. The Forlorn Hope: Brigadier General Andrew A. Humphreys' Pennsylvania Division at Fredericksburg. In *The Fredericksburg Campaign—Decision on the Rappahannock*. Gary Gallagher, ed. Durham: University of North Carolina Press, 1995.

Rhea, Gordon C. *The Battle of the Wilderness*. Baton Rouge, La.: Louisiana State University Press, 1994.

Rhodes, John H. *The History of Battery B, First Regiment, Rhode Island Artillery*. Providence: Snow and Farnham, Printers, 1914.

Roback, Henry. *The Veteran Volunteers of Herkemer and Oswego Counties in the War of the Rebellion*. Utica, N.Y.: L. C. Childs, 1888.

Robertson, James, I., ed. *The Civil War Letters of General Robert McAllister*. New Brunswick, N.J.: Rutgers University Press, 1965.

Rollins, Richard. *The Damned Red Flags of the Rebellion*. Redondo Beach, Ca.: Rank and File, 1997.

Rumkel, William. "The Philadelphia Brigade. Its Part, Under Sedgwick and Howard, in the Battle of Antietam." *Philadelphia Weekly Times*, April 8, 1882.

Sandburg, Carl. *Abraham Lincoln: The War Years.* Volume 1. New York: Harcourt, Brace, and World, 1939.

Sauers, Richard A. *Advance the Colors: Pennsylvania Civil War Battle Flags.* Harrisburg: Capital Preservation Committee, 1987.

Sears, Stephen W. *George B. McClellan: The Young Napoleon.* New York: Ticknor and Fields, 1988.

Sears, Stephen W. *To the Gates of Richmond.* New York: Ticknor and Fields, 1992.

Sears, Stephen W. *The Landscape Turned Red.* New Haven, Conn.: Ticknor and Fields, 1983.

Sears, Stephen W. *Chancellorsville.* Boston: Houghton Mifflin Company, 1996.

Shotwell, R. A. "The Battle of Ball's Bluff." *The Philadelphia Weekly Times,* April 6, 1878.

Sifakis, Stewart. *Who Was Who in the Civil War.* New York: Facts on File, 1988.

Smith, Asa diary. *American Heritage,* February 1971.

Smith, R. Penn. "The Battle: The Part Taken by the Philadelphia Brigade in the Battle." *Gettysburg Compiler,* June 7, 1887.

Stewart, George R. *Pickett's Charge: A Microhistory of the Final Attack at Gettysburg, July 3, 1863.* Boston: Houghton Mifflin Co., 1959.

Sturtevant, Ralph O. *Pictorial History, Thirteenth Vermont Volunteers.* Burlington, Vt.: Regimental Association, 1910.

Sword, Wiley. "Defending the Codori House and Cemetery Ridge: Two Swords with Harrow's Brigade in the Gettysburg Campaign." *Gettysburg Magazine* 13 (July 1995): 43–49.

Taylor, Frank H. *Philadelphia in the Civil War, 1861–1865.* Philadelphia: Dunlap Printing Company, 1913.

Tucker, Glenn. *High Tide at Gettysburg: The Campaign in Pennsylvania.* Indianapolis: Bobbs-Merrill, 1958.

United States War Department. *War of the Rebellion: A Compilation of the Official Records of the Union and Confederate Armies,* 70 vols. in 128 parts Washington, D.C.: Government Printing Office, 1880–1901.

Vanderslice, Catherine. *The Civil War Letters of George Washington Biedleman.* New York: Vantage Press, 1978.

Walker, Francis. *History of the Second Army Corps.* New York: Charles Scribner's and Sons, 1886.

Ward, Joseph R. *History of the One Hundred and Sixth Regiment, Pennsylvania Volunteers.* Philadelphia: Grant, Faires, and Rogers, 1883.

Webb, Alexander S. *The Peninsula.* New York: Jack Brussel, n.d.

Weld, Stephen. *War Diary and Letters of Stephen Minot Weld, 1861–1865.* Boston: Massachusetts Historical Society, 1979.

Weland, Gerald. *O. O. Howard, Union General.* Jefferson, N.C.: McFarland & Company, 1995.

Whan, Vorin. *Fiasco at Fredericksburg.* State College, Pennsylvania: Pennsylvania State University Press, 1961.

Wiley, Bell. *The Life of Billy Yank.* Bobbs-Merrill: New York, 1951.

Wistar, Isaac J. *Autobiography of Isaac Jones Wistar, 1827–1905.* Philadelphia: Wistar Institute of Anatomy and Biology, 1937.

Wyckoff, Mac. *A History of the 3rd South Carolina Infantry.* Fredericksburg, Va.: Sargent Kirkland's Museum, 1995.

INDEX

O'Kane, Col. Dennis, 22, 124, 127, 147,
168–69, 238 n. 16
Orange and Alexander RR, 149, 185
Orange Turnpike, Va., 194, 195, 196, 197, 200
Orchard Station, Va., 83
Osborne's Battery, 87
Oswald, Captain, 71
Otter, William, 38, 240 n. 23
Owen, Gen. Joshua, forms 3rd California,
13; during winter of 1861–62, 42, 53;
at Seven Days' battles, 93; during
Antietam campaign, 118, 119, 120;
takes command of brigade, 123–24,
147, 185, 192, 194; during Fredericksburg campaign, 125, 127, 131, 133,
134, 135, 246 n. 12; during winter of
1862–63, 139, 140; at Chancellorsville,
146; relieved of command, 151–52,
218–19, 226, 229; at Gettysburg, 166;
during Wilderness campaign, 196, 197,
198; during Spotsylvania campaign,
201, 203, 204, 205, 206; during
Totopotomoy Creek campaign, 212,
213; during Cold Harbor campaign,
214, 215, 216; as commander, 230
Ox Ford, 209

P

Palfrey, Col. Francis, 114, 115, 118, 120
Palmer, Col. Oliver, 130
Pamunkey River, Va., 69, 212
Paris, Va., 125
Parker's Store, Va., 195
Parksburg, Md., 109
Parrish, Maj. Robert, 22, 42, 99
Patterson, Gen. Robert, 1, 236 n. 1
Peach Orchard, Va., 84, 98, 124, 158
Peacock Hill, Va., 26
Peninsula, Va., 10, 11, 59, 97, 102, 104,
139, 191, 220
Pennsylvania Regiments
22nd, forerunner of 106th Pennsylvania,
1, 13; at Baltimore, 2
24th, forerunner of 69th Pennsylvania, 1,
13
28th, along Potomac River, 45; on
Loudoun Heights, 51; at Antietam, 114
53rd, at Orchard Station, 84, 243 n. 5
69th, name change, 42, 237 n. 1, 238 n.
2; during winter of 1861–62, 44, 46,
53; during Yorktown campaign, 56,
58, 67; at Fair Oaks, 74, 75, 77, 79,
81, 244 n. 6; during Seven Days'
battles, 83, 88, 89, 92, 93, 94; at
Harrison's Landing, 101; during the
relief of Pope, 106; during Antietam

campaign, 113, 119; refitting, 123,
124; during the Fredericksburg
campaign, 127, 130, 135, 136; during
winter of 1862–63, 136, 138, 139;
during Chancellorsville campaign,
142, 146; march to Gettysburg, 148,
150, 153; Gettysburg—July 2, 156,
157, 158, 161, 163; Gettysburg—July
3, 167, 168, 169, 170, 172, 173, 174,
175, 177, 178, 179, 249 n. 10, 250 n.
11, 250 n. 15; during fall 1863
campaign, 187, 190, 251 n. 7; during
winter of 1863–64, 191, 192, 193;
during Wilderness campaign, 200;
during Spotsylvania campaign, 201,
202, 205, 207, 252 n. 11; during
Totopotomoy campaign, 211, 212,
during Cold Harbor campaign, 213,
218, 219; during Petersburg campaign, 221, 222, 223, 226, 227, 253 n.
5; disbanding, 228; analysis, 230, 235
71st, name change, 42; during winter of
1861–62, 43, 44, 46, 49, 51, 52;
during Yorktown campaign, 56, 58,
62, 65, 66; at Fair Oaks, 70, 71, 73,
77, 78, 79; during Seven Days'
battles, 83, 84, 88, 89, 93, 95, 243 n.
5; at Harrison's Landing, 97, 98, 99;
during the relief of Pope, 103, 105;
during Antietam campaign, 112, 113,
114, 119, 120; refitting, 123, 124;
during the Fredericksburg campaign,
127, 129, 130, 134, 135, 136; during
Chancellorsville campaign, 141, 143,
145; march to Gettysburg, 148, 150,
153; Gettysburg—July 2, 156, 158,
161, 163, 164, 166; Gettysburg—July
3, 168, 169, 170, 172, 173, 176, 177,
178, 181, 183, 249 n. 10, 249 n. 16,
250 n. 11; during fall 1863 campaign,
187, 190, 251 n. 7; during winter of
1863–64, 193; during Wilderness
campaign, 194, 198, 200; during
Spotsylvania campaign, 207; during
Totopotomoy campaign, 212, 213;
during Cold Harbor campaign, 218,
219, 225; analysis, 229, 230
72nd, name change, 42, 237 n. 1; during
winter of 1861–62, 43, 44, 46, 52;
during Yorktown campaign, 58, 60, 62;
at Fair Oaks, 74, 75, 77, 78, 81; during
Seven Days' battles, 87, 88, 89, 91, 93,
95; at Harrison's Landing, 98, 99;
during Antietam campaign, 113, 116,
119, 120; during the Fredericksburg
campaign, 125, 127, 129, 130, 135,
136; during winter of 1862–63, 139;